The Euro

In this book, leading financial professionals and academics examine the prospects for the European single currency, widely seen as heralding a 'quantum leap' for European financial markets.

The impact of the euro, and its implications for European market integration, are examined in terms of three core factors:

- risks and opportunities for financial intermediaries
- challenges for monetary and supervisory authorities
- issues for portfolio management and corporate finance.

The discussion embraces key topics such as the Maastricht Treaty design for the European Bank, and its possible loopholes, and the assumption that the European capital market will emerge to challenge the US market in scale and liquidity.

This book is based on the proceedings of the Twenty-First Colloquium of the Société Universitaire Européenne de Recherches Financières (SUERF), held in association with the Center for Financial Studies (CFS), Frankfurt.

Michael Artis is currently Professor of Economics at the European University Insititute, Florence, during a leave from Manchester University. He has published widely in the areas of macroeconomics and monetary economics.

Axel Weber is Professor of Economics at Johann Wolfgang Goethe University and Director, Center for Financial Studies (CFS), Frankfurt.

Elizabeth Hennessy is managing editor of *Central Banking* magazine, and an editor on the periodical *Treasury Management International*. Her publications include twelve corporate and institutional histories. She is currently working on a history of the London Stock Exchange.

Routledge international studies in money and banking

The Euro

A challenge and opportunity for financial markets

**Edited by
Michael Artis,
Axel Weber and
Elizabeth Hennessy**

London and New York

First published 2000
by Routledge
11 New Fetter Lane, London EC4P 4EE

Simultaneously published in the USA and Canada
by Routledge
29 West 35th Street, New York, NY 10001

Routledge is an imprint of the Taylor & Francis Group

Typeset in Baskerville
by Curran Publishing Services Ltd
Printed and bound in Great Britain
by MPG Books Ltd, Bodmin

British Library Cataloguing in Publication Data
A catalogue record for this book is available
from the British Library.

Library of Congress Cataloging-in-Publication Data
  The Euro: a challenge and opportunity for financial
  markets/[edited by] Michael Artis, Axel Weber and Elizabeth
  Hennessy.
  416 pp. 15.6 x 23.4 cm
  Includes bibliographical references and index.
  1. Euro. 2. Capital movements – Europe. 3. Banks and banking –
  Europe. I. Artis, Michael J. II. Weber, Axel A.
  III. Hennessy, Elizabeth.
  HG925.E8667 2000
  332.4'5—dc 21   99-054586

ISBN 0–415–21710–5

Contents

vi *Contents*

Figures

Tables

Contributors

John Arrowsmith is a Senior Research Fellow at the National Institute of Economic and Social Research, London.

Michael Artis is currently Professor of Economics at the European University Insititute, Florence, during a leave from Manchester University.

Olivier De Bandt is head of unit in the Research Department of the Banque de France (SEMEF).

Ray Barrell is director of the World Economy team at the National Institute of Economic and Social Research, London.

Andrea Beltratti is Associate Professor of Economics at Bocconi University.

Graham Bishop is Adviser on European Financial Affairs at Salomon Smith Barney, London.

Martin Brookes is an International Economist and Executive Director at Goldman Sachs International, London.

E. Philip Davis is a Senior Economist at the Bank of England.

Jean Dermine is Professor of Banking and Finance at INSEAD, Fontainebleu.

Daniel Gros is Senior Research Fellow and Deputy Director at the Center for Economic Policy Studies, Brussels.

Christopher Huhne is Vice Chairman of the Sovereign Department, Fitch IBCA, and a Member of the European Parliament.

Ernst-Moritz Lipp is a member of the Board of Directors of the Dresdner Bank.

Robert N. McCauley is Senior Economic and Financial Representative of the Bank for International Settlements' Representative Office for Asia and the Pacific, Hong Kong.

Alessandro Prati is an economist in the International Capital Markets and

Financial Studies Division in the Research Department of the International Monetary Fund.

Sinikka Salo is a Senior Economist at the Bank of Finland, currently on secondment to the European Central Bank.

Garry Schinasi is Chief of the International Capital Markets and Financial Studies Division in the Research Department of the International Monetary Fund.

Franziska Schobert is a Ph.D. student in the Department of Monetary Economics, Goethe University.

Christopher Taylor is a Visiting Fellow at the National Institute of Economic and Social Research, London.

Niels Thygesen is Danske Bank Professor of International Economics at the University of Copenhagen.

Hans Tietmeyer was President of the Deutsche Bundesbank from 1993 to 1999.

Rudi Vander Vennet is Professor of Financial Economics at the University of Ghent.

Acknowledgements

The success of the Twenty-First Colloquium of the Société Universitaire Européenne de Recherches Financières (SUERF) owes much to many hands, not least of course to those who gave speeches and presented papers. A special vote of thanks goes, however, to those who organized the conference on the ground, and to the good offices of the Center for Financial Studies in Frankfurt with which the SUERF jointly organized its Twenty-First Colloquium.

Figure 5.1, 'Hypothetical cost structure in banking', and Figure 5.2, 'Excess capacity in US banking', are reproduced by permission of the Federal Reserve Bank of New York.

Acknowledgement is made to Salomon Smith Barney for permission to reprint Graham Bishop, 'Delivering the benefits of EMU: securitization', as Chapter 13 of this volume.

An earlier version of Chapter 16, Robert N. McCauley, 'Prospects for the exchange rate of the euro', was published in the *Open Economies Review* in February 1999 under the title 'The Euro and the dollar, 1998', Acknowledgement is made to Kluwer Academic Publishers for permission to reprint this material.

Abbreviations

ACH	Automated Clearing House (US)
ATM	automatic teller machine
BHCs	bank holding companies
BIS	Bank for International Settlements
CFS	Center for Financial Studies, Frankfurt
DTB	Deutsche Terminbörse (German Futures Exchange)
ECB	European Central Bank
ECU	European Currency Unit
EIB	European Investment Bank
EMBI	Emerging Bonds Market Index
EMI	European Monetary Institute
EMS	European Monetary System
EMU	European Economic and Monetary Union
ERM	Exchange Rate Mechanism
ESCB	European System of Central Banks
FDIs	foreign direct investments
G7	Group of Seven (countries)
G10	Group of Ten (countries)
HICP	harmonized index of consumer prices
IFS	International Financial Statistics
IMF	International Monetary Fund
LOLR	lender of last resort
MATIF	Marché à Terme International de France (International Futures Market of France)
MMFs	money market funds
MPIPs	Monetary Policy Instruments and Procedures
NCB	national central banks
OCA	optimum currency area
OEEC	Organization for European Economic Co-operation
ROAA	return on average assets
ROAE	return on average equity
RTGS	real-time gross settlement
SOMA	System Open Market Account
SUERF	Société Universitaire Européenne de Recherches Financières
UCITS	Undertakings for Collective Investment in Transferable Securities

Introduction

The papers reproduced in this volume are selected from those given at the Twenty-First Colloquium of the Société Universitaire Européenne de Recherches Financières (SUERF). When the location and theme of that colloquium were first discussed, it seemed that there was little real choice but to take as a theme the advent of the new currency for Europe, and to hold the conference where the new European Central Bank would be located, in Frankfurt. Conferences as large as that of SUERF take some time to plan, though, and it was still just possible at the time that this location and theme were first discussed to entertain a doubt as to whether the new currency would be born on time. But by October 1998, when the colloquium took place, any residual doubts had been all but removed: the first participating members of the Eurozone had been nominated, the foreign exchange markets had calmly accepted the project and the new currency was on course to be introduced in the New Year.

The adventurous quality of the project to introduce a new currency for Europe cannot be doubted; nothing like it has happened before. At the same time the scope of an agenda devoted to such a large subject could be enormous. SUERF chose to ensure that the theme would be treated in a way which respected the comparative advantage of its members, while stressing the adventurous quality of the enterprise. Hence the aptness of the title for the colloquium: *The Euro: A Challenge and Opportunity for Financial Markets*.

The two sides of the theme were immediately reflected in the three keynote addresses which are reproduced here. Hans Tietmeyer stressed the underlying need, for the success of the euro to be assured, for policy to be stable and consistent with the goal of price stability; to this end, he noted, monetary policy will need the support of other areas of economic policy. Dwelling on the turbulence in global financial markets associated with the South East Asian crises, he noted that the stability of the prospective Eurozone suggested that the euro had passed its first test. The second keynote speaker, Professor Lipp, emphasized that the 'the euro will mean a quantum leap for the European financial system', with the elimination of exchange risk and the increase in transparency produced by the new currency leading to a much broader, deeper and more liquid single European financial market. The present fragmentation of the capital markets in Europe would give way to the emergence of a unified market.

Professor Artis, the third keynote speaker, addressed the issue of the internal strains faced by countries inside the Eurozone in adapting to a single monetary policy in circumstances where their conjectural situations varied. If this sounded like a warning he also pointed out that the coherence of the core of the Eurozone was a favourable sign for the success of the euro.

Following the keynote addresses the colloquium got down to its work of discussing the papers presented in three 'commissions'. This feature of the SUERF colloquium organization is relatively unusual and worth mentioning. The idea is to divide the papers into relatively homogenous groups assigned to a corresponding commission, with members 'belonging' to a particular commission and committed to pursuing the theme of that commission through its papers, to some kind of conclusion. While the arrangement seeks to deny the indulgence of serendipity, which some conference-goers like, it has the distinct virtue that it promotes the construction of a body of knowledge and critical ability in a particular area, and aims to raise the level of discussion. The papers in this volume are arranged according to the commission in which they were delivered. The titles of the commissions themselves reflect some of the issues raised by the keynote speakers, in particular by Professor Lipp. His judgment that the coming of the euro would make for 'a quantum leap' in the integration of European financial markets underlies the more detailed look at the prospects for this outcome implicit in the commission titles.

Thus, Commission 1 was devoted to risks and opportunities for banks and other financial intermediaries. The authors of the four papers from this commission which are published here all agree, more or less explicitly, that the coming of the single currency implies a regime shift for commercial banking in Europe, making the creation of a single market in banking irreversible. Jean Dermine makes the point that in the new conditions the sources of competitive advantage will change. Olivier de Bandt argues that while the trend towards consolidation by merger in the European financial market will increase, competition will at the same time also increase, when assessed at the now more appropriate European, rather than domestic, market level. Philip Davis and Sinikka Salo note that the process of merger and concentration, and the increase in competitive pressure may have a destabilizing effect on the prosecution of monetary policy (echoing a comment of Tietmeyer's in the latter's keynote address).

A particular source of concern has been whether the new competitive pressures will favour a homogenization of banking organization, and in particular whether they will threaten the survival of the European style of 'universal banking', in favour of more specialized banking. Rudi Vander Vennet looks at this issue by examining the cost and profit of European banking in relation to its organizational form. His finding is that universal banking structures have in the past proven more efficient; in the absence of a 'Lucas critique' effect (which perhaps cannot be ruled out here); this suggests that universalistic structures may be the ones that survive.

Commission 2 was directed towards challenges to monetary and supervisory authorities. Three papers from this commission are reproduced here. One of the main concerns with the 'Maastricht design' for the European Central Bank has always been that it omits mention of any lender of last resort function for the bank, and beyond that, also fails to make any other clear and unambiguous suggestion for the location of such a function in the Eurozone. The difficulty with this is made more acute to the extent that transitional problems of the adjustment of the private sector to the new setting may induce crisis situations. According to the critique of Alessandro Prati and Garry Schinasi, the allocation of clear responsibilities in this regard is an urgent necessity. The need for a rearrangement of national central bank balance sheets in the new regime is another left-over item on the agenda. Daniel Gros and Franziska Schobert explore the Byzantine accounts of these banks with a critical force aimed at a recommendation that national central banks should change entirely the presentation of their balance sheets to reflect their role in the European System of Central Banks' (ESCB's) monetary policy framework. John Arrowsmith, with Ray Barrell and Christopher Taylor, addresses yet a further 'black hole' in the Eurozone set-up: that is, the relationship between the euro and other currencies. They advocate a strategy in which the moderation of instability in Euro-exchange rates is made an explicit target for policy.

Commission 3 concerned issues for portfolio management and corporate finance. There is a widely-shared background assumption that the formation of the Eurozone will permit the creation of a Eurozone capital market as big and as liquid as that in the United States, with the definition of the 'home market' (and thus some elements of the well-known 'home bias' in portfolio investment) expanding to the European plane. The colloquium papers expand on, and in some cases qualify, this theme. Beltratti's paper, for example, draws attention to the fact that risk-spreading diversification will imply the need, for some investors, to move out of European securities into securities denominated in other currencies. Martin Brookes argues that concerns in the equities market should now move from investigation of national issues to a concentration on sectoral fortunes. In a similar way, Christopher Huhne argues that the concerns of rating agencies will now move from currencies to fiscal policies; highly indebted sovereigns are advised to fund their debt in order to diminish their exposure to pressures arising in the financial markets.

Graham Bishop stresses the potential for European capital markets to rival the American, emphasising the key role played by government bond markets in providing a highly liquid base. The securitization of debt instruments, which had developed to a high level in the US, can be expected to proceed in the European markets also, with important implications. One of these is that securitization is likely to lead to a more uniform financial structure across Europe (which would be a facilitating factor for UK entry).

Among the big questions raised by the advent of the euro have been the prospects for the volatility of the new currency and for its relative strength in the medium term. Among the scenarios that have been rehearsed are the possibilities of large portfolio shifts as the euro becomes an accepted world currency, and of large swings in the euro/dollar exchange rate as the ECB joins the Fed in playing 'benign neglect'. In his large and carefully detailed paper on these issues, Robert McCauley emerges with a relatively sober assessment. Downplaying the more spectacular scenarios as unrealistic, his assessment is that the euro in the medium term is likely to be regarded as an inherently strong currency; with the support of a continued current account surplus of modest to large size, a trend for medium-run real appreciation is possible.

The Prix Marjolin

The Council of SUERF awarded the Prix Marjolin to Dr Rudi Vander Vennet, Professor of Financial Accounting at the University of Ghent, Belgium, for the best colloquium contribution from an author under forty years of age. The award was presented by Neils Thygesen, Danske Professor of International Economics at the University of Copenhagen and past President of SUERF (1988–91).

The Marjolin Lecture

Neils Thygesen also gave the 1998 Marjolin Lecture which he entitled 'Evolving Ambitions in Europe's Monetary Unification'. Taking his cue from the Marjolin report (1975) and the later comments on that report that appear in Marjolin's memoirs, Thygesen identifies five major ambitions of monetary integration, of which two (or, as Thygesen puts it, 'two and a half') have been realized: the elimination of exchange rate fluctuations, the elimination of inflation and the development (half-development) of coordination across countries of non-monetary policies. Two remain to be achieved: the development of a role in the international monetary system and the development of a European financial regulation regime.

Conclusions

The title of the colloquium accurately conveyed the two sides of the euro project: the risks and threats that any new endeavour entails, and the new opportunities that are likewise implied. Perhaps for reasons to do with the self-selection of individuals to their chosen professions, it might appear that the threats and risks seem bigger in the papers coming from academics and those working in the capacity of international civil servants, while the attractiveness of the new opportunities looms larger in the papers coming from those working in commercial and financial environments. How well the balance of views stands up to the test of time should become apparent to readers of this volume in the fullness of time.

Michael Artis, EUI, Florence
Axel Weber, CFS, Frankfurt
Elizabeth Hennessy

Keynote speeches

1 The euro

A challenge to, and opportunity for, financial markets

Hans Tietmeyer

I

> Educational institutions – explicitly including universities – are not philanthropic islands of abstract debate.

This maxim of the German President is borne out by this colloquium, for this is not merely an 'abstract debate'. The subject is of great practical relevance: 'the euro: a challenge to, and opportunity for, the financial markets'. And there can be no talk of an 'island', either, for this is a cross-border, joint meeting of SUERF and the CFS. Incidentally, the motive is the exchange of knowledge with the financial community (including central banks), thus avoiding all suspicion of insular ivory-tower erudition. There can be no doubt that the financial community will likewise benefit from an exchange of knowledge. After all, the euro was and is an intellectual challenge for all those concerned with it. An interesting exchange of views is therefore to be expected, and a debate based on two fundamental perceptions may be fruitful:

- A consistent monetary policy, committed primarily to the target of stability, is the best contribution a central bank – no matter whether the Bundesbank or the European Central Bank (ECB) – can make to the viability of the financial markets. Without stable money, the financial markets cannot function properly.
- Conversely, it must also be said that monetary policy needs an efficient, highly competitive and stable financial system. In the first place, a financial sector that is susceptible to disruption poses risks to the entire monetary system, and thus also to the safety of the currency. Second, in a stable environment, monetary policy impinges on economic activity more smoothly. That was and is true of the Bundesbank's monetary policy. It is bound to apply to the European System of Central Banks' (ESCB's) monetary policy as well.

II

Clarity now obtains in some matters of significance to financial market players concerning the euro. The future framework for economic policy action is now emerging ever more clearly.

Since its constitutive meeting in June 1998, the ECB Governing Council has taken a multitude of important decisions. There is broad clarity today about the arsenal of instruments with which the ESCB will operate. The primary buttress of refinancing will be repo transactions, which have been so successful at the national level. The interest rate for this main source of finance will lie within the corridor whose ceiling and floor are marked out by the interest rates for the marginal lending and deposit facilities. These principal elements of the range of instruments have been designed with the intention of the money market developing as steadily as possible, so that recourse to fine-tuning instruments can be relatively rare.

The same purpose is served by minimum reserves, which are often criticized in banking circles. At a rate of 2 per cent, the cost burden is kept within very narrow bounds, especially considering that, owing to the envisaged payment of interest on minimum reserves, the banks' working balances, which will have to be held anyway, will yield interest. In the envisaged form (a reserve to be maintained as a monthly average) they will act as a buffer in the money market. They can therefore largely cushion unforeseen fluctuations in the demand for liquid funds without any major central bank intervention.

A very important step on the way to a single monetary policy is the agreement on the main elements of the monetary policy strategy which was reached in the ECB Governing Council on 13 October 1998. These elements comprise the quantitative definition of price stability as the primary objective of the single monetary policy: 'Price stability shall be defined as a year-on-year increase in the Harmonised Index of Consumer Prices for the euro area of below 2%.' This price stability is to be maintained over the medium term. Money will be assigned a prominent role, with a reference value for the growth of a broad monetary aggregate. This reference value will be derived in a manner which is consistent with – and will serve to achieve – price stability. Under normal circumstances, deviations of the current monetary growth rate from the reference value signal risks to price stability. This concept of a reference value, of course, does not imply a commitment to mechanistically correct deviations over the short term, because this was not the case in the Bundesbank policy.

Besides this prominent reference value for the growth of broad money, a broadly-based assessment of the outlook for price developments and the risks to price stability will play a major role in the ESCB's strategy. However, a forecast figure will not be published. By this decision, the ECB Governing Council is following up to a large degree the Bundesbank's successful strategy, while at the same time taking due account of the specific conditions prevailing in the euro area, especially at the start of EMU.

By and large, the institutional and technical preparations are making substantial progress. On 1 January 1999 the ESCB will certainly be fully operational. Happily, there is broad agreement in the ECB Governing Council on the basic orientation of anti-inflation policy. Economically speaking, the Eurozone has been in a *de facto* monetary union anyway since the eleven participating states were determined and the bilateral entry rates defined. Not later than 1 January 1999, central bank interest rates must be running at a single level, but where that common level will be cannot, of course, be said with any certainty today, some eleven weeks before the start of monetary union. However, given our current knowledge of monetary trends and other economic prospects, the interest rates are likely to converge towards the lower end of the current range in the euro area. In the past few weeks, a number of central banks of the future Eurozone whose interest rates are still relatively high have undertaken significant interest-rate cuts. That process will continue in the course of the next two months. On the average, such convergence will result in a further not inconsiderable reduction in interest rates in Europe.

With its 'steady-as-she-goes' interest-rate policy, the Bundesbank has contributed to a stable monetary and economic situation in Germany and the Eurozone as a whole. That is why the IMF expressly 'commended' the Bundesbank a month ago 'for having led the way in establishing price stability in Germany as well as throughout much of the European Union'. In the process, it had created favourable conditions for the introduction of the euro. The Bundesbank's monetary policy was even characterized at that time as 'somewhat accommodative'. Gratifyingly, the target of price stability has virtually been reached in Germany and Europe alike. For the immediate future, neither particular inflation risks nor particular deflation risks are detectable at present. That must remain so. But the Bundesbank still remains vigilant: vigilant as to the extent to which new constraints might arise, and of course, vigilant as to the extent to which new room for manoeuvre might materialize.

Monetary policy must always pay heed to the specific conditions prevailing. For instance, the conditions for monetary policy in the future euro area differ to some extent from those in the United States and also in the United Kingdom. Beside the different levels of central bank rates, there are differences in the position in the business cycle and in the intensity of the trade relations with the crisis regions, not to mention the specifically European subject of the convergence of central bank rates.

III

However, there can be no doubt that the global environment has become harsher and more turbulent for Germany, and Europe as well, in the past few weeks and months. A number of East Asian countries are beset by a deep-seated, persistent financial crisis. Happily, in some countries that have initiated far-reaching adjustments, encouraging signs of consolidation are meanwhile to be seen. Russia is in the grip of a profound economic crisis, which naturally has a very worrying political dimension. In Latin America, despite considerable efforts at adjustment in some countries, there are still latent risks of contagion, and the markets have, alas, so far not taken sufficient account of the differences in conditions. And in Japan a severe crisis of confidence still prevails, involving substantial potential risks to the world economy. The recent measures to remedy the weaknesses in the banking sector might, however, constitute an important step towards overcoming the difficulties.

On the continent of Europe, by contrast, conditions have so far been distinctly more favourable. The economic upswing in the future euro area is now more broadly based. Internal expansionary forces are in the ascendant. Our trade relations with the crisis regions are not so close that the crises there are bound to trigger a recession in Europe. But besides the comparatively reassuring perception that those crises are unlikely to spill over to us (at least in the short run) through the channel of trade relations, there is increasing concern that the crises might, instead, come right into our 'front room' through the channel of financial relations, via the global financial markets.

That concern also owes something to the fiasco of the hedge fund Long-Term Capital Management, and to the response it triggered. Many people are wondering whether the greater part of the problem is not still floating below the surface, as with an iceberg. And many people fear that the present crises might result in a structural weakness of the financial system with regard to appropriate risk transformation. The first aspect concerns the emerging countries. There is a danger that, as it were, the financial markets will now withdraw from a whole category of countries without distinguishing sufficiently carefully to what extent individual countries have made structural progress.

A second aspect – albeit very vague – might be seen in the fact that banks may be less willing to run risks in extending credit, especially to enterprises. But it is not only the financial markets that should differentiate appropriately when taking investment decisions and assuming risks. The responsible politicians and central bankers should likewise make adequate distinctions in their analyses.

General panic is unwarranted, and there is no reason for lapsing into an apocalyptic mood. A dispassionate analysis shows that there are a number of factors stabilizing the world economy. They certainly include the high degree of monetary stability world-wide. They also include the favourable overall performance in the future euro area, and they likewise include the still favourable course of business activity, by and large, in the English-speaking area. What is more, many analysts make far too little distinction between developments of crisis proportions, on the one hand, and adjustments of previous exaggerations, which may even be desirable in the medium run, on the other hand. That applies, for instance, in part to some equity markets.

It is also wrong to regard the recent annual meetings of the IMF and the World Bank as a failure, as has widely been claimed. It may be true that certain incautious statements in the wings aroused some unrealistic expectations, but the results achieved in Washington should not necessarily be judged by that. Distinct progress was definitely made in Washington with regard to the future work of those organizations, and I hope very much that in the near future the US Congress will clear the hurdle and remove the obstacle to a better financial endowment of the IMF.

IV

Unwarranted though panic in the assessment of the situation is, blind political hyperactivity, with the aim of inordinately large financial programmes, would be equally undesirable. For the essential prerequisite for steering a country out of a crisis of confidence is sound domestic policies. After all, it cannot be denied that some of the emerging countries affected by the turmoil had previously made serious domestic mistakes. Not infrequently, the public and private sectors were interlinked. Foreign investors, as well as domestic financial institutions, could therefore take it for granted that they would be bailed out by the state or by IMF programmes in the event of a crisis. Unfortunately, moral hazards and the lack of financial supervision have in the past often prompted overly risky behaviour. Asset prices – especially those of real property and equities – have sky-rocketed in some cases. Investments were made which were not duly geared to the return that could realistically be expected.

Moreover, many countries had overly rigid exchange rate links. Such links may be dangerous. After all, they obstruct monetary policy. Under such a system, massive current account deficits may accumulate if a persistent inflation differential exists, and one's own currency therefore appreciates sharply in real terms. Some countries have also shown unsustainable budget deficits. All these weaknesses of domestic policies are points calling for action. The therapy and conditionality of the IMF must likewise make appropriate distinctions, and take action to deal with the actual causes of the problems. In some countries, investors' confidence can only be regained by a sustained consolidation of the national budget. In other cases, it will be necessary to settle a domestic banking crisis. In some places that may entail, not least, the creation of a stable legal system, with a clear dividing line between the private and public sectors. And in very many, if not all, cases domestic financial market supervision must be improved. It must at least meet international standards, such as have been laid down by the G10 in its Core Principles. Enhanced and efficient surveillance is likewise necessary in this context.

Not blind political hyperactivity, but action in steps, albeit target-oriented action, is on the agenda, because there have for some time been a number of sound and promising approaches at the level of international cooperation. Those approaches must be implemented. That builds more confidence in the markets than all new announcements of generous financial programmes. There are likewise reasonable approaches to making what many people regard as over-sensitive financial markets more resilient again. It is generally agreed that the global financial markets need greater transparency in order to improve their viability. Firstly, more transparency at the national level is required: beside macroeconomic data, financial market data must be monitored more carefully than before. Above all, more, and more up-to-date, particulars on national debts in foreign currencies, and on maturities, are required. This is a challenge to borrowers and lenders alike. Second, more transparency is needed at the level of market players. The experience of the past few days has shown that there seems to be a particular need to take action in the case of hedge funds. How this is to be done can still be discussed. An indirect solution has been proposed: banking supervisors monitor the lending of an individual bank to a hedge fund. The data are then compiled through an international credit register.

Taking hedge funds as the starting point has been proposed. It may well be true that they are so flexible that they can elude direct supervision whenever they want, but when it becomes apparent which hedge fund discloses data and which does not, then the market can discipline itself. Then it is competition that determines the degree of transparency. Be that as it may, if hedge funds are as important for the overall system as those responsible in the United States judge them to be, then they cannot remain exempt from supervision.

Third, more transparency is necessary about the financial instruments posing risks. That applies, for instance, to derivatives in bank balance sheets. And fourth, more transparency about the activities of the international financial institutions themselves can do no harm. On the one hand, it is true, the confidentiality of discussions must be upheld. On the other hand, the recipients of public funds must be subject to a strict assessment of performance.

V

A cool head rather than a hot heart: that would, by the way, even be appropriate – or would be particularly appropriate – if the crises in the global financial system were to spread further (though I sincerely hope, and believe, they will not). That goes for the IMF. There must be no more panic-stricken rescue operations in which private creditors are not involved. It also goes for the countries concerned. Thus, debt moratoriums announced unilaterally – that is, without including the creditors – are highly questionable. After all, a country beset by a crisis has to try to regain investors' confidence as soon as possible. Utmost caution is required on the subject of controls on capital movements, too. Trying to control, let alone to limit, the outflow of capital *ex post* in a crisis is extremely risky. Quite apart from the limited technical options, the far-reaching effects of such controls must also be borne in mind. On this point, Rudi Dornbusch has rightly said:

> In a global setting *ad hoc* capital controls in one country will immediately cause contagion not only to the 'usual subjects' but even beyond. Fearful that the crisis might spread, investors will act pre-emptively everywhere. They will pull out their money without waiting for more bad news.

A clear target-oriented stance, rather than hyper-activity: that motto likewise applies to monetary policy. A relaxation beyond the degree that is consistent with domestic stability is beneficial to nobody. In the medium and long run, it actually does harm, not only to the country itself but to the global economy as a whole. That is a lesson taught by the current problems in Japan. They are due not least to the overly expansionary monetary policy pursued in the late 1980s. At the time, Japan regarded that policy as a contribution to international cooperation, and it was actually called for by the United States. That does not mean that monetary policy should bury its head in the sand. In the Communiqué of the Interim Committee, it says: 'Should there be a worsening of the crisis or a further slowdown in economic activity, additional action on both domestic and international grounds would be required by both emerging market countries and industrial countries.' However, upheavals in the financial markets cannot be tackled by monetary policy instruments alone. Monetary policy in the industrial countries must preserve the high level of confidence and credibility it now enjoys in the financial markets. Otherwise, any measures could backfire.

VI

Without any doubt, given the crises besetting many parts of the world, the euro has passed its first acid test. That is gratifying. The markets regard the euro as a safe haven. In that respect, it has already become a serious rival to the dollar. Exchange rates in the EMS between the future euro currencies have remained stable. That demonstrates two things: the markets have accepted the transition to monetary union as being irreversible, and the euro and the independent European Central Bank are enjoying a high degree of confidence in investors' eyes.

The continuous, and sometimes exasperating, insistence on the achievement of the necessary stability conditions has thereby borne its first fruit. However, maintaining those conditions for success is a long-term task. The role of the euro as an international investment currency, anchor currency and reserve currency is inseparably associated with its internal stability. The markets will focus their attention on that. And that is the criterion whereby the markets, and also the man in the street, will judge European monetary policy at the end of the day. It is this anti-inflationary basic orientation by which the Governing Council of the European Central Bank will be guided; that emerged very clearly again from the debate we held on strategy two days ago (13 October 1998). However, for a durably stable monetary union, European monetary policy also needs the support of the other areas of economic policy, not only at the start of monetary union but also in the future. In that case, the euro has a good chance of becoming a lastingly stable currency, respected by the markets and the population alike. Domestic stability is at the same time the best contribution the euro can make to a sound, viable and stable global financial system in which the financial market players can act in a spirit of responsibility.

2 Critical years for the global financial markets

Ernst-Moritz Lipp

Factors which drive the global financial crisis

Global financial markets in the last months have been driven by two main events. The emerging market economies during the last fifteen months (of late 1997 and 1998) have witnessed turbulences unparalleled since 1945. What began as a local currency crisis in Thailand in July 1997 has evolved into a full-fledged crisis with global dimensions. It cannot be denied that this crisis poses dangers even for economic growth in the industrialized countries.

In the mature financial markets the most distinguishing feature has been the run-up to European Monetary Union (EMU), with the euro integrating the markets of eleven European countries. Even though EMU will officially start in seventy-seven days from now, the advent of the common currency has already triggered important adjustment processes on money, bond, equity and forex markets.

The financial crisis and the forthcoming EMU will be the driving forces for the future architecture of the international capital markets.

First, the introduction of the euro itself will be much more problematic if the euro area does not prove to be resistant against the contagious effects of the current crisis. This would not only impede EMU's positive effects for growth perspectives and financial development of the EU economy, but in addition create unfavourable repercussion effects for the world economy.

Second, the reintegration of the emerging market economies into the international financial system is of crucial importance for an efficient allocation of capital, which is a precondition for the future growth and wealth not only of the affected countries but of the world as a whole.

Third, the international financial system can look forward to momentous change with the launch of monetary union. EMU will integrate the monetary sphere of an economic area whose real economy is roughly comparable to that of the United States. But as a new currency, the euro will have its most direct effects in those spheres where money and money-related products are traded, that is, on European financial markets. Measured by relevant indicators the euro will give rise to the second-largest capital market in the world. However, merely adding up current data on market capitalization does not help one grasp the true potential of the monetary union project. The common currency will intensify integrative and competitive pressures and thus act as a catalyst for existing structural changes. The abolition of inner-European exchange rate risks will remove frontiers for cross-border investments. Not only the EMU participants, but also countries outside the euro area, will profit from these likely effects.

Finally, the ongoing intense public debate about the lessons to be learned from the current emerging markets crisis will have profound consequences for the future financial architecture. Questions of informational transparency, prudent supervision and systemic risks, for example, not only lie at the centre of the current crisis but must also be addressed in the context of monetary union. The decision about imposing capital controls will influence the shape of the world economy in the years to come.

Background

The decision by the central bank of Thailand to stop defending the external value of the baht on 2 July 1997 triggered a first round of depreciation in South East Asia. The immediate consequences seemed to be nothing more than a necessary correction of previously over-valued currencies. When in October 1997 it became clear that with South Korea, the eleventh biggest economy in the world, and Hong Kong, the crisis was spreading internationally, nervousness grew.

The first quarter of 1998 brought a little relief, but with increasing cyclical and structural problems of the Japanese economy, and political problems in Indonesia, the crisis intensified. In August the Russian authorities decided to abandon the rouble's dollar peg and declared a debt moratorium. Currently, there are widespread fears that the economies in Latin America, especially Brazil, will not be able to withstand contagion.

In the affected countries the currencies have depreciated by double-digit numbers, interest rates have sky-rocketed and the real economy is shrinking markedly. Banks and other financial institutions are experiencing an unprecedented liquidity-crunch after international capital flows came to a virtual standstill, interest rates rose and equity markets collapsed. IMF support, bilateral and multilateral agreements for Indonesia, Thailand and Korea alone reached US$ 118 billion.

Although the Asian crisis resembled some of the common features of past international currency crises – surges in private capital inflows, heavily reduced interest rate spreads, and large unhedged foreign currency exposures by domestic borrowers – the dimension of the crisis makes previous events like the Latin American debt and Mexican crises look like minor nuisances.

The depreciations of affected currencies are well above what even the most pessimistic observers regarded as a necessary correction. The intensity and speed of contagion exceeded those predictable by macro-economic and trade linkages. Private capital flows, which grew from US$ 31 billion in 1990 to US$ 241 billion in 1996, were reduced by US$ 70 billion in 1997. The affected Asian countries which received US$ 73 billion in 1996 had to cope with an outflow of US$ 11 billion. Capital flows to Asia as a whole shrank by US$ 100 billion, a 90 per cent reduction.

The rapid disintegration of emerging and developed capital markets as a result of the chain of events just described raises important questions. What are the reasons for such erratic market behaviour, and – assuming that potential high volatility in capital movements will accompany us in the future – what are the necessary policy responses?

There is thus an immediate need to gain a deeper understanding of the forces behind abrupt swings in international capital flows and market confidence. The issue has not been settled yet, neither theoretically nor empirically; or as the IMF aptly phrased it, 'The increasingly integrated global financial system has produced important efficiency gains, but the new system's market dynamics are not fully understood.'

The 1990s have seen net private capital flows to emerging markets in an amount of US$ 1.2 trillion. One-third of these flows was directed to Asia. The growth in private flows went along with the declining relative importance of official capital flows. These official flows accounted for 50 per cent of all flows in the 1970s, compared to 10 per cent for the period 1990 to 1996.

Nearly half of the recent net flows have been foreign direct investments (FDIs), a total of US$ 580 billion. The other half consisted of portfolio investments and net bank lending. Especially important in that context is the fact that the sharp turn-around in capital flows ocurred only in short-term portfolio investments and bank lending. FDIs still grew at 20 per cent last year. Equally remarkable, short-term flows have been significantly more volatile than FDIs.

The increasing volume of capital inflows was accompanied by improving conditions for market access. Bond issues by emerging markets soared steadily during the 1990s with an average yearly growth rate of nearly 130 per cent. The same can be said – with less impressive growth rates, however – for equity issues and syndicated loans. Financing conditions for emerging market bonds improved since the Mexican crisis. Spreads of the Emerging Bonds Market Index (EMBI) reached an all-time low of 335 base points in the first week of October 1997, the spread on the Eurobond market narrowed down to 200 base points or less for Russia, Asian and Latin American countries.

These improvements were, by and large, based on a shift in market sentiment in favour of these countries. Recent econometric research supports the view that the observed spread declines can be explained not by improved economic fundamentals but by a change in market confi-dence. There is therefore a strong indication that international credit markets have difficulty in pricing risks adequately.

Diverse explanations have been given for these deficiencies: asymmetric information, moral hazard on the part of borrowers and lenders, the liberalization of capital markets with imprudently supervised and weakly regulated financial institutions, and finally, irrational herding by international investors. Of course, there is some grain of truth in all these arguments.

Financial markets allocate savings into investments, and financial intermediaries exist to overcome the inherent problem of asymmetric information between the two sides of the market. When international investors have incomplete information about the health of those intermediaries, and/or they believe in an implicit bail-out in case of a crisis, an external shock in form of a currency depreciation can throw a weak financial system from apparent stability into disaster. The serious blow to investors' confidence, coupled with incomplete information, leads to a reassesment of investment strategies in countries perceived to be similar to the one in crisis, thereby setting into motion a fatal herding.

If this is an accurate description of the current crisis story, the lessons to be learned are obvious, although their implementation will certainly prove to be difficult. As most of these topics will certainly be a major theme of the SUERF congress, just let me briefly mention what I regard as the most important lessons and reform proposals:

1   More or less sound macroeconomic policies are no guarantee against a major economic crisis.
2   Capital account liberalization necessitates a healthy domestic financial system. Without efficient surveillance and prudential supervision, financial deregulation is a dangerous game. Investing countries should demand that an effective supervisory framework – for example, the 'Core Principles for Effective Banking Supervision' by the Basle Committee for Banking Supervision – is established.
3   The flow of information in the international financial system needs to be improved. The standardization of relevant data in the SDDS programme of the IMF is a first step in the right direction.
4   Private investors should be more involved in crisis management, to prevent both moral hazard and irrational herding.
5   Capital controls should be implemented carefully, when necessary. They might prove necessary in order to discriminate between excessive inflows of short-term capital and long-term capital flows resulting from FDIs. Capital controls as an *ex post* measure to prevent further capital flights need to be evaluated even more critically. The basic reason for such controls is that they make it possible to lower interest rates without provoking a new round of depreciation. However, the economic costs are enormous: credibility to foreign investors might be permanently destroyed, and the bureaucratic expenditures to carry through the instrument are immense. Therefore, controls

implemented in the face of a crisis are a kind of political sledgehammer and should only be used as an *ultima ratio*. Moreover, if imposed they should be irrevocably terminated.

EMU against this background

At the same time as most emerging economies are suffering from their worst recession in decades, eleven countries of the European Union merge their national currencies and surrender monetary autonomy. The members of the ECB's Governing Council could not have found a more difficult time to formulate and implement the rules governing the new monetary regime. Even without the current international turbulences, the introduction of the euro would have been a more than awkward task, but with a view to the economic slump in nearly 40 per cent of the world economy, careful monetary management in the early stages of EMU has become even more important.

Hitherto, the USA and the EU countries, which together make up 60 per cent of the world economy, have been affected by the crisis mainly through increasing asset-market volatility. The real economy of both areas seems to be strong enough to resist the negative external pressures. Of course that is no certainty, however, and the Asian crisis has remarkably proven Murphy's Law: what can go wrong, does go wrong. Thus, the critical question at the moment is: which political instruments do the industrialized countries have to withstand contagion?

A central role will be played by the monetary policy authorities in the USA and Europe. The fundamental problem is not whether to cut rates and by what magnitude, but how to guide markets in an environment in which self-fulfilling prophecies reign. The danger of a significant slowdown in economic growth in both regions, fed by pessimistic expectations, is clearly undeniable.

In order effectively to guide expecatations, the ECB must gain the credibility of markets. As a new institution, by definition it can not rely on a historic track-record. Even more important is a coherent, practicable strategy and a transparent use of instruments.

The difficult economic environment has shown that financial markets have given the ECB marked trust. There is no other economic explanation for the fact that the future euro area is functioning as a safe haven in the current turbulences. None of the eleven national EMU currencies were put under pressure in September 1998. Although Norway had to devalue the krona by 10 per cent in the aftermath of the Russian crisis, the Finnmark remained stable. This is even more surprising when one considers that the trade linkages between Russia and Finland are more intense than those between Russia and Norway.

The euro has passed its first critical test even before it comes into existence, but the experiences of the Asian tiger states have shown that every trust must be earned *ex post*.

As far as contagion is concerned, in my view the monetary policy responses of both the Fed and the ECB are clearly adequate. The rate cut by the Fed and the convergence of money market rates of the euro countries at the low German level mean expansionary monetary impulses in both regions.

The impact on the European financial system

The euro will strongly influence the future design of the international monetary system. With the creation of the euro area, at one fell swoop the second-largest capital market of the world emerges. At the moment capitalization of the US bond and stock market is over two-and-a-half times higher than in Europe, reflecting the fact that the US financial market exhibits the greatest market depth, breadth and liquidity worldwide. But the euro will mean a quantum leap for the European financial system.

The elimination of exchange risk will boost market transparency on the money, bond and stock markets and foster the Europeanization of investment and issuing behaviour. Ensuing competition among issuers for investment capital that can move freely around Europe will harmonize market techniques and cut the transaction costs of direct market access. This will foster the tendency towards securitization in Europe, which is still under-developed compared to the United States.

EMU will make the single European financial market deeper, broader and more liquid than the sum total of the eleven national EMU markets at present. Integrative pressure will, however, differ in intensity on the markets. Let me therefore briefly describe some of the consequences of monetary union for the European money, bond and stock market.

The liquidity and volume of the money market will be dependent largely on the technical features of the ECB's monetary policy. It is already foreseeable that liquidity will be supplied by the ECB using market techniques. Repo agreements in the form of weekly standard tenders with fortnightly maturities will act as the main funding instrument.

The EMU money market is currently dominated largely by interbank dealings and the sale of short-term national debt. Until recently the German money market in particular was almost exclusively a strictly interbank market. Not until 1996 did the German government also begin issuing national debt instruments in the lower maturity range. The lack of liquidity of the term structure of German interest rates in the lower maturity segment is explained by the Bundesbank's aversion to any form of short-term national debt for fear of a conflict between fiscal and monetary policy.

Companies outside the financial sector have hitherto made scarcely any use of money market transactions for their liquidity management. The only exception is French firms, who have currently issued over 60 per cent of the euro-joiners' commercial paper holdings. On the euro money market largeish German companies are likely to have greater recourse to the market for commercial paper, especially since they will find more developed markets for the procurement of securitized liquidity in other euro countries (notably France).

EMU will likewise see the emergence of the second largest market for bonds with medium and long maturities. At the moment the bond and medium-term note segment of the eurobond market has a volume of not quite 50 per cent of the US market and 128 per cent of the Japanese market. Government issues dominate the European market. In comparison with the USA, the market for corporate bonds in particular is clearly underdeveloped. Again, this reflects the strong significance of the European banking sector as a source of external financing for companies, which has already been mentioned.

At present there is no liquid corporate bond market in Europe. Only big, internationally operative corporations tap the commercial paper and corporate bond market as a source of financing. But the advent of EMU will create a favourable regulatory framework for the emergence of just such a market segment. The absence of exchange risk will increase pressure to design an efficient rating system. This will be to the benefit of the potential market for corporate bonds, because it needs detailed rating.

The increased market transparency resulting from the euro and falling transaction costs will make financing with funds borrowed directly on the capital market more attractive. The demand for capital by the corporate sector which this may possibly generate will meet with appropriate supply, for two reasons in particular:

1   EMU will reduce the scope for spreading government bond risks Europe-wide. Investors will therefore need alternative investments in order to optimize the risk/earnings structure of their portfolios.
2   The Amsterdam stability pact and the necessity of fiscal consolidation in many EMU countries are reducing government recourse to the bond market.

Issuing their own bonds on a pan-European market will, however, presumably be a privilege reserved for big companies only. For by far the greater majority of small and medium-size companies, traditional financing through the local banking sector will remain the most efficient and cost-effective alternative.

At present the European stock markets are similarly fragmented to the bond markets. On an international comparison, EMU will create a stock market with capitalization equivalent to roughly 30 per cent of the US volume. The United Kingdom's absence will have significant implications here, because the EU-15 achieve a capitalization ratio of almost 50 per cent of the American market.

The euro will tend to release the same integrative forces on to the stock markets as have been outlined for the bond market, but the process of market homogenization will be slower than on the money and bond markets. The differences still existing in the tax, accounting and legal systems of the various EMU members will persistently run counter to rapid and complete market integration.

The attitude towards stock investment, and hence the willingness to take risk, is still not particularly pronounced on the Continent. But in this respect, too, developments have begun to gather momentum ahead of EMU, suggesting that the EMU countries are in the process of catching up. Given that capital market rates remain lower, and as the funding predicament besetting state pension schemes comes ever more clearly into focus, European stock markets will attract more attention from investors in future.

Here, too, the elimination of exchange risk will lead to an improvement in the risk/earnings profile. The portfolio restructuring which this induces will go hand in hand with greater cross-frontier sectoral orientation instead of traditional risk weighting by countries. Extra liquidity will be available for the Europeanization of investment decisions, since EMU will, by and large, eliminate the legal restrictions on cross-border investment within Europe in the form of various currency-matching rules, which presently confront institutional investors (life assurance companies and investment funds).

International liquidity will concentrate on European blue chips, but in the wake of rising price/earnings ratios for these equities, growth-oriented small caps will also come into focus for investment decisions.

Events in the recent past offer empirical evidence of this in Germany. Admittedly, there too around 90 per cent of share turnover is in only 5 per cent of the listed companies. But in recent months high liquidity and the removal of various legal impediments have turned Germany into a sought-after location for medium-size companies in forward-looking industries to procure equity capital through the stock market (New Market).

By international standards, it is obvious that the stock markets in Europe have much ground to make up in the medium to long term, and they are only at the beginning of this process.

All this will, of course, have direct effects on the competitive environment of banks and other financial institutions. The Europeanization of financial industries ultimately raises important questions concerning supervision and crisis management. I know the Colloquium will discuss these topics in detail, so I do not want to anticipate them. I am sure this congress will provide new interesting insights, and I hope it will also allow delegates enough time to get some impression of 'Mainhattan', the city where the euro is going to be managed.

3 'One size fits all?'

EMU and Procrustes

Michael Artis

Introduction

The myth of Procrustes is well known. According to the *Oxford Companion to Classical Literature*, Procrustes was 'a legendary brigand of Eleusis, who used to lay travellers on a bed, and if they were too long for it, cut short their limbs; but if the bed was longer, stretch them to make their length equal to it'. This legend holds a moral for member countries of the Eurozone: whatever their individual preferences and needs there will be only one monetary policy, only one interest rate structure, a 'one size fits all' monetary policy.

In the transition to Stage Three it has already been decided to embark on the Procrustean process. Figure 3.1, based on the 'Euroconvergence' series printed in the *Financial Times*, shows the configuration of Central Bank interest rates in September 1998, when the expectation was that the ECB interest rate would settle at 3.75 per cent on 4 January 1999, and illustrates the dimensions of the Procrustean task. Several countries were then chosen as being required to reduce their interest rates (Ireland, Italy, Spain and Portugal) while others were expected to raise them. In the event, the South East Asian and Russian crises reduced the convergence rate to 3.3 per cent, eliminating the immediate need for many countries to raise their rates. But the basic Procrustean problem remained; and the legend suggests that the Procrustean bed can be uncomfortable, even painful, for some.

The focus of this address is on this issue and, more specifically, on the issue of the homogeneity of the Eurozone elect, the EU-11 forming the 'first wave' of monetary union, with the remaining EU countries currently staying outside the monetary union. By measuring the homogeneity of the groupings, we can obtain some impression of where the strains and difficulties are most likely to come, and what might be done to ease the problems of adjustment. The fact that some inhomogeneities can indeed be found by no means implies that monetary union is unsustainable or that members will secede; such a scenario is an extreme case. In the more general case, it simply follows from the fact that participation in the Union

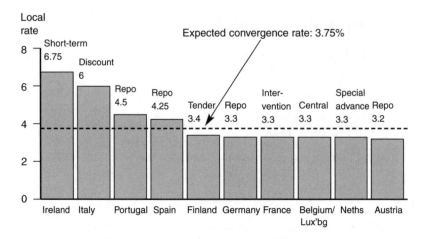

Figure 3.1 Eurozone interest rate convergence, September 1998

Note: This chart shows the official interest rates of the eleven countries that will
participate in Europe's forthcoming single currency. Analysts surveyed by
Standard and Poor's MMS expect the short-term interest rates of the eleven
countries to converge at a 3.75% initial rate for the European Central Bank
at the beginning of 1999

is a cost–benefit calculation for each country, that some countries will be
observed to face some costs; the positive way to view this is to ask what
policy adjustments can be made to minimize those costs. Another purpose
of the analysis is to enquire into the rationality of the decision to remain
outside the Eurozone which Denmark, Sweden and the UK have taken,
while the position of Greece will also come under the spotlight.

The contribution of OCA theory

Economists approaching the issue of monetary union have relied heavily
on 'optimal currency area theory' to guide them. Although open to
important qualifications, this approach, pioneered by such figures as
Mundell, McKinnon and Kenen, continues to provide important insights
into the *desiderata* of currency union. I appeal to it here to provide us with
some dimensions by which to judge the homogeneity of the EU-11 and
prospective EU-15 Eurozone. The framework within which those dimensions will be used here to assess the homogeneity of the current and
prospective Eurozones is provided by cluster analysis. In what follows I
shall draw extensively on joint work, using cluster analysis, that I have
carried out in cooperation with my colleague Wenda Zhang. It is reported
more formally in two Discussion Papers of the European University
Institute, 'Core and Periphery in EMU: A Cluster Analysis' (Artis and
Zhang 1998) and 'Membership of EMU: A Fuzzy Clustering Analysis of

Alternative Criteria' (Artis and Zhang 1999), where further references to the relevant literature may also be found.

It is useful to look very briefly here at the framework of cluster analysis. The simplest illustration I can give of it is shown in Figure 3.2. In this figure, five points are plotted in two dimensions, *x1* and *x2*. The task is to group the 'objects' A, B, C, D and E defined in *x1*, *x2* space into clusters of 'similar' objects. To do this we might first put A and B together into a cluster ('cluster 1'), then C and D ('cluster 2'). Object E might be put into cluster 1, but with the misgiving that E is nearly as much like objects in cluster 2 as it is like those in cluster 1. In fact we might well prefer to say something like, 'object E belongs 60 per cent to cluster 1 and 40 per cent to cluster 2'. This is a neat example of the merits of 'soft' (or fuzzy) clustering as against hard clustering. Hard clustering forces the allocation of each object to a cluster; soft clustering produces statements of 'belong-ingness'. I shall subsequently apply both approaches to the actual and prospective Eurozone countries. Before I do so, it is necessary to elucidate some relevant characteristics or dimensions, by reference to which 'similarity' can be assessed.

The dimensions

In Figure 3.2, clustering was performed on the basis of an 'eyeball' assessment of the minimum distance between the objects in the two-dimensional space provided. By invoking the appropriate economic theory it is possible to isolate six dimensions for which appropriate data exist for countries, and to proceed in an analogous way to form clusters by mini-mizing the distance between the countries. Formally, the distance minimized is the Euclidean one (the square root of the sum of the squared distance in each dimension). To provide a control on the procedure and to ensure that the results are not nonsensical, the set of countries used

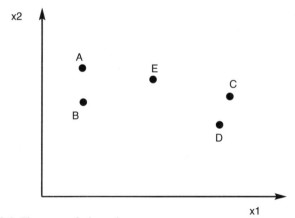

Figure 3.2 Cluster analysis options

here is the EU-15 together with the US, Canada and Japan and two non-
EU European countries, Norway and Switzerland. It is assumed that
Germany is the prospective centre country of the Union, and the variables
are measured accordingly, with respect to Germany.

These variables are:

1 the differential between a country's rate of inflation and that in
   Germany
2 the proportion of a country's trade which is transacted with Germany
3 the volatility of a country's real DM exchange rate
4 the synchronization of a country's business cycle with that in Germany
5 the synchronization of a country's monetary policy (measured by its
   real interest rate) with that in Germany
6 the flexibility of a country's labour market with respect to Germany's
   (measured by the ranking of the severity of its employment protection
   legislation).

The data have been derived at monthly frequencies, generally over the
period from April 1979 to September/October 1995.

The reasoning behind this choice of variables deserves an exposition.
The first variable – inflation convergence – is the only one not to be
explicit in the traditional optimum currency area literature. That literature
was first conceived in the era of 'fix-price' economics, so price stability was
in a sense simply assumed. In any case it has become quite clear – not least
from the negotiations leading up to the Maastricht Treaty – that convergence on low inflation is a *sine qua non* of monetary union; hence it is
essential to include it here. (The panoply of fiscal, interest rate and
exchange rate criteria that appears in the Maastricht Treaty itself may be
viewed as a supportive extension of the inflation convergence criterion
which also appears there). The remaining variables are all suggested by the
principal arguments of OCA theory. The trade criterion, for example,
directly reflects the idea in the OCA literature that the principal benefit of
a currency area (the elimination of exchange costs) is the greater, the
greater the extent of trade with the partner country. The variables 3, 4 and
5 relate directly to the main perceived costs of currency union, which are
the renunciation of a separate monetary policy, and the possibility of
exchange rate change to cope with shocks that impact differently on the
country concerned and its prospective partners: so-called asymmetric
shocks. So, in this instance, the less the volatility of a country's real DM
exchange rate (variable 3) the less there is to lose by entering a currency
union with Germany. In similar fashion, the more highly synchronized a
country's business cycle is with that in Germany (variable 4), the less the
need for an independent monetary policy; then (variable 5), the greater
the synchronization of a country's monetary policy with that in Germany,
the less is the loss of resigning monetary policy independence. The final

variable considered is labour market flexibility. Theoretical considerations suggest that labour market flexibility enables adjustment to shocks to take place with less need for macro-policy adjustment.

To summarize, I have suggested six dimensions along which clustering, or the detection of similarity, may be reviewed most relevantly. All are expressed with respect to Germany, which is regarded as the centre country. The clustering algorithms thus provide clusters of countries which are similar in respect of these variables. Notice that similarity in being very far from Germany (with, for example, little trade with Germany, low business cycle synchronization, and a volatile DM exchange rate) is just as relevant as similarity in being very close to Germany for detecting a cluster as such. The clusters are just clusters of 'similar' objects.

The results

First, the results of a 'hard clustering' approach are shown in Table 3.1.

For the *cognoscenti* it may be noted that these results are those obtained when hard clustering is pursued using the so-called 'group average' agglomerative algorithm, but a very similar result is obtained when the so-called 'centroid' method is used in the agglomerative algorithm. In any case, the results indicate a clear cohesive 'core group' and two peripheral groups among the European countries – a Northern and a Southern group – while North America and Japan are clearly indicated as separate groups, distinct from the others.

Before the important respects in which the groups differ are discussed, it should be noticed that the 'fuzzy' clustering approach yields highly supportive results. For the 'fuzzy' clustering approach, the example concentrates solely on the EU-15 countries, but using the same six dimensions as for the hard clustering approach. The method yields 'membership coefficients', or 'degrees of belongingness' for each country, summing to 100 per cent across three possible clusters. Table 3.2 gives an excerpt from these results. The figures in italics show the highest degree of 'belongingness' of a country to one of the groups. These identify exactly the country-membership of the three European clusters given by the hard

Table 3.1 Clusters of countries detected under hard clustering

1	Core group	{France, Netherlands, Belgium, Austria}	RMS: .56
2	Northern periphery	{Denmark, Ireland, Switzerland, Sweden, Norway, Finland, UK}	RMS: .81
3	Southern periphery	{Italy, Spain, Portugal, Greece}	RMS: .47
4	North America	{USA, Canada}	RMS: .18
5	Japan	{Japan}	

Table 3.2 Fuzzy clustering: membership coefficients

	Group I (Core)	Group II (Northern)	Group III (Southern)
France	62.7	19.9	17.4
Italy	11.6	18.5	69.9
Netherlands	87.3	7.0	5.7
Belgium	87.9	6.1	6.0
Denmark	22.8	58.7	18.5
Austria	66.7	16.2	17.1
Ireland	8.4	75.8	15.8
Spain	8.1	28.7	63.2
Portugal	2.1	4.9	93.0
Sweden	3.2	86.8	10.0
Finland	6.1	82.5	11.4
Greece	8.1	15.5	76.4
UK	5.3	82.9	11.8

clustering approach. The most marginal country is Denmark which has a 22.8 per cent membership coefficient for the core group.

From the viewpoint of the cohesiveness of the EU-11 'first-wave' monetary union, the good news is that there is a strong core of countries around Germany, including France, Austria, Belgium and the Netherlands. (Notice that, strictly speaking, what the clustering algorithms identify is a group of countries similar to each other in respect of the six dimensions, all measured with respect to Germany. Germany can be added to the core group, however, since this group is 'close' to Germany in the relevant senses.) These countries have been those identified in most other studies of monetary union in Europe. In such studies (of which those by Bayoumi and Eichengreen are the best known: e.g. Bayoumi and Eichengreen 1993, 1996), Denmark is a 'swing' member of the core, sometimes in and sometimes out, while France also is sometimes placed on the margin. In our results France is a more marginal member of the core group than any of the others identified in this group, but none the less is decisively more attached to the core than to the peripheral groups. By the same token there is the concern that there is a quite strongly identified 'Northern periphery' group which includes two member countries of the EU-11 (Ireland and Finland) as well as three of the 'pre-in' or 'out' countries (Denmark, Sweden and the UK). A distinctive characteristic of this group is that its business cycle is poorly correlated with that of Germany, while its real DM exchange rate has exhibited a good deal of volatility.

The 'Southern periphery' group distances itself from the core in different respects: inflation convergence is weak, labour markets are less flexible and the monetary policy cycle is weakly correlated with Germany's.

Finally, it is worth noting that the method fares well in identifying the North American and Japanese groups as quite separate from the European groups. In fact, as the RMS distance measure indicates (see the hard clustering results) the US–Canada group is a very cohesive one, detected when the critical distance is very small.

Implications

The data thus distinguish some clear inhomogeneities among the EU-15. How much do they matter? Some observers would claim that past data are a poor guide, at least in this instance, to the future. There is even a disturbing tendency to invoke an 'ever-optimistic Lucas-critique', to argue that wherever past data suggest a bad problem, the severity of the problem itself will produce a solution. This kind of approach exemplifies wishful thinking to an unreasonable degree.

I prefer a more measured approach. The data sample used here includes all of the 1980s and the first part of the 1990s. The Maastricht Treaty created incentives for countries to satisfy its criteria in order to qualify for participation in monetary union. In particular, inflation was much more convergent towards the end of the sample period than it was on average. This is especially true of the Southern periphery group. To the extent that the convergence indicates a sustainable change in stability culture, the pre-Maastricht data are indeed a poor guide, but to the extent that the Maastricht qualification date induced temporary and unsustainable adjustments, the past data provide a better guide to the underlying position.

The position of the Northern periphery group is rather different. A principal issue here is the lack of synchronization with the German business cycle. This has shown no recent sign of changing. Nevertheless, it is important to recall that this criterion might prove endogenous: that is to say, it may be that a major component in the asymmetry of the cycles is asymmetry in policy, which will automatically be removed by the monetary union's single policy, while further trade growth may itself be conducive to more cyclical synchronization. Jeff Frankel and Andy Rose are among those who have recently argued in this fashion (e.g. Frankel and Rose 1998). If they are right, then this 'cost' of monetary union will be transitory rather than permanent, and treated on a discounted basis, it should therefore have much less salience than it has been given. But it would be premature to count on this.

Policy adjustments

Meanwhile, consideration has to be given to the issue of substitute policies for the loss of independent monetary policy by those countries for which it is likely to matter most. This applies as much to those countries, presently out as to those that are in, since all four 'out' countries 'belong' on the analysis here to one of the 'periphery' groups, three of them to the Northern periphery group for which cyclical desynchronization is an important consideration. The most important macro-policy weapons left in national hands after monetary union are fiscal policy (within the limits allowed by the Growth and Stability Pact) and wages policy, though regional policy may constitute an important third prospective entry.

An important characteristic of monetary policy which fiscal policy may need to be 'trained' to share is that of flexibility. A long struggle against the former dominance of fine-tuning considerations in the formation of fiscal policy has led to a perverse situation of excessive rigidity in this respect, which now needs to be qualified. The role of wages policies can be seen as one which smaller countries may best be placed to exploit. They may be in a better position to internalize the necessities of adjustment when an important macro-policy adjustment avenue is blocked. Observers should be looking to note instances of flexible and adaptable fiscal policy, wage concertation and constructive wage negotiating, for they may prove the key to the success of montary union. They will also provide relevant lessons for those countries now outside the monetary union which are contemplating joining.

Conclusions

In this address I have sought to bring forward some considerations on the homogeneity of the current and prospective future Eurozone. Some implications have been explored, but interested readers may think of more, or different, ones.

A companion technique to that of cluster analysis in the pattern recognition field is the so-called 'faces' representation of multivariate data. It is a commonplace of everyday life that we can identify (albeit sometimes with error) groups of people by their facial characteristics. That facility can be exploited here. Rendering each of the six dimensions of currency area suitability as facial characteristics produces the cartoon faces of Figure 3.3.

Specifically, business cycle correlation is represented by the fatness of the face; exchange rate volatility by the curve of the mouth; interest rate synchronization by the distance between the eyes; trade intensity by the length of the nose; inflation differentials by the shape of the eyebrows; and labour market flexibility by the size of the ears. That the groups are relatively homogeneous and distinct from one another stands out in this representation. That the core group appears to be smiling might be worth discussion . . .

Bibliography

Artis, M. and Zhang, W. (1998) 'Core and Periphery in EMU: A Cluster Analysis', *EUI Working Papers RSC no. 98/37*, European University Institute, Florence.

Artis, M. and Zhang, W. (1999) 'Membership of EMU: A Fuzzy Clustering Analysis of Alternative Criteria', *EUI Working Papers RSC no. 98/52*, European University Institute, Florence.

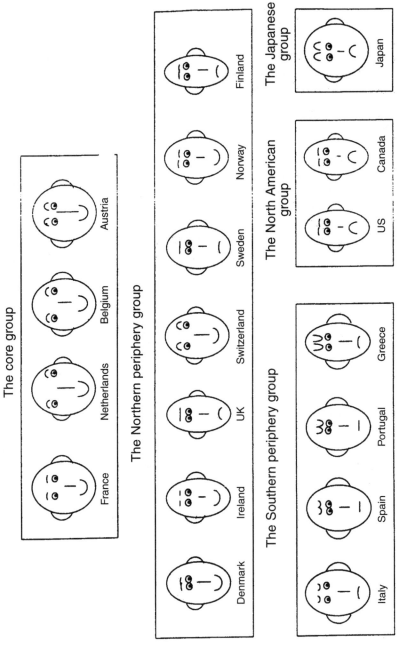

Figure 3.3 Faces representation of OCA criteria

Bayoumi, T. and Eichengreen, B. (1993) 'Shocking Aspects of European Monetary Integration', in F. Torres and F. Giavazzi (eds), *Adjustment and Growth in the European Monetary Union*, Cambridge University Press, Cambridge.

Bayoumi, T. and Eichengreen, B. (1996) 'Operationalising the Theory of Optimum Currency Areas', *CEPR Discussion papers no. 1484*, Centre for Economic Policy Research, London.

Frankel, J. and Rose, A. (1998) 'The Endogeneity of The Optimum Currency Area Criteria', *Economic Journal* 108: 1009–25.

4 Evolving ambitions in Europe's monetary unification

The Robert Marjolin Lecture

Niels Thygesen

When I received the kind invitation of SUERF to give the Marjolin Lecture at the Frankfurt Colloquium of SUERF I became enthusiastic, because there is for me a close link between Economic and Monetary Union (EMU) in Europe and the name of Robert Marjolin. My introduction to the subject of Europe's monetary integration in fact goes back to my participation in a group headed by Robert Marjolin in 1974–5, exactly twenty-five years ago.

At that time the Werner plan, drawn up in 1970 by a group of high European officials, was in disarray. The eruption of high inflation following the oil price hike of 1973–4 and the transition to floating exchange rates had made the international environment for this ambitious undertaking too hostile. In the winter of 1973–4 the European Commission therefore decided to have a group of independent experts study whether introducing EMU by 1980 was still possible.

Several prominent economists with highly sceptical views about EMU joined the group. Notable among them were Professor Herbert Giersch of Kiel and Sir Donald McDougall, then Chief Adviser to the Confederation of British Industries. There were also more positive voices such as Professor Hans Bosman, already then Secretary-General of SUERF, whose presence in this colloquium I deeply miss. Hans Bosman was a great European and contributed substantially to the debates in the Marjolin group. There was also Bernard Clappier, later to become Governor of the Banque de France and an architect of the European Monetary System (EMS). His view was that EMU might have been feasible if officials had been bolder in 1970 and had moved much more rapidly to lock up exchange rates. I also count myself among the optimistic members of the group in these dark moments of the 1970s. But in the end we were all persuaded to sign up to a sceptical report in April 1975 (see Marjolin *et al.* 1975). Robert Marjolin himself has briefly and brutally summarized the conclusions from this report in his memoirs written shortly before his death in 1986, a decade later (see Marjolin 1986).

In his memoirs Marjolin does not devote many pages to his presidency of the EMU group named after him. This of course was to be expected for someone who had achieved much greater things in life than chairing a committee. Robert Marjolin came to the group with his rich experience, first as Secretary General of the OEEC from 1948 when he was only thirty-seven, then ten years later as the first Vice-President for Economic Affairs of the new European Commission. Marjolin also brought, particularly from the former of these experiences and from his many links to the United States, a global perspective to Europe's integration. He speaks in his memoirs of 'the illusion of Economic and Monetary Union' and he criticizes politicians for seeing EMU as a substitute for political union. Marjolin further noted that 'national economic and monetary policies have never in 25 years been more discordant' (Marjolin *et al.* 1975). Indeed, 1975 when the report appeared was marked not only by double-digit inflation, but by inflation rates of 20–25 per cent in Italy and the United Kingdom. Europe was about to enter a cycle of devaluation and inflation. While we worked in the group France was mostly outside the currency snake, the rudimentary exchange-rate arrangement that had been put in place in 1972 as the main legacy of the Werner Report. The Marjolin Report pointed to an absence on the part of politicians of any real understanding of what was involved in EMU and it encouraged governments 'to concentrate on the immediate problems of inflation, balance of payment deficits and unemployment' (ibid.).

With a certain pride Marjolin noted in 1986 that the report he presided over had its effect: 'there was no more talk of EMU'. He specu-lates whether the report may have contributed indirectly to the creation of the EMS three years later, but he also states that it would absurd to speak of a practical arrangement such as the EMS as being a step towards full monetary union.

I wish Robert Marjolin were still here to continue the argument. Some of the conclusions of his report have stood the test of time; others have not. The EMS did in the end turn out to be a step towards EMU, both in its long and successful survival and, more paradoxically, in its demise in 1992–3. And in the long run, EMU may well turn out to be the best possible solution to preserving the priorities of low inflation and the containment of balance-of-payment imbalances, and hence to meeting a precondition for addressing Europe's current main problem: unemployment.

In the following I want to trace the ambitions of European monetary integration as they evolved over the past twenty-five years. I note five major ambitions and survey how they evolved, gradually gaining ground and overcoming the opposition, mostly from national policy makers, but also – and sadly from my point of view – from a majority of academic economists. The five evolving ambitions are the following:

- reducing, then eliminating nominal exchange-rate fluctuations
- reducing, then eliminating inflation
- developing rules for non-monetary national policies, then scope for coordinating them without undermining the rules

- developing a potential role in the international monetary system, then adjusting it to the realities of today
- developing a European profile in financial regulation.

Truthfully only the first three, or maybe more correctly two and a half, of these ambitions can be said to have been fulfilled with EMU as it has started on 1 January 1999. There are still unfulfilled ambitions. In any case, to start the discussion it is necessary to go back to the origins of the EMS or even further. In doing so I rely heavily on joint work with Daniel Gros, embodied in a book that we first published in 1992 and have now published in a significantly revised second edition (Gros and Thygesen 1998).[1]

Reducing, then eliminating nominal exchange rate fluctuations

The reduction – and finally elimination – of exchange-rate fluctuations must be said to have been the core achievement of the two decades since 1978. The European Monetary System evolved gradually from damage limitation via joint exchange-rate management to almost stable rates in the beginning of the 1990s. In the first four years of the system, exchange-rate changes were still frequent; seven of them occurred in these four years. The system gradually firmed up over the next four years from March 1983, constraining exchange-rate fluctuations quite successfully, as countries tried to converge on Germany. From January 1987 a period of fully stabilized exchange rates followed, and it lasted until September 1992. Towards the end of that period it even became fashionable to talk as if Europe was already in a quasi-monetary union.

A common currency was identified in the Delors Report (Committee for the Study of EMU 1989) as necessary for the final stage of Europe's monetary unification. This was a remarkable development; in the late 1980s the ambition talked about was initially just to have fully locked exchange rates. But it was recognized that it was very difficult to foresee that exchange rates would become 'irrevocably' locked in the absence of a common monetary authority, and indeed a common monetary unit. The evolution of the ambition to go all the way to a common currency implied that one moved from coordinating national policies and integrating financial markets to full-scale unification. That in turn implied a significant simplification of the task of monetary policy, because one would then move to a more familiar 'national' model.

In his remarkable book *The Road to Monetary Union in Europe* Tommaso Padoa-Schioppa (1994) notes that the utopian perspective of full currency union was confirmed as a realistic option by the 1992–3 crises in the EMS. With the degree of capital mobility achieved at the end of the 1980s, fixed-but-adjustable exchange rates might have become impossible to maintain. Central bankers found it difficult to face this issue, and claimed in most cases that the experience with the EMS was sufficiently promising to justify aiming no further than a well functioning EMS. It is more surprising that many, if not most, academic economists also found it extremely difficult to accept this ambition as reasonable in economic terms. I suggest that this is due to two important biases in much of the economic analysis of full monetary union. The first is that the alternative to EMU is viewed in too optimistic a perspective. The second is that the issue of asymmetric shocks affecting the participants in EMU in a differential way has been played up too much in the economic debate, confounding the possible with the probable. Finally, most of the academic discussion seems to have under-estimated the benefits of fully eliminating exchange-rate fluctuations.

The theory of optimum currency areas (OCA) has provided the econ-omist with a useful checklist for the evaluation of whether an economy could derive net benefits from participating in a monetary union with one or more of its trading partners. Unfortunately the vagueness and the static character of the proposed criteria, as well as their failure to give full attention to the alternative to monetary union, have in my view imparted a certain bias against EMU in much of the academic literature on the subject. That in turn has left many economists and non-economists alike with the conclusion that EMU must be a project that can only be under-stood in political terms.

Nobody will deny that EMU has a political inspiration which may well have been dominant for some of the main actors in the process, such as Chancellor Kohl. But monetary union would not have come about if it did not have a stronger backing than the bulk of the professional economics literature suggests in economic arguments, as perceived by large segments of business, trade unions and financial market participants. What are the causes of this gap in perceptions? And who is closer to reality?

Maybe the main weakness of the analytical framework of OCA theory lies in its inadequate attention to the alternative. It implicitly assumes that the alternative to a country's participation in a monetary union is *either* a well-functioning system of tightly managed exchange rates, where rare realignments of parities are undertaken in situations of major country-specific or asymmetric disturbances without upsetting otherwise stable foreign-exchange markets, *or* a system of floating rates reminiscent of the ideal state of Friedman's classic 1953 case for flexible rates, where markets smoothly provide a safety valve for the adjustment to residual differences between economic performances and/or policies in two areas. Both of these benchmark cases appear excessively optimistic when one considers a realistic overall alternative to EMU.

On important occasions the former of the two benchmarks received official status. The European Commission, usually not suspected of bias against monetary union, no doubt in its major report *One Market, One Money* (Emerson *et al.* 1990) considerably underestimated the potential gains of realizing EMU by comparing it to a continuation of the apparently successful tight EMS which existed at the time. The benefits of eliminating the small residual exchange-rate variability of the early 1990s were perceived to be small, though larger than the additional costs which had already been borne. In a surprising show of confidence some central bankers even said that should EMU fail to be implemented, the informal and pragmatic cooperation between central banks in the EMS had become sufficiently robust largely to reproduce the effect desired with EMU.

The foreign exchange turmoil in 1992–3 demonstrated that any such confidence was misplaced. A system of fixed exchange rates where the possibility of realignments has not been excluded is very vulnerable in a state of high capital mobility, which pushes countries beyond cooperation towards full-scale abolition of national monetary autonomy. Without this final step, the ERM would remain prone to speculative attacks, as Padoa-Schioppa had already argued in 1988.

Models for such attacks had originally been inspired by observations of national monetary policies gradually leading to the exhaustion of international reserves required to defend the parity. Since financial market participants would be able to foresee the time of exhaustion they would attack earlier and precipitate a collapse. The crises for some currencies in 1992 – lira, peseta and Swedish krona – provide illustrations of this so-called 'first-generation model' of speculative attacks. Many European officials were reluctant to admit the relevance of this model, because the EMS was in principle based on unlimited mandatory interventions, while at the same time the access to borrowing was growing rapidly for the participants. However, in September 1992 the Bundesbank reminded others that interventions could not in practice be unlimited as long as monetary policies were only imperfectly coordinated. The reminder has been repeated in the framework arrangement for cooperation between the euro area and non-participating EU currencies which has replaced the EMS at the start of EMU.

In the early months of 1993 and again over the summer there were new speculative attacks, this time on several currencies believed to have sufficiently sound fundamentals for the first-generation models to be inapplicable. These attacks can be illustrated by the so-called 'second-generation models': speculators gain if they have correctly anticipated reluctance among the officials responsible to continue to bear the costs of defending the parity by means of high domestic interest rates. As recession dragged on, France was seen to develop such reluctance and a growing temptation to follow the British example of exit from the system in the previous year.

These expectations proved unfounded in 1993: there was no easing of monetary policy in France or in other EMS countries, even after governments and central banks in August 1993 took the unexpected, but in retrospect logical, step of widening the margins of fluctuation to ±15 per cent. That created 'two-way risk' for speculators, while the maintenance of the central rates indicated that fundamentals were unchanged. This lax system functioned well over more than five years until it became ever tighter, but one should not interpret this as evidence that the participants have finally found a robust compromise between fixed and flexible exchange rates: the disciplining force of approaching the final deadline for monetary union had then become the major factor constraining behaviour.

If the calls from Britain and from Continental critics for postponing the start of EMU to await a longer period of convergence had been accommodated, the EMU participants would no doubt have tried to hold on to central rates within wide margins for an extended transition. But it is unrealistic to expect that such a strategy could have continued to convince financial markets of its stability. Minor policy shifts in divergent directions would have become subject to over-interpretations; it is particularly doubtful if the system could have survived one or more realignments.

A system of managed exchange rates, where changes are confined to relatively rare occasions of 'fundamental disequilibrium', would for these reasons have been unable to provide an acceptable alternative to monetary union. Could the other benchmark of flexible exchange rates have done so, provided fluctuations were dampened by a commitment of the countries concerned to low and broadly parallel inflation rates? This is of particular interest to countries such as the United Kingdom and Sweden which have chosen initially to stand apart from EMU, but have introduced national inflation targets, apparently fully consistent with stable exchange rates *vis-à-vis* the euro.

Unfortunately the answer appears to be negative. The experience with inflation targets suggests that even when the policy delivers the main result intended – a low and stable inflation rate – it does not deliver a high degree of exchange-rate stability at the same time. Canada has had an impressive inflation record over a number of years, similar to or better than that of the United States. This has not prevented the Canadian dollar from fluctuating very significantly against the US dollar. More to the point, UK inflation broadly parallel to Continental European inflation has not prevented sterling from moving over a wide range between DM 2.25 and 3.18 over the past three years. If the mid-point of this range is taken to be close to a longer-run equilibrium, it is necessary to reflect on the cost both to the UK economy and to those of its trading partners of swings of ±15 per cent in both directions. There is certainly no evidence to suggest that the movements observed in sterling since 1992 can be explained primarily by movements in relative fundamentals. Even the Bank of England described the strength of sterling in early 1998 as 'erratic'.

If one presents the alternative to monetary union as *either* a system of managed exchange rates prone to recurrent speculative attacks *or* a régime of flexible rates marked, even in relatively propitious circumstances, by excess volatility of rates, the conclusion changes from that where EMU is compared either to a well-managed discretionary system where exchange-rate changes remain as a useful instrument of macroeconomic adjustment, or to a flexible system where the exchange rate functions as a safety valve. It should be a cause for soul-searching to economists why they emphasize the random and volatile nature of exchange rates when teaching international economics, while adopting a very different posture when they review the pros and cons of EMU. A less biased question would be whether monetary union eliminates costly exchange-rate volatility to a degree which makes acceptable the lost opportunity of allowing the exchange rate to move in the rare cases when such changes could provide an important element in the macroeconomic adjustment. As you will have gathered my own answer to this question is yes.

Let me now turn to the second source of bias in the evaluation of the net benefits of EMU: the assumed prominence of asymmetric shocks affecting the participants in a differential way. Here again I refer to classical OCA theory. When are changes in the nominal exchange rate appropriate as part of macroeconomic adjustment? The celebrated asymmetric or country-specific shocks are seen by many as *the* essential argument for preserving national currencies and hence the possibility of adjusting their external value.

Mundell's pioneering article (1961) took as its starting point demand shifts between domestic and foreign products in a world of sticky prices and very limited factor (labour) mobility. Such shifts become more likely, the more specialized the economy is in its productive structure; Kenen (1969) extended Mundell's model, which had assumed full specialization, to diversified economies between which demand shifts are less likely, and in which supply shocks have more similar effects. Whatever will pose a threat to the survival of EMU, it will hardly be significant demand shift from, say, German to Italian or Spanish goods, and even less so after the start of EMU has unified monetary policy and imposed constraints on divergences between national budgetary policies. In EMU one will no doubt continue to observe non-policy disturbances which have a particularly strong impact on some sectors and industries, and hence on regions in which these sectors or industries are strongly represented. But such regions are unlikely to correspond to national states participating in EMU, and their problems could not, as Mundell himself was the first to point out – and as he has recently repeated (see Mundell 1998) – be corrected by a realignment between national currencies. They should lead to changes in relative prices and in relative remunerations of the factors used in the production of the sector's output. The main question is therefore – in EMU as it was before the project was launched – whether these mechanisms work more or less well *inside* any particular country.

This puts the most used argument against EMU – the singling out of asymmetric shocks as the main obstacle to the single currency – into a more realistic perspective. It is not enough to demonstrate that over the past two or three decades the correlation between GDP growth rates and changes in unemployment in the EU countries has been much less than perfect. In order to evaluate the need for retaining the exchange rate as an adjustment mechanism, it is necessary to isolate those disturbances which are truly external in nature, because it is with the purpose of softening the impact of the latter that OCA theory advocates reliance on exchange-rate changes. Yet it is only rarely that this distinction is made. Some researchers adopt an indirect approach by distinguishing between supply shocks, which should in principle be independent of domestic macroeconomic policies, and demand shocks which clearly are not (see notably Bayoumi and Eichengreen 1993). But this does not go far enough; some shocks to supply such as wage explosions have also been generated by divergent economic policies.

Gros and I (Gros and Thygesen 1998) use a crude method for identifying externally-generated shocks, by looking at the difference between the growth rates of exports from an EU member state and from the whole of the EU, and we report some rather striking examples of differential performance. Yet such a measure also exaggerates the problem that will be faced in EMU, as can be illustrated by the example most often quoted of an asymmetric external shock: the impact of the dissolution of the Soviet Union on the Finnish economy around 1991. The standard presentation of this case is that the virtual disappearance of an important trading partner was a decisive asymmetric shock requiring the major devaluations of the Finnish markka observed in 1991–2.

The facts are that Finnish export volumes overall fell by 6 per cent in 1991; when compared to a growth rate of exports from EU as a whole of 4.8 per cent this was indeed the largest single discrepancy in national export performance ever observed. However, the main reason was less specific and less external than implied by the standard presentation: if the Soviet market had developed in line with all Finland's other export markets, total exports would still have fallen by just over 5 per cent. The dissolution of the USSR, however dramatic and unique, was not the main explanatory factor: a long inflationary boom in Finland, fuelled by expansionary policies, had weakened competitiveness and exposed Finnish industry as recession struck in 1991. Finnish policy makers have obviously been content to endorse the OCA perspective of an asymmetric external shock, but this does not make the story more convincing. Even in this apparently unique case it is necessary to qualify the measure of the external asymmetric shock in order to make an assessment relevant to the challenges conceivable in EMU.

Have external, that is export, shocks, regardless of their origin, been important in shaping *internal* balance, as measured by the most politically sensitive indicator, the unemployment rate? Somewhat surprisingly, it is not straightforward to demonstrate such an impact. Among the EU countries the relationship was statistically significant only for Belgium.

If one can not confirm the importance of export shocks for employment changes, that must weaken the assertion that retaining the instrument of exchange-rate adjustments is essential to good macroeconomic management in the sense of maintaining broadly satisfactory employment levels.

The implication of this conclusion is, at a minimum, that external shocks would have to be very large before they had a significant impact on employment. The point can also be illustrated by the size of the *real* devaluation required to lower the unemployment rate by one percentage point in a typical medium-sized EU economy, where the share of exports in GDP is about 30 per cent. Over a two to three-year horizon, most macromodels estimate the elasticity of exports with respect to the *real* exchange rate at about 0.5. It would then take a 20 per cent real devaluation to produce the increase of output of approximately 3 per cent which, according to Okun's Law, is required to cut one percentage point off the unemployment rate. Although this back-of-the-envelope calculation disregards the impact on output and employment via imports, public finances and other indirect channels, it does suggest that giving up the use of exchange-rate changes makes only a modest difference to the macroeconomic performance of the EU economies.

My final point in the rationalization of why many economists have been critical of the move to full monetary union is that economic analysis has largely neglected the costs of short-term exchange rate volatility. While the costs of longer-term swings into misalignments of currencies have generally been recognized, short-term volatility is mostly not seen as costly, simply because it is assumed that such disturbances can easily be hedged through the foreign-exchange market.

It should, however, be uncontroversial that there are transaction costs and other costs related to exchange-rate volatility which can only be eliminated by the emergence of the single currency. These costs depend on the degree of variability, since bid–ask spreads in the foreign-exchange market, as well as hedging costs, are directly related to the latter. The most recent research-based estimate, in view of the experience of the early and mid-1990s, is about 1 per cent of EU GDP (see IFO 1997); European multinationals typically regard this as too low a figure. Even disregarding this latter view, the potential gain from the euro is not negligible – one to two years' benefits of this order would be enough to offset the once-and-for-all costs of introducing the euro – though it may not provide a decisive argument in favour of going all the way to monetary union. There is, however, an additional argument.

Economists have tended to dismiss further macroeconomic effects of the elimination of exchange-rate variability with reference to the difficulties experienced in documenting any major impact on trade flows. Even the least agnostic findings have suggested a boost to intra-European trade flows of only about 1 per cent as a result of reducing volatility, measured by, say, monthly variability of rates to zero. These modest effects have been rationalized primarily with reference to the ever-extending scope for hedging currency risks.

I have long had doubts whether the macroeconomic effects of exchange-rate variability are really as limited as these studies suggest. Inspired on the one hand by the work of Krugman (1989) on the implications of variability for the evolution of a wait-and-see attitude to international trade, where firms follow a 'pricing to market' strategy and hence experience major changes in profit margins when the exchange rate moves, and on the other hand by the recurrent German debate about the value to Germany of very stable exchange rates *vis-à-vis* important European trading partners, Daniel Gros and I (Gros and Thygesen 1998) tried to see if we could observe for Germany as well as for other EU member states a direct linkage from monthly exchange-rate variability between the EMU currencies to changes in the unemployment rate, or in the percentage rate of change of employment in manufacturing. Somewhat to our surprise we initially found significant and quantitatively important effects on these important indicators of macroeconomic performance for Germany. As an illustration, the increase in the monthly variability of the DM against an index of the other EMU currencies from 1994 to 1995, when European currency markets again experienced some tensions, may explain a rise of one percentage point in the overall German unemployment rate, say from 8 to 9 per cent. Subsequently, broadly similar results have been found by Belke and Gros (1998) for the three other large countries in the first EMU group (France, Italy and Spain), though not for the United Kingdom.

Obviously these results are preliminary and suggestive only. Some colleagues have found them implausible, not least when seen in conjunction with the relatively low estimates of price elasticities in the trade flows of the EMU countries which we have also reported. But the paradox can be explained. It is entirely possible that trade flows could be more sensitive to changes in the volatility of exchange rates than to changes in their level; there may even be a trade-off between these two dimensions to the extent that an increase in volatility, by generating more uncertainty about the more permanent level of the exchange rate, will tend to reduce price elasticities. That is indeed the argument of Krugman (1989) in his analysis of inertia in observed trade flows when volatility in the dollar–yen exchange rate shot up in the 1980s, admittedly more dramatically than anything witnessed in Europe. This line of reasoning may also help to explain the underlying support of German industry and trade unions for the participation of Germany in EMU, in contrast to the usually more vociferous skepticism voiced by German savers regarding the project.

It is accordingly not adequate to dismiss the macroeconomic benefits of the single currency by viewing them as arising only from some relatively modest savings in transaction and hedging costs. The latter may be the easiest to quantify, but they are not the most important.

My conclusion is that the case for fully eliminating exchange-rate fluctuations by forming a full monetary union is much stronger on purely
economic grounds that has yet generally been accepted by economists.
This does not imply that one should overlook the political motivations for
creating Europe's common currency, only that these political motivations,
strong as they may have been for some actors, can not explain why this
objective achieved steady support in the business community, as clearly has
been the case. The first ambition of EMU has been fulfilled, and there are
good arguments for being satisfied with this outcome.

Let me now turn to the second ambition which is more generally
accepted by economists as desirable, namely that of the reducing the
inflation rate to a very low rate, maybe even to zero.

Reducing, then eliminating inflation

When the discussion of EMU surfaced during the turbulent years of the
1970s, the ambition of using European monetary integration as a means of
reinforcing anti-inflationary policies in the member states was initially
appealing to liberal academic economists such as Herbert Giersch, Roland
Vaubel, Pascal Salin and Paul de Grauwe, all of whom have subsequently
been skeptical about EMU itself (see Giersch 1975, Vaubel 1978, Salin *et al.*
1975, de Grauwe 1975).

I had an early experience with discussions of an ambitious liberal
approach to a European single currency through my participation in a
group that drafted the so-called 'All Saints Day Manifesto' which was
published by the *Economist* on 1 November 1975 (see Basevi *et al.* 1975).
The group of nine European economists behind this statement based their
opinions on the Hayekian view that competition between different issuers
of national currencies was the best way of reducing the scope for irre-
sponsible and divergent policies such as those that marked the earlier
period of the 1970s. European monetary integration could do that by
offering citizens in inflation-prone countries the choice of an alternative
currency of superior quality.

Hayek elaborated the idea of competition between different currency
issuers in his little volume *The Denationalization of Money* (Hayek 1976), and
he endorsed the idea of competition between national currencies in
Europe in a paper presented in 1980 (see Salin 1984). Briefly the idea was
to expose nationally-issued currencies to competition from a new
European unit – he called it the Europa – the purchasing power of which
was to be guaranteed jointly by the European authorities. More precisely,
all consumers and firms in Europe would be offered the opportunity of
using a unit which appreciated against any individual European currency,
in step with its superior inflation performance as measured by national
consumer price indices. This would have put enormous pressure on countries permitting high inflation rates whereas those with low inflation rates

might have been able successfully to defend their national currency domain for quite some time. The proposal was arguably naive and excessively brutal. It seems unlikely that European governments could ever have agreed to the joint issue of a completely stable currency in competition with their own much weaker ones; that would no doubt have been perceived as too risky. The group had considerable difficulties in persuading the *Economist* to publish this radical idea, not least for this reason. There was also a major weakness in the scheme, soon pointed out in the subsequent debate: the plan was designed for the transition to the single currency rather than for managing the single currency subsequently. During the transition period the constant purchasing power of the new unit could be guaranteed in a technically easy way by the rule of appreciation against national currencies. However, once the new unit had replaced national currencies, one was left with the problem of managing a single European currency according to the same principle of stable purchasing power. Once conversion rates could no longer be relied upon, the supply of the single currency would have to be managed tightly.

Anyway, a much more gradualist and managed approach was preferred by European officials when the EMS was started, notably after 1982–3 when inflation convergence was put high on the agenda. The emphasis was put on tightening central bank cooperation, gradually to eliminate the inflation differential between the high inflation countries and those at the low end, particularly Germany. In other words, central bank collaboration was preferred to the competitive process inherent in the currency competition of the All Saints Day Manifesto. Most of my co-signatories of the latter disliked this alternative approach which they tended to label a central-bank cartel, unlikely to have the same beneficial effect of reducing inflation as unfettered currency competition. The suspicion was that there would be incentives for such a cartel to inflate together. The stability of exchange rates would then endanger the achievement of low inflation even in the prudent member states. Such a conflict could, in the view of the liberal economists, only be resolved by subordinating exchange-rate objectives to the overriding aim of price stability.

In retrospect, the liberal economists underestimated the capacity of the European policy makers to strive simultaneously for external and internal stability, though it must be admitted that their concerns did not seem unfounded for an important part of the history of European monetary unification, arguably until the post-1992 period. Although Germany was obviously happy to see other EMS countries trying to emulate their relatively better inflation performance through attachment to German monetary policy via a fixed rate for the DM, 'borrowing the credibility of the Bundesbank' was not a complete solution to the potential conflict between the external and internal dimensions of price stability. Two outcomes could be envisaged: either inflation rates would converge at a low level – in which case German monetary leadership would inevitably be called into question by demands to share that leadership in a joint European framework – or some inflation differentials would remain and gradually undermine the credibility of fixed exchange rates. In the latter alternative, countries with excess inflation might well succeed in temporarily taking over the leadership from Germany and other low-inflation countries, because the tendency of the former group to maintain higher nominal interest rates would keep their currencies strong inside the EMS. For a while in 1989–90 the Spanish and Italian currencies were typically trading at rates stronger than their central rate for the DM, despite continuing excess inflation in Southern Europe. Such a situation could endure for a while, but not indefinitely.

German unification from 1990 on gradually pushed up German inflation and obliged the Bundesbank to raise interest rates. Monetary leadership was, at least in part, restored, but the higher average inflation rate in the EMS removed some of the pressure to reduce inflation elsewhere in Europe and opened up a debate as to what rate to aim for. Was a rate of 4–5 per cent, as observed in the early phase of the recession of 1991–3, about as far as one ought to raise ambitions, or would progress towards zero inflation be justified after weighing the output costs of reducing inflation against the benefits of a more stable monetary unit?

The political answer came first and most clearly; an academic rationalization had to wait a few more years. As recession spread there were few illusions that it could be contained by more expansionary macroeconomic policies. Budgetary policies were constrained by past excesses, notably the failure to consolidate significantly during the upswing of the late 1980s, which had left little room for manoeuvre when it subsequently became desirable to expand. Monetary policy was applied with great caution, maybe in retrospect excessive caution, in 1993–4, out of fear of rekindling inflation. The countries that chose to abandon a fixed exchange rate for their currency, notably the United Kingdom, Italy and Sweden, all opted for maintaining or reducing inflation. These three countries adopted broadly similar anti-inflationary strategies with explicit inflation targets below any recent historical experience as the focus. The task for them, as for those countries which remained in the EMS, was much eased by the slack in their economies, by structural improvements in their labour markets and, not least, by a favourable international climate, marked by low prices of raw materials and increasing competition from low-cost producers of manufactured goods outside the industrial countries. In the most recent period inflation has fallen even below the rate of 2 per cent which was long regarded as fully satisfactory by the Bundesbank and recently referred to as the upper threshold of a target range by the European Central Bank. We do not yet have in Europe any thorough study of the size of the likely upward bias in the measurement of inflation conveyed by national consumer price indices, or *a fortiori* by the harmonized index (HICP) calculated by the ECB, but surely measured inflation of about 1 per cent is for practical purposes an indication of price stability.[2] If anyone had suggested ten years ago, not to mention at even earlier stages of Europe's monetary integration, that such an objective should be set and maintained over a long horizon, such a proposal would have attracted derision, protests or both.

Why has political opinion and a large part of academic opinion endorsed a high priority for price stability, and how has monetary policy come to be seen almost solely as a means for maintaining a stable nominal framework, regardless of the exchange rate régime? These are the fundamental questions for anyone wanting to evaluate the soundness of EMU as designed. Trying to provide answers would take me far beyond the limits of this lecture. Let me just offer a rationalization for the objective of price stability. It has not influenced the design of the Maastricht Treaty, yet it is not unreasonable to suggest that policy makers in this, as in some other cases – insistence on full elimination of exchange-rate uncertainty is another example discussed in the previous section – are capable of developing solutions to policy issues which only somewhat later find more complete justifications in the academic literature.

At least some recent efforts at evaluating the net benefits of reducing the inflation rate all the way to zero – corrected for possible inflation bias in the consumer price or other index being used – should offer food for thought. There is an older literature, mostly from three decades ago, on the optimal rate of inflation. The central contribution (Friedman 1969), stressed that the optimal rate of inflation was slightly negative, in view of the argument that if not, the public would hold less than the optimum quantity of monetary base (which can be produced costlessly). Others, notably Phelps (1973), criticized this view by pointing out that in a second-best world, inflation tax on money holdings might be less distortionary than the alternative taxes which might otherwise be imposed. But a comprehensive discussion of the costs and benefits of low inflation had to wait for the recent period.

In a pioneering article, Martin Feldstein (1996) performed an elaborate evaluation of the net benefits of reducing inflation from 2 per cent to zero, allowing for possible bias in the measure of inflation. The costs are the temporary loss of output as inflation falls; they depend crucially on the sluggishness of prices and wages. The benefits come from several sources, one of which, but less important than others, is the increased willingness of the public to hold a larger volume of non-interest bearing money at zero inflation. The most important benefit is that zero inflation minimizes the distortionary effects of a nominal tax system. Other benefits come from the impact on private saving and on demand for housing, the main long-term asset in private portfolios. Feldstein estimates the net benefit from zero rather than 2 per cent inflation in a steady state to be equivalent to an increase in the level of GDP of approximately 1 per cent year after year.

Given the presumed high degree of price and wage flexibility in the US economy, one would expect the costs of implementing such a policy strategy to be more modest than in Europe, where sluggishness in nominal variables is undoubtedly greater than in the United States. This conclusion is borne out in studies of two European countries – Germany and Spain – but at the same time the benefits of zero inflation also seem to be larger (see Tödler and Ziebarth 1997 and Dolado *et al.* 1997, who follow the empirical methodology of Feldstein). In Germany and Spain the net benefits of eliminating the residual two percentage points of inflation therefore turn out to be very similar to, or a bit larger than, those found for the United States. A third study for a European country has been carried out for the United Kingdom; here the net benefits are also found to be positive, but only marginally so. Yet the main conclusion from this set of studies is that there are indeed probable gains from going all the way to price stability in the full sense of the term.

It is necessary to repeat that this research remains preliminary despite all the work that has gone into it. If taken at face value, it nevertheless suggests a net gain of an order of magnitude similar to that found from the complete elimination of exchange-rate variability inside Europe. In that case EMU presents a double gain to which external and internal stability have contributed about equally, and the total effect – a level of GDP a couple of percentage points higher than would otherwise have been observed – is certainly considerable. The ambition of European policy makers in making a monetary union with *de facto* zero inflation would then seem to be vindicated.

This double achievement is the core result of EMU with a stable currency. Achieving also the other ambitions to which I now turn is clearly subsidiary to the elimination of both exchange-rate variability and inflation. It is well known, however, that in order to make these two main achievements sustainable, threats to them should be minimized. Such threats may come from three sources that could each potentially undermine EMU: from large imbalances in the main other type of macro-economic policy, budget deficits; from large-scale interventions in the foreign-exchange market for the single currency against other currencies; and from efforts to prevent financial instability.

Developing rules for non-monetary policies, then scope for coordinating them

From the start of this past decade's debates on the design of EMU, the role of budgetary policies was controversial. Some – and I readily admit to having been among them – thought that once exchange rates were locked definitively, the longer-term constraints on budgetary decision makers would be sufficiently severe to make outright rules for budget deficits and debt superfluous. But I became convinced by the discussions in the Delors Committee that this view was too sanguine. The argument in favour of some form of 'binding guidelines' for the upper limit to budget deficits in

the member states participating in EMU was primarily based on the likelihood that national governments, when freed of the risk of higher interest
rates and possibly a currency crisis, would react by relaxing any effort to
contain their public sector deficits. Any textbook analysis suggests that the
efficiency of tax and expenditure policies increases with the degree of
fixity of the exchange rate.

If only one member state – or a few smaller ones – were to succumb
to this temptation, there might not be any important distortion to the
aggregate policy stance. But there is no mechanism to assure that the
temptation will not be widespread in a monetary union. We may already
have seen this mechanism at work towards the end of the 1990s, when
several member states failed to consolidate their budgets at a time of a
relatively strong upswing. As the EMS firmed up and governments
became confident of the stability of the exchange-rate framework,
discretionary expansion largely offset the automatic improvements on
the revenue side, as clearly illustrated in Buti and Sapir (1998).[3] This
mechanism was not yet clearly perceived in the Delors Report, but the
basic argument was presented as a plausible hypothesis by Lamfalussy
(1989) in an Annex to the Report, and it convinced at least the central
bankers that peer pressure based on clear rules of budgetary conduct to
contain divergent national behaviour had to substitute for some of the
market discipline imposed through higher premia in national interest
rates. The idea was incorporated into the Maastricht Treaty and further
elaborated in the Growth and Stability Pact (GSP or 'Stability Pact')
proposed by Germany in 1995 and agreed at the Amsterdam European
Council in 1997. This final elaboration clarified both the procedure to
be followed in evaluating whether an excessive deficit had emerged in a
country participating in EMU, and the precise nature of the sanctions to
be imposed on a deviant country, issues that had been left vague in the
Treaty itself.

On balance, and having considered the alternatives, governments
found it difficult to escape the conclusion that mandatory upper limits to
budget deficits – except in well-defined 'exceptional circumstances' –
would be warranted in order to bolster the capacity of the ECB to conduct
a monetary policy directed at price stability as a primary objective. Judging
from the experience around the start of EMU, it is easy to see that they
were well justified in not relying solely on the remaining elements of
market discipline to contain a plausible expansionary bias in budgetary
policies; differentials between long-term government bond rates narrowed
over the final months of 1998 to 20–30 basis points despite a remarkable
decline in the benchmark rate of the German Bunds. In contrast to what
some economists and market practitioners had argued, rising credit risk
premia far from substituted for rapidly declining currency risk premia,
hence vindicating the skepticism of central bankers that the former would
constitute reliable discipline.

The main criticism of the admittedly somewhat arbitrary mechanism introduced by the adoption of the Stability Pact is, however, that macro-economic stabilization policies may become too constrained if EMU participants, having lost their capacity to conduct monetary and exchange-rate policies independently, also become unable to protect themselves against the impact of asymmetric shocks through the working of automatic budgetary stabilizers, occasionally supplemented by discretionary action. Here it is necessary to distinguish between transitional problems and the longer-run properties of the Stability Pact. For the more immediate future the problem is that several countries, not least the two largest member states, have entered EMU with budget deficits which are perilously high relative to their output gaps. Even a modest worsening of the economic outlook in 1999–2000 could bring Germany and possibly France in conflict with the 3 per cent limit to budget deficits.[4] Hence the room for manoeuvre is extremely small, and it would clearly be damaging to confidence if the budgetary limit were to be breached within two years of the start of EMU. The ECB faces a difficult task in persuading governments that for it to maintain – or even further ease – the stance of monetary policy is contingent on more efforts at budget consolidation.

In a longer-term perspective the mechanism of the Stability Pact seems unobjectionable. Its central element is the declared intention of governments to aim for budget balance, or a small surplus on average, over the business cycle. This is a sensible objective which marks a clear improvement over past behaviour. If adhered to, it would leave considerable room for automatic stabilizers to work, particularly if countries where deficits are most sensitive to the cycle accept that they have to aim for a small surplus as the normal state of affairs. Focusing on the average budget position over the cycle would bring the budgetary rule close to the concept most economists would prefer to see at centre stage: structural deficits. It would be far superior to sole focus on the measured deficit and to the balanced budget amendments in existence for example in US states, though such a rule can be justified in federations where the lower levels of government have little or no macroeconomic stabilization functions.

Large federal states use a variety of methods for imposing discipline on sub-federal levels of government, ranging from administrative controls in many developing and transition countries to monitoring by financial markets in countries where the latter are most developed, such as Canada.[5] Intermediate forms, such as rules or a cooperative approach in annual negotiations, are also observed. The Stability Pact clearly relies primarily on rules, at least in the initial stage.

On balance, the Stability Pact with its apparently rigid rules and procedures should help to put budgetary policies closer to the kind of medium-term stable path which is already the aim of the joint monetary policy. As such it deserves to be credited, rather than merely being regarded as a side condition to monetary union which it became necessary to fulfil simply because the German government insisted on it in order to placate its own domestic opinion, still hostile to the single currency in the run-up to EMU. This latter interpretation, not implausible in view of the zeal with which the Stability Pact was presented by and in Germany, should not be the full story. The mandatory budgetary rules and procedures have improved the prospects for an appropriate policy mix. They offer some protection against erosion of the central achievement of very low and stable inflation outlined in the previous section, and ultimately against threats to a break-up of the single-currency area.

It is still questionable whether that in itself can be labelled as an achievement meeting a fundamental ambition of EMU. Whatever one may think of the imposition of constraints on national budgetary policies, this step does not qualify as coordination of macroeconomic policies in the traditional sense of that term. At first sight the Stability Pact appears to have superseded coordination of budgetary policies; the situation looks similar to the position of the ECB, which is committed to price stability as a primary objective, leaving scope for output stabilization only when that objective is beyond danger. But the analogy runs deeper than that; both the ECB and the national budgetary authorities will need from time to time to decide upon the desirable speed at which economic disturbances that cause temporary departures from expected achievements – for budgetary policies with respect to the output gap and unemployment – should be eliminated. If, say, a negative output disturbance with potential inflationary consequence is observed for (most of) the EMU participants, the ECB will need to consider how rapidly future inflation can be brought back to its desired trajectory; analogously, the ECOFIN Council, while continuing to insist on national budgetary deficits staying below 3 per cent of GDP, will need to apply judgment in evaluating departures from previously submitted stability programmes. In the opposite case, where both inflation and budgetary targets are undershot, there may be a case for initiatives to shift the policy stance in a less contractionary direction. Therefore, simple rule-bound budgetary policies prominent in the Maastricht Treaty and the Stability Pact, useful as they are, will hardly be the full story of economic policy-making in EMU, nor would they be accepted as such in the European policy debate. They will in reality be supplemented by efforts at coordination of a cooperative nature, as outlined in the literature on fiscal federalism.

The ECOFIN Council has a natural mandate, in addition, to look at EMU-wide aggregates, as the ECB is already obliged to do. Important indicators here are the aggregate output gap and unemployment rate, the current account position of the euro area, and movements in the euro *vis-à-vis* the major currencies (see also the following section). There have over the recent months been several signs that the ECOFIN Council, led by the Euro-11 finance ministers, will wish to rise to this challenge and not just confine its activities to the monitoring of compliance with the Stability

Pact. This would make economic sense and should bring two types of benefit, the first economic – to improve macroeconomic policies – and the second political: to protect the ECB better against a backlash of frustration of public opinion, if central bankers are perceived to be virtually alone on the European policy stage. Some visible role for ECOFIN, or rather the Euro-11 Council, in the coordination of non-monetary policies, may in fact protect rather than endanger the independence of the ECB.

Supplementing the Stability Pact by extended policy coordination, with the double purpose of monitoring both individual budgetary behaviour inside the Stability Pact limits and the aggregate policy stance, is today the unfulfilled second half of the third ambition for EMU which I have listed. It is of more recent vintage than the first two ambitions already discussed, but it has surfaced in earlier discussions of EMU as well. The Werner Report of 1970 which presented the first outline of the final stage of EMU outlined an advanced form of centralization of budgetary authority at the EU level. That went beyond what was politically feasible for a number of member states, and the idea was explicitly rejected as superfluous in the Delors Report. An additional reason for the change, rooted in economic analysis, was that over the twenty years between the publication of the two reports, the degree of optimism concerning the capacity of budgetary policy to fine-tune an economy had been significantly modified. This made the idea of vesting authority to try to manage the tax and expenditure policies of a number of countries at the European level look economically naive as well. When Roy Jenkins as Commission President in 1977 proposed to resume the debate on EMU, his main concern was to develop a budgetary stabilization function at the European level, through a much expanded EU budget to finance public goods and effect transfers between the participating states, in analogy to what is found in many large federal states. The amounts required were regarded as far beyond the politically realistic, and the debate on the Jenkins proposal soon ended. The present ambition is in this perspective more realistic, modest and constructive. The strong push now given to the recent version of the budgetary ambition, not least by France and Germany, suggests that the ambition is firmly on the agenda.

Developing a potential role in the international monetary system

This fourth ambition has been present in Europe's monetary unification at least since the start of the EMS in 1978–9. To the fathers of that project, Chancellor Helmut Schmidt and President Valéry Giscard d'Estaing, tighter monetary integration was initially a defensive move made necessary by unstable policies in the United States, and in the long-term a means of enhancing Europe's role in the global monetary system. The first part of that ambition has been fulfilled; as the EMS firmed up gradually, intra-EMS exchange rates became less sensitive to movements in the US dollar than had been the case with particular virulence in 1977–8; now EMU is formed, the last traces of the capacity of US dollar swings to push European cross rates apart have by definition disappeared. This is in itself a major achievement; with only a small part of the foreign trade of the EMU participants being with the United States and countries that link their currency to the US dollar, the potential harm to the EMU partici-pants from global instability has been sharply reduced, though certainly not eliminated.

The second part of the international ambition remains unfulfilled, but the potential to fulfil it is now available. Some of the initial EMU partici-pants, notably France, have always regarded EMU as a stepping-stone to global monetary reform; the emergence of a single European currency could finally make a more managed international monetary system feasible. This view was until recently not shared by German leaders – with the exception of Helmut Schmidt – but with the change of government in September 1998, German attitudes have converged much more closely with French views, and both governments have indicated an interest in exam-ining the case for a target zone for the euro's exchange rate against the US dollar and possibly the yen. In the case of the latter, the Japanese authorities have voiced sympathy for the initiative, whereas the attitude of the US authorities remains negative. The ECB has also poured cold water on the idea, fearing that any obligation to maintain the euro within intervention margins against other international currencies could prove incompatible with the ECB's primary objective of maintaining price stability.

The formal procedures governing any initiative by the EMU participants with respect to exchange rates are outlined in Article 109 of the Maastricht Treaty, which distinguishes between 'formal arrangements' and other situations.[6] In the former case the ECOFIN Council can unanimously decide to enter into them, having sought the view of the ECB as to the consistency of the proposed arrangement with price stability. Once the formal arrangements are in place, the ECOFIN Council can decide to 'adopt, adjust or abandon' the central rate of the euro by qualified majority. In the absence of an exchange-rate system in relation to one or more non-EU currencies, the Euro-11 Council may by qualified majority 'formulate general orientations for exchange rate policy', again following consultations with the ECB. The Council has recently indicated that it will discuss general orientations – the latter term was chosen in preference to 'guidelines' used elsewhere in the Treaty – in cases where the euro's exchange rate is beginning to look misaligned. Given the reluctance of both the ECB and the US authorities to engage in exchange-rate stabi-lization, it is highly doubtful whether these provisions will lead to anything really new. A unilaterally-declared target zone for the euro could hardly qualify as 'formal arrangements', and would therefore imply only 'general orientations' from the Euro-11 Council. Even the Louvre Accord of 1987, which is the closest the main industrial countries have come to agreeing on a target zone, would presumably have to be a lot more specific and transparent before it could be regarded as formal. If the euro were to appreciate sharply against other important currencies, mainly because it was taking market share from the US dollar in private world financial might obviously sway the attitude of the ECB and make it more receptive to 'general orientations' from the Euro-11 Council.

Europe's role in the international monetary system does not, however, stand or fall with its capacity to negotiate a target-zone-like arrangement with the US authorities, although the avoidance of major unwarranted swings in the exchange rate between the world's two major currencies remains an important test. Fortunately the days when European policy makers could rightly lament major imbalances in the US economy have been over for some time. (The sharp weakening of the US dollar in 1977–8, and the gyrations of the US dollar in the 1980s, closely linked first to the emergence of the massive budget deficits under President Reagan, and subsequently to the market perceptions that the position was unsustainable and the US dollar grossly overvalued, are the main examples.) Europeans have much less to criticize at a time when the US Federal budget has swung into substantial (and appropriate) surplus and the Fed's monetary policy has succeeded in keeping US output and employment performance much better than Europe's, and without signs of a pick-up in inflation. Old confrontational attitudes die hard, but it may well be that the past attractions of being able to challenge the United States through the emergence of a strong European currency to compete with the dollar are no longer relevant. This would certainly be true if the growth rate of output in the euro area were to begin to match more closely that of the United States, and the dollar were to weaken moderately. Both factors would then reduce the US current account deficit and the European external surplus. These two factors will no doubt be seen to operate over the next couple of years. But even the glaring current imbalance between the two regions is difficult for the Europeans to criticize, at a time when the US economy must be credited with imparting the bulk of the remaining growth in world demand.

What is then the main challenge for Europe to meet in reinforcing the international monetary system, in the next few years, or maybe decade? It is to cooperate more efficiently with the United States to contain international financial instability and improve the much-talked-about international financial architecture. Most urgently, it is to contribute constructively to the containment of financial crises outside the industrial countries, of which a number of examples have been provided since the currency and banking problems in Asia came to the attention of the international community in mid-1997.

The euro area needs to meet three conditions in order to become an effective player in the present difficult phase for the international monetary system. It has clearly met the first by creating a unified currency area. It is beginning to meet the second – to develop a tight rules-based system of regional surveillance, comprising also budgetary policies – and hence the policy mix. Together, these two first elements already have a positive impact, simply by showing to other regions in the world the value of tight regional integration comprising fully fixed exchange rates, non-zero inflation and a certain degree of macroeconomic policy coordination. There will be a long way for other regions to go in order even to begin to emulate some of these achievements, yet the example will be important. But Europe has hardly begun to meet the third condition for exercising an influence commensurate with its economic and financial weight. The euro area needs to develop an effective representation of its views in global fora.

Put crudely, there are currently far too many Europeans in the traditional international fora: the G7 (or G8, as it has recently become with the inclusion of Russia), the G10, and the Executive Board and the Interim Committee of the International Monetary Fund (IMF). The fragmentation of the European presence paradoxically implies a loss of influence, despite the European capacity to outnumber others.

With the set-up of the ECB things are beginning to change, but very slowly. Central bankers from the four large European countries apparently still intend to participate in G7 meetings and other meetings with central bank input.[7] On the side of the budgetary authorities, European representation will even be enlarged; the four large countries' finance ministers will be accompanied by the President of ECOFIN (if he is not from one of the four large countries) and a representative of the European Commission.[8] This is the arrangement laboriously worked out and announced at the European Council in Austria in December 1998. To American and other non-EU officials this makes matters worse rather than better; from an outsider's point of view the President of the ECB and the President of ECOFIN would suffice, even though the short tenure of six months of the latter does not exactly assure the kind of continuity in personal relations which is important in international policy coordination.

Irritation among US officials over the numerically strong EU presence in the G7 and the G10 no doubt contributed in 1998 to the setting-up of a new informal framework for discussing some of the issues most central to reform of the international monetary system. The US Secretary of the Treasury, at the time of the spring meeting of the IMF Interim Committee, convened three working parties consisting of representatives from the G7 countries and fifteen emerging market countries, to consider three sets of issues from the agenda of the IMF (transparency, financial reforms, and private sector participation in financial support packages). That structure squeezed out all the smaller EU member states (and Spain); four of them subsequently fought their way back into the caucus, the future of which is reportedly uncertain at the present stage.[9] Finally, the EU constituencies in the IMF bodies do not reflect present realities after the start of EMU; some constituencies mix EU and non-EU member states, while one EU country (Ireland) is in the Canadian constituency.

Some of these deficiencies – at least from the viewpoint of effective EU representation – are clearly less serious than others, and will anyway take some time to remedy. Others could be addressed with some urgency. The excessive central bank representation in the G7 reflects the highly decentralized way in which the ECB has initially been implemented, operationally as well as in its analytic and policy-formulating role. That may gradually be rectified, as will the surprising continuation of the representation of the national central banks of the euro area in the Economic and Financial Committee (formerly the Monetary Committee) which prepares issues on the agenda of the ECOFIN Council. In view of the likely international agenda with emphasis on containing international financial crises, the composition of these bodies and their international representation is of considerable interest to the outside world.

The US Treasury is usually able to act quickly and decisively in international crises because it has a unified political leadership; Secretary Robert Rubin and his Deputy, now successor, Larry Summers, were necessarily at the centre of international economic efforts. The Europeans may be jealous – and sometimes critical – of their efforts, and they would like to have more of an active role, rather than to be informed subse-quently, when events and financial rescue packages have already taken shape. If the European finance ministers can not for some time designate an external representation which is both effective and acceptable to all member states, is it too much to hope that they could at least designate someone just below their level to coordinate European views? There has been much discussion in recent months about the designation of a high-level representative for the common foreign and security policy, where national attitudes are typically further apart than in the international economic area. There seems to be a strong case for a similar figure in international economic affairs. A natural candidate for such a 'State Secretary for International Economic Affairs' could be the chair of the Economic and Financial Committee; that might be preferable to a representative of the European Commission (in analogy to the role of the Commission in the trade policy field), since the Commission's authority in economic policy is not strongly developed. Of course, such a European official would have some congenital weaknesses relative to his US counterpart until the euro area had advanced further in its non-monetary integration and co-ordination. But the point is that such a process could be advanced significantly by such a procedural step.

In short, it takes more than establishing a solid single currency to develop Europe's potential role in today's international monetary system. Given the institutional complexities of external representation, the euro area – and even more the EU as a whole – is still far from 'speaking with one voice' in international fora. Maybe it will take a major international crisis to bring this about.

Developing a European profile in financial supervision

One may discuss whether this final ambition should have been included at all. Not only is it largely unrealized, it is not even an ambition widely shared by European officials. Rather, it is a task which financial instability is likely to thrust upon financial supervisors and the ECB. Therefore I would argue that it *should* be an ambition.

When the Maastricht Treaty and the ECB Statute annexed thereto were negotiated nearly a decade ago, the majority view was that the ECB should not be considered directly responsible for financial stability. Prudential control of financial institutions and markets was to remain in the hands of national authorities. The reasons for this design were complex. As in the area of budgetary policy, the general principle of subsidiarity appeared to suggest leaving responsibility for financial stability in the hands of those closest to the problems. Two additional reasons were also given. First, some central banks were not in charge of financial supervision in their domain, hence making it institutionally more difficult to envisage vesting this authority in the ECB after the start of EMU. Second, some important central banks, notably the Bundesbank, and several political authorities felt that responsibility for monetary stability – the main task of the ECB – could be undermined by widening the list of objectives. Anyway, the issue of who is in charge of financial supervision – central banks or separate agencies – is subsidiary to whether the task is sufficiently well coordinated at the European level, in view of the higher level of financial integration after the start of EMU.[10]

Coordination between national supervisors in the EU is today based on bilateral memoranda of understanding. It seems important in EMU to intensify cooperation between supervisors and central banks, and to underpin it by clear EU-wide agreement on a code of conduct covering supervisory responsibilities and standards, in order to avoid misunderstandings, institutional rivalry, and excessive forbearance by national supervisors, and to ensure that all financial institutions are adequately supervised by a lead regulator. The ECB could play a role as a clearing house for such a cooperative arrangement, which should, in particular, make clear provisions for the allocation of responsibilities in times of crises. Such coordination at the EU level would represent an important contribution to global financial stability.

There is a surprising degree of ambiguity in the framework of the ECB and the national central banks participating in EMU with respect to lender-of-last-resort operations. Financial stability may occasionally require the capacity to conduct such operations.

The decentralized framework, with operational activities carried out through the national central banks, implies that conflicts may arise between the provision of liquidity to national institutions and the ECB's responsibility for determining liquidity in the euro area as a whole. An interest-rate subsidy to a local problem bank may in the end be paid for by banks in other EMU countries and by their customers. For these reasons, and because of the need to preserve competitive equity, procedures for lender-of-last-resort operations should be allocated clearly between the ECB and national central banks. These agreed procedures should include adequate collateral, penal interest rates and prior authorization, rather than simple monitoring by the ECB for the injection of liquidity by a participating national central bank.

Conclusions

There is today a much clearer perception of what EMU implies than Robert Marjolin foresaw in his critical review of 1975 and in his memoirs a decade later (Marjolin 1986).

I listed five ambitions which have gradually evolved as the project progressed towards realization. There is a logical order in them, as we look back over the past two decades since the start of the EMS. Increasingly rigid exchange rates – an important benefit in themselves – required convergence of national inflation rates, hence raising the issue of who should exercise the n-th degree of freedom in an increasingly joint monetary policy. Basically, such a policy required an explicit stand on the principal objective of monetary policy: to provide a stable nominal framework for the area as a whole. With the inflationary experience of the 1970s and early 1980s still fresh in the minds of policy makers, this issue was settled in a clear and forceful way in the Maastricht Treaty. Recent research has confirmed that the gains of near-zero inflation are likely to be substantial and must not be put at undue risk.

Even the most virtuous central bank is not, however, fully in charge of the factors that may cause inflation. A monetary policy aiming at price stability can be undermined by large-scale public sector deficits, intervention obligations *vis-à-vis* other important currencies, and financial crises which appear to require significant injections of liquidity. A purist might say that, in order to preserve to the maximum the capacity of the ECB to meet its primary objective, monetary policy should be protected fully against these three factors. The tools for assuring that are, respectively, rules for maximum public sector deficits, no obligations to intervene in foreign-exchange markets, and no role for the ECB in solving financial crises.

The Maastricht Treaty is imbued with this spirit. It emphasizes constraints on deviant national budgetary policies, subsequently reinforced by the Stability Pact, it makes an exchange-rate policy for the euro area very difficult to envisage, and it gives no important role to the ECB in financial supervision. The degree to which these purist side-conditions for EMU was imposed was impressive, and surprising given the ambitions which were also present, though less prominently, to improve the coordination of non-monetary policies among the EMU-participants, to allow the euro area to fill its potential role in the international monetary system, and to assure a high degree of financial stability.

We are now entering an interesting phase where these three remaining ambitions reassert themselves. The EU-11 finance ministers will push the Euro-11 Council towards additional budgetary coordination and towards a more aggregate view of the EMU policy mix, particularly in a more global context. With a less conflictual international agenda, there is scope for a constructive contribution from the euro area to the resolution of global economic problems, notably financial crises, but the issue of more effective external representation remains to be resolved. Finally, there is increasing (though still only moderate) awareness that financial supervision needs to be better coordinated after the arrival of the euro, and that the role of the lender-of-last-resort function needs to be specified and allocated more clearly.

The re-emergence of these three ambitions – or at least of the first two of them – is natural now that the two major and most important achievements of eliminating all exchange-rate variability and, for practical purposes, all inflation in the euro area, have been obtained. There is some scope for realizing the remaining three ambitions while still ensuring that the first two are always kept in mind.

Notes

Support for the Economic Policy Research Unit (EPRU), University of Copenhagen, by a grant from the Danish National Research Federation is gratefully acknowledged.

1 Some of the subsequent analysis has been developed in two earlier papers presenting our work on European monetary integration: Thygesen 1998 and Thygesen 1999.
2 In the United states a commission chaired by Michael Boskin reported in 1995 that the US consumer price index may overstate the inflation rate to the extent of at least one percentage point.
3 See notably Buti and Sapir 1998, Figure 7.2, p. 87.
4 In the German case the major transfer from the Bundesbank to the government in 1998 reflecting the revaluation of gold reserves temporarily boosted the budgetary position by about 0.4 per cent of GDP.
5 For an useful survey see Ter-Minassian 1997.
6 Article 111 of the Amsterdam Treaty.
7 Following a compromise reached in 1999 with the US, Japan and Canada, the three national central bank governors from Euro-11 countries (France, Germany and Italy) who had earlier participated fully in sixty-seven meetings, will henceforth not take part in the discussions of trends in the world economy, multilateral surveillance and exchange rates, but only in the exchange on other financial issues.
8 The representative of the Commission will onlyu participate at the discretion of the ECOFIN/Euro-11 President.
9 The working parties of the G22/26 were disbanded after reporting in late 1998. A new forum, the G20, consisting of the G7 plus eleven systemically important emerging market countries, the EU Presidency and the IMF, was launched in September 1999.
10 The comments in the next section are largely based on Statement no. 2 by the European Shadow Regulatory Committee, of which I am a member.

Bibliography

Basevi, G. *et al.* (1975) 'The All Saints Day Manifesto', *Economist*, 1 November.

Bayoumi, T. and Eichengreen, B. (1993) 'Shocking Aspects of European Monetary Integration', in F. Torres and F. Giavazzi (eds), *Adjustment and Growth in the European Monetary Union*, Cambridge University Press, Cambridge: 193–210.

Belke, A. and Gros, D. (1998) 'Evidence on the Costs of Intra-European Exchange Rate Variability', *CEPS Working Document no. 121*, Centre for European Policy Studies, Brussels.

Buti, M. and Sapir, A. (eds) (1998) *Economic Policy in EMU, A Study by the European Commission Services*, Oxford University Press, Oxford.

Committee for the Study of EMU (1989) *Report on Economic and Monetary Union* (the Delors Report), EC Publications Office, Luxembourg.

Dolado, J., Gonzalez-Paramo, F. M. and Viñalo, J. (1997) 'A Cost-Benefit Analysis of Going From Low Inflation to Price Stability', *Documento de Trabajo no. 9728*, Banco de España, Servicio de Estudios, Madrid.

Emerson, M. *et al.* (1990) *One Market, One Money*, European Economy no. 44, Commission of the European Communities, Brussels.

European Shadow Financial Regulatory Committee (1998) 'EMU, the ECB and Financial Supervision', Statement no. 2 (19 October).

Feldstein, M. (1996) 'The Costs and Benefits of Going from Low Inflation to Price Stability', *NBER Working Paper no. 5469*, National Bureau of Economic Research, Cambridge, Mass.

Friedman, M. (1969) 'The Optimum Quantity of Money', in *The Optimum Quantity of Money and Other Essays*, Aldine, Chicago.

Giersch, H. (1975) 'The Case for a European Parallel Currency', in *Report of the Study Group 'Economic and Monetary Union 1980'* (Marjolin Report), Annex II, EC Commission (DG II), Brussels: 77–83.

de Grauwe, P., Heremans, D. and van Rompny, E. 'Vers une velance de l'union monétaire européenne', in Textes et Documents, *Collection Idées Études* no. 305, Ministère des Affaires Étrangères, de Commerce Extérieur et de la Cooperation et Développement, Brussels.

Gros, D. and Thygesen, N. (1998) *European Monetary Integration – From the EMS to EMU*, Addison-Wesley Longman, London and New York.

Hayek, F. von (1976) 'Denationalization of Money', *Hobart Paper no. 70*, Institute of Economic Affairs, London.

IFO (1997) 'Intra-EU Multi-Currency Management Costs', Study for the European Commission DG XY, *IFO Schenelldienst no. 19*, Munich: 3–17.

Kenen, P. B. (1969) 'The Theory of Optimum Currency Areas: An Eclectic View', in Mundell, R. A. and Swoboda, A. K. (eds) *Monetary Problems of the International Economy*, University of Chicago Press, Chicago: 41–60.

Krugman, P. (1989) 'The Declining of Exchange Rates from Reality', in *Exchange Rate Instability*, MIT Press, Cambridge, Mass.: 36–75.

Lamfalussy, A. (1989) 'Macro-Coordination of Fiscal Policies in an Economic and Monetary Union', in Committee for the Study of EMU, *Report on Economic and Monetary Union* (the Delors Report), EC Publications Office, Luxembourg.

Marjolin, R. (1986), *Le travail d'une vie*, Editions Robert Lafforet, Paris. (*Robert Marjolin: Architect of European Unity, Memoirs 1911–86*, trans. W. Hall, Weidenfeld and Nicholson, London 1989).

Marjolin, R. *et al.* (1975) *Report of the Study Group on Economic and Monetary Union 1980* (the Marjolin Report), Commission of the European Communities, Brussels.

Mundell, R. A. (1961) 'A Theory of Optimum Currency Areas', *American Economic Review* 51: 657–75.

Mundell, R. A. (1998) 'Great Expectations for the Euro', *Wall Street Journal*, 24 March.

Padoa-Schioppa, T. (1988) 'The European Monetary System: A Long-Term View', in F. Giavazzi, S. Milcossi and M. Miller (eds), *The European Monetary System*, Cambridge University Press, Cambridge.

Padoa-Schioppa, T. (1994) *The Road to Monetary Union in Europe*, Oxford University Press, Oxford.

Phelps, E. S. (1973), 'Inflation in the Theory of Public Finance', *Scandinavian Journal of Economics* 75: 67–82.

Salin, P. (1975) 'Roads to Monetary Union', in 'Comments on Economic Policy for the European Community – The Way Forward', *Kiel Discussion Papers* 38/39, Institut für Weltwirtschaft, Kiel: 27–41.

Salin, P. (ed.) (1984), *Currency, Competition and Monetary Union*, Martinus Nijnhoff, The Hague.

Ter-Minassian, T. (ed.) (1997), *Fiscal Federation in Theory and Practice*, International Monetary Fund, Washington, D.C.

Thygesen, N. (1998) 'EMU, Britain and Other Outsiders', *Special Paper no. 102*, Financial Markets Group, London School of Economics.

Thygesen, N. (1999) 'Fiscal Institutions in EMU and the Stability Pact', in Hughes-Hallett, A., Hutchison, M. M. and Hougaard Jensen, S. E. (eds) *Fiscal Aspects of European Monetary Integration*, Cambridge University Press, Cambridge.

Tödter, K.-H. and Ziebarth, G. (1997) 'Price Stability vs. Low-Inflation in Germany: An Analysis of Costs and Benefits', *NBER Working Paper no. 6170*, National Bureau of Economic Research, Cambridge, Mass.

Vaubel, R. (1978) *Strategies for Currency Unification*, J. C. B. Mohr (Paul Siebech), Tübingen.

Werner, P. *et al.* (1970) *Report to the Council and the Commission on the Realization by Stages of Economic and Monetary Union in the Community* (Werner Report), Supplement to Bulletin II-1970 of the European Communities, Brussels.

Commission 1

Risks and opportunities for commercial banks and other financial intermediaries

5   Indicators of potential excess capacity in EU and US banking sectors

E. Philip Davis and Sinikka Salo

Introduction

The issue of potential excess capacity in banking is a topic of interest to supervisors and central banks, as well as to the banking industry itself. In recent years, many commentators have suggested a relation between the emergence of such excess capacity and the development of banking in an increasingly global and deregulated situation with rapid technological development. In this context, excess capacity might on the one hand be seen as making excessive risk taking in order to maintain profitability more likely (see BIS 1996), while on the other the potentially disruptive consequences of a rapid removal of capacity from the banking sector can also be seen as a cause for concern. From a viewpoint of competition policy, there is also the issue of whether the removal of excess capacity may lead to concentration and risks of anti-competitive behaviour. In this overall context, this paper considers the conceptual and policy issues raised by excess capacity in banking, and illustrates the various indicators of potential excess capacity using data for EU countries, with comparative data provided from the US. For EU countries, such indicators are, it is suggested, of interest notably in the light of the advent of EMU, which will act to integrate banking sectors across the Union much more closely.

The paper is structured as follows. The first section considers conceptual aspects of excess capacity. It shows that the concept is by no means straightforward, and is linked both to technological and market conditions. The second section addresses empirical measurement of excess capacity and underlying factors, using information from the US as well as the EU. In the final section the paper assesses policy issues.

Conceptual and measurement issues relating to excess capacity

This section looks at the concept of excess capacity both in general and in the specific industry of banking. It is shown that, while the concept of excess capacity has intuitive appeal, it is difficult to define and measure for all industries. It is also closely linked to the underlying competitive structure of the sector. Two separate concepts can be distinguished, as outlined by Frydl (1993), namely 'engineering' excess capacity and 'economic' excess capacity.

The concept of 'engineering' excess capacity

'Engineering' excess capacity is closely related to the concept of the 'output gap' in macroeconomics, measured on the 'short term' assumption that the supply of factors of production – labour and capital – is fixed. In the 'output gap' paradigm, excess capacity emerges at a macroeconomic level when aggregate demand falls below that needed to employ all available resources in terms of labour and capital. Excess capacity is then the difference between maximum potential output and prevailing output, where the former is usually defined by means of a trend calculation or explicit production function. Alternatively, an estimate of excess capacity in this sense may be derived from forms of survey, which pose the question whether firms could increase their outputs without increasing investment.

Such an engineering approach can in principle also be applied at the level of an individual industry, at least when output is well defined. The problem that arises in such a case is that the amount of factor resources cannot be considered as fixed even in the short term; so-called 'variable' factors of production such as labour can always shift between industries. Indeed, assuming, as is reasonable, that the relationship between capital and labour inputs is not entirely fixed, the employment of labour and other variable factors in a given industry will depend on the level of demand and relative output prices in the industry. Such shifts will, however, be limited if factors of production are highly specialized and hence 'specific' to the given industry. With regard to the application of this approach to banking and other financial services, several problems arise, namely that output is itself ill defined (see Colwell and Davis 1992), so statistical trend-fitting to the time series of actual output – the usual method of calculation – cannot give a meaningful approximation to potential output. Moreover, and following the general point noted above, banking and financial services use a certain amount of 'non-specific' capital, such as office buildings, whose usage may respond even in the short run to output price changes.

The 'economic' concept of excess capacity and its link to competitive conditions

This discussion brings us to the 'economic' concept of excess capacity and leads to the question whether it is a superior approach in the case of banking and other financial services. 'Economic' refers to the fact that the concept rests on economic criteria of profit maximization or cost minimization. Standard industrial organization analysis shows that firms typically face a U-shaped relationship between costs and output for a given scale of output, that is, there is a level of output which minimizes average costs. There may also be economies of scale, that is, average costs may be lower at a larger scale of operations (see Figure 5.1). The implications of these patterns vary depending on the industrial structure, in particular whether new competitors may or may not enter the industry.

The case of free entry

In a competitive industry, with free entry of new firms, any level of output below the cost minimizing one is not viable in the long run, as the firm in question would be earning less than 'normal economic profits', that is, the minimum needed to stay in the industry given profit opportunities elsewhere in the economy. Following this argument, excess capacity may be said to exist when at least one firm in an industry is operating in the short run at an output level which is below the optimum for the firm's scale of operations (Shapiro 1989). Full capacity for a firm is defined as the output level at which variable costs per unit output are minimized.

However, an industry may be free of excess capacity in the sense that firms are minimizing costs at their short-term equilibrium level of output, but it may be operating at a non-optimal firm size, if there are long-run economies of scale in the industry (in other words, larger banks have lower average costs). Such a situation may persist if small firms do not wish to

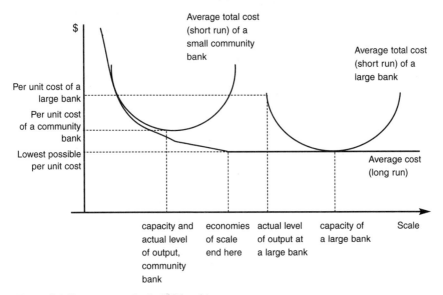

Figure 5.1 Excess capacity in US banking

Source: Frydl 1993. Reproduced by permission of the Federal Reserve Bank of New York

take the risks associated with rapid expansion, such as the need for heavy external financing. So firm size may remain inefficiently low. It may indeed be the emergence of sizeable excess capacity when competition intensifies, which forces the industry into a rationalization through large-scale mergers and acquisitions. On the other hand, in the case of banking the evidence for the existence of economies of scale is not overwhelming. Certainly, empirical studies suggest that economies of scale may be exhausted well below the actual size of current 'large banks' (see Molyneux *et al.* 1996 and references); beyond an asset size of US$ 0.2–4.0 billion, there may be rather few benefits in terms of average costs to be reaped. Very large banks may have diseconomies of scale, with average costs tending to rise, thus implying that they are best advised to *reduce* the scale and/or scope of their operations.

The case where entry is restricted

In a non-competitive industry, where entry is restricted by regulation and output prices are artificially high, perhaps also with extensive cross-subsidies, cost minimization cannot be assumed to hold, and the concept of excess capacity becomes more complex. Two firms in the same industry and with the same technology may be operating at the same scale, but one may have higher costs owing to so-called X-inefficiencies (differences in average costs arising from differing quality of management and organization of work). Such X-inefficiencies may be durable where entry is restricted, as firms are not under pressure to minimize costs. X-inefficiencies may have been rife in banking prior to deregulation (Berger and Humphrey 1990). Equally, where entry is restricted, firms may have a combination of X-inefficiency and inappropriate levels of output, while managing to survive given the inappropriately-high level of output prices. The situation may entail overproduction of 'quality' of banking services. One illustration could be the case of deposit regulation, which gives incentives to cross-subsidize activities (leading for example to overbranching). Such latent excess capacity may, however, become more threatening when an industry is deregulated, profitability declines and excess capacity becomes 'open'.

Other paradigms of competition

It should be noted that the discussion so far is oversimplified. Industrial organization cannot be considered solely in terms of the polar alternatives of free and restricted entry. Even when entry has been liberalized, there are three possible alternatives to the traditional 'perfect competition' paradigm, namely monopolistic competition, contestable markets and strategic competition.

The idea of 'monopolistic competition' may have a role to play, in that banks may be seen as having a form of 'spatial monopoly' in their local area, which implies that there is a degree of product differentiation even with free entry to the sector as a whole (Dietsch 1994, Vesala 1995). Then, given product differentiation, firms may maximize profits when producing at a level below the cost-minimizing level, and there is 'sustainable' excess capacity. Technically, the firm faces a downward sloping demand curve, such that restricting output may raise prices and thus be profit maximizing. Because of free entry and lower production per bank, more banks enter the sector than would be the case under perfect competition. In principle such a situation can be an equilibrium, but if such 'spatial monopoly' also links to restrictions on competition, or if it depends on a certain technology, there may be an excess capacity problem when the forces of competition are set free or technology advances.

The theory of contestable markets (assuming free entry and exit to the market, but also substantial economies of scale) can also be used for banking markets, because it can be applied to markets with only few players and potential competition, which is often the case in banking (Baumol 1982). Sunk costs may be important in retail banking (that is, costs that may not be recovered when leaving the industry, such as relationships, reputation and expertise). This suggests that there also may be elements of strategic interaction among banks to take into account (Tirole 1989), in particular where banks will forgo short-term profit maximization for the long term benefit of, for example, discouraging market entry.

However, it is evident from the literature (discussed later in this paper) that the operational implications of the theory of competition in banking and of financial intermediation are difficult to implement, and thus in practice the concept of excess capacity is in general discussed simply by comparing different overall indicators of banking markets.

Measurement issues arising from the economic concept of excess capacity

If one assumes that competitive conditions and free entry prevail, one may employ a corollary of economic excess capacity to good effect, namely that in an industry where there is free entry, and hence output prices are at a competitive level, banks in excess capacity will be earning negative economic profits. Thus, less than normal reported earnings may provide a summary of excess capacity in the industry. An alternative index of excess capacity – particularly relevant for banking – is the provisions/net income ratio. The underlying argument is that firms are driven by excess capacity to make risky loans at inadequate spreads, hence in a recession banks are unable to earn sufficient interest income to cover their losses. Nevertheless, it should be noted that this measure can also reflect other factors, such as poor credit assessment, inadequate pricing and market distortions. On the other hand, for a non-competitive industry the link of profitability or risk to capacity may not be close. If entry is restricted, either for market or regulatory reasons, and/or each firm has a degree of local monopoly power, subnormal profits imply excess capacity, but the opposite is not necessarily the case (higher than normal profits do not necessarily mean lack of capacity). Also, if firms can make satisfactory profits regardless of their cost situation, they will not be driven to recover profitability by making risky loans. Thus, if entry is restricted it may be appropriate to focus directly on the dispersion (and in cross-country comparisons the level) of cost/income ratios in order to assess the potential degree of excess capacity in the context of artificially-high output prices and X-inefficiencies. Other proxies may include the staffing and density of branches of a banking sector. In effect, such measures indicate the degree to which excess capacity may become evident – and potentially disruptive – when the sector is deregulated. These points are developed later in this paper.

Causes of excess capacity

Employing the above framework, it is evident that emergence of a situation where the level of demand is insufficient to maintain normal profitability at the current scale of operations may result from various causes which may be interrelated and reinforce each other, as follows:

1   There may be a cyclical or structural decline in demand for the industry's product.
2   Technological shocks may make existing capacity redundant. Regarding the banking sector, this may be particularly relevant for deposit collecting, which was traditionally rather dependent on branches, and may be more easily done by using telebanking, the Internet and similar methods. Moreover, such developments reduce entry barriers for outside competition.
3   The distribution of demand may shift between firms, with successful firms gaining market share at the expense of unsuccessful ones, with the latter being pushed into a situation of excess capacity, even if demand at the industry level is unchanged.
4   New competitors may enter the industry, attracted by profit opportunities, and by reductions in the costs of entry and of exit. But this may lead some weaker producers to a situation of excess capacity; or if entry is sufficiently large scale, such problems may arise for the entire industry.
5   Changes in regulation or economic policies are a potential cause of excess capacity, which affect the costs, or even the feasibility, of entry and exit.
6   Where there are sunk costs, firms may engage in forms of strategic competition (such as build-up of capacity to discourage new entry) which may themselves lead to excess capacity.

7   Excess capacity of a benign type may even hold in a rapidly growing industry. Firms may expand the scale of operation and take short-term losses or low profits in a hope of profiting from anticipated increases in demand, which will remove excess capacity. This underlines the fact that a 'snapshot' of an industry may not capture excess capacity well. Rather, to be a cause for concern, excess capacity needs to be unanticipated, unusual, chronic and not diminishing of its own accord.

As is shown later, elements 1, 2, 4, 5 and 6 may have been important in banking difficulties and excess capacity in the US, and may be so in the EU, especially after EMU. The final section of this paper suggests that differing causes of excess capacity may also condition the appropriate policy response.

Conclusion

It has been shown that the concept of excess capacity is closely related to those of efficiency: both productive efficiency and allocative efficiency. The former requires that whatever is produced, it should be at minimum cost; the latter implies that what is done should meet consumer/market needs at prices which reflect the cost of provision (see Neven 1992). When entry is restricted, the pressures to be efficient are weak or absent, and latent excess capacity may develop at the industry level, but a firm in a competitive product market has in general incentives to pursue efficiency, and hence in due course to eliminate excess capacity. The main incentive to productive efficiency will be the threat of bankruptcy or a hostile takeover owing to inadequate profitability. The firm must also pursue allocative efficiency, since otherwise consumers would shift to other firms offering lower product prices. The fact that excess capacity is related to both aspects of efficiency also points up the close relation of the concept to competitive conditions as well as technology. Meanwhile, a possible summary criterion for defining excess capacity at the firm level (Dietsch 1994) is that to be in excess, the installation of the relevant capacity must later be a matter of regret to management. Such a criterion would also distinguish the type of excess capacity resulting from consumer choice (so-called 'monopolistic competition') from forms where it reflects types of market failure.

Measurement of excess capacity and underlying factors

Summary of methodological issues

Most studies look at overall measures of the performance of the banking sector, either using aggregate data *per se* or summarizing data on individual banks, implicitly ignoring the precise competitive situation prevailing in the market: be it free or restricted entry, monopolistic competition, contestable markets or strategic competition (for an exception, see Shaffer 1995). In some ways this approach can be justified. As long as the distribution of market power remains stable, summary measures of changes in levels of profitability may, for example, give an indicator of excess capacity regardless of the precise competitive paradigm. Also if small firms tend to be monopolistic and large firms competitive, there may be little impact at an industry level. Such a pattern may prevail in banking, where in many countries local banks have some monopoly power while larger institutions operate in competitive international markets. Caution is still needed in selecting a time period, however. If it is too short, there is a risk that it will be dominated by cyclical and one-off events. This justifies looking at periods of five years or more, if the data allow. Also, overall measures may be of particular interest in a cross-country analysis.

However, it is not clear that industry-average profitability using aggregate data is always the ideal measure for excess capacity, even for a competitive industry. On the one hand, if the whole industry shows low profitability or makes losses, it is an *a priori* indicator of excess capacity. But the existence of constant, positive profitability on average may not indicate the absence of excess capacity. If demand weakens moderately, some firms may face excess capacity, while others raise productivity, shift scale and product mix, and thus improve profitability. Then average profits may not change, and the appropriate measure of excess capacity would be the share of firms with below normal or unusually low profitability. Thus, summary measures using data derived at the level of the bank may have a useful role to play. How many banks are making 'adequate' levels of profitability? Such an exercise, of course, requires a benchmark for adequacy of profitability; a measure is suggested and employed later.

More generally, a problem with a profits-based measure is that in the financial sector, declines in profitability can at least in a cyclical upturn be offset by increasing the level of risk. A complementary approach is to look at the level of risk in the banking sector, on the view that excess capacity exists if risk increases sharply in relation to profitability. This implies that the bank in question – or the sector as a whole – is choosing a more risky position on the risk/return frontier in order to compensate for the loss of earnings. Once a downturn occurs, provisions compared with profitability of lending would be a possible *ex post* measure. Of course, such a measure needs to be employed carefully, as financial deregulation would itself tend to be associated with some increase in risk. Also, unforeseen macroeconomic shocks may generate losses on loans even if spreads were adequate *ex ante*.

Use of data on banks' size and cost structures is a third microeconomic approach to examining excess capacity. It is particularly useful where entry to the sector is restricted, since in this case profitability data may be uninformative about excess capacity (in other words there may be 'incipient' excess capacity). The dispersion of size in a competitive industry, for example, gives a view as to whether efficient and inefficient firm sizes coexist. In a cross-country context, detailed aspects of the cost structure, such as the scope of branching, may offer complementary indicators, although care is needed in selecting a benchmark. It is also warranted to look at cost—income ratios generally, as well as their dispersion for a given size of firm. This may indicate existence of excess capacity (accompanying X-inefficiency) even where entry is restricted. Note that given lags in adjustment of capacity, such cost-based measures may also provide helpful information for some time after competitive conditions prevail.

Excess capacity in US banking: some evidence and underlying factors

In the light of the above discussion, this section presents results of some empirical indicators of excess capacity for the US. Note that for both the US and European countries, the history of the banking system is in many ways rather similar. Before deregulation and the liberalization of financial markets, banks competed under conditions of low price competition under tight structural regulation. Under such conditions, banks tended to compete by providing 'free' services and in branch proliferation; there was high capacity in terms of employees, and salaries were high in the banking sector. In this way the rents due to low competition were eliminated, while leaving X-inefficiency in banking. However, as a result of deregulation, securitization and market integration, these features were eliminated. The monopoly position and corresponding franchise of the banking industry were eroded, and fierce competition among banks and disintermediation led to a narrowing of the interest margin and emergence of excess capacity.

Frydl (1993) notes that excess capacity is widely considered to have emerged in the US financial services sector in the 1980s and 1990s. Following the suggestion made earlier that a profit-based measure of excess capacity can be used once entry barriers are removed, a summary measure of this was the proportion of banks and of bank assets held by low-earning banks, where low earning is defined as a return on total assets of 5 per cent of the real Treasury bill rate (assuming own funds of 5 per cent, capital should earn at least the same rate as such a risk-free asset). The use of a risk-free rate which varies over time with inflation and the stance of monetary policy, rather than a fixed threshold, may allow in a rough and ready manner for the likely cyclical nature of banks' profits. This measure (see Figure 5.2) showed a marked rise over the 1980s, with the asset measure rising particularly strongly, suggesting problems for larger banks (reflecting, in effect, their delayed provisioning for LDC (less developed country) debt). Such a surmise is confirmed by a separate examination of different size classes of banks. Branching in the US also gave indications of excess capacity (Radecki 1993). In the US, the branch-to-population ratio

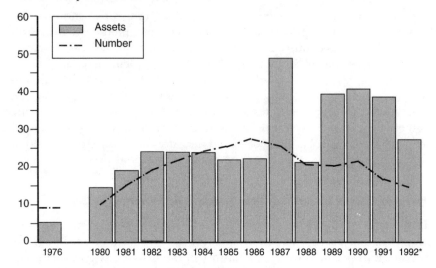

Figure 5.2 Assets and number of low-earnings banks as a percentage share of
        banking system totals

Notes: Low-earnings banks have ROA <.05r, where r equals the average 1-year T-bill rate
        minus the annual growth in the GDP implicit price deflator
*   Estimate based on earnings 1991 Q4 through 1992 Q3

Source: Frydl 1993; originally from Call Reports, Board of Governors, and Bureau of
        Economic Analysis. Reproduced by permission of the Federal Bank of New York

showed no sign of falling over the 1980s, even though the deposit share of
household financial wealth shrank.[1] In terms of headquarters-based operations, transaction-processing capacity was also seen as an area in which to
reap scale economies and gains from consolidation.

As regards underlying factors, excess capacity in banking in the US was
held to be the result of a variety of factors, notably:

1   new competitors
2   diversification on the part of households away from bank deposits
3   adverse shifts in the macroeconomic environment
4   errors in regulation
5   agency conflicts between managers and shareholders.

Points 1 and 2 in particular may be anticipated in the EU in the future, and
hence are worth considering in detail.

New credit sources in the US competing against commercial banks
included foreign banks, finance companies and direct credit markets.
Foreign banks might be at an advantage if they faced a lower cost of funds
or (prior to Basle) lighter capital regulation, and their entry could thereby
lead to excess capacity for domestic banks. Finance companies could make
inroads on banks' business especially in the area of lease finance, which

was tax advantaged. And most crucially, direct credit markets were growing along with the expanding size and influence of institutional investors, reducing the cost of direct issuance of debt (and equity) on the part of firms. Commercial paper and junk bonds were considered to be particularly close substitutes for bank loans. Industrial and commercial companies also entered financial services in specific areas such as consumer loans. Financial innovation, facilitating securitization of claims, increased further the comparative advantage of markets. Although banks still played a role in many of these developments (for example by providing backup lines of credit), they were not able to profit as much as if the loans had remained on the balance sheet.

Banks also faced intense competition on the liabilities side, as institutionalization took hold, leading to a sharp fall in deposits as a share of households' gross financial wealth. Money market mutual funds offered banks direct competition in offering liquid transaction balances. Previously, such liquid transaction balances had been a source of relatively cheap funds for banks. Yet more important, there was a shift in preferences to the longer end as life insurers and pension funds accounted for an increasing share of household assets. Given the ageing of the population, such shifts are likely to persist (see Davis 1995a, 1996).

Macroeconomic developments in the US were also unpropitious for banks, and may have aggravated excess capacity. Bank credit is by nature relational, and suited to immature businesses facing high credit risks. Monitoring is used to control credit risk. Market credit relies on reputation or collateral to secure credit risk. High stable economic growth tends to help banks' share of business credit, since in such a situation a high share of credit demand comes from young growing firms of low reputation. Low economic growth favours the ageing of companies, growing reputation and hence use of direct credit. Volatile growth will tend to lead to high bankruptcies of smaller firms, thus damaging bank assets disproportionately, given their focus on this type of borrower. The period from the first oil shock to the early 1990s saw low and volatile growth, in contrast to the preceding period of sustained high growth, which has implied a deterioration in the environment for banks.

In the US, undue safety-net protection and inadequate prudential supervision were also seen as leading to excess capacity, especially among large banks. The limit for deposit insurance was raised; 'brokered' deposits developed, packaging wholesale deposits so they were fully insured; the 'too big to fail' doctrine entered market perceptions with the rescue of Continental Illinois in 1984.[2]

The particular vulnerability of large US banks to excess capacity in the later 1980s was noted earlier. While the late realization of losses on LDC debt was a key factor in this, others, following the arguments made above, may include the intrusion of new competitors such as foreign banks and investment banks. Large banks may have been operating in a region of diseconomies of scale in terms of lines of business, having been slow to gauge the fact that overall market conditions for bank credit would not support their large size. They may have made losses due to heightened risk-taking, given the moral hazard of 'too big to fail'; and the agency conflict between managers and shareholders may have been increased by the prevalence of syndicated loans, which tend to lead to a front-loading of managerial compensation (as big banks typically organized the syndicate) but a back-loading of credit risk (for banks which participate). Meanwhile, there is some evidence in terms of the profitability of US banks since 1993, that suggests that the worst of the excess capacity has been eliminated.[3]

Indicators of excess capacity in banking in EU countries

Based on the above considerations, we go on to present indicators of potential excess capacity in EU member states. We employ data at both an aggregate and an individual bank level. The indicators do not separate various types of banking with varying functions, and thus need to be interpreted cautiously.[4] Nor is any specific allowance made for the state of competition, although it is noted that some indicators are more suited to certain market situations than others. We conclude by focusing on the degree to which capacity has been rationalized.

Profitability of banks has tended to be low recently

Using aggregate data, Tables 5.1a and 5.1b show that viewed in a long-term perspective, average profit margins in banking have tended to decline at least since the mid-1980s, according to OECD data. Belgium, Denmark, France and Finland showed low returns on assets in 1990–4. The tables also show that there has also been an overall decline in returns on equity. Denmark, France and Finland, and to a lesser extent Belgium, Spain and Austria show up in 1990–4, according to this measure. Meanwhile Table 5.2 indicates that share prices in the banking sector have lagged behind the overall index since 1980 (Belgium and the UK are the main exceptions). This is an a priori indicator that profitability has been below that which the market would require in the long term.

Table 5.3a follows the suggestion in the first part of this paper and the results for the US discussed earlier, and uses a profit-based measure of excess capacity. As was noted, profit-based measures are not appropriate when entry is restricted; however, for the period shown, 1989–95, such a measure is appropriate in most cases in the light of the deregulation of EU banking markets. A summary measure of this is the proportion of banks and of bank assets held by low-earning banks, where low earning is defined as a return on total assets of no more than 5 per cent of the real money market rate (assuming own funds of 5 per cent, capital should earn at least the same rate as such a risk-free asset; that is, the benchmark rate is 0.05

Table 5.1a Profitability measures for banking sectors: all banks

	Profit before tax (% of average balance sheet total)			Return on equity		
	1979–84	*1985–9*	*1990–4*	*1979–84*	*1985–9*	*1990–4*
Belgium	0.35	0.32	0.31	14.64	10.92	8.18
Germany	0.64	0.62	0.55	19.28	16.76	13.78
Spain	0.78	1.07	0.98	10.17	12.75	10.33
France	—	0.44	0.23	—	14.52	5.62
Italy	—	1.17	0.92	—	15.90	11.03
Netherlands	0.48	0.70	0.55	14.63	16.99	13.41
Austria	—	0.60	0.41	—	15.42	8.40
Portugal	0.44	0.59	1.09	15.55	14.11	16.62
Finland	0.32	0.40	-1.12	5.55	6.28	-19.15
Arithmetic average	0.50	0.66	0.41	10.92	12.41	6.65

Table 5.1b Profitability measures for banking sectors: commercial banks

	Profit before tax (% of average balance sheet total)			Return on equity		
	1979–84	*1985–9*	*1990–4*	*1979–84*	*1985–9*	*1990–4*
Denmark	1.22	0.99	-0.17	13.32	11.34	-2.61
Germany	0.53	0.73	0.55	13.35	15.84	10.60
Greece	—	0.46	1.20	—	14.65	26.55
Spain	0.69	1.09	0.98	8.77	12.34	9.72
France	—	0.31	0.06	—	13.48	1.95
Luxembourg	0.34	0.34	0.37	11.04	10.12	12.25
Finland	0.48	0.49	-1.06	6.81	6.90	-17.97
Sweden	0.37	0.63	0.89	8.19	9.53	16.82
UK	0.88	0.84	0.66	22.00	16.28	15.68
Arithmetic average	0.64	0.65	0.39	11.29	11.73	7.34

Table 5.2 Long-term movements in bank share prices

	Ratio of bank index to overall index, 1980=100					
	1970	*1980–2*	*1984–6*	*1990–2*	*1993–5*	*1995*
Germany	93	94	83	75	78	72
Italy	—	138	96	86	72	67
UK	85	97	90	83	118	127
Belgium	110	97	92	88	107	112
Finland	85	98	84	47	22	15
Netherlands	—	92	77	56	61	60
Spain	56	112	78	85	76	72
Sweden	66	99	84	68	66	61
US	142	111	120	69	92	96

Source: BIS

Table 5.3a A profitability-based measure of potential excess capacity using returns on assets

Benchmark for low earnings (= 0.05* real money market rate) percentage points

	1989	1990	1991	1992	1993	1994	1995	Average
Belgium	0.14	0.14	0.15	0.19	0.15	0.12	0.16	0.15
Denmark	0.10	0.21	0.20	0.27	0.43	0.16	0.15	0.22
Germany	0.13	0.16	0.13	0.09	0.08	0.10	0.12	0.12
Greece	0.06	0.04	0.05	0.06	0.07	0.12	0.09	0.07
Spain	0.11	0.11	0.11	0.13	0.08	0.10	0.10	0.11
France	0.13	0.15	0.15	0.22	0.20	0.18	0.18	0.17
Ireland	0.12	0.17	0.16	0.20	0.33	0.12	0.13	0.18
Italy	0.10	0.10	0.09	0.13	0.12	0.11	0.10	0.11
Netherlands	0.34	0.18	0.15	0.15	0.13	0.09	0.11	0.16
Austria	0.16	0.14	0.14	0.12	0.10	0.09	0.10	0.12
Portugal	0.06	0.06	0.08	0.09	0.10	0.11	0.12	0.09
Finland	0.10	0.11	0.15	0.23	0.18	0.24	0.29	0.19
Sweden	0.09	0.07	0.06	0.25	0.09	0.16	0.15	0.12
UK	0.12	0.09	0.09	0.10	0.10	0.12	0.12	0.11

Percentage of banks having returns on assets below the benchmark

	1989	1990	1991	1992	1993	1994	1995	Average
Belgium	21.1	32.4	29.0	42.1	27.0	27.9	33.7	30.4
Denmark	33.3	53.6	28.1	55.0	18.1	24.7	2.2	30.7
Germany	32.8	40.2	29.4	16.6	8.8	14.7	11.3	22.0
Greece	21.4	21.4	23.5	20.0	31.8	27.3	23.8	24.2
Spain	73.6	46.3	10.7	9.7	15.3	22.5	15.8	27.7
France	24.1	37.5	34.8	47.9	39.7	43.3	40.4	38.2
Ireland	—	—	0.0	33.3	45.5	30.0	23.8	26.5
Italy	3.9	3.1	5.9	13.5	11.7	23.8	14.3	10.9
Netherlands	69.2	64.3	28.6	28.6	38.1	14.3	9.8	36.1
Austria	30.0	20.9	21.7	21.5	15.4	15.4	15.2	20.0
Portugal	0.0	0.0	8.0	21.4	19.4	15.2	15.6	11.4
Finland	20.0	40.0	66.7	83.3	70.0	72.7	70.0	60.4
Sweden	0.0	0.0	50.0	45.5	50.0	35.0	15.0	27.9
UK	23.9	20.0	21.3	19.4	24.2	31.3	27.8	24.0

Percentage of bank assets held by banks having returns on assets below the benchmark

	1989	1990	1991	1992	1993	1994	1995	Average
Belgium	23.7	21.5	23.9	38.8	21.7	6.8	11.8	21.2
Denmark	89.6	92.8	63.6	94.0	68.7	55.6	0.3	66.3
Germany	18.0	40.8	22.5	16.7	11.4	14.3	17.9	20.2
Greece	54.2	53.2	6.6	14.7	30.1	23.0	8.4	27.2
Spain	28.2	13.2	4.3	2.6	12.0	14.0	17.8	13.2
France	15.7	25.8	25.1	60.3	62.7	61.8	51.4	43.3
Ireland	—	—	0.0	3.8	79.8	20.5	15.3	23.9
Italy	12.7	12.4	11.9	22.1	22.7	34.2	21.8	19.7
Netherlands	94.5	41.9	11.6	14.5	15.5	6.6	6.4	27.3
Austria	22.8	15.9	10.8	6.4	4.1	4.1	2.4	9.5
Portugal	0.0	0.0	0.8	13.6	9.5	3.8	4.6	4.6
Finland	21.5	45.9	79.2	87.7	87.7	88.3	91.9	71.7
Sweden	0.0	0.0	57.3	22.6	54.0	15.7	8.1	22.5
UK	25.2	15.0	40.0	51.7	45.9	56.0	48.3	40.3

Source: IBCA

times the real money market rate).[5] Benchmark rates are shown in the first part of the table. The data source for banks' balance sheets and profit and loss is the rating agency Fitch IBCA's Bankscope Database (henceforth IBCA), which implies that coverage of smaller banks may be incomplete, although most large banks should be included.

The analysis of the central section of Table 5.3a shows that for 1989–95, over 30 per cent of banks earned less than the real money market rate (divided by 20) on their assets on average in Belgium, Denmark, France, the Netherlands and Finland. The figure is 20–30 per cent for the remaining countries other than Italy and Portugal, where only a small proportion of the IBCA sample suffered from low profitability (bearing in mind that the benchmark varies between countries). This may of course link to rather recent timing of deregulation – and possible latent excess capacity – in these countries. The percentage of assets figures (in the last section of Table 5.3a) illustrate the extent to which it is small or large banks that are afflicted by low profitability. On average, the asset figure exceeds that for numbers – indicating particular problems for large banks – in Denmark, Greece, France, Italy, Finland and the UK.

Table 5.3b shows similar calculations for the return on equity. This time the benchmark is the real money market rate itself. Such a measure allows more sensitivity than returns on assets for the differing profitability of balance-sheet components (where otherwise a bank with many interbank assets will appear relatively unprofitable). The central section of the table shows that similar results are obtained to those found in Table 5.3a. Over the period 1989–95 over 30 per cent of banks earned less than the real money market rate on their capital in Belgium, Denmark, France and Finland, and 20–30 per cent did so in Greece, Spain, Ireland, the Netherlands, Sweden and the UK. Results for assets are again consistent, except they show up less severely for the large banks in France.

On balance, according to these data, low profitability was a particular problem for the banking sector as a whole in Denmark, France and Finland. These averages over six years of course mask divergent behaviour within the period, which varies with the amplitude and timing of the economic cycle, for example, as well as with the benchmark itself. In many cases there was an improvement over time; the impact of banking crises in the Nordic countries and France is also apparent. Some deterioration over time is, moreover, apparent in countries such as Italy and Portugal, which may link to the fairly recent date of deregulation in those countries. As outlined in BIS (1996), in the EU as in the US, underlying factors behind these profitability-based indicators of excess capacity include the quickening pace of innovation and the scope of deregulation, both of which have unleashed heightened competitive forces. Sources of financial capital have become more expensive, the cost of retail funds has risen; collateralization of interbank and wholesale financing has spread, as shown by growth of repos; institutional shareholders are more assertive in their

Table 5.3b A profitability-based measure of potential excess capacity using returns on equity

Benchmark for low earnings (= real money market rate) percentage points

	1989	1990	1991	1992	1993	1994	1995	Average
Belgium	2.80	2.80	3.00	3.80	3.00	2.40	3.20	3.00
Denmark	2.00	4.20	4.00	5.40	8.60	3.20	3.00	4.34
Germany	2.60	3.20	2.60	1.80	1.60	2.00	2.40	2.31
Greece	1.20	0.80	1.00	1.20	1.40	2.40	1.80	1.40
Spain	2.20	2.20	2.20	2.60	1.60	2.00	2.00	2.11
France	2.60	3.00	3.00	4.40	4.00	3.60	3.60	3.46
Ireland	2.40	3.40	3.20	4.00	6.60	2.40	2.60	3.51
Italy	2.00	2.00	1.80	2.60	2.40	2.20	2.00	2.14
Netherlands	6.80	3.60	3.00	3.00	2.60	1.80	2.20	3.29
Austria	3.20	2.80	2.80	2.40	2.00	1.80	2.00	2.43
Portugal	1.20	1.20	1.60	1.80	2.00	2.20	2.40	1.77
Finland	2.00	2.20	3.00	4.60	3.60	4.80	5.80	3.71
Sweden	1.80	1.40	1.20	5.00	1.80	3.20	3.00	2.49
UK	2.40	1.80	1.80	2.00	2.00	2.40	2.40	2.11

Percentage of banks having returns on equity below the benchmark

	1989	1990	1991	1992	1993	1994	1995	Average
Belgium	23.68	21.62	26.32	42.11	35.35	30.77	34.65	30.64
Denmark	40.74	57.14	38.97	77.11	38.30	36.56	2.17	41.57
Germany	25.81	32.67	26.25	17.84	9.31	13.02	11.79	19.53
Greece	21.43	21.43	23.53	25.00	31.82	27.27	23.81	24.90
Spain	73.55	46.27	12.16	12.58	17.11	25.99	22.22	29.98
France	26.05	34.57	33.33	44.61	41.98	44.86	42.42	38.26
Ireland	0.00	0.00	33.33	42.86	61.54	40.00	30.43	29.74
Italy	3.85	3.05	7.60	10.81	8.52	31.85	18.75	12.06
Netherlands	61.54	42.86	21.43	28.57	28.13	15.91	6.98	29.34
Austria	21.95	17.07	17.02	22.73	10.96	19.77	17.05	18.08
Portugal	6.67	4.55	8.00	17.86	25.81	26.47	24.24	16.23
Finland	20.00	40.00	66.67	83.33	70.00	75.00	81.82	62.40
Sweden	0.00	0.00	37.50	27.27	43.75	27.27	12.50	21.19
UK	23.91	20.00	22.95	26.61	28.89	36.45	34.10	27.56

Percentage of bank assets held by banks having returns on equity below the benchmark

	1989	1990	1991	1992	1993	1994	1995	Average
Belgium	23.11	6.01	7.41	37.58	6.37	3.99	9.33	13.40
Denmark	90.05	92.88	65.13	96.92	17.77	30.12	0.08	56.14
Germany	6.91	14.28	11.45	12.10	8.83	7.82	6.02	9.63
Greece	54.16	53.24	6.59	15.00	30.07	23.00	8.41	27.21
Spain	28.17	13.18	4.45	2.97	8.85	6.98	18.89	11.93
France	9.72	12.60	11.85	35.75	39.54	43.28	40.91	27.66
Ireland	0.00	0.00	8.78	8.64	87.57	50.47	44.43	28.55
Italy	9.13	0.76	8.95	21.58	24.50	53.81	23.41	20.31
Netherlands	39.64	13.18	6.55	8.80	3.74	0.91	0.94	10.57
Austria	10.81	5.87	2.15	5.64	1.23	10.92	2.99	5.66
Portugal	1.26	0.56	0.82	5.94	12.54	5.02	5.88	4.58
Finland	21.45	45.85	79.15	87.74	87.72	97.98	99.22	74.16
Sweden	0.00	0.00	52.78	17.66	53.48	13.39	8.14	20.78
UK	25.22	15.00	40.02	52.24	47.41	56.45	44.75	40.16

Source: IBCA

dealings with management; and regulators are alert to the need for banks to operate with adequate capital.

A risk-based measure of excess capacity

Table 5.4 seeks to show whether banks have made sufficient interest income to cover the provisions considered necessary to cover loan losses. For 1994 and 1995, this indicates the percentage of banks which had provision/net interest ratios of over 50 per cent and 100 per cent respectively. Clearly, the latter may be in danger of failure, depending on costs and other sources of income; the former may be an accurate indicator of the overall level of (uncovered) risks taken in the past. Caution is warranted, in that only a subset of the IBCA banks provide these data, and in some countries the overall sample is hence rather small. With this caveat

Table 5.4 Percentage of banks with loan loss provision/net interest ratios of over 50% and 100%

		Over 50%	Over 100%	No. of banks in the sample
Belgium	1994	4	0	74
	1995	6	4	73
Denmark	1994	5	1	88
	1995	1	0	85
Germany	1994	3	1	1692
	1995	2	1	1403
Greece	1994	19	6	16
	1995	6	6	17
Spain	1994	8	2	144
	1995	6	1	136
France	1994	20	11	368
	1995	16	9	323
Ireland	1994	0	0	3
	1995	0	0	3
Italy	1994	7	1	284
	1995	8	2	234
Netherlands	1994	4	0	22
	1995	0	0	17
Austria	1994	23	6	52
	1995	15	4	75
Portugal	1994	16	3	30
	1995	10	0	29
Finland	1994	42	42	7
	1995	25	12	8
Sweden	1994	29	12	17
	1995	13	7	15
UK	1994	5	3	66
	1995	5	2	58

Source: IBCA

in mind, the results do show some marked differences between EU countries. The proportion of banks with ratios of over 50 per cent exceeds one in ten in Greece (in 1994), France, Austria, Portugal, Finland and Sweden. Notably in France, Finland and Sweden, severe difficulties of this nature are apparent, with provision/net interest ratios of over 100 per cent for a number of banks.

Aspects of industry structure

In this section we focus on aspects of the structure of the industry which may give some evidence on overall capacity. This is of particular interest in an uncompetitive sector, as such capacity may become excessive and cause difficulties for profitability as competition intensifies. Table 5.5 seeks to follow the logic that excess capacity may be linked to insufficient exploitation of economies of scale. It was noted that US$ 1 billion is often quoted as the minimum asset size needed to reap all available economies of scale in banking. How important is the 'tail' of small banks, in other words, and hence what scope could there be for consolidation in a more competitive environment, even if banks are viable in the current situation owing to 'local monopoly power'? IBCA data are used to give the number of large banks (over US$ 1 billion), while total numbers of institutions were taken from OECD or BIS data. The number of small banks, both absolutely and as a percentage of the total, varies widely. In most cases, it is around 80 per cent; exceptionally high ratios are seen in Finland and Austria, while it is particularly low in Greece and Portugal.

Table 5.5 Indicators of economies of scale in EU banking sectors (1995)

	Banks with assets of under US$ 1 billion	
	Percentage of total	*Number*
Belgium	74	111
Denmark	85	96
Germany	87	3035
Greece	57	10
Spain	71	226
France	65	384
Ireland	n/a	11
Italy	87	814
Netherlands	88	154
Austria	96	1013
Portugal	52	24
Finland	98	345
Sweden	86	96
UK	90	504

Source: (left column: IBCA for large banks, OECD/BIS for total)

Table 5.6 provides supplementary information on overall banking structure, namely the ratio of population to number of institutions, branches, automatic teller machines (ATMs) and employees in banking. As supporting information, the population per square km is given (in a sparsely populated country more branches may be needed). Although such comparisons should be made with caution, given differing banking activities, regulations and customer preferences, they tentatively show whether capital and labour are used more or less economically.[6] The insularity of EU banking sectors will of course break down with the advent of EMU, making such comparisons yet more relevant. These show that the average size of institution is largest relative to population in Greece, Portugal, the UK and Spain. Germany, Austria the US and Finland have many more small institutions. In terms of population per branch, Greece, Sweden, the UK and the US have the least branches, and Spain, Austria and Belgium the most. The level of employment in banking relative to population is more even, with Sweden standing out as having the lowest employment given the population. Population per employee is relatively low in Denmark, Germany and Austria.

Note in this context that employment may reflect not excess capacity but rather a sector which is highly internationally competitive and heavily involved in the export of banking services. Also, staff may vary in terms of their flexibility and qualifications; overstaffing may be either alleviated or compounded by the structural composition of bank personnel. When assessing banking capacity, the size of the ATM network may also play a

Table 5.6 Indicators of banking capacity

	Population per institution	Population per branch	Population per employee	Population per ATM/ cash dispenser	Population density per sq.km
Belgium	67,333	1,315	133	2,778	352
Denmark	46,044	2,381	112	4,830	121
Germany	23,400	1,719 *	108	2,283	229
Greece	584,105	4,545	260	7,757	79
Spain	123,270	1,190	168	1,468	78
France	97,800	2,272	142	2,544	106
Ireland	61,661	3,100	175	3,891	51
Italy	60,786	2,326	159	2,695	190
Netherlands	89,080	2,325	138	2,816	379
Austria	7,626	1,402	106	2,380	96
Portugal	212,704	2,778	162	2,688	107
Finland	14,488	2,632	159	1,123	15
Sweden	78,571	3,448	204	3,759	20
UK	104,285	3,572	144	2,793	239
US	11,025	3,778	139	2,143	28

Note: *excluding Deutsche Postbank.

Source: BIS, National data, OECD

role. For Spain and Finland the network is dense. If a country has a dense network of ATMs and at the same time a dense network of branches and plenty of employees, that might signal overcapacity in distributing networks. On the other hand, ATMs may be a useful means of saving staff; inferences cannot hence be drawn solely from the ATM data. In fact, both Spain and Finland have average rather than high ratios of population to employees.

Cost-to-income ratio and its dispersion points to inefficiencies and/or excess capacity in particular in small banks

As noted, the rationale of looking at cost-to-income ratios and their dispersion as an indicator of relative excess capacity is based on the assumption that where there is no free entry into banking, banks may (continue to) have different types of X-inefficiencies and nevertheless remain in the market.[7] At the least, deregulation may be too recent to have had a major impact on behaviour. First, we compare cost-efficiency on average across the member states (see Table 5.7) to see whether there are differences between countries with regard to 'efficiency' as measured by the cost-to-income ratio.[8] Second, cost-to-income ratios by size class may also give some indication of unused economies of scale, if the ratio is higher for larger banks (and standard deviations are not too spread).[9] Third, we look at standard deviations across size classes, a rough measure of X-inefficiency, albeit also linked to competition. The data again come from the IBCA database.[10] The majority (around 64 per cent) of the EU banks identified by IBCA are 'small', if the criterion for 'small' is taken to be total assets below US$ 1 billion (as discussed earlier). Only 23 per cent are medium-size, that is, with total assets between US$ 1 and 4 billion, and 13 per cent of banks are 'large' with total assets more than US$ 4 billion.

The results for 1994 are summarized in Table 5.7. Cost–income ratios of all banks varied between countries from 44 per cent to 78 per cent. Ratios of over 70 per cent were present in Belgium, Greece, Spain, France, Italy, and Austria. In most countries the average cost-to-income ratio tends to decline slightly with the size of the bank, which would point to economies of scale. Nevertheless, the standard deviations are rather high, so this conclusion should be interpreted with caution. The average cost–income ratios for different sizes of banks are similar between the EU as a whole and the US. As regards results disaggregated by size of institution, in Belgium, Greece, Spain, Italy, the Netherlands and Austria the average cost-to-income ratio for small banks is clearly above the EU average of 67 per cent in 1994, and in all of these countries it is above 70 per cent. With regard to medium-size banks, the average cost-to-income ratio is above the EU average of 67 per cent in 1994 in Belgium, Greece, Spain, France, Italy, Austria, Portugal and

Table 5.7 Cost-to-income ratio in small, medium and large banks in 1994 (%)

		Small	Medium	Large	All
Belgium	Average	76	71	70	74
	Standard deviation	21	23	35	24
Denmark	Average	65	61	37	62
	Standard deviation	45	30	22	43
Germany	Average	66	61	50	64
	Standard deviation	28	19	26	27
Greece	Average	88	82	56	77
	Standard deviation	40	41	37	73
Spain	Average	72	71	65	71
	Standard deviation	113	24	23	79
France	Average	69	69	75	71
	Standard deviation	50	44	35	46
Ireland	Average	38	54	n/a	44
	Standard deviation	28	23	n/a	24
Italy	Average	76	75	77	76
	Standard deviation	15	23	38	23
Netherlands	Average	70	49	30	60
	Standard deviation	25	28	24	28
Austria	Average	83	74	74	78
	Standard deviation	55	14	8	38
Portugal	Average	57	72	59	63
	Standard deviation	19	26	10	19
Finland	Average	68	99	111	60
	Standard deviation	13	n/a	61	83
Sweden	Average	49	48	45	48
	Standard deviation	16	25	23	20
UK	Average	62	53	61	59
	Standard deviation	28	72	49	43
EU	Average	67	67	62	65
	Standard deviation	28	16	16	22
US	Average	66	62	62	64
	Standard deviation	23	13	14	15

Note: Small banks have assets of below US$ 1 billion, medium US$ 1–4 billion, and large over US$ 4 billion

Source: IBCA database

Finland, and above 70 per cent in most of these countries. As regards large banks, the EU average is 62 per cent in 1994. Belgium, Spain, France, Italy, Austria and Finland are above average in this regard.

We may interpret standard deviations of cost–income ratios as a measure of potential inefficiency, albeit linked to competition, in the sense that the smaller the standard deviation, the more intensive is the competition (forcing the banks to a similar 'optimal' cost-to-income structure). The data show that the standard deviation tends to be smaller in medium-sized and large banks than in small banks. This may link to competition being less intense among small banks, which is in accordance with a general perception that they often benefit from local market power.[11] However, a complementary explanation is that there is potential excess capacity. A third explanation, which may be relevant for some countries, is that there may be an 'arithmetic' element to the results, with a higher mean linking to a higher standard deviation. Subject to this caveat, we note that standard deviations among small banks are relatively high in Denmark, Greece, Spain, France and Austria.

We also examine various types of banks separately. Table 5.8 presents cost-to-income ratios for savings banks and commercial banks. For savings banks, the ratio is above the EU average in Belgium, France, Italy and Finland, while for commercial banks Belgium, Germany, Greece,

Table 5.8   Cost-to-income ratio in savings banks and commercial banks in 1994 (%)

		Savings banks	Commercial banks	All banks
Belgium	Average	71	76	74
	Standard deviation	25	24	24
Denmark	Average	56	59	62
	Standard deviation	7	16	43
Germany	Average	60	73	64
	Standard deviation	8	59	27
Greece	Average	n/a	85	77
	Standard deviation	n/a	35	73
Spain	Average	66	76	71
	Standard deviation	10	101	79
France	Average	91	73	71
	Standard deviation	11	52	46
Ireland	Average	71	20	44
	Standard deviation	1	7	24
Italy	Average	79	83	76
	Standard deviation	9	22	23
Netherlands	Average	65	60	60
	Standard deviation	18	30	28
Austria	Average	70	72	78
	Standard deviation	6	25	38
Portugal	Average	55	63	63
	Standard deviation	16	20	19
Finland	Average	99	59	60
	Standard deviation	n/a	29	83
Sweden	Average	60	52	48
	Standard deviation	n/a	20	20
UK	Average	71	62	59
	Standard deviation	n/a	21	43
EU	Average	70	65	65
	Standard deviation	7	24	22
US	Average	62	64	64
	Standard deviation	26	14	15

Note: Only 3 or fewer banks are included in a group

Source: IBCA database and own calculations.

Spain, Italy and Austria show figures above the EU average. Considering the EU as a whole as compared to the US, results for average cost–income ratios appear rather similar (with the average cost-to-income ratio of medium-sized banks being slightly lower in the US). Smaller standard deviations within all size groups in the US may indicate more intensive competition compared to the average situation in Europe. Nevertheless, ratios for savings banks and commercial banks seem to be above the respective ratios in the US.[12]

Some elimination of excess capacity has taken place

Tables 5.9 to 5.12 give an indication of the degree to which excess capacity has already been eliminated and by what means, again using aggregate data for nine countries (see pages 81–3). They show that restructuring has proceeded in an uneven manner, which according to BIS (1996) links both to differing initial conditions – including the intensity of competition as well as banking market structures – and the strength of the obstacles to the required adjustment. Table 5.9 shows that there has been a fall in the number of institutions in all the EU countries shown since the 1980s (except for Belgium, where numbers peaked in 1992 and have fallen only a little since then). The number of institutions still differs enormously (and is even more out of line in the US). Size concentration has not always tended to rise, however, as a consequence of restructuring. Only in Finland, the Netherlands, Spain and Sweden is there a clear upward trend in concentration, although concentration has also increased in Italy since 1990. Branch networks have been cut back (Table 5.10), except in Italy and Spain, where

Table 5.9 Banks' restructuring: number of institutions and size concentration

	Number of institutions						Concentration: 5-firm (10-firm)		
	1980	*1990*	*1995*	*Peak (since 1980)*			*1980*	*1990*	*1995*
	number				*year*	*%*	*percentage share*		
						change	*in total assets*		
Germany	5,355	4,180	3,487	5,355	1980	-35	—	—	17 (28)
France	1,033	786	593	1,033	1984	-43	57 (69)	52 (66)	47 (63)
Italy	1,071	1,067	941	1,109	1987	-15	26 (42)	24 (39)	29 (45)
UK	796	665	560	796	1983	-30	63 (80)	58 (79)	57 (78)
Austria	1,595	1,210	1,041	—	—	—	—	—	—
Belgium	148	129	150	163	1992	-8	64 (76)	58 (74)	59 (73)
Finland	631	498	352	631	1985	-44	63 (68)	65 (69)	74 (83)
Netherlands	200	180	174	200	1980	-13	73 (81)	77 (86)	81 (89)
Spain	357	327	318	378	1982	-16	38 (58)	38 (58)	49 (62)
Sweden	598	498	112	598	1980	-81	64 (71)	70 (82)	86 (93)
US	35,875	27,864	23,854	35,875	1980	-34	9 (14)	9 (15)	13 (21)

Source: BIS

Table 5.10 Banks' restructuring: number of branches

	1980	1990	1995	Peak	Year	% change
	Number (in thousands)					
Germany	39.3	39.8	37.9	40.0	1985	-5
France	24.3	25.7	25.5	25.9	1987	-2
Italy	12.2	17.7	23.9	23.9	1995	—
UK	20.4	19.0	16.6	21.2	1985	-22
Austria	3.4	4.5	4.7	—	—	—
Belgium	7.80	8.3	7.8	8.5	1989	-8
Finland	3.4	3.3	2.1	3.5	1988	-39
Netherlands	6.6	8.0	7.3	8.5	1986	-14
Spain	25.8	35.2	36.0	36.0	1995	—
Sweden	3.7	3.3	2.7	3.7	1980	-27
US	58.3	67.7	69.6	69.6	1994	—

Source: BIS

branching restrictions have been lifted slowly or recently. In most cases, EU countries are ahead of the US in cutting back on branches. Table 5.11 shows that employment has fallen in most EU countries, and staff costs have been reduced as a percentage of gross income. Falls in employment are most marked in the UK and Finland (as well as in the US); in Germany and Italy employment is at a peak which, in combination with high employment per head of population (Table 5.6), suggests a risk of excess capacity. This lack of adjustment may relate to the impact of employment protection legislation although, especially in Italy, relatively weak competition was also a factor till recently. Table 5.12 indicates that the scope of restructuring via mergers and acquisitions is

Table 5.11 Banks' restructuring: employment and staff costs

	Employment						Staff costs		
	1980	1990	1994	Peak			1980–2	1986–8	1992–4
	number (in thousands)				year	% change	as a percentage of gross income		
Germany	533	621	658	658	1994	—	48	44	39
France	399	399	382	401	1988	-5	47	44	44
Italy	277	324	332	333	1993	-0.3	46	48	44
UK	324	425	368	430	1989	-15	47	38	36
Austria	59	76	76	79	1995	—	—	—	—
Belgium	68	79	76	79	1990	-5	41	33	34
Finland	42	50	36	53	1989	-32	43	33	24
Netherlands	113	118	112	119	1991	-6	42	41	38
Spain	252	252	245	256	1991	-4	47	43	37
Sweden	39	45	42	46	1991	-5	29	23	22
US	1,900	1,979	1,891	2,136	1987	-12	36	31	27

Source: BIS

Table 5.12 Merger and acquisition activity in banking

	Number			
	1989–90	*1991–2*	*1993–4*	*1995–6*
Germany	19	71	83	27
France	52	133	71	43
Italy	41	122	105	65
UK	86	71	40	28
Belgium	11	22	18	12
Finland	6	51	16	4
Netherlands	12	20	13	7
Spain	30	76	44	26
Sweden	10	38	23	8
US	1,501	1,354	1,477	1,176

	Value							
	in billions of US dollars				*as a percentage of all mergers and acquisitions*			
	1989 –90	*1991 –92*	*1993 –94*	*1995 –96*	*1989 –90*	*1991 –92*	*1993 –94*	*1995 –96*
Germany	1.1	3.5	1.9	0.7	4.5	6.5	7.6	3.5
France	2.7	2.4	0.5	3.2	5.1	4.3	1.0	10.4
Italy	8.2	5.3	6.1	3.0	22.7	15.6	17.7	19.7
UK	6.4	7.5	3.3	21.7	2.6	6.5	3.4	12.4
Belgium	0.0	1.0	0.6	0.4	0.2	14.1	7.0	7.9
Finland	0.4	0.9	1.0	0.8	13.9	22.3	21.7	11.3
Netherlands	10.9	0.1	0.1	0.8	56.3	0.2	0.5	9.5
Spain	4.0	4.3	4.5	2.1	18.5	13.5	21.5	34.1
Sweden	2.0	1.1	0.4	0.1	8.8	3.8	2.0	0.4
US	37.8	56.8	55.3	82.5	7.3	18.7	9.0	13.5

Source: BIS

again highly uneven, with the UK, Spain and Italy (as well as the US) standing out to some degree.

As in the US, the differential patterns of restructuring, and the outturns, partly reflect the impact of public policy in the EU (BIS 1996). Notably, in the Nordic countries the authorities have actively promoted rationalization of the banking industry following banking crises which, it can be argued, were themselves partly a symptom of excess capacity following deregulation (Davis 1995b). On the other hand, some of the reasons for relatively slow adjustments in other EU countries may also link to policy. One barrier to adjustment is continuing public ownership of a wide range of financial institutions, which are much less amenable than private institutions to market signals. Mutual institutions may be subject to similar difficulties. Regulatory constraints on the takeover mechanism exist. There remains inflexibility in the labour market, which hinders restructuring of financial services. Lack of disclosure on the part of banks still makes assessment of credit risk difficult, as well as operation of corporate control. The next section discusses these policy issues in a more systematic manner.

Policy issues

Can market forces resolve excess capacity?

There are three ways by which an excess capacity problem can be resolved: productivity improvements, restructuring and exit.

Productivity improvements are most readily available to firms which were inefficient prior to the emergence of excess capacity. Banking sectors are quite commonly inefficient before deregulation, as witness the rationalization of staff and branching that often occurs thereafter. Elimination may also involve removal of existing X-inefficiency, such as improved management practices and better organization of work. However, such changes may not be readily or easily introduced, and may require changes of management to be effected.

Restructuring may entail changing the scale of the firm to a more efficient one, or changing the product mix. The former is by definition an option which is always available, but losses made during periods of excess capacity may make the necessary adjustments more likely to occur. They may be difficult to achieve for firms which are too small to be fully efficient, as such firms may be constrained in the availability of external finance for such a move. Shrinkage of large firms to a more efficient size is more readily achieved. On the other hand, sunk costs such as reputation may limit speeds of adjustment; if pulling out of certain areas is thought to weaken such a reputation, for example.

In either case, achievement of scale economies may require mergers and acquisitions of other firms. This may reduce the problem of limits on external finance for small firms which wish to grow.[13] Mergers may also be a favoured way of achieving shrinkage to a more efficient scale. In banking, this may help to eliminate complex strategic forms of excess capacity such as competing branch networks, which the firms by themselves could not rationalize without becoming unviable. In other words, mergers may overcome what amount to elements of wasteful strategic competition among oligopolists. Mergers may also lead to changes in management structure which may facilitate the aggressive pursuit of economies.

Exit of firms is the third way to remove excess capacity. Mobility of capital (absence of 'sunk costs' which cannot be recovered when leaving the industry) is essential to exit. If the industry is dominated by firms having immobile capital, excess capacity may persist. It was highlighted above that sunk costs may be more pervasive in banking than might appear at first blush.

If market forces could be relied on to eliminate excess capacity in the ways outlined, then from the point of view of competition policy, such developments would be desirable, so long as they do not lead to such a degree of concentration as to threaten to cause a monopoly situation. Existence of excess capacity would be an issue only to the extent that its elimination may prove disruptive, as in the case of banking, threatening to lead to systemic risk and affecting the economy as a whole.

Speeds of adjustment of excess capacity

It is useful to continue by assessing factors underlying differing speeds of adjustment of banking sectors to excess capacity. Clearly, excess capacity needs to be reasonably long-lasting in order to raise policy concerns. According to the description in the first section of this paper, the economic concept of excess capacity is a form of disequilibrium which requires a firm to make an adjustment, such as a change of scale of production, of product mix or of productive efficiency. The adjustment is inevitable in the long run. But the speed of adjustment may depend on various factors, such as the following.

1   Whether firms expect demand and the market price to rapidly return to the full capacity level, which would lead to a delay in adjustment in the hope of 'better times returning'. This may be typical of adjustment to recessions.
2   Costs of adjustment, such as the length of labour contracts and employment protection legislation.
3   Regulatory restrictions that may limit changes in the product mix, or even exit *per se.*
4   The proportion of costs which are sunk (that is, having a low recovery rate if the investment is unwound), which give an incentive to continue to operate in the short run even if normal profits are not being made. (Note that sunk costs in financial markets include not just fixed investments but also reputation, expertise and relationships developed over time.)
5   Pressures on management to maintain normal profits, which depend on the leverage which shareholders have over them.
6   Strategic interactions, such that banks which are in oligopolistic competition have no incentive to reduce capacity where rivals will benefit as much as themselves. This may lead to 'wars of attrition'.

As noted, the first factor is typical of the response of any firm to a recession, while the second is also typically a feature of an entire economy. The remaining factors 3 to 6 have particular applications to banking.

Regulation does limit the ability of banks to switch into new product areas, and to combine with non-financial companies. Regulators may also seek to restrict or delay exit from the industry, even in cases of financial distress, if they consider that a failure of one bank may violate the credibility of the whole banking system. The safety net, if it offers protection without forms of oversight, may lead to incentives to take risks when losses are made, rather than exit from the industry ('betting the bank' or 'gambling for resurrection' in the style of the US thrifts).

Sunk costs are arguably quite sizeable in retail banking, stemming from factors such as computer hardware and software specific to the institution in question, the branch network and, crucially, on the deposit side marketing expenditures, and on the loan side, the corps of lending officers/customer relationships/knowledge about customers' creditworthiness. Note that these items are not all or predominantly, fixed capital *per se*. They also, as discussed later, have an impact on competitive conditions. They are arguably much less important in investment or wholesale banking. Also technological developments such as the advent of telephone banking and credit-scoring techniques are significantly reducing the extent to which such sunk costs are also effective barriers to entry.

It is the case in any industry that the interests of managers and shareholders are not always well aligned. Managers may pursue their own interests, for example pursuing growth-oriented strategies which are not in the interests of shareholders. There are a number of reasons why shareholders have less control over management in banking than elsewhere, and hence banks may be less amenable to the operation of market forces than other industries. First, there is the prevalence of public or mutual ownership of banks, or implicit public guarantees (some banks may be 'too big to fail', deposit insurance systems and so on). Second, there is the fact that banks' balance sheets, involving illiquid assets and complex offsetting exposures using marketable assets such as derivatives, are by nature less transparent than those of a typical firm, even for banks that are owned by private shareholders. It is, for example, relatively costly to evaluate a loan portfolio, given the private information the bank has about its clients, a problem that also militates against take-overs. Such problems may be aggravated by inadequate disclosure of banks' balance sheets and risk management practices, and/or lack of comparability of accounting methods across countries. Third, the operation of the takeover mechanism is often limited in the banking sector, partly by the ownership structure *per se*, but often also by regulation. In the case of strategic interactions, the number of branches is an obvious area where oligopolistic banks build up large capacities (Dietsch 1994) and are unwilling to 'disarm' when competitive conditions change, because their competitors would benefit disproportionately. It is argued in BIS (1996) that these elements are sufficiently severe to bias the banking industry to permanent excess capacity even if there are no technological pressures.

Public policy issues

If market forces are weak, public policy may act to promote a more efficient industrial structure by lifting regulatory restrictions, facilitating mergers and/or reducing exit costs, while guarding against the danger that failures may be disruptive. In theory they may also, as in the past, protect the industry from external competitors. But this implies not obtaining the full benefits of a competitive financial services sector, with a threat of 'hidden excess capacity' and widespread X-inefficiency. We now outline the options, using examples from the US and the EU.

Widening of banking powers into securities and insurance is a potential way to improve a situation of excess capacity. It could enable economies of scope to be realized. The realization of such economies requires use of an existing resource that is in excess supply. The branch network, rather than the credit department or transactions processing capacity, may be best suited to this function. Again, the EU is more liberalized in this respect, as in most countries the 'universal banking' tradition enables banks to operate freely in a variety of business areas. This tradition was enshrined in the Single Market legislation, whereas the Glass Steagall Act, which forbids universal banking, is still in force in the US.[14] Universal banking as a flexible model, with wide possibilities for exploiting economies of scope and maximal use of cumulating information from its many functions and counterparts, may indeed prove to be crucial for survival strategies in European banking. However, the empirical evidence of scope economies is again uncertain, and increasing dissociation of financial services from branch distribution due to technological advances may lower the potential for realizing economies of scope linked to joint production and distribution by branch networks. Moreover, efficiency might not be the only *raison d'être* of the universal bank as it may well – as a provider of multitude of services – enhance concentration in the financial sector.[15] Consequently, to guarantee market discipline, outside competition and the threat of takeover are all the more crucial.

Ownership restrictions could be waived. At present there are limits to banks' holdings in non financial firms. However, lifting of such limits could be ill advised, as banks may not be best suited to realize efficiency gains in non-financial businesses, given their lack of knowledge of these industries. Also, industrial ownership of banks may lead to major conflicts of interest.

Policies to boost bank mergers may reduce excess capacity.[16] Two types of merger can be distinguished. Diversification mergers joins banks with different geographical balance sheet exposures, thus making the institution less vulnerable to localized economic problems. Such mergers should reduce the emergence of excess capacity. Consolidation mergers combine banks with competing operations. Benefits can be achieved by consolidating branch networks, consolidating transactions processing and imposing superior management practices.[17] However, there is also skepticism as regards mergers, except those combining very small banks. For example Revell (1987) and Berger and Humphrey (1994) argue that in practice, efficiency gains are proved to be rather negligible. There is clearly a trade-off at some point between mergers and concentration, although this will be less threatening in the euro area than individual countries (depending on how important 'local banking markets' are in EMU).

Following on from this discussion, it is also important to provide shareholders with sufficient leverage over management to ensure that policies which are contrary to their interests are not pursued. Governments would clearly need to avoid artificial restrictions on takeovers. The privatization of public banks, and the transformation of mutual banks to public limited companies or their equivalent, could increase the role of market forces.[18] Public and mutual banks may have less reason to pursue 'shareholder value' or adequate returns on investment, thus heightening the risk of excess capacity. They may raise supervisory issues when they also benefit from an implicit public guarantee (which may be the case for large institutions) or where small banks enter unfamiliar areas such as derivatives.[19] Meanwhile, better disclosure of information would enable shareholders better to evaluate policies being pursued by management, and would facilitate takeovers. Capital adequacy ratios must be maintained, to prevent it being in shareholders' interests to allow management to 'bet the bank'. In these respects, it may be noted that the EU has more public and mutual banks, a more restrictive approach to takeovers, less disclosure than in the US and fewer organized (and concentrated) institutional shareholders to impose discipline on management. (For a discussion of the 'corporate governance movement' in the US and EU see Davis 1995a.) On the other hand, a number of EU countries impose differential capital requirements on small banks to allow for risk, which can be helpful in removing excess capacity by encouraging small banks to merge.

Lowering exit costs will address excess capacity by encouraging firms to leave the sector. It does not seem easy to lower the exit costs as they are to an extent unavoidable, but regulators could strive to establish 'neutral' or 'normal' exit conditions. They should avoid, to the extent possible, regulatory incentives which keep banks alive artificially till a buyer can be found for the capacity (as might occur, for example, if the losses from liquidation are borne by the public sector). A requirement to close banks when capital reaches a certain low level may be helpful, as in the US. As a side-effect, it should also reduce the tendency for capital to flow into banking in the first place.

A general point that could be made is that public policy should on the one hand allow market forces to operate, but on the other ensure that the process is smooth and not disruptive. These tendencies may of course go in the same direction, for example if delay were to make the adjustment sharper and more abrupt. Supervisors may in this context need to ask about the business viability of banks and their profitability relative to a peer group, while recognizing the danger of close involvement in business activities.

Conclusions

Despite conceptual problems in the measurement of excess capacity in banking, some indicators may none the less be derived and these have been presented in this article for EU countries and the US. As has been noted, the potential existence of excess capacity raises policy implications, to the extent that elimination of excess capacity may be a source of disruption of the financial sector and hence the economy as a whole. In this respect, appropriate regulatory policies related to mergers and takeovers, as well as ownership of banking sectors, are important to resolution of excess capacity problems, while nevertheless keeping in mind the danger of 'too much' concentration and ensuring that any removal of excess capacity is orderly. The perspective of EMU, which may well lead to a further intensification of competition, thus heightening the problem of redundant capacity, could increase the importance of orderly removal of capacity, although it may reduce concerns regarding the effect of concentration on competition.

Notes

The authors thank C. Ostergaard for helpful comments. Views expressed are those of the authors and not necessarily those of the European Central Bank, to which both authors were on secondment at the time this paper was prepared.

1 More recent data are shown in Table 5.6.
2 The case for 'too big to fail' has to be made carefully, as it can be argued that the shareholders are still vulnerable in such cases. If banks do engage in excessively risky business, it may link rather to lack of control of managers by shareholders.
3 Interestingly, the US securities and insurance sectors were not seen to have faced the same excess capacity problems as banking. In securities, a high risk and high return sector with volatile earnings, excess capacity appears to be rapidly eliminated when it emerges. This is helped by rather low fixed costs. In insurance also, no excess capacity is seen to have emerged. In both securities and in insurance, the costs of exit are relatively low compared to banking. Unlike in banking, there is no 'too big to fail' doctrine, as the collapse of Drexels showed, so liquidation can be an integral part of the elimination of excess capacity. Foreign entry did not affect capacity as directly as for banking, and there are no impediments to nation-wide operation, leading to a more efficient industrial structure than for banking.
4 Davis and Salo (1998) show preliminary results of an overall comparison of financial sectors.
5 Note that measuring a return on total assets may underestimate profitability for banks with low-risk assets, which require less capital than other banks. An alternative measure is provided later.
6 Important differences relate, for example, to whether banks are intermediating housing finance, and the extent to which the payment system of a country is based on bank giro or post giro system.
7 Another possibility would be to examine cost-to-asset ratios as a rough measure of productivity.
8 The cost-to-income ratio is calculated as a ratio of overheads (excluding depreciation) to the sum of net interest income and other operating income for non-consolidated banks.
9 It should be noted that data do not allow differentiation of banks with

branches and those without, which may have an impact on the potential for making use of economies of scale and scope.

10 Medium-to-large sized institutions are disproportionately represented. The coverage (with regard to the number of banks) varies between 60 and 100 per cent for the medium to large institutions in the majority of EU countries, and between 25 and 40 per cent for small institutions. The coverage for small banks is limited for Austria, Portugal, Finland and Sweden (between 1 and 5 per cent).

11 It should also be noted that the analysis does not take into account the branches of large banks which are competing with small banks in local markets.

12 More detailed time-series results are shown in Davis and Salo 1998.

13 It should be borne in mind, however, that such small firms may have very immobile capital, leading them to persist in business even if they are making below-normal profits, as long as they are not actually losing money.

14 Note that US restrictions on interstate banking were largely eliminated in 1997. Glass-Steagal was abolished in 1999.

15 The benefits and costs of the universal bank model may suggest incentives to restructure an 'ordinary' integrated universal bank into separate units under a holding company, with the argument that in this kind of organisation 'risk management would improve, regulation is easier and conflicts of interests (resulting from a universal bank acting simultaneously as a supplier of savings services and an investor) are reduced'.

16 Not all mergers are equally desirable. 'Defensive mergers' which involve buying a 'local monopoly' to shelter rents may not be viable in the long run.

17 The US literature is inconclusive as to whether such benefits have actually been achieved via merger to a greater extent than would have been the case if banks had not merged.

18 On the other hand, arguments have been presented for preserving at least one public bank for competitive reasons in a local market, if the number of 'core' banks is too small to maintain sufficient competition and efficiency. It is also argued that enhanced competition may sometimes lead to 'short-termism' as the profitability of banks is tested continuously, and thus worsen the financing of longer-term contracts. It has been argued that a public bank can mend these potential flaws of the market mechanism under basically the same conditions as private banks just by its existence, as a threat.

19 This implies in turn a high credit rating and access to cheap funds.

Bibliography

Baumol, W. (1982) 'Contestable Markets: An Uprising in the Theory of Industrial Markets', *American Economic Review* 72.

Berger, A. N. and Humphrey, D. B. (1990) 'The Dominance of Inefficiencies over Scale and Product Mix Economies in Banking', *Finance and Economies Discussion Series no. 107*, Federal Reserve Board, Washington, D.C.

Berger, A. N. and Humphrey, D. B. (1994) 'Bank Scale Economies, Mergers, Concentration and Efficiency: The US Experience', *Finance and Economies Discussion Series no. 94–23*, Federal Reserve Board, Washington, D.C.

BIS (1996) '66th Annual Report', Bank for International Settlements, Basle.

Colwell, R. J. and Davis, E. P. (1992) 'Output and Productivity in Banking', *Scandinavian Journal of Economics* 94 Supplement, 111–29.

Davis, E. P. (1995a) *Pension Funds, Retirement-Income Security and Capital Markets – An*

International Perspective, Oxford University Press, Oxford.

Davis, E. P. (1995b) *Debt, Financial Fragility and Systemic Risk*, revd and extended edn, Oxford University Press, Oxford.

Davis, E. P. (1996), 'The Role of Institutional Investors in the Evolution of Financial Structure and Behaviour', in *The Future of the Financial System*, proceedings of a conference held at the Reserve Bank of Australia, RBA, Sydney.

Davis, E. P. and Salo, S. (1998) *Excess Capacity in EU and US Banking Sectors – Conceptual, Measurement and Policy Issues*, Special Paper, Financial Markets Group, London School of Economics.

Dietsch, M. (1994) 'Les surcapacités bancaires en France', in D. Fair and R. Raymond (eds), *The Competitiveness of Financial Institutions and Centres in Europe*, Kluwer Academic, Netherlands.

Frydl, E. J. (1993) 'Excess Capacity in the Financial Sector, Causes and Issues', in *Studies on Excess Capacity in the Financial Sector*, Federal Reserve Bank of New York.

Molyneux, P., Altunbas, Y. and Gardener, E. (1996) *Efficiency in European Banking*, Wiley, Chichester.

Neven, D. (1992) 'Structural Adjustment in European Retail Banking: Some Views from Industrial Organization', in J. Dermine (ed.), *European Banking in the 1990s*, Blackwell, Oxford.

Radecki, L. J. (1993) 'The Proximate Causes for the Emergence of Excess Capacity in the US Banking System', in *Studies on Excess Capacity in the Financial Sector*, Federal Reserve Bank of New York.

Revell, J. (1987) *Mergers and the Role of Large Banks*, University College of North Wales, Bangor.

Shaffer, S. (1995) 'Market Conduct and Excess Capacity in Banking: A Cross-Country Comparison', *Working Paper 93-28/R*, Economic Research Division, Federal Reserve Bank of Philadelphia.

Shapiro, M. D. (1989) 'Assessing the Federal Reserve's Measures of Capacity and Utilisation', *Brookings Papers on Economic Activity* 1/89.

Tirole, J. (1989) *The Theory of Industrial Organisation*, MIT Press, Cambridge, Mass.

Vesala, J. (1995) 'Testing for Competition in Banking: Behavioural Evidence from Finland', *Bank of Finland Studies E:1*.

6   EMU and the structure of the European banking system

Olivier De Bandt

Introduction

The advent of European Economic and Monetary Union (EMU) represents new opportunities and challenges for financial institutions in Europe. The purpose of this study is to assess its importance as a factor provoking changes in banking structure and performance, against the background of the various trends affecting the medium-long run prospects of the banking industry around the world (liberalization, internationalization, technological change, disintermediation and concentration).

There are several different ways to consider these changes. First, EMU may be seen as the extension to the European context of the aforementioned world trends by way of progress towards frontier opening, pressures on regulatory differences, and respect of market principles. Second, EMU may be viewed as a further step in the direction of European economic and financial integration, so that it may be difficult to distinguish its effects from those of the Single Market and the Second Banking Co-ordination Directive. In particular, one may argue that one of the major gains of the single currency is that it makes the single market real. Third – and this is the approach chosen in this paper – one can consider that EMU may, in itself, have very direct and specific consequences on the European banking system, for instance by exacerbating underlying trends or even having a catalytic role. Of course, EMU should not be seen as the only driving force behind current developments in the European banking industry. The study attempts therefore to assess the relative impact of monetary union and to ponder its effects as compared with the other drivers of change. The analysis distinguishes between the aggregate impact of monetary union on the whole EU-wide banking system and its differential effect on national or sectoral components.

The overall conclusion of the study is that EMU may have some important effects on the nature of banking activities and the level of competition, at the retail as well as wholesale level, although there remains some uncertainty, notably regarding, one, how large the returns to scale are in the different activities, and two, how fast retail markets are going to change.

In order to provide a comprehensive assessment of the future of the European banking industry in Stage Three of EMU, it is convenient to follow the standard – albeit sometimes criticized – paradigm in industrial economics, namely the structure–conduct–performance approach. As a consequence, the paper studies the effect of EMU on different banking activities such as foreign exchange, money market and payment systems, before taking a more comprehensive view of banking strategy and profitability.

The direct effect of EMU on the structure of banking activities

EMU will probably require significant adjustments in the supply of financial services and banks' products, with possible substitution among activities. In that respect, it may be useful to understand the dynamics of EMU in terms of the creation of a level playing field for market activities, which will foster the convergence of financial structures and help to integrate other asset management activities. This motivates successive reviews of market and other banking activities.

EMU will have direct and significant effects on market activities

Foreign exchange transactions

Concerning market activities, the most immediate changes will affect the foreign exchange markets, since cross-trades between currencies participating in the monetary union will disappear. The need for currency-hedging transactions will also decrease, although they have already done so with the reduction of volatility among currencies participating in the ERM, so that the bulk of hedging transactions currently involve the US dollar. New activities may emerge, in particular associated with the use of the euro as a reserve currency, although this will only occur as the euro becomes established. (See Table 6.1.)

It is difficult to find reliable information on the importance of intra-European cross trades (for example, on volumes involved and effects on profits).[1] The main reason is that the US dollar, being a dominant currency, may be used as a vehicle for trades between European currencies, although the DM has progressively become the main vehicle currency for cross-trades in Europe.[2] According to the 1995 BIS survey on forex activity (BIS 1995), the share of spot trading involving the dollar against EU currencies in each country's total turnover for Germany, France and the UK was equal to 62.8 per cent, 55.8 per cent and 53 per cent respectively in 1995, among which transactions with countries outside the zone cannot be distinguished from those where the US dollar is used as a vehicle currency.[3] At the same time, forex trading involving the

Table 6.1 Impact of EMU on foreign exchange transactions

	Share in total transactions reported by the country (%)	
	Transactions between DM and EU currencies	*Transactions with non-EU currencies**
UK	9.5	36.6
Germany	15.4	21.8
France	27.1	13.7
Denmark	13.5	29.5
Belgium	13.5	14.7
Netherlands	21.4	14.4
Italy	17.1	4.5
Sweden	24.4	16.6
Luxembourg	13.0	21.6
Spain	20.4	4.0
Austria	11.3	15.0
Finland	33.5	12.4
Ireland	37.7	9.1
Greece	13.1	22.1
Portugal	26.8	6.7
Total EU-15	13.4	28.3

Note: * Transactions between US$ or DM and non-EU currencies + 50 per cent of
transactions between non-EU currencies and other currencies than US$ and DM

Source: BIS (1995 *Survey on Foreign Exchange Activity*), author's calculations

domestic currency against other EU currencies accounted for 3.6 per cent
of total forex turnover in the UK, 15.3 per cent in Germany and 24.6 per
cent in France. Keeping in mind that direct cross-trades between EU
currencies usually involve the DM, trades between the DM and one of the
other EU currencies (including the domestic currency) were 9.5 per cent
of total turnover in the UK, compared to 13.4 per cent at the EU-15 level
and 19 per cent for the European Union outside the UK (see Table 6.1,
left-hand column). This may provide a measure of the immediate effect of
EMU as a reduction between 10 per cent and 15 per cent of forex trades
in EU countries.[4] A part of this reduction, as estimated on the basis of data
for 1995, may have already occurred to the extent that currency traders
have reduced their trading and hedging activity as a result of the decrease
in volatility and arbitrage opportunities.

The various EU countries also exhibit significant differences. In
general, financial centres dealing with non-European currencies will be
less affected than others. In particular, London is the most active forex
market in the world. In 1995, its total turnover in the spot market was six
times larger than in Frankfurt and eight times larger than in Paris. In
addition, the currencies traded in London are far more diversified than in
Frankfurt or Paris, despite the fact that 41.6 per cent of cross-trades
between European currencies that involve the DM and take place in
Europe originate in London (see Table 6.1 for the market share of the

different EU financial centres). More generally, in the UK and Germany, 36.6 per cent and 21.8 per cent respectively of total turnover, involves non-European currencies. In the latter case, the importance of non EU-currency trades is due to the prominent role of the DM, while the corresponding figure is only 13.7 per cent for France (see Table 6.1, right-hand column).

Concerning the development of new activities, independently of the evolution of forex transactions motivated by speculative objectives, opinions differ widely regarding the expected role of the euro as a reserve and transactions currency. Given the relative autarky of the European Union as a commercial zone, trade invoicing in euro may not be a source of large development in forex activities.[5] However, it is well known that the latter transactions tend to be more dependent on portfolio flows. In addition, if the larger size and lower external-trade-to-GDP ratio in the Euro area induces an increase in the day-to-day volatility of the bilateral euro exchange rates with the dollar and the Japanese yen, derivative markets would develop more significantly. The use of the euro as an international or as a reserve currency will also depend, of course, upon the willingness of investors outside the monetary union – both official and private – to hold the currency in their portfolio. To the extent that the euro would rapidly become fully credible, more transactions could effectively take place in euro, providing a competitive advantage to banks in the euro area.[6] The final impact for banks will depend on their ability to reposition themselves for trading the euro against third currencies, although the Asian crisis has made clearer the risks associated with emerging markets. It is possible that such additional transactions in the foreign exchange market of the euro would be mostly located in London, even if the UK does not participate in the Union.

Money markets

EMU will have very significant effects on the money markets. The single monetary policy will create a new environment, to which the banks will have to adapt.

THE SINGLE MONETARY POLICY FRAMEWORK WILL CREATE A NEW ENVIRONMENT

The new framework for the implementation of the single monetary policy will create the necessary conditions for the integration of European money markets.

First, the technical infrastructure to support a large European money market will be provided by the interlinking of real-time gross settlement (RTGS) systems through TARGET. Large cross-border payments denominated in euros will therefore be processed as smoothly as if they were domestic payments. Initially designed to carry out the single monetary policy, TARGET might also be available for other kinds of transfers as an alternative to private net settlement or non-real-time systems (such as the ECU Clearing), mainly at the wholesale level, and should therefore contribute substantially to reducing the kind of systemic dangers to which netting systems are exposed.

Second, the ESCB will rely on monetary policy instruments designed to create a deep and liquid money market at the EU level. As indicated in the 'Framework Report' published in January 1997 by the European Monetary Institute (EMI 1997a), and explained in more detail in the so-called 'General Documentation' published in September 1997 (EMI 1997b), the ESCB will rely on open market operations as well as on standing facilities. The interest rate corridor between the latter (the deposit and the marginal lending facilities) is designed to bind overnight market rates, while leaving significant leeway to banks to manage their interest exposure, therefore encouraging market development. The ESCB will also rely on a broad range of counterparties. In addition, the ECB Governing Council has decided to make use of fully remunerated reserve requirements, and the averaging provisions mechanism might be viewed as contributing to an increase in the volume of the interbank market. Compared with alternative ways of controlling volatility in the interbank market, reserves with averaging facilities will have the advantages of assigning a central role to market forces and of not requiring the central bank to be frequently active in the market. Equal treatment of counterparties and the reliance on market-based policy instruments are consistent with the requirement, enshrined in the Maastricht Treaty, that the ESCB 'shall act in accordance with the principles of an open market economy with free competition'.

THE NEW ENVIRONMENT WILL REQUIRE BANKS TO ADAPT

The single monetary policy will, however, require market participants to adapt to the new environment.

First, the harmonization of Monetary Policy Instruments and Procedures (MPIPs) at the start of Stage Three will have an impact on banks' refinancing. New refinancing operations and facilities will be introduced, requiring further adjustment of techniques towards a greater use of interventions at market rates in some countries. Of course, some countries have already made some adjustment (such as the development of the short-term money market in Germany) and changes realized in the past did not prove to be too difficult to implement for many countries. For a few other countries, however, the adjustment is more significant.

Second, in order to accommodate differences in financial structures across countries, two tiers of eligible collateral are to be allowed for monetary policy operations: the first one includes instruments that are common to all countries, while the second comprises assets which are of particular importance for national banking systems, and includes marketable and non-marketable financial obligations as well as, in some cases, equities. In the case of the second tier, the assets and eligibility criteria are established by each NCB, under ECB guidelines and with its approval. This would, for example, allow the inclusion of a relatively large volume of trade bills and bank loans in Germany and France.

Third, one might anticipate that not only the harmonization effect of the single monetary policy, but also the greater level of competition, will progressively reduce arbitrage opportunities linked to liquidity differentials across money markets. However, the US case shows that it has not hindered the development of large money markets. In particular, the decision that the ECB will use reverse transactions as the main instrument for implementing monetary policy might provide a strong incentive for the development of an EMU-wide private 'repo' market, where financial and non-financial entities may engage in short-term collateralized refinancing operations for conducting day-to-day treasury management (see Schinasi and Prati 1997).

Securities markets

EMU will also have an impact on securities markets, where banks, especially the largest ones, are major participants either through the management of their own portfolio or as intermediaries in investment banking activities. EMU will create the potential for the emergence of deeper and more liquid financial markets; it may also have effects on the nature of products offered. The development of large European 'domestic' markets will provide an opportunity to banks to diversify their revenues towards a larger share of non-interest income.

Regarding the size of financial markets, EMU will offer EU institutions an easy access to a really global financial market, and the opportunity to compete on an equal footing with US and Japanese banks. The capitalization of existing (domestic and international) debt securities and equities in the EU-15 area amounted to US$ 12,500 billion at the end of 1995, as compared to US$ 27,000 billion for the US and Japanese markets taken together, on account of the large size of the EU domestic bond markets (see Schinasi and Prati 1997). The current process of harmonization of market conventions and codes of practices (day counts, business days, reference rates and so on) will not only ensure the continuity of operations when moving to Stage Three of EMU and the smooth functioning of the area-wide money market based on the euro, it will also promote the fungibility of instruments across countries, a necessary condition for the creation of deeper financial markets (see the Giovannini Report (EC 1997)). The greater depth and liquidity of EU markets after the introduction of the single currency, as well as the strength and the stability of the euro, may also attract additional investors from outside the

EMU may have significant effects on the nature of products offered on EU securities markets.

First, one can expect that the disappearance of foreign exchange risk will mean that credit risk will become more important in relative terms, which may lead to the emergence of a 'credit risk culture' in the management of debt instruments. Investors, as well as banks, may therefore switch from a country to a sectoral approach. While this will be favoured, in particular by the implementation of the 'no bail-out' clause – which will have an impact on the rating of public debt, in the sense that domestic issues are likely to receive ratings similar to those currently attributed to foreign issues (see BIS 1996) – fiscal discipline and the strict application of the Stability and Growth Pact should *per se* reduce credit differentials to a minimum.[7] In countries where banks hold a significant proportion of government bonds (France, Germany, Belgium and Luxembourg), banks will have to adjust their portfolios in the light of perceived variations in this credit risk. At the same time, the zero credit risk weighting for zone A government debt (which includes all EU countries' government debt) in the solvency ratio regimes will provide a strong incentive to invest in government bonds. Investors will also pay more attention to the liquidity characteristics of securities.

Second, one could witness in the very near future the creation of a unified European capital market for prime borrowers, partly as a consequence of international co-operation among European exchanges. Although EMU provides a strong incentive for such a restructuring for 'in' countries, other countries such as the UK, but also Switzerland, would be associated. This would include the emergence of a single reference bond yield curve, as well as a European equity market for blue-chip stocks. Such markets would, however, not cover the whole spectrum of issuers, since securities from small and medium-sized companies would probably remain national. The latter compartment of the market will probably remain to a large extent separated, since investors' home bias is likely to remain important, because of asymmetric information, tax differences, or attempts by national centres to protect their market shares.

Third, other markets may also develop. The Stability and Growth Pact will, by constraining fiscal policy and imposing limits on government deficits, reduce governments' recourse to the capital market, hence creating room for other issuers. In addition to population ageing, it will put additional pressures on pay-as-you-go pension systems in favour of funded ones. Non-government bond and equity markets should therefore grow, accelerating the general movement towards disintermediation. In addition, to the extent that the operational framework for monetary policy increases the demand for private paper, it will have an effect on financial market structures, by creating the critical mass which will allow new products to be sufficiently competitive to expand significantly. This will increase the scope for securitization; it might even lead to the emergence of a low-grade bond market in addition to the market for prime borrowers.

Fourth, EMU will also have an impact on derivatives markets. Products linked with short-term interest rates are likely to suffer falls in trading volumes in many cases, since the single monetary policy in Stage Three implies that there will be only room for one leading short-term contract. This may have severe consequences for the sixteen European futures or options markets (including Switzerland). As far as long-term contracts are concerned, the coexistence of more than one reference bond market will not be a durable feature, so that one can anticipate either a single contract – although this may imply co-operation between financial centres – or several identical ones with similar characteristics (margins, opening hours). Banks may have to reconsider their degree of participation to the exchanges providing such derivatives contracts, in particular regarding seat ownership.

EMU will also trigger substantial changes in traditional banking activities

EMU will also have an impact on 'core' banking activities, that is, payment activities, as well as credit and deposit-taking business. It may also have an effect on the regulatory environment. The analysis focuses here on banks as a whole, leaving to the next part of this paper an analysis of how competition among banks is likely to evolve.

Further progress in payment systems

EMU will induce further progress in payment systems, even if technological innovation remains the major driving force behind changes in payment systems as evidenced, not only by the case of electronic money, but also by many other money transmission services. For instance, technological innovation may itself be fostered by the transition to the single currency. In particular, the liberalization of telecommunications, favoured by the single market that EMU is due to complete, may lead to a more widespread use of phone, PC and Internet banking. Network-based e-money payments may also benefit from a global and highly contestable market. Some observers expect, indeed, that, because of the non-availability of euro bank notes during the transition period, electronic money might grow significantly.

Regarding revenues, banks' profitability will be adversely affected since revenues from money transmission services will be reduced with the disappearance of correspondent banking fees derived from intra-European forex operations.[8] In addition, the structure of traditional correspondent banking activities will have to adjust to the new environment. The new payment systems will allow balances associated with correspondent banking to be reduced, but also the rents associated with it. This will affect large banks, more significantly involved in such activities; conversely small banks will benefit from competition in payment systems. At the same time, if the euro were to gain an international role, single currency area banks would be in a position to increase correspondent banking activity. These changes may also affect former alliances among groups of banks based on correspondent services (see the last part of this paper). Finally, due to the interlinking of national RTGS, payment systems at the national level will operate in a much more competitive environment, with a possible reduction in the 'float'.[9] In particular, national RTGS will be under the pressure of corporate clients who will take advantage of EMU to organize treasury and risk management on a European scale. Differences across countries may also imply diversion of traffic. Therefore, much of the evolution will depend on the pricing policy of payment operations, characterized by more important returns to scale in wholesale activities than in retail operations.[10] Overall, this background implies that network effects propagated by revenue changes may potentially be significant. In addition, if securities markets are to expand and become more diversified to compete on an equal basis with the United States, securities settlement systems will have to improve further and develop significantly. In that context, national securities depositories will face the competition of international depositories (Cedel, Euroclear).

Effects on credit and deposit activities

It is also necessary to study to what extent EMU will affect traditional intermediation activities. EMU is likely to increase the size of securities markets so that securitization in the 'narrow sense' – the transformation of banking assets into tradable securities through financial engineering – will make further progress, offering banks more flexibility in terms of asset/liability management. At the same time, with securitization in the 'broad sense' (the larger use of instruments tradable in deeper financial markets), the competitive disadvantage of traditional bank intermediation *vis-à-vis* financial markets and non-banks is likely to increase, with differential effects on deposit collection and credit activities.

On the deposit side, banks are likely increasingly to face competition from institutional investors. Following the disappearance of foreign exchange risk, limits on portfolio diversification by institutional investors, like the 'currency matching rules', are likely to be applied only outside the euro area.[11] This will boost the cross-border investment activity of institutional investors. As a consequence of the changing nature of demand, with the greater use of mutual funds, the maturity of banks' deposit-taking may become shorter, and deposit collection more costly.

On the asset side, greater competition in the securities business will coexist with the persistence of asymmetric information in lending activities. In the latter case, the need to have a direct link with borrowers means that traditional financial intermediation is likely to remain substantial, in particular lending to small and medium-sized enterprises, for whom access to the securities markets is more difficult. Nevertheless, banks face competition also in their traditional lending activities, because of the dramatic reduction in transaction costs and the improved possibilities to evaluate risk brought about by information technology. In the not too distant future, the development of securitization – fostered by EMU – and the growth of mutual funds may increase the challenge posed to banks by rating agencies using computerized credit scoring techniques. Even for small and medium-sized enterprises (as well as technology firms), increasingly connected securities markets with improved disclosure rules might also diminish the information advantage of banks. In that respect, securitization in the 'broad sense' may reinforce securitization in the 'narrow sense' targeted at small and medium-sized companies. The risk is also that banks will only keep in their portfolio the less profitable fraction of their traditional customers. To counter this evolution, banks may therefore decide to 'unbundle' their products, and to concentrate on activities where they keep comparative advantages, namely monitoring borrowers and the provision of liquidity insurance to them (through back-up lines), without effectively funding the loans (Rajan 1996).[12] To summarize, banks' competitive advantages may be reduced, while EMU will intensify challenges for assets transformation and uncertainty management.

Liberalization and harmonization of the regulatory environment

EMU, by increasing competition among financial systems, is likely to trigger further steps towards the liberalization of banking regulation. On the one hand, deregulation favours financial innovation and the development of financial markets. In general, it enables other financial and non-financial institutions to compete with banks, thereby increasing disintermediation (see the previous paragraph). On the other hand, if it may be argued that EU directives fostering the single market have, in most cases, been implemented in national legislation, there remains scope for further harmonization in many countries, in particular in the tax and social area, or regarding UCITS and pension funds. In the absence of regulatory harmonization, each country may try to enhance the attractiveness of its home market by introducing structural reforms that will affect competition. In addition, being more visible in the single currency area, regulatory differences will face further pressures leading to their progressive disappearance. It may therefore create a level playing field, via international competition, which would be more favourable to banking activity. In particular, the deregulation of the remuneration of deposits may, in France for instance, enable banks to compete more effectively with MMFs. An associated issue is whether banks organized under private law will not be better equipped than publicly owned or co-operative banks to manage the transition to EMU.

Effects on banking strategies and performance

Taking into account possible externalities across activities, I now consider the overall effect of EMU on banking institutions. First, I investigate the strategies that European banks may develop in order to accompany changes in their basic activities. Second, I assess the effect of EMU on banking profitability.

EMU imposes new strategic choices

The possible effects of EMU on banking capacity, in particular whether banks will try to exploit possible economies of scale, is now discussed, as well as the level of competition in the banking system and how European banking may adapt to the new environment.

Banking capacities

Concerning banking capacity, it is important to investigate whether banks, facing a larger market as a consequence of EMU, will try to exploit economies of scale or scope in banking activities, if any.

The economic literature is not very conclusive regarding the existence of returns to scale at the level of the banking firm. Although the analysis of the previous section of this paper indicates that, in some product lines, there exist potential returns to scale which EMU will help banks to exploit, the economic literature offers generally conflicting evidence regarding the returns to scale at the level of the banking unit. One of the reasons is that returns to scale in banking may relate not to institutions themselves but rather to processes and functions.[13] It is also interesting to notice that returns to scale of non-bank competitors, like pensions and mutual funds, are not substantial either (Dermine 1996). It should be kept in mind, however, that returns to scale may not be very substantial in retail banking, but current measures may also not be totally reliable, in the sense that they may be influenced by the regulatory environment which is about to change with EMU. The success of possible mega-mergers intended to exploit returns to scale at the EU level would therefore require a substantial reorganization of banks in order to cut duplicated costs. Otherwise, diseconomies of scale might appear.

There exist clear externalities between activities, although the literature on whether such economies of scope may justify the existence of large universal banks is again inconclusive. While specialist providers are often more efficient than others, there is, at most, evidence of small gains of joint production. It may be useful to distinguish, on the one hand, activities that are more conducive to concentration (liquidity and portfolio management, treasury and dealing activities, payment systems) and, on the other hand, those which do not lead to further concentration. As regards the first type of activities, Vander Vennet (1994) notes that off-balance-sheet activity may provide banks with cost economies. There is also anecdotal evidence that returns to scale in money market operations may also imply concentration of other activities. In addition, financial markets induce strong network externality effects, based on liquidity and the supply of infrastructure (experienced labour force, availability of ancillary services). As a consequence, the concentration of financial centres may also have strong effects on the location of banking activity. For instance, if financial markets were mostly concentrated in one location (London, for instance), banks would have a strong incentive to locate their money market activities in this financial centre, and geographic concentration will therefore also imply a reduction in the number of banks. On the other hand, and conversely, if financial market activities remain spread out in several centres (Frankfurt, Paris), banking location may be more evenly distributed across countries. This trend would be fostered by the decentralization of monetary policy, since national central banks use institutions active in their own countries as their most natural counterparties.

Concerning activities that are less likely to increase concentration, it should be noted that there are other factors which may offset the effects of geographic concentration of money market activities. For instance, a large part of retail banking activities would remain decentralized anyway, although easy remote electronic access would support concentration. Moreover, the US experience shows that, given the progress made by telecommunication technology and the persistence of wage differentials across the EU, banks may choose to locate their most labour-intensive activities, as well as their back offices, outside the main financial centres.

Competition in banking and future prospects

DIFFERENTIAL EFFECTS OF EMU ON COMPETITION IN VARIOUS BANKING SEGMENTS

EMU will increase competition among financial institutions. To assess the overall effect of EMU, it is useful to distinguish between wholesale and retail markets.

Wholesale markets are already significantly internationalized and competitive, but competition in these markets will nevertheless evolve over time. The single currency will imply a further redistribution of banking activities to the extent that competitive advantages, partly based on the existence of national currencies, will disappear. In particular, the 'anchoring principle' imposed by some central banks and requiring domestic financial institutions to lead manage bond issues will, if maintained, be enlarged to a wider zone, or even disappear.[14] In addition, the main currency-based competitive factor, namely the expertise in the domestic monetary environment will, according to Dermine (1996), disappear. However, other competitive factors are likely to be unaffected by the single currency in the short run. These include the existence of a distribution network of customers, as well as access to information on supply/demand flows, which help to assess the direction of price movements. Regarding mergers and acquisitions, the knowledge of the accounting, legal and fiscal environment also remains an important determinant. However, all these competitive advantages are not irreversible and may be progressively eroded. In addition, in the context of the development of a pan-European trading system linking the different exchanges, the importance of the size factor in terms of market power (the cumulative advantage of operating on a larger scale through the ability to control a larger market share) indicates that current positions at the national level may progressively be overturned by European or even by other global players, especially US institutions.

In retail banking markets, changes in competition may therefore be expected to be more pronounced on the liabilities than on the assets side. In particular, remote access to banks in other member states will become very easy in the context of a single currency, and the relevance of branches as distribution centres of deposit products may be reduced. Regarding the assets side, monetary union will enable operations in any national market to be financed through deposits obtained in the home country, hence also facilitating the remote supply of financial services. Consequently, competition in some segments of the market is likely to increase. This is the case of activities which are relatively homogeneous and closely related to the deposit function, like consumer credit and standard mortgage loans, as opposed to small-scale commercial loans and specialized consumer loans, which require more direct contact with customers. On the other hand, there still exist legal, fiscal and institutional obstacles to full integration which will limit the effects of competition. This explain why, if one excludes the particular role of countries like Ireland, Luxembourg and the United Kingdom, the level of internationalization of banking networks is currently lower than in the United States, where foreign penetration was around 20 per cent in 1993. (See Table 6.2 for EU countries and Ettin 1995 for the US.)

INDICATORS OF CONCENTRATION AND CONTESTABILITY

To assess future trends in terms of competition, this paper uses two types of analysis: first, a computation of concentration indicators at the euro-area level, then a report of the results of tests of contestability at the national level, based on rigorous microeconomic foundations. This dual approach is motivated by some of the drawbacks of concentration indicators – the market share of the top five or ten largest institutions – which are relatively easy to compute, but are purely static. In addition, concentration indicators impose a view of the relevant geographic dimension of

Table 6.2a Internationalization of European banking networks: market share of foreign institutions as a percentage of total domestic assets

	Branches from EEC countries			Branches from other countries			Total branches			Subsidiaries from EEC countries			Subsidiaries from other countries			Total subsidiaries			Total branches and subsidiaries		
	1985	1990	1995	1985	1990	1995	1985	1990	1995	1985	1990	1995	1985	1990	1995	1985	1990	1995	1985	1990	1995
Belgium	—	10.0	9.1	—	10.0	7.8	—	20.0	16.9	—	8.0	9.8	—	1.7	1.3	—	9.7	11.1	—	29.7	28.0
Germany	—	—	0.7	—	—	0.6	—	—	1.4	—	—	1.5	—	—	1.4	—	—	2.9	—	—	4.3
Greece	4.5	6.9	8.8	9.1	5.2	7.2	13.6	12.1	16.0	0.3	0.7	1.7	0.7	0.2	0.8	1.0	0.9	2.5	14.5	13.0	18.5
France	—	—	3.4	—	—	3.6	—	—	7.0	—	—	18.4	—	—	3.9	—	—	5.2	—	—	12.2
Ireland	—	—	16.5	—	—	1.8	—	—	18.3	—	—	18.4	—	—	3.9	—	—	22.3	—	—	40.6
Italy	1.6	1.0	2.9	0.1	0.4	0.8	1.7	1.4	3.7	0.2	0.5	1.5	0.7	0.9	0.3	0.9	1.4	1.8	2.6	2.8	5.5
Luxembourg	—	—	20.0	—	—	1.0	—	—	21.0	—	—	70.9	—	—	7.8	—	—	78.7	91*	—	99.7
Netherlands	2.7	3.1	2.9	1.3	0.7	0.7	4.0	3.7	3.5	4.2	5.4	3.7	6.5	3.4	2.5	10.7	8.8	6.2	14.6	12.6	9.8
Austria	0.1	0.1	0.6	0.7	0.1	0.1	0.8	0.2	0.7	—	1.2	2.1	—	1.4	0.7	—	2.6	2.8	0.8	2.8	3.5
Portugal	1.6	0.5	3.0	0.0	0.2	0.1	1.6	0.7	3.1	0.0	2.1	4.9	0.6	1.0	1.4	0.6	3.1	6.3	2.3	3.8	9.4
Finland	—	—	6.5	0.6	0.6	—	—	—	—	—	—	—	—	—	—	—	—	—	—	—	—
Sweden	0.0	0.0	1.6	0.0	0.0	0.1	0.0	0.0	1.7	0.0	0.0	0.8	0.0	0.0	0.0	0.0	0.0	0.8	0.0	0.0	2.5
UK	8.6	14.2	21.7	40.0	34.0	23.2	48.6	48.2	44.9	—	—	1.5	—	—	5.2	—	—	6.7	—	—	51.6

Note: * 1987 (Steinhert and Gilibert 1989)

Source: National central banks and supervisory authorities, unless otherwise indicated

Table 6.2b Internationalization of European banking networks: assets of foreign branches and subsidiaries of domestic instititutions as a percentage of total domestic assets

	Branches in EEC countries			Branches in other countries			Total branches			Subsidiaries in EEC countries			Subsidiaries in other countries			Total subsidiaries			Total branches and subsidiaries		
	1985	1990	1995	1985	1990	1995	1985	1990	1995	1985	1990	1995	1985	1990	1995	1985	1990	1995	1985	1990	1995
Germany	–	–	9.6	–	–	4.8	–	–	14.4	–	–	6.8	–	–	0.7	–	–	7.5	–	–	21.9
Greece	3.0	1.7	2.9	1.1	0.7	0.2	4.1	2.4	3.1	0.8	0.9	2.3	2.5	2.2	1.7	3.3	3.1	3.6	7.3	5.5	6.7
France	–	–	8.0	–	–	9.2	0.0	0.0	17.2	–	–	7.4	–	–	3.5	0.0	–	–	0.0	0.0	17.2
Ireland	–	–	11.9	–	–	0.8	–	–	12.7	–	–	6.3	–	–	12.9	–	–	14.2	–	–	26.9
Italy	–	11.0	8.0	–	7.4	4.7	–	18.4	12.7	–	3.2	3.9	–	0.8	2.1	–	4.0	6.4	–	22.4	19.1
Luxembourg	–	–	0.3	–	–	0.7	–	–	1.0	–	–	–	–	–	–	–	–	–	–	–	–
Austria	–	1.7	1.9	–	1.8	2.8	–	3.5	4.7	–	–	–	–	–	–	–	–	–	–	–	–
Portugal	9.9	12.4	10.3	9.3	5.0	5.2	19.2	17.4	15.5	–	–	3.5	–	–	3.6	0.0	0.0	8.3	19.2	17.4	23.8
Finland	4.0	6.0	4.4	0.1	3.7	4.6	4.0	9.7	9.0	6.5	3.0	0.3	3.0	2.3	0.4	9.5	5.3	0.9	13.5	15.0	9.9
Sweden	–	2.4	7.5	–	1.7	3.0	–	4.1	10.5	–	–	–	–	–	–	–	–	–	–	–	–

Source: National central banks and supervisory authorities, unless otherwise indicated

banking markets in a context where, as was indicated earlier, deposit markets are more likely to extend to the euro area while loan markets may keep some of their local/national features. Finally, only the contestability of retail banking markets is linked to the concentration of the sector, because of sunk costs associated with relationship banking – based on reputation and the role of brand names – and asymmetric information. This may not be true for wholesale markets.[15]

Tables 6.3 and 6.4 reveal that the level of concentration is different across countries, with a significantly lower concentration in Germany and Italy and, in general, in the larger countries.[16] However, one could characterize European banking markets by a high level of concentration within national boundaries which are scheduled to disappear. Conversely, the Eurozone is expected, at least at the beginning of EMU, to follow the rule of lower concentration in the larger areas. As is indicated in Table 6.4a, based on individual bank data from IBCA, an upper limit for the level of concentration of assets, loans and deposits, measured by the share of the assets of the five largest EU credit institutions in the total cumulative assets of all EU institutions was between 10 and 11 per cent in 1996 (between 16 and 17 per cent for universal banks).[17] This should be compared to 18 per cent in the US in 1993 (Ettin 1995). Although one should remain cautious when using figures derived from different sources, this reveals that there may exist some scope for consolidation in Europe.[18] Such a movement towards the constitution of EU global players also appears in Table 6.3, since in most countries, concentration increased between 1990 and 1997 (and, in many cases, continuously since 1985). In addition, the contestability of retail banking has certainly increased. If, as indicated above,

Table 6.3 Indicators of concentration in %: country analysis

	Total assets				Loans				Non-bank deposits			
	1985	*1990*	*1995*	*1997*	*1985*	*1990*	*1995*	*1997*	*1985*	*1990*	*1995*	*1997*
Belgium	48.0	48.0	54.0	57.0	54.0	58.0	61.0	66.0	62.0	67.0	62.0	64.0
Denmark	61.0	76.0	74.0	78.0	71.0	82.0	79.0	75.0	70.0	82.0	76.0	72.0
Germany	n/a	13.9	16.7	16.1	n/a	13.5	13.8	13.7	n/a	11.6	12.6	14.2
Greece	82.1	83.3	75.7	71.0	93.2	89.7	80.8	77.0	89.2	87.7	83.0	79.6
France	46.0	42.5	41.3	40.3	48.7	44.7	46.8	48.3	46.0	58.7	68.1	68.6
Ireland	47.5	44.2	44.4	40.7	47.7	42.9	47.5	46.8	62.6	43.7	52.6	50.2
Italy	20.9	19.1	26.1	24.6	16.6	15.1	26.3	26.6	19.9	18.6	42.1	36.7
Luxembourg	26.8	n/a	21.2	21.8	n/a	n/a	15.1	28.6	n/a	n/a	22.5	28.0
Netherlands	69.3	73.4	76.1	79.4	67.1	76.6	78.5	80.6	85.0	79.5	81.9	84.2
Austria	35.9	34.6	39.2	48.3	28.9	30.1	34.0	39.3	32.0	32.0	36.4	39.1
Portugal	61.0	58.0	74.0	80.0	60.0	57.0	73.0	75.0	64.0	62.0	76.0	79.0
Finland	51.7	53.5	68.6	77.8	49.7	49.7	60.0	56.2	54.2	46.1	64.2	63.1
Sweden	60.2	70.0	85.9	89.7	62.6	64.9	90.1	87.8	58.0	61.4	84.3	86.9
UK	n/a	n/a	27.0	28.0	n/a	n/a	25.0	26.0	n/a	n/a	25.0	26.0

Source: National central banks and supervisory authorites; share of the 5 largest institutions in assets/liabilities held by credit institutions

Table 6.4a Indicators of concentration: EU analysis, total assets, loans and deposits (1996)

	Total assets						Loans					
	C5			C10			C5			C10		
	All bks	All bks*	Univ. bks	All bks	All bks*	Univ. bks	All bks	All bks*	Univ. bks	All bks	All bks*	Univ. bks
Belgium	68.0	65.3	73.0	84.0	80.7	88.3	70.5	67.7	78.6	85.8	82.5	89.6
Denmark	77.6	72.3	89.7	92.9	86.6	99.2	76.4	71.1	89.1	94.9	88.4	99.7
Germany	24.4	20.9	42.0	38.9	33.2	52.9	21.2	18.1	44.3	34.3	29.3	n.s.
Greece	83.1	74.8	n.s.	n.s.	n.s.	n.s.	83.0	74.7	n.s.	n.s.	n.s.	n.s.
Spain	39.3	36.1	42.8	55.1	50.5	59.3	34.5	31.7	37.8	49.7	45.6	55.3
France	38.2	36.0	49.7	53.4	50.3	60.8	35.0	33.0	50.3	52.6	49.5	54.2
Ireland	57.0	51.8	n.s.	94.2	85.6	n.s.	65.3	59.4	n.s.	94.9	86.2	n.s.
Italy	34.3	30.9	40.5	50.8	45.8	57.3	33.8	30.4	42.5	50.8	45.7	59.8
Luxembourg	30.2	27.2	30.8	48.7	43.7	49.5	26.0	23.3	27.1	52.2	46.9	54.5
Netherlands	62.8	61.1	80.2	83.0	80.7	95.0	62.9	61.2	86.5	87.1	84.8	96.8
Austria	52.9	41.5	57.7	73.8	57.9	80.4	44.9	35.2	51.9	66.5	52.2	76.9
Portugal	61.5	57.0	71.7	84.9	78.8	95.3	53.8	49.9	62.8	84.0	77.9	95.5
Finland	n.s.	n.s.	n.s.	n.s.	n.s.	n.s.	n.s.	n.s.	n.s.	n.s.	n.s.	n.s.
Sweden	73.8	70.2	90.9	93.9	89.2	n.s.	75.3	71.6	87.8	91.3	86.8	n.s.
UK	50.6	49.0	72.0	65.7	63.7	83.5	56.7	54.9	71.6	75.4	73.1	86.1
EU-11	11.8	10.8	16.3	19.3	17.6	25.7	11.0	10.0	16.8	18.6	17.0	27.8
EU-15	10.1	9.2	14.6	16.9	15.4	23.3	9.5	8.7	14.7	16.9	15.4	25.1

	Deposits					
	C5			C10		
	All bks	All bks*	Univ. bks	All bks	All bks*	Univ. bks
Belgium	67.5	64.9	73.5	83.0	79.8	87.0
Denmark	n/a	n/a	n/a	n/a	n/a	n/a
Germany	29.3	25.0	40.2	41.3	35.3	44.5
Greece	83.3	74.9	n.s.	n.s.	n.s.	n.s.
Spain	36.7	33.6	37.4	50.2	46.1	53.1
France	42.0	39.5	47.7	54.4	51.2	53.1
Ireland	49.7	45.2	n.s.	94.4	85.9	n.s.
Italy	30.4	27.4	33.3	46.9	42.2	50.9
Luxembourg	35.6	32.0	35.8	50.9	45.7	51.2
Netherlands	37.3	36.3	65.3	76.3	74.2	92.7
Austria	45.3	35.5	48.5	70.4	55.2	75.4
Portugal	61.3	56.9	68.1	89.6	83.1	97.2
Finland	n.s.	n.s.	n.s.	n.s.	n.s.	n.s.
Sweden	81.9	77.9	91.3	96.7	91.9	n.s.
UK	63.5	61.6	75.4	76.8	74.4	88.7
EU-11	12.6	10.6	16.6	19.3	16.2	23.4
EU-15	11.0	9.3	14.7	18.5	15.6	21.8

C5   market share of the 5
         largest institutions
C10 market share of the 10
         largest institutions
n/a   not available
n.s. not significant owing to the
         low coverage of the country
         by the database

Source: Fitch-IBCA Bankscope CD-ROM, author's calculations

Table 6.4b Indicators of concentration: EU analysis, off-balance-sheet items and securities (1996)

	Off-balance-sheet items						Securities					
	C5			C10			C5			C10		
	All bks	All bks*	Univ. bks	All bks	All bks*	Univ. bks	All bks	All bks*	Univ. bks	All bks	All bks*	Univ. bks
Belgium	79.5	76.4	80.8	92.1	88.5	92.6	63.7	61.2	67.1	79.8	76.7	85.5
Denmark	85.1	79.2	92.6	93.4	87.0	99.9	79.2	73.7	90.4	87.1	81.2	98.3
Germany	41.7	35.7	58.3	57.9	49.5	65.4	26.6	22.8	33.3	41.4	35.4	49.7
Greece	85.0	76.5	n.s.	n.s.	n.s.	n.s.	86.3	77.6	n.s.	n.s.	n.s.	n.s.
Spain	47.6	43.6	54.5	60.0	55.0	71.4	45.3	41.6	47.2	57.1	52.4	60.4
France	51.9	48.9	65.0	62.0	58.4	73.4	40.2	37.8	49.2	56.0	52.7	65.3
Ireland	n/a	n/a	n/a	n/a	n/a	n/a	48.5	44.1	n.s.	98.3	89.3	n.s.
Italy	43.8	39.4	50.5	64.1	57.7	68.9	29.1	26.2	32.2	44.7	40.3	48.5
Luxembourg	9.7	8.8	9.7	14.9	13.4	14.9	38.9	35.0	39.8	50.2	45.1	51.4
Netherlands	40.3	39.2	64.3	66.4	64.6	83.3	68.4	66.6	84.9	86.7	84.3	97.4
Austria	57.6	45.2	61.5	77.8	61.0	83.1	54.4	42.7	57.9	75.1	58.9	79.8
Portugal	60.7	56.3	70.4	89.2	82.7	99.5	60.7	56.2	75.6	77.3	71.7	92.7
Finland	n/a	n/a	n/a	n/a	n/a	n/a	n.s.	n.s.	n.s.	n.s.	n.s.	n.s.
Sweden	93.7	89.1	97.8	97.8	93.0	n.s.	77.9	74.0	93.0	98.2	93.3	n.s.
UK	77.2	74.8	82.0	83.2	80.7	86.2	45.3	44.0	77.5	57.2	55.5	82.6
EU-11	18.9	17.2	23.7	28.4	25.9	32.7	11.4	10.4	14.1	18.4	16.8	21.5
EU-15	15.1	13.8	20.1	24.0	21.9	28.3	9.8	8.9	12.8	15.5	14.1	19.6

Source: Fitch -IBCA Bankscope CD-ROM, author's calculations

technological change has played a major role in this evolution, EMU will reinforce these trends.

Regarding off-balance-sheet operations and interbank lending, which are more contestable, concentration indicators may explain the incentives for institutions to evolve or enter other national markets. As is shown in Table 6.4b, concentrations in off-balance-sheet operations and interbank lending/borrowing also appear to be more pronounced than for other activities. One may therefore anticipate some consolidation in that area. One could, for instance, argue that an efficient interbank market rarely has more than ten prominent market makers. In that case, the start of EMU could lead to competitive pressures towards a restricted number of EU-wide money market makers.[19]

To assess the effective level of competition, it is necessary to implement more formal tests of contestability. The 'new industrial organization' literature has stressed the need to test competition by measuring the elasticity of bank revenues to changes in costs, the intuition behind these tests being that for monopolistic banking markets, revenues respond less than proportionately to changes in costs. A possible drawback is that these tests are based on reduced form equations, so that they cannot cope with the regime shift associated with EMU. Consequently, they provide only a measure of the current level of competition in the EU banking system and a benchmark against which the effects of EMU can be tested. Molyneux *et al.* (1994) conclude that during the period 1986–9, banks in Germany, the UK, France and Spain earned revenues as if in monopolistic competition, while in the case of Italy, monopoly power is not discounted. For Finland, Vesala (1995) concludes that deregulation triggered a short period of price war among banks but banks reverted later to a somewhat monopolistic competition. On the more recent period, De Bandt and Davis (1998), using a sample of banks in France, Germany and Italy during the period 1992–6, conclude that banking markets are still characterized by monopolistic competition.

To conclude this section, it can be noted that the monitoring of concentration at the EU level and its impact on competition, through the definition of the appropriate market segments, will certainly be a crucial issue in the years to come.

STRATEGIC RESPONSES BY BANKS

Against the background of an increase in competition ushered in by EMU, it is important to investigate how banks will react to potential competition. It is not obvious that EMU will induce the concentration of all banking institutions. Given the existence of asymmetric information, one possible scenario is therefore the coexistence of a few Europe-based global players, alongside smaller institutions, specializing either in given product groups or in specific regions. It is difficult to predict which strategy will be preferred by banks after EMU, between, one, specializing in specific 'niches' involving particular skills; or two, building new alliances among universal banks either for strategic motives, with a view to limiting entry and softening competition in particular markets, or for technological reasons, mainly to use more efficiently existing banking networks; or three, accelerating the movement of concentration to reach a critical size through mergers and acquisition. There is no dominant model in my view. On the one hand, the experience of the Single Market shows that the last two choices are the most likely to be fostered by EMU. However the motivation for the current wave of mergers in the different EU banking systems may be partly independent of EMU, and new types of alliances may also be fostered by technological change, as was indicated earlier.[20] On the other hand, if there is evidence that successful mergers are a consequence of cost-cutting rather than revenue-enhancing strategies, there remains uncertainty regarding the reality of returns to scale and legal obstacles to restructuring (in particular regarding employment status). The final question is therefore whether EMU will induce a significant development of cross-border mergers. If the motivations are not different from mergers at the national level, the need to accommodate national differences of legal and accounting systems may increase the risk of duplication of costs in the case of cross-border mergers. It is probable that, at least in the short run, a consolidation of the banking systems in the smaller countries will take place.[21]

EMU may have a significant impact on the performance of the banking industry

The analysis of the overall effect of EMU on banking performance should distinguish between the short and medium-run effects of EMU on banking profitability. In the short run, EMU will have a limited impact on banks' costs, due to the need to complete the changeover to the euro, while in the medium term, EMU will affect banks' profits, as well as their distribution across institutions.

EMU implies one-off costs associated with the changeover

In the short run, banks will have to face the one-off costs of changeover. Experts do not fully agree about the importance of those costs. According to estimates by the Fédération Bancaire Européenne, changeover costs, excluding adaptation of national payment systems, would amount to ECU 8–10 billion, or 2 per cent of annual operating costs for three to four years. On the other hand, for firms active in securities business, switchover costs would appear to be small and amount to an average of 0.06 per cent of total operating costs of financial institutions (ISMA 1997). Such a difference may be explained by the fact that costs are higher for institutions specialized at the retail level, since half these costs would come from the adaptation of information technology, and the need to offer to retail customers, during Stage Three A, services in the euro and in national currency. Securities firms already operate in a multi-currency environment. It is interesting to note that various estimates tend to show that smaller and/or more specialized institutions may not always be disadvantaged, although their lower cost of organization may in some cases be more than offset by limited expertise. Adequate planning and timing of the changeover seems to make a difference, since some changes are due to be made independently of the occurrence of EMU, in particular preparations for the year 2000.

Medium-term effects on profitability

From a structural point of view, EMU will create a new environment which will have positive effects on the competitiveness of EU institutions. It may at the same time increase disparities among institutions.

EMU will have positive effects on the competitiveness of banks. First, the move to Stage Three may help reveal organizational deficiencies at the level of institutions, the solution of which will, in the end, prove decisive in improving the competitiveness of European institutions.

Second, from a more macroeconomic point of view, the introduction of a single currency in the place of multiple currencies will reduce trans-action costs and eliminate the foreign exchange risk that previously existed among the currencies of the euro area, so that the commercial and financial unification of the European Union will be enhanced and cross-border trade in goods and services, including financial services, stimulated. This should complement the growth effect associated with the frontier-opening process of the Single Market. In addition, the priority given to price stability in Stage Three should provide an enhanced environment for the production of financial services. Less volatile inflation and interest rates are good for bank customers, and hence for banks. Both banks and customers will also benefit from higher expected economic growth caused by lower interest rates supported by a strong euro. Thus, EMU may increase the competitiveness of the whole European banking industry, and in particular of the international banking groups.

For EU institutions in general, EMU will take place in an environment where intermediation margins and profitability are lower than at the end of the 1980s, marking a reallocation of margins from banks to customers. As is shown in Figures 6.1 and 6.2, which are based on aggregate data from IBCA, there is a clear convergence across EU countries. The movement was particularly pronounced in Spain, a country enjoying above average margins in the early 1990s.[22] The improvement in profitability in 1995–6 partly attenuated this movement in connection with the satisfactory performance of securities markets.[23]

However, EMU may not affect all institutions similarly. One usual prediction of increasing competition is that some banks will lose and others will gain. EMU will therefore have the effect of reallocating intermediation margins among banks, which will have to focus even more on

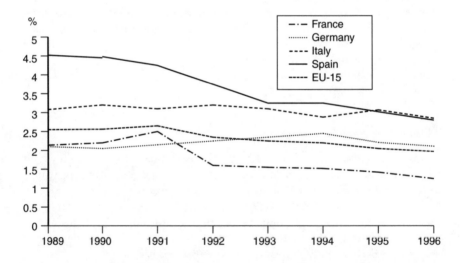

Figure 6.1 Bank intermediation margin (net interest revenue/total earning assets): all universal banks

Source: Fitch IBCA Bankscope CD-ROM, author's calculations

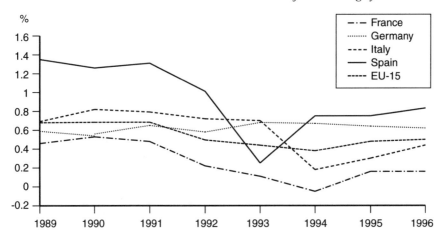

Figure 6.2 Bank profitability (profit before tax/total assets): all universal banks

Note: 1993 figures for Spain are affected by the negative results of BANESTO

Source: Fitch IBCA Bankscope CD-ROM, author's calculations

non-interest income and fee-generating activities. All banks are not equally prepared to make this transition. The final result might therefore be to introduce more diversity across banks in terms of profitability.

As a test exercise of the possible effects of EMU, it may be worthwhile to consider the distribution of profitability across institutions during the period of implementation of the Single Market programme. Using data from IBCA, it is possible to investigate differences in profitability across banks. Profitability is measured by the return on asset (ROAA) or equity (ROAE) and three classes of banks are distinguished: large banks with total assets above ECU 5 billion, medium-sized banks with total assets between ECU 1 and 5 billion, and small banks (assets below ECU 1 billion). Two separate years are considered, 1994 (Table 6.5a and 6.5b) and 1996 (Table 6.6), in order to correct for the possible influence of business cycle conditions. Different hypotheses are tested for the various sub-samples of banks.[24]

First, for each country sample, the average profitability is compared to its standard deviation (both unweighted). If the population is normal, 95 per cent of banks have their profitability in the interval defined by the average plus or minus two times the standard deviation. A double star (**) in column AV indicates therefore whether the average profitability is greater than twice its standard deviation.[25] At the 95 per cent confidence level, it appears that in 1994 and 1996, profits are significantly positive only for the largest banks in Germany, while this was also the case in 1996 for medium-sized and large banks in Denmark and Austria. Large banks in Belgium experienced significantly positive profits in 1994 only, while the Netherlands saw an improvement in the profitability of medium-sized as well as large banks between 1994 and 1996. In Spain, the improvement in 1996 was limited to

Table 6.5a Profitability indicators in 1994: all banks

	Total				Banks < 1 bn ECU				Banks 1–5 bn ECU						Banks > 5 bn ECU					
	ROAA		ROAE		ROAA		ROAE		ROAA			ROAE			ROAA			ROAE		
	AV	SD	AV	SD	AV	SD	AV	SD	AV	SD	F1	AV	SD	F1	AV	SD	F2	AV	SD	F2
Belgium	0.42	0.80	7.90	21.30	0.48	0.95	5.01	10.25	0.35	0.38	##	8.35	9.74		0.22	0.13	##	21.95	51.37	
Denmark	0.54	1.89	2.89	13.44	0.54	1.98	3.01	14.21	0.87	1.68		0.92	10.32		0.16	0.06	##	3.64	0.70	##
Germany	0.33	0.60	6.74	5.70	0.33	0.65	6.57	5.49	0.33	0.42	##	7.50	6.92		0.24	0.19	##	6.80*	4.03	##
Spain	0.59	2.11	7.42	18.82	0.47	2.74	3.43	14.11	0.74	1.38	##	8.70	15.99		0.65	0.45	##	17.55	30.93	
France	0.21	4.73	-2.93	46.59	0.25	6.19	-0.24	42.31	0.19	1.34	##	-8.38	57.51		0.02	0.90	##	-1.10	29.17	##
Italy	0.33	0.87	1.82	13.34	0.49	0.97	3.26	13.16	0.20	0.76		0.86	13.07		0.08	0.56	##	-1.14	14.18	
Luxembourg	0.67	1.29	9.76	9.02	0.75	1.49	7.49	8.24	0.60	1.08		12.28	10.20		0.46	0.30	##	14.73**	6.09	##
Netherlands	0.63	1.49	8.82	9.32	0.46	0.62	7.30	7.29	0.35	0.46		7.94	6.37		1.83	3.77		17.04	16.99	
Austria	0.40	2.69	6.23	21.96	0.49	3.73	4.35	29.10	0.33	0.34	##	8.00	9.01	##	0.22	0.08	##	9.26	10.05	
Portugal	0.23	1.56	4.72	7.59	-0.01	2.27	1.66	8.15	0.30	0.49	##	5.36	5.85		0.69	0.33		11.10	5.45	
UK	0.75	1.60	6.89	11.20	0.95	1.93	7.22	10.15	0.55	0.73	##	7.60	11.32		0.23	0.50	##	4.25	14.96	
EU-15	0.38	2.29	5.04	20.34	0.42	2.67	5.24	17.15	0.31	1.29	##	3.81	27.44		0.27	0.74		6.60	21.12	##

Notes:
Universal banks = commercial banks + savings banks + cooperative banks (countries where the coverage by IBCA is lower than 30 banks are not exhibited)
ROAA   return on average assets
ROAE   return on average equity
AV   mean (unweighted) (*:significantly greater than zero at 10% level; **:significantly greater than zero at 5% level)
SD   standard deviation (unweighted)
F1   Fisher one-sided test of difference of variances between banks with assets < ECU 1 billion and assets included in ECU (1–5 billion)
F2   as F1 for banks in assets size ECU (1– 5 billion) and > ECU 5 billion
smaller banks have significantly higher variance at 10%
smaller banks have significantly higher variance at 5%

Source: Fitch IBCA Bankscope CD-ROM (unconsolidated accounts), author's calculations

Table 6.5b Profitability indicators in 1994: universal banks

	Total				Banks < 1 bn ECU				Banks 1–5 bn ECU						Banks > 5 bn ECU					
	ROAA		ROAE		ROAA		ROAE		ROAA			ROAE			ROAA			ROAE		
	AV	SD	AV	SD	AV	SD	AV	SD	AV	SD	F1	AV	SD	F1	AV	SD	F2	AV	SD	F2
Belgium	0.37	0.80	5.97	10.51	0.40	1.00	4.43	11.69	0.36	0.39	##	8.23	10.01		0.25	0.12	##	8.48	3.75	##
Denmark	0.50	1.93	2.40	13.39	0.54	1.99	2.64	13.61	-0.25	0.93		-4.93	15.09		0.21	0.05	##	3.72	0.79	##
Germany	0.33	0.55	6.79	5.73	0.32	0.58	6.61	5.44	0.34	0.43	##	7.63	7.03		0.30	0.20	##	7.06	4.63	##
Spain	0.53	2.06	7.32	19.21	0.43	2.75	3.38	14.25	0.63	0.96	##	8.89	16.47		0.65	0.45	##	17.72	32.61	
France	0.12	4.88	-1.51	37.25	0.12	6.60	0.24	28.36	0.12	1.06	##	-5.06	50.63		0.13	0.41	##	2.06	14.36	##
Italy	0.35	0.89	1.94	13.89	0.52	0.95	3.61	12.94	0.19	0.81	#	0.69	14.44		0.02	0.61	##	-2.40	15.67	
Luxembourg	0.48	0.97	9.62	8.98	0.54	1.24	7.01	7.81	0.38	0.39	##	12.44	10.52		0.46	0.30	##	14.73**	6.09	##
Netherlands	0.39	0.54	8.58	9.90	0.47	0.66	7.29	7.29	0.25	0.17	##	7.09	6.53		0.26	0.22		19.01	21.49	
Austria	0.70	2.12	8.49	15.06	0.99	2.78	8.58	18.03	0.36	0.39	##	7.98	10.59	##	0.22	0.08	##	9.26	10.05	
Portugal	0.11	1.61	4.07	7.72	-0.17	2.27	0.65	7.42	0.17	0.45	##	4.71	6.51		0.69	0.33		11.10	5.45	
UK	0.43	1.13	6.44	10.18	0.48	1.40	5.35	9.16	0.43	0.55	##	8.48	11.23		0.26	0.49		7.18	12.41	
EU-15	0.33	2.01	5.35	16.46	0.34	2.36	5.35	12.67	0.30	0.72	##	4.77	24.81		0.29	0.46	##	7.13	16.38	##

Notes and source: as for Table 6.5a

Table 6.6 Profitability indicators in 1996

	Total				Banks < 1 bn ECU				Banks 1–5 bn ECU						Banks > 5 bn ECU					
	ROAA		ROAE		ROAA		ROAE		ROAA			ROAE			ROAA			ROAE		
	AV	SD	AV	SD	AV	SD	AV	SD	AV	SD	F1	AV	SD	F1	AV	SD	F2	AV	SD	F2
All banks:																				
Belgium	0.96	3.16	8.93	13.77	0.97	3.15	6.60	9.39	1.33	4.00		11.81	7.81	##	0.21	0.32	##	19.31	32.53	
Denmark	1.51	1.54	10.47	8.19	1.50	1.36	10.33	8.48	2.78	4.26		11.29 **	2.30		0.69 **	0.31	##	12.55 **	4.68	##
Germany	0.30	1.34	6.80	4.97	0.31	1.49	6.73	4.73	0.29	0.34	##	6.96	6.05		0.24	0.20	##	7.51	4.88	##
Spain	0.98	1.73	10.06	9.76	1.05	2.11	9.59	9.94	0.98	1.18	##	10.65	11.09		0.70 *	0.42	##	10.80 **	4.89	##
France	0.10	3.48	1.52	44.05	0.07	4.41	4.04	46.27	0.15	1.65	##	-2.80	46.82		0.07	0.71	##	0.57	17.45	##
Italy	1.29	2.31	9.26	14.55	1.57	2.51	11.63	6.65	0.43	0.50	##	4.55	6.48		0.06	1.26		-6.85	45.96	
Luxembourg	0.64	1.19	10.70	8.70	0.76	1.50	8.25	7.60	0.42	0.30	##	14.26	10.16		0.54 *	0.30		14.91 **	4.23	##
Netherlands	2.03	3.95	9.61	6.10	1.85	3.80	8.60	7.13	1.49	3.39		10.44 **	4.39	##	0.37	0.54		12.23 **	2.76	
Austria	0.65	1.78	8.92	12.77	0.93	2.33	10.14	16.54	0.30*	0.16	##	7.04 *	4.23		0.24 **	0.08	##	8.09 **	3.49	
UK	1.70	4.99	11.34	15.78	1.87	5.76	9.91	16.30	1.60	2.76	##	14.21	14.63		0.48	0.47	##	15.80	13.02	
EU-11	0.59	2.27	7.25	21.42	0.66	2.55	7.95	20.73	0.41	1.28	##	5.60	22.90		0.34	1.29		4.90	23.38	
EU-15	0.69	2.45	7.70	20.66	0.78	2.74	8.21	19.94	0.51	1.50	##	6.28	22.44		0.38	1.22	##	6.44	22.49	
Universal banks:																				
Belgium	0.58	1.09	8.20	9.45	0.69	1.33	6.37	9.64	0.46	0.34	##	12.31	8.03	##	0.24	0.35		10.15	8.98	
Denmark	1.42	1.06	10.35	7.98	1.45	1.07	10.18	8.12	0.81 **	0.24	##	11.83 **	1.64	##	0.90 **	0.21		15.02 **	3.54	
Germany	0.31	1.38	6.77	4.82	0.31	1.51	6.75	4.60	0.29	0.35	##	6.88	6.05		0.27 **	0.10	##	6.66 **	1.96	##
Spain	0.96	1.73	10.19	9.93	1.04	2.14	9.62	10.11	0.91	1.01	##	10.67	11.20		0.74 *	0.43	##	11.78 **	3.94	##
France	-0.12	3.54	1.06	41.80	-0.30	4.73	2.17	48.27	0.07	1.34	##	-1.08	37.99	##	0.04	0.80	##	2.84	10.28	##
Italy	1.36	2.35	9.77	14.65	1.60	2.53	11.84	6.43	0.53	0.31	##	5.98 *	3.08	##	0.00	1.39		-9.56	50.63	
Luxembourg	0.45	0.52	10.83	8.70	0.44	0.64	8.09	7.42	0.42	0.30	##	14.26	10.16		0.54 *	0.30		14.91 **	4.23	##
Netherlands	1.11	2.35	7.93	5.39	0.89	1.12	6.77	5.90	0.41 *	0.23	##	8.45 **	3.97		0.32	0.57		11.95 **	3.16	
Austria	0.71	1.91	9.12	13.50	0.96	2.38	10.49	16.73	0.30 **	0.13	##	6.15 **	2.82	##	0.24 *	0.08	#	8.09 **	3.49	
UK	1.36	4.33	11.06	10.77	1.63	5.10	10.00	10.40	0.63	0.60	##	11.30	12.05		0.83	0.56		20.00 **	7.71	
EU-11	0.54	2.03	7.38	20.07	0.60	2.29	7.96	19.89	0.35	0.78	##	6.11	19.09		0.35	1.34		4.43	24.72	
EU-15	0.61	2.07	7.71	19.39	0.69	2.32	8.16	19.09	0.37	0.78	##	6.42	18.92		0.41	1.29		6.00	24.09	

Notes and source: as for Table 6.5a

large banks. Actually, in many cases the distribution of banks' profitability is not normal, so that the high value of the ratio standard deviation/average measures the high dispersion of profits among banks.

Next, the dispersion of profitability across classes of banks is studied, comparing the standard deviation of profits between small and medium-sized banks (column F1) as well as between medium-sized and large banks (column F2) using a F-test. It appears that in most countries, the variability of returns was statistically decreasing across size classes of banks, with the highest dispersion among banks with assets below ECU 1 billion. It is not clear, however, whether such a result reflects the fact that small banks remain sheltered from competition, or signals more structural problems of lower efficiency of some small banks.[26] Returns on assets or equity, which are more significantly positive for large banks, may tend to favour the second hypothesis. It can therefore be expected that EMU may further increase the variability of profits across institutions, fostering the restructuring of some segments of the market.

Conclusion

EMU will certainly have a major impact on the European banking system. Admittedly, banking systems in many countries are experiencing a restructuring phase as a response to worldwide trends affecting the industry. However, the single monetary policy will generate new activities, in particular in connection with the emergence of larger and deeper financial markets. This will require changes in the strategic focus of banks operating in the euro area. In addition, competition is likely to increase significantly with the single currency, as one of the major obstacles to financial integration will disappear, although retail banking markets will keep, at least at the beginning of EMU, many of their 'local' features, in particular those due to tax differences.

Market participants are adapting their accounting and operational systems and can now define their strategies. One realistic scenario is therefore that the final impact of EMU will be to increase the competitiveness of banks in the Single Currency area and to favour the emergence of some large Europe-based global banking groups, while at the same time, smaller institutions may develop profitable 'niches'. Provided that the supply of financial services is adequately priced *ex ante* (this would require that not all banks decide to invest in the same sectors, and that banks do not lend imprudently to new customers), successful financial institutions will soon reap the benefits of EMU.

Notes

Comments on an earlier draft of the paper by Lorenzo Bini-Smaghi, E. P. Davis, Vítor Gaspar, Johannes Priesemann, D. T. Llewellyn, Philippe Moutot and

Benjamin Sahel are gratefully acknowledged. Salvatore Marrocco provided excellent research assistance. The article expresses the author's own opinions and does not necessarily reflect the position of the European Central Bank.

1   In most countries, margins on forex transactions are very low, so that the final reduction in revenues should be limited. Salomon Brothers (1995, quoted by McCauley and White 1997) estimate that revenues derived from foreign exchange might fall by up to 10 per cent, but this would only imply a 1 per cent reduction in total revenues. However, a distinction has to be made between the wholesale business and retail transactions, which are much more profitable. This may explain differences across countries: in Finland, forex losses would amount to only 2–4 per cent of banks' total income.

2   The literature on market microstructures shows that forex markets may be viewed as a network between currencies. In order to maximize liquidity, these markets tend to be organized in a hierarchical way, with a limited number of 'nodes' (vehicle currencies) connected to the other 'satellite' currencies by liquid bilateral markets, whereas exchanges between 'satellite' currencies imply two transactions involving the vehicle currency on one side (see Hartmann 1996). The gains from higher liquidity have however to be balanced by the need to pay bid–ask spreads twice. An informal survey of practices in EU forex markets has shown that the DM has progressively become the dominant vehicle currency for intra-European spot trades, supplanting the US dollar, with a market share between one half and two thirds in the UK, around two thirds in France, while most trades would involve the DM for Denmark, Belgium, Austria, and maybe also for Italy and Ireland. On the other hand, Portugal and Greece seem to use the US dollar more extensively.

3   As a consequence the estimates presented here only provide, *ceteris paribus*, a lower bound of the reduction in forex activity.

4   The 67th BIS *Annual Report* estimates that the world forex market could be reduced by 10 per cent.

5   Hartmann (1996), on the basis of several assumptions, estimates that, with fifteen participating countries at the start of EMU, 24 per cent of world trade would be invoiced in euros. However, the currency of invoicing may depend on the size of the exporting/importing country, so that the size of the Single Currency Area may induce a larger share of invoicing in euros.

6   If the euro becomes an international currency, Europe-based banks, which will have both assets and liabilities (in particular capital) in euros, may have a competitive advantage over US and 'pre-in' global institutions.

7   Differences in rating across Canadian states may be taken as evidence of the likelihood of such an effect, although the effective bankruptcy of a European government would only occur after running through the alternative assistance mechanisms, including those from the IMF.

8   The Boston Consulting Group (1996) estimated that forex fees account for 50 per cent of the $ 10 billion of intra-European cross-border revenues.

9   According to the Boston Consulting Group (1996), revenues derived from the 'float' should be reduced from 10 per cent to 5 per cent of wholesale payment revenues, but they represent a much higher fraction of retail payments.

10 On wholesale activities, see Bauer and Hancock 1995 for US ACH (Automated Clearing House, the US, nation-wide, value-dated, electronic fund transfer system used for recurring consumer and commercial payment). On retail operations, see Humphrey 1994 for a description of the 'excessive' use of ATMs in the US, although 'cybermoney' may effectively help reduce costs.

11 Currency matching rules require insurance companies, for example, not to hold more than 20 per cent of their assets in foreign currencies, unless they

are matched by liabilities denominated in the same currency. The Single Market and the constitution of international groups of institutional investors have already limited the relevance of such rules.

12 However, 'unbundling' has the additional effect of reducing entry barriers. This may favour the growth of 'supermarket banking' (where food retailers offer competitive deposit facilities and an increasing array of other financial services in-house), as in the United Kingdom.

13 See in particular Llewellyn 1998. Schaffer and David (1991) found evidence of returns to scale in interstate banking for the US. Periods of branching deregulation were usually followed, as expected, by a significant increase in out-of-state branches (Humphrey 1994). The conclusion of the subsequent literature is either that scale economies are usually exhausted at a small scale (maximum gains from risk diversification are obtained at a low size level and offset by organization costs, so that fixed costs are a relatively small fraction of total costs), or that evidence of returns to scale is generally based on specification errors (Berger and Humphrey 1991 find evidence of diseconomies of scale). Concerning the EU, under the caveat that the number of studies is smaller, similar conflicting results are found. There is evidence of returns to scale in France (Dietsch 1994). However, Lang and Welzel (1995) conclude that scale economies in German banks exist up to a certain size, and Vander Vennet (1994), that, for a sample of EU banks, the average costs are minimized between US\$ 3 and 10 billion.

14 The anchoring principle, initiated by some central banks to protect their currency, has traditionally restricted the lead management of bond issues to banks incorporated in the country whose currency is being used.

15 Applied researchers have not generally been able to show a significant relationship between concentration and profits in banking, nor to identify the true geographic market associated with a given measure of concentration. Following Baumol's 1982 critique that competition depends *in fine* on the 'contestability' of the market (that is, on the absence of sunk costs), the 'new' industrial organisation (NIO) literature has argued in favour of a set of tests based on rigorous microeconomic foundations. In particular, the Rosse–Panzar test relies on the fact that an individual bank will respond differently in response to a change in costs, in a way that depends on whether the bank enjoys some monopoly power or instead is operating in a competitive market (see Schaffer 1994 for a survey).

16 Table 6.3 is based on exhaustive information from central banks and supervisory authorities, while Table 6.4 is derived from the Fitch IBCA Bankscope CD-ROM (henceforth IBCA). The latter indicators diverge slightly from the former ones since the coverage is partial for small banks: which, however, only represent a small fraction of cumulative assets. They are presented here in order to derive an estimate of the EU-wide level of concentration (last row in each sub-table). See the notes with the tables for details. The most substantial divergence between the two tables arises in the UK, given that the international sector is not considered in IBCA.

17 Universal banks are defined as commercial, co-operative and savings banks.

18 Such a movement should be even more pronounced if one takes into account the effects of competition policy which is traditionally more severe in the US than in Europe.

19 The concentration indicators in Table 6.4 are computed using data from Fitch-IBCA for banks with total assets above ECU 1 billion (indicators 'all banks' and 'universal banks'), as well as additional information indicating the share of banks with assets above ECU 1 billion in the total assets of the whole banking sector. The latter information was obtained from national central banks (indicators 'all banks*').

Formally: 'all banks' or 'univ. banks' = $\sum^{5\text{ or }10}_{i=1}Ai \, / \, \sum^{N1}_{i=1} Ai$
where Ai is the balance-sheet item (total assets, deposits, loans, etc.) of bank i and N1 is the number of institutions with total assets above ECU 1bn as recorded by IBCA.

'All banks*' = 'All banks' x $\sum^{N2}_{i=1} Ai \, / \, \sum^{N}_{i=1}Ai$
with N, the total number of institutions and N2 , the total number of institutions with assets above ECU 1 bn. 'Universal banks' is defined as commercial banks, cooperative banks and savings banks.

20 Small banks with a significant presence in local markets have so far not been concerned by the movement of mergers and aquisitions.

21 Recently observed cross-border mergers in Europe (e.g. the merger between Fortis (Netherlands) and Générale de Banque (Belgium), the purchase of BBL (Belgium) by ING (Netherlands) and the merger between Merita (Finland) and Nordbanken (Sweden)) occurred in countries with a relatively more concentrated banking sector and fewer opportunities for national alliances.

22 The intermediation margin is defined as the ratio of net interest revenue to total earning assets, and profitability is measured as the ratio of profit before tax to total assets.

23 Indicators are computed on the sample of banks provided by IBCA (see note 19 for details), using 'ratios of average', i.e. dividing the cumulative sum of profits across banks by the cumulative sum of assets.

Formally $(\sum^n_i P_i \,)/(\sum^n_i A_i \,)$, where P_i is profit and A_i is total asset of bank i and n is the number of banks.

24 As this study is concerned with the distribution across institutions, the profitability of bank I is P_i/A_i using the same notation as in note 23. The unweighted average is $(1/n) \sum^n_i P_i \,/A_i$.

25 Given the low coverage of some countries by IBCA, the results are only reported when the sub-sample includes at least thirty observations (banks).

26 See Davis and Salo, chapter 5 of this volume.

Bibliography

Bauer, P., Berger, A. and Humphrey, D. (1993) 'Efficiency and Productivity Growth in US Banking Industry', in H. Fried, K. Lovell and S. Schmidt (eds), *The Measurement of Productive Efficiency: Techniques and Applications*, Oxford University Press, Oxford.

Bauer, P. and Hancock, D. (1995) 'Scale Economies and Technological Change in Federal Reserve Ach Payment Processing', *Economic Review*, Federal Reserve Bank of Cleveland, 31(3), 14–29.

Baumol, R. J. (1982) 'Contestable Markets, An Uprising in the Theory of Industrial Structure', *American Economic Review* 72: 1–15.

Berger, A. N. and Humphrey, D. B. (1991) 'The Dominance of Inefficiencies over Scale and Product Mix Economies in Banking', *Journal of Monetary Economics:* 17–148.

Berger, A. N. and Humphrey, D. B. (1994) 'Bank Scale Economies, Mergers, Concentration and Efficiency: The USA Experience', *FRB Finance and Economic Series* no. 94–23, Federal Reserve Bank, New York.

BIS (1995) *Survey of Foreign Exchange and Derivations Market Activity*, Bank for International Settlements, Basle.

BIS (1996) *International Banking and Financial Market Developments* (August), Bank for International Settlements, Basle.

BIS (1997) 66th and 67th *Annual Report*, Bank for International Settlements, Basle.

Boston Consulting Group (1996) 'Payment Systems: Recreating the Franchise', Payment Systems International Conference.

Chiappori, P. A., Perez-Castillo, D. and Verdier, T. (1995) 'Spatial Competition in the Banking System: Localization, Cross Subsidies and the Regulation of Deposit Rates' *European Economic Review* 39: 889–918.

De Bandt, O. and Davis, E. P. (1998) 'Competition, Contestability and Market Structure in European Banking Sectors on the Eve of EMU: Evidence from France, Germany and Italy, With a Perspective on the United States', mimeo, European Central Bank, Frankfurt. Forthcoming in *Journal of Banking and Finance*.

Dietsch, M. (1994), 'Les surcapacités bancaires' in D. E. Fair and R. Raymond (eds), *The Competitiveness of Financial Institutions and Centres in Europe*, 73–95, Kluwer Academic, Netherlands.

Dermine, J. (1996) *European Banking with a Single Currency*, paper presented at Wharton Financial Institutions' Center Seminar: Risk Management in Banking, 13/15 Oct. 1996, Philadelphia.

EC (1997) *The Impact of the Introduction of the Euro on Capital Markets*, (Giovannini Report), European Commission, Brussels.

Ettin, E. C. (1995) 'The Evolution of the North American Banking System' in *The New Financial Landscape*, OECD, Paris.

EMI (1997a) *The Single Monetary Policy in Stage Three: Elements of the Monetary Policy of the ESCB*, European Monetary Institute, Frankfurt (February).

EMI (1997b) *The Single Monetary Policy in Stage Three: General Documentation on ESCB Instruments and Procedures*, European Monetary Institute, Frankfurt (September).

Hartmann, P. (1996) 'The Future of the Euro as an International Currency: A Transactions Perspective', *LSE Financial Markets Group Special Paper no. 91*, London School of Economics.

Humphrey, D. B. (1994) 'Delivering Deposit Services: ATMs versus Branches', *Federal Reserve Bank of Richmond Economic Quarterly* 80: 59–81.

ISMA (1997) *The Cost and Timescale for the Switchover to the European Single Currency for the International Securities Market*, European Economics and Financial Centre (H. M. Scobie) for the International Securities Market Association, London.

Lang, G. and Welzel, P. (1995) 'Strukturschwäche oder X-Ineffizienz? Cost-Frontier-Analyse der bayerischen Genossenschaftsbanken' (Structural Disadvantages or X-Inefficiency? A Cost Frontier Analysis for German Cooperative Banks. With English Summary), *Kredit und Kapital* 28(3): 403–30.

Llewellyn, D. T. (1998) 'Banking in the 21st Century: The Transformation of an Industry', *Repères* vol. 2.

McCauley, R. N. and White, W. R. (1997) 'The Euro and European Financial Markets', *Bank for International Settlements Working Papers no. 41*, Basle.

Molyneux, P. D., Lloyd-Williams, M. and Thornton, J. (1994) 'Competitive Conditions in European Banking', *Journal of Banking and Finance* 18(3): 433–43.

Rajan, R. G. (1996) 'Why Banks Have A Future: An Economic Rationale' *Temi di discussione*, Banca d'Italia.

Schaffer, S. (1993) 'Market Conduct and Excess Capacity in Banking: A Cross-Country Comparison', Federal Reserve Bank of Philadelphia, Economic Research Division, *Working Paper no. 93–28*.

Schaffer, S. (1994) 'Bank Competition in Concentrated Markets', Federal Reserve Bank of Philadelphia *Business Review* (March–April): 3–16.

Schaffer, S. and David, E. (1991) 'Economies of Superscale in Commercial Banking', *Applied Economics* 23: 283–93.

Schmid, F. (1994) 'Should Bank Branching be Regulated? Theory and Empirical Evidence from Four European Countries', *Journal of Regulatory Economics* 6(2): 137–49.

Schinasi, G. J. and Prati, A. (1997) 'European Monetary Union and International Capital Markets: Structural Implications and Risk', paper presented to the conference EMU and the International Monetary System, IMF and Fondation Camille Gutt, Washington, D.C., March.

Steinhert, A. and P. L. Gilibert (1989) *The Impact of Financial Market Integration on the European Banking Industry, Research Report, Financial Markets Unit*, Centre for European Policy Studies.

Vander Vennet, R. (1994), 'Economies of Scale and Scope in EC Institutions' *Cahiers Economiques de Bruxelles*, 144: 507–48.

Vander Vennet, R. (1994), 'Concentration, Efficiency and Entry Barriers As Determinants of EC Bank Profitability', *Journal of International Financial Markets, Institutions and Money*, 4(3/4): 21–46.

Vesala, J. (1995), 'Testing for Competition in Banking: Behavioral Evidence from Finland', *Bank of Finland Studies E:1*.

7 Eurobanking

The strategic issues

Jean Dermine

Anyone who wants to conquer the markets of the future cannot stay locked into the defensive territorial thinking of the past.

(Mr Thiemann, Chairman of DG Bank, 1998)

Introduction

Although a large series of papers have been concerned with macroeconomic issues such as price stability or employment, very few studies have discussed the impact of the euro on the competitive structure of European banking markets. Two questions are addressed in this paper. How does the move from national currencies to the euro alter the sources of competitive advantage of banks? What are the main strategic options available to financial firms?

A structural analysis of the banking industry raises the question of the importance of a national currency factor. For instance, the markets for pension funds and mutual funds management, and the euro-francs and euro-lira bond markets, are quite fragmented, with domestic institutions capturing a very large market share. Although this fragmentation is explained in part by regulations and history, it could reflect the importance of national currencies. Another example is the leading role of American institutions in the dollar-denominated Eurobond market. Will the emergence of a new world currency competing with the US dollar help the competitiveness of European banks? This paper will attempt to show how, besides an obvious loss of intra-European currencies trading business, the introduction of a common currency will change fundamentally the sources of competitive advantage of banks. This calls for a major review of strategic options.

The paper is structured in two parts. In the first part, eight impacts of the euro are identified and analysed. In the second, the strategic options are discussed.

Banking with a single currency

The first six impacts analysed concern capital markets, including the government bond market and its fast-growing appendage the interest rate derivative market, the corporate bond and equity markets, institutional fund management, the Euromarket, the foreign exchange market, and the competition between the euro and the US dollar as international reserve currencies. The last two effects concern commercial banking: the impact of the single currency on credit risk, and on bank profitability in a low inflation environment.[1]

The government bond market, underwriting and trading

It is apparent that the government bond market in Europe is a very fragmented market, with domestic players capturing a large market share of the underwriting and secondary trading business. This raises the question of the sources of competitive advantage for local banks.

As concerns the underwriting and trading of government bonds, Feldman and Stephenson (1988), a Federal Reserve Study (FRB 1991), and Fox (1992) show that the dominance of local players is the result of three main factors. The first is historical, with local players having a privileged access to the public debt issuer; the second is domestic currency denomination, which facilitates the access to a large investor home base, providing a significant advantage not only in placing, but also in understanding the demand/supply order flows. Finally, expertise in the domestic monetary environment provides essential information for operating on the secondary bond market.

Will these sources of competitive advantage survive with a single currency? As domestic currency denomination, the main source of competitive advantage identified for local banks in the literature, will disappear, it is quite likely that we shall observe the emergence of a truly integrated European bond market. If access to a Europe-wide investor base does facilitate placement, and if access to information on the supply/demand order flows seems essential for secondary trading, then it is very likely that operations on a large scale and at a European-wide level will become a necessity, and there will be a consolidation of the government bond underwriting and trading businesses.[2]

The corporate bond and equity markets, underwriting and trading

As is the case for government bonds, a key issue concerns the sources of competitive advantage of local institutions in corporate bond and equity underwriting and secondary trading. As explained earlier, customer relationship, assessment of credit (business) risk, and currency denomination are critical sources of competitive advantage. The Eurobond market presents an interesting case. A study by the Federal Reserve Bank of New York (FRB 1991), confirmed in Dermine (1996), McCauley and White (1997) and Harm (1998), reports a strong correlation for non-dollar issue between the currency denomination and the nationality of the lead bank manager. This is illustrated in Table 7.1 which shows that, for instance,

French banks are the lead managers 86 per cent of the time for French franc-denominated eurobonds issued by French companies, and 75 per cent of the time for similar bonds issued by non-French borrowers. The domestic currency denomination facilitating the access to an home-investor base is a key source of competitive advantage for placement and also for secondary trading. Indeed, an understanding of local monetary policy gives a competitive advantage in forecasting interest rates and price movements. The leading role of American institutions in the dollar-denominated Eurobond market is explained not only by large issues by American companies, with their expertise developed in their home corporate securities markets, but also by the important advantage linked to the dollar denomination of many bonds. Indeed, access to home investors, and an understanding of US order flows and US monetary policy provide a decisive advantage in secondary trading as they help to predict price movements.

A single currency in Europe will change fundamentally the competitive structure of the corporate bond and equity markets, as one key source of competitive advantage, namely home currency, will disappear. Indeed, savers will diversify their portfolio across European markets, the exchange rate risk being eradicated. Moreover, a single currency will suppress

Table 7.1 Currency and home-country relationship in the choice of the bond bookrunner (1996)
Percentage market share won by bookrunners of indicated nationality

German bookrunners			*French bookrunners*		
Borrower	*Currency*		*Borrower*	*Currency*	
	Mark	*Other*		*French francs*	*Other*
German	44	16	French	86	10
Other	37	2	Other	75	2
All	39	4	All	77	2
UK bookrunners			*Dutch bookrunners*		
Borrower	*Currency*		*Borrower*	*Currency*	
	Pound	*Other*		*Guilder*	*Other*
UK	40	21	Dutch	83	26
Other	48	3	Other	85	2
All	44	4	All	84	2
US bookrunners			*Japanese bookrunners*		
Borrower	*Currency*		*Borrower*	*Currency*	
	Dollar	*Other*		*Yen*	*Other*
US	86	46	Japanese	75	46
Other	54	13	Other	87	6
All	64	16	All	84	8

Source: McCauley and White (1997)

the secondary trading advantage for domestic banks derived from a better understanding of order flows and monetary policy in the domestic country. Therefore, the two main sources of comparative advantage remaining for local players will be historical customer relationship and the understanding of credit (business) risk through a better knowledge of the accounting, legal and fiscal (not to mention language) environment. Whenever the business risk embedded in corporate securities can better be assessed by domestic banks, these players will control underwriting and secondary trading. Local expertise would be particularly valuable for smaller companies, venture capital and the real estate market. However, for larger corporations, worldwide industry expertise will most likely dominate any national advantage. For instance, to serve a Volvo corporation, it is unlikely that Swedish expertise is of great help to local institutions. What is needed is expertise in the global automobile industry.

To conclude this analysis of the impact of a single currency on the corporate bond and equity markets, it seems that customer relationship and an understanding of business risk could remain two sources of strength for domestic firms in some segments of the market. But placing power and trading across Europe, coupled with global industry expertise, are forces that lead to consolidation in a major part of the securities industry. As a tentative base for comparison, it is symptomatic to observe in Table 7.2 that the top ten American underwriters of investment grade debt control 87 per cent of the US market.

Fund management

An important segment of the capital markets business is the fund management industry, handling pensions funds and mutual funds. As

Table 7.2 Top underwriters of investment grade in the USA (1996)

Manager	1996 ECU bn	Market share %
Merrill Lynch	79	18.3
Salomon Brothers	54	12.5
Goldman Sachs	46.9	10.8
J. P. Morgan	45	10.4
Lehman Bros	43.7	10.1
Morgan Stanley	40.8	9.4
CSFB	29	6.7
Bear Stearns	29	3.1
Smith Barney	12.8	3.0
NationsBank	12.3	2.8

Source: Securities Data Co. Taking into account the merger of Smith Barney and Salomon Brothers, the five largest have a cumulative market share of 65.1%

Table 7.3a illustrates for France and Table 7.3b for the United Kingdom, it is symptomatic to see the total dominance of the fund management industry by local firms.[3] In view of this extreme fragmentation, especially in comparison with other segments of the capital markets, it is worth considering the impact of the single currency on the fund management industry. In this case too, an understanding of the main sources of competitive advantage needs to be developed. These concern the retail distribution network, the home-currency preference, research expertise, and the existence of economies of scale (Kay, Laslett and Duffy 1994).

The first source of competitive advantage in the retail segment is the control of the distribution network, which is in the hands of local banks in several countries. Domestic control of distribution is even protected under current European legislation framework, which gives national authorities the right to regulate the marketing of funds into their own territory. Obviously the advantage derived from the control of the distribution

Table 7.3a Mutual fund (OPCVM) managers in France (December 1996)

	ECU bn	*Market share (%)*
Société Générale	31.3	7.4
Crédit Agricole	25.1	5.9
Crédit Lyonnais	24.1	5.7
BNP	23.96	5.68
CDC-Trésor	18.5	4.4
La Poste	16.3	3.9
CIC-Banque	14	3.3
Caisses d'Epargne	12.9	3.1
Banques Populaires	12.3	2.9
Paribas	8.2	1.95

Source: EuroPerformance, AFG-ASSFI.

Table 7.3b UK league of fund managers: total assets under management

	ECU bn	*Market share %*
Prudential	123.4	9.6
Schroder	119.3	9.3
MAM	116.6	9.1
Morgan Grenfell	93.6	7.3
Commercial Union	92.2	7.2
Fleming	78.6	6.1
Invesco	78.6	6.1
PDFM	77.3	6
Gartmore	69.2	5.4
Standard Union	65	5

Note: excludes the assets managed by Wells Fargo Nikko, the US fund management arm of Barclays

128   *Jean Dermine*

network applies to retail investors only, as it will not be a barrier to entry in the institutional market.

A second source of competitive advantage is the customer preference for home-currency assets, often imposed by regulation. A single currency will of course eliminate this factor and reinforce the need for Europe-wide portfolios. A large part of these will be provided by index-tracking investment funds.

A third source of success is excellence in research-based management. As to the existence of economies of scale and scope in the fund management industry, it is still a subject of debate (Bonanni, Dermine and Röller 1998). If scale seems important for index-tracking funds, it could be less relevant for actively-managed funds.

A single currency will eliminate the obstacle to international diversification. It is quite likely that we will see very large low-cost European index-tracking funds competing with smaller research-based funds. On the retail distribution side, domestic banks will keep their competitive advantage as long as the branch network remains a significant channel of distribution.

The euro-deposit market

An extremely efficient euro-deposit market was created thirty years ago to circumvent various forms of domestic regulations.[4] A first issue concerns the size, coverage and remuneration of the reserve requirement on euro-denominated deposits in the future. Indeed, foreign-currency-denominated deposits are not subject to reserve requirements in most countries. A second and more significant issue will be the fiscal treatment of the income earned on these assets in the future. The imposition of a 20 per cent witholding tax, or information sharing between tax authorities on interest paid to EU citizens, would no doubt affect the location of the euro-markets.

Foreign exchange markets

A direct effect of the single currency is that not only will intra-European foreign exchange transactions disappear, but the competitive advantage of a particular bank in its home currency *vis-à-vis* third country currencies will change as well. As an example, a Belgian bank operating in New York will no longer be a Belgian franc specialist, but will compete with other European banks for euro/dollar business. As is the case for the government bond markets, for which an understanding of the supply/demand order flows is important in predicting the direction of price movements, there is likely to be a consolidation of the commodity-type low-cost spot foreign exchange business. This conjecture is consistent with the analysis by Tschoegl (1996) of the sources of competitive advantage in the currency market, namely size and the international status of the home currency. Differentiated products based on quality of service, and innovations such as options, will be other sources of competitive advantage.

The euro as an international currency: the benefits for banks

One of the asserted benefits of EMU is that the single currency will become a challenger to the US dollar as the dominant international currency, used for units of accounts, store of value and means of payments (Emerson 1990, Alogoskoufis and Portes, 1991, Maas 1995). However, it must be appreciated that contrary to a national currency which is imposed as sole tender by national legislation, the role of an international currency is fixed by demand and supply on world capital markets. Two questions arise. First, is the euro likely to compete against the US dollar in international financial markets? Second, from the perspective of this paper, what are the benefits for banks of the euro having an international currency status?

Whether one looks at the role of the dollar as a unit of account, a store of value, or a means of payment, it still is today by far the prime international currency. For instance, 60 per cent of the foreign exchange reserves of central banks are denominated in dollars, while US exports represent only 12 per cent of world exports. To assess the probability of the euro accelerating the relative decline in the dollar, it is instructive look at history, and the relative fall of sterling and rise of the dollar in the international payment system.

In 1914, on the eve of the First World War, the City of London was indisputably the world's leading international financial centre, with the pound sterling the major international currency. According to economic historians, the weakness of the pound started with the First World War. The war of 1914–18 saw the emergence of large bond financing in the USA. There followed the events of 1931, the insolvency of the Creditanstalt in Vienna and the inconvertibility of the pound. The Second World War increased even more the stature of the dollar, which was confirmed in its international role by the 1944 Bretton Woods agreement.[5] It can be concluded that the rise of the dollar over a thirty-year period was very much helped by the two world wars, and that despite the abandoning of convertibility into gold in 1971 and continuous devaluation, the dollar twenty-five years later still maintains a leading role as an international currency. On the basis of the last two decades, which have seen a progressive erosion of the dollar and a slow rise of the DM, in view of the relative economic size of Europe, and building on the potential for growth in the eastern part of Europe, one can extrapolate and forecast that the euro will replace the DM and be a strong competitor to the dollar. But in my opinion, any forecast of the future relative importance of the US dollar and the euro is premature.

It is possible to identify three benefits to banks of having the euro as an international currency. The first is that an increased volume of euro-denominated assets or liabilities will ease the foreign exchange risk management of bank equity. Indeed, a large part of bank assets will be denominated in the same currency as the equity base, easing the control of currency-driven asset growth and capital management. Second, access to a discount window at the European Central Bank will make the liquidity management of euro-based liabilities marginally cheaper. Finally, if third countries issue assets denominated in the euro, or use the European currency as a vehicle, European banks will be well positioned for secondary trading, for the reasons mentioned earlier.

EMU and credit risk

Many of the channels which have been identified concern the money and capital markets. An additional impact of the euro is its potential effect on credit risk. There are reasons to believe that the nature of credit risk could change under a single currency. The argument is based on the theory of optimum currency areas and on the objective of price stability inscribed in the Treaty on European Union.

There is an old debate on the economic rationale that leads a group of countries to adopt a common currency.[6] The argument is that the more countries are subject to asymmetric economic shocks, the more they would appreciate monetary autonomy to cancel the shock. Indeed, with symmetric shock there would be a consensus among the members of a currency union on economic policy, but with asymmetric shocks the policy run from the centre may not be adequate to all the members of the union. Recent economic developments have strengthend the argument. For instance, it is arguable that the rapid recovery enjoyed by British banks in 1994 has been helped by the 1992 devaluation, which reduced a bad debt problem. Similarly, the devaluation of the Finnish markka has helped the restructuring of the country after the collapse of one of its major trading partners, the Soviet Union.

How could the introduction of a single currency affect credit risk? If a bank concentrates its business in its home country, and if that country is subject to asymmetric shocks, it is quite possible that a central monetary policy will not be able to soften the shock. Some have argued that the adverse consequences of such shocks could be dealt with at the European level, and that in any case, these shocks would be quite rare. Indeed, severe asymmetric shocks could in principle be mitigated by fiscal transfers across Europe. However, this is only a possibility that remains to be verified. As to the argument that asymmetric shocks are rare events, it is indeed the case, but a fundamental mission of any bank risk management system is to ensure the solvency of financial institutions following precisely those rare but significant events.

An indirect and interesting corollary of the optimum currency area theory is that for banks operating in a single currency area, the need to diversify their loan portfolio increases the more their home country is likely to be subject to asymmetric (uncorrelated) shocks. This can be achieved through international diversification, or with the use of credit derivatives.

A related effect of EMU on credit risk is that the statute of the European Central Bank will prevent inflationary policies. *Ceteris paribus*, this could increase the potential for losses resulting from default, as it becomes no longer possible to count on a predictable positive drift for the value of collateral assets.[7] The inability of a country to devalue, and the very strict anti-inflationary policy of the ECB, imply that whenever a need to restore competitiveness arises in a particular region, the only tool available will be a reduction of nominal wages and prices. This will change fundamentally the nature of credit risk, as firms and individuals will no longer be able to rely on the nominal growth of their revenue to reduce the real value of their debt. This new world calls for innovative techniques to handle potential deflations.[8]

Banking in a low-inflation environment

The last effect of a single currency discussed in this paper concerns the impact on bank profitability of doing business in a low-inflation environment. Indeed, in the last twenty years, higher inflation and interest rates have provided substantial interest margins on price-regulated deposits. For instance, as is shown in Table 7.4 for the 1980–5 period, interest margins on demand deposits were above 10 per cent in Belgium, France, Denmark and Spain. If new products, such as money market funds, competed with these deposits, it is important to notice that these demand and savings deposits still represent more than 40 per cent of client resources collected by banks in Belgium and France (Commission Bancaire 1996; Banque de France 1996). As Table 7.4 documents, margins on these products have been seriously eroded with the overall decrease in the interest rate level in recent years. It can safely be concluded that the objectives of monetary stability and low inflation pursued by an independent European Central Bank will reduce the source of profitability on the deposit funding business. However, if this effect is quite significant in a large number of countries, two additional effects of a low-inflation environment might soften the impact of lower margins on deposits.

The first is that a low-interest-rate environment leads usually to a much higher margin on personal loans, because of the relative inelasticity of the interest rate on personal loans. For instance, in France, loan rate stickiness has raised the margin on hire purchase (consumer) loans from 6.3 per cent in 1990 to 10.1 per cent in 1996, over a period of rapidly-declining market rates (Banque de France 1996). A second positive impact of a low-inflation

Table 7.4 Interest margins of commercial banks (%)

	Belgium	Denmark	France	Germany	Spain
Average margin on demand deposits:[1]					
1980–5	11.2	16.2	11.7	6.5	14.5
1987–92	8.7	9.0	9.7	7.2	6.0
1994–5	5.0	n/a	6.1	4.8	3.6
Average margin on savings deposits:[1]					
1980–5	5.6	8.9	4.3	2.8	10.7
1987–92	3.9	7.0	5.2	2.2	9.0
1994–5	1.9	n/a	1.6	2.9	5.0

Note: 1 Current short-term rate minus interest rate paid on deposits.
Source: OECD

environment is that the so-called 'inflation tax' will be much smaller (Fisher and Modigliani 1978). A simple example will show the argument behind the inflation tax. Consider a case with no inflation, in which equity is invested in a 3 per cent coupon bond. After a 30 per cent corporate tax is deducted, the revenue is 2.1 per cent ((1–0.3) x 3%). The full profit can be paid as a dividend, as there is no need for retained earnings and higher capital since there is no growth of assets. If because of 10 per cent inflation, the same equity is invested in a 13 per cent coupon bond, the profit after tax is only 9.1 per cent ((1–0.3) x 13%), a figure too small to finance the necessary equity growth of 10 per cent. No dividend can be paid in this case, and equity holders have suffered from an 'inflation-tax'.

Therefore, the impact of a low-inflation environment on the profitability of banks will depend on the relative importance of reduced margins on deposits and higher profit on personal loans, and on the significance of the 'inflation tax'.

The strategic issues

As Table 7.5 shows, a considerable amount of domestic restructuring has already taken place in Europe. This was driven by the creation of the single market in 1992. In most cases, domestic mergers were driven by cost cutting. For instance, White (1998) reports that the restructuring of the Finnish banking system, undertaken after a severe financial crisis, has reduced employment by 32 per cent.[9] These domestic mergers have increased concentration and produced firms of bigger size, albeit at a national level. A first series of cross-border deals, documented in Table 7.6a and 7.6b, took place in the merchant banking area, where independent merchant banks (many of them British) were purchased by continental banks. These acquisitions were no doubt motivated by the wish to acquire rapidly the necessary expertise in securities-based corporate

Table 7.5 Domestic mergers in Europe (not complete: for illustration only)

Belgium	1992	CGER–AG (Fortis)
	1995	Fortis–SNCI
	1995	KB–Bank van Roeselaere
	1997	BACOB–Paribas Belgium
		CERA–Indosuez Belgium
	1998	KBC (KB–CERA–ABB)
Denmark	1990	Den Danske Bank
		Unibank (Privatbanken, Sparekassen, Andelsbanken)
Finland	1995	Meritabank (KOP–Union Bank of Finland)
France	1996	Crédit Agricole–Indosuez
Germany	1997	Bayerische Vereinsbank–Hypo-Bank
Italy	1992	Banca di Roma (Banco di Roma, Cassa di Risparmio di Roma, Banco di Santo Spirito)
		IMI–Cariplo
		San Paolo–Crediop
	1995	Credito Romagnolo (Rolo)–Credit Italiano
	1997	Ambroveneto–Cariplo
Netherlands	1990	ABN–AMRO
	1991	NMB–PostBank–ING
	1998	Rabobank–Achmea
Portugal	1995	BCP–BPA
Spain	1988	BBV (Banco de Vizcaya–Banco de Bilbao)
	1989	Caja de Barcelona–La Caixa
	1992	Banco Central–Banco Hispano
	1994	Santander–Banesto
Sweden	1993	Nordbanken–Gota Bank
Switzerland	1993	CS–Volksbank–Winterthur
	1997	SBC–UBS
United Kingdom	1995	Lloyds–C&G–TSB

finance and asset management. Until quite recently, cross-border mergers of commercial banks of significant size have been rare. The difficulty in merging two national cultures was often put forward as a barrier to cross-border mergers. However, two noticeable deals have taken place recently: the purchase of the Belgian Banque Bruxelles Lambert (BBL) by the Dutch Internationale Nederland Groep (ING), and the merger of the Swedish Nordbanken with the Finnish Meritabank. These cross-border deals are noticeable because they involve very large domestic players. It is worth noticing that these deals involve small countries with banks attempting to create a larger home base.

As was discussed in the second section of this paper, the arrival of the euro will change rapidly the sources of competitive advantage in various segments of the capital markets, namely government bonds, corporate securities (bonds, shares, asset-backed securities), foreign exchange, and asset management. If the argument that size will matter on some of these

Table 7.6a International mergers in Europe (not complete: for illustration only)

Buyer	Target
Deutsche Bank	Morgan Grenfell
ING Bank	Barings
Swiss Bank Corp	Warburg, O'Connor, Brinson, Dillon Read
Dresdner	Kleinwort Benson
ABN–AMRO	Hoare Govett
Unibank	ABB Aros
Merrill Lynch	Smith New Court (UK), FG (Spain), MAM
CSFB	BZW (equity part)
Société Générale	Hambros (UK)

Table 7.6b International mergers in Europe

Buyer	Target
DEXIA (France, Belgium, Luxemburg, Italy)	Crédit Communal, Crédit Local, BIL, Crediop
BACOB (Belgium)	Paribas (Netherlands)
ING (Netherlands)	BBL (Belgium)
Fortis (Belgium, Netherlands)	AMEV+Mees Pierson (Netherlands) /CGER/SNCI (Belgium)/Générale Bank
Nordbanken (Sweden)	Meritabank (Finland)
Générale Bank (Belgium)	Crédit Lyonnais (Netherlands), Hambros (UK, corporate)

markets is accepted, then the options for the players are either to exit (outsource) part of these activities, or to reach the appropriate size. Moreover, it should be borne in mind that an additional, potentially much more significant, change concerns information technology. IT should allow, in principle, the distribution of financial services to retail clients across borders and without a physical presence. The key issue is the speed of acceptance of this new delivery channel by customers, and their willingness to entrust a significant part of their financial affairs to a foreign supplier. In this new Eurobanking world, banks will face three major strategic options: to become a national champion, to pursue an European strategy through cross-border acquisition or merger, or to pursue an European strategy through a cooperative structure.

Becoming a national (or regional) champion

A firm achieves this by acquiring through takeovers or mergers a significant market share on its domestic market. It outsources part of its capital market activities to larger international firms. Domestic size will provide the ability to achieve cost efficiency and to offer high quality services. This strategy can survive until new technology allows large foreign firms to target directly local clients, disintermediating the local financial supermarket. Under such a scenario, the domestic champion will be absorbed sooner or later by a large international player who benefits from a large low-cost operating platform. Given the loyalty of retail clients and the particular nature of financial services, for which trust is an essential element which cannot be acquired rapidly, one could take the view that significant competition from foreign competitors on the retail market will not take place for several years. This domestic strategy could be adopted by national banks or even by some regional banks, such as the *Cajas* in Spain, which have a very strong local retail franchise.

A policy of cross-border merger or acquisition

This allows the institution to reach size and international coverage rapidly. Corporate control can be efficient, as the process is managed with authority from a centre, but the allocation of responsibilities in the newly-created entity appears to have been a very difficult process for many financial firms.[10] This is the top-down approach.

The cooperative strategy

This is the bottom-up approach. Local cooperatives created national centres several decades ago to serve their treasury or international needs (as in the case of the Rabobank in the Netherlands, or of the Crédit Agricole in France). In a similar way, groups of national institutions could create European centres taking care of asset management and, potentially, large international corporates. This approach has the merit of being decentralized at the national retail level, with efficient management of capital market activities at the international centre. As history has shown (such as that of European American Bank or European Asian Bank), the danger is a lack of control or speed of decision by the various members.

A premise of the above analysis has been that size will be important for operation in some segments of the markets, and that a European coverage will be necessary. This premise demands identification of the major competitive difference between large *domestic* size and large size at the *European* level. Indeed, it could be argued that two large banks of an equal size (one domestic and the other European) would have the same leverage on the bond or currency markets. That question is indeed relevant, as no doubt it will be much more difficult to create an international institution than a domestic one. It is the author's belief that European coverage dominates a domestic one for two major reasons. The first is that some corporate clients become increasingly international, giving preference to banks with an international coverage. The second, more significant, argument in favour of a European coverage is that it provides a most welcome source of diversification. This is of course necessary to reduce credit risk, but is also relevant to stabilizing the demand for services in capital markets. Indeed, if because of a recession or change in the legal–fiscal environment, the demand for foreign exchange services for instance, or pension funds investment in bonds, changed dramatically, a large domestic bank would rapidly lose what was deemed necessary to compete: sufficient size to analyze the supply/order flows or to have the placing power. A European coverage would be a way to stabilize business flows, allowing an adequate size to be retained permanently.

Conclusions

The objective of this paper has been to identify the various ways in which the euro will alter the sources of competitive advantage of European banks, and to analyse the various strategic options available. Besides the obvious fall in revenue from intra-European currencies trading, the analysis has identified significant and permanent effects on several segments of the industry. Among these are rapid consolidations of the commodity-type business, government bonds, interest rate derivatives, and spot currency trading. Banks will be motivated by the loss of a main domestic source of competitive advantage, namely the national currency. If domestic expertise in the accounting, legal and fiscal environment gives a competitive advantage to domestic players in some segments of the corporate bond and equity markets, other factors such as placing power across Europe, trading capacity, and global industry expertise will lead to consolidation of that industry. On the fund management side, very large European-wide index-tracking funds will compete with specialized funds. As concerns the euro-deposits market, the rules of monetary and fiscal policies will have to be known before it is possible to assess the impact of a single currency on the size and location of this market. On the commercial banking side, the nature of credit risk is likely to change as one of the instruments of monetary policy, devaluation, will not be available. Finally, the impact of a low-inflation environment on bank profitability will work through reduced margins on deposits, higher profits on personal loans, and a lower 'inflation tax'.

Furthermore, it is important to highlight the obvious but important fact that the single currency will make *irreversible* the creation of a single European banking market. A more predictable environment will facilitate the exploitation of economies of scale and the optimal location of processing units.

If the premises underlying the above analysis are verified in the future, one can anticipate the creation of a new Eurobanking world. A major international consolidation of the European banking industry will take place in the capital market business, and further domestic rationalization of commercial banking will be needed. An important premise of the analysis has been that European size will dominate domestic size because it enables diversification benefits to be realized.

The objective of the 1992 single market programme was to reinforce the efficiency and competitiveness of European firms. As concerns banking, it is a clear conclusion that the introduction of a single currency will not only make the creation of a single market irreversible, but that it will, besides the obvious fall in revenue from intra-European currencies trading, alter fundamentally the nature of several businesses. A new banking world will emerge with very different sources of competitive advantage. If this challenge is met successfully by European banks, there is little doubt that it will reinforce the competitiveness of European banks operating in the capital markets of third countries such as those of Asia, Latin America and the United States.

Notes

1 This section on impacts draws on Dermine 1997, 1998 and Dermine and Hillion 1999.
2 The relative merits of large domestic scale versus large European scale are discussed in the third section of this paper.
3 Some of these, such as Morgan Grenfell, have been purchased by continental firms.
4 Some creative wording is needed as it is important to distinguish *euro-deposits*, deposits from non-residents, from *euro-denominated deposits*.
5 According to McKinnon (1993), a key factor increasing the role of the dollar was the European Payments Union established in September 1950 for clearing payments multilaterally, using the US dollar as the unit of account and as the means of payment.
6 See Mundell 1961, McKinnon 1963.
7 However an argument can be made that non-inflationary policies will reduce the amplitude of business cycles.
8 A tool could be the creation of securities indexed on regional prices.
9 This should be compared with a drop in bank employment of 5 per cent in France and 0.3 per cent in Germany (White 1998).
10 An interesting case in 1998 is that of the highly praised Wells Fargo failing to integrate FirstInterstate successfully, and recently being forced into a merger by Norwest.

Bibliography

Alogoskoufis, G. and Portes, R. (1991) 'International Costs and Benefits from EMU', in *The Economics of EMU*, European Economy.
Banque de France (1996) *Bulletin Trimestriel* (December).
Bonanni, C., Dermine, J. and Röller, L. H. (1998) 'Some Evidence on Customer "Lock-in" in the French Mutual Funds Industry', *Applied Economics Letters* (5): 275–9.
Commission Bancaire (1996) *Rapport Annuel*, Commission Bancaire, Brussels.
Dermine, J. (1996) 'European Banking with a Single Currency', *Financial Markets, Institutions and Instruments* 5 (5).
Dermine, J. (1997) 'Eurobanking, a New World', Laureate of the 1997 EIB Prize, *EIB Papers* (2).
Dermine, J. (1998) *The Euro World, A Strategic Analysis*, Video Management, Brussels.

Dermine, J. and Hillion, P. (eds) (1999) *European Capital Markets with a Single Currency, An ECMI Report*, Oxford University Press, Oxford.

Eichengreen, B. (1993) 'European Monetary Unification', *Journal of Economic Literature* 31: 1321–57.

Emerson, M. (1990) 'One Market, One Money', *European Economy* 44 (October).

Feldman, L. and Stephenson, J. (1988) 'Stay Small or Get Huge – Lessons from Securities Trading', *Harvard Business Review* (May–June): 116–23.

Fisher, S. and Modigliani, F. (1978) 'Towards an Understanding of the Real Effects and Costs of Inflation', *Weltwirtschaftliches Archiv* 114: 810–33.

Fox, M. (1992) 'Aspects of Barriers to International Integrated Securities Markets', *Journal of International Securities Markets* (Autumn): 209–17.

FRB (1991) *International Competitiveness of US Financial Firms*, Federal Reserve Bank of New York, staff study.

Harm, C. (1998) 'European Financial Markets Integration: The Case of Private Sector Bonds and Syndicated Loans', mimeo, Copenhagen Business School: 1–26.

Kay, J., Laslett, R. and Duffy, N. (1994) *The Competitive Advantage of the Fund Management Industry in the City of London*, City Research Project, London.

Maas, C. (1995) *Progress Report on the Preparation of the Changeover to the single Currency*, Brussels.

McCauley, R. and White, W. (1997) 'The Euro and European Financial Markets', *BIS Working Paper no. 41*, Bank for International Settlements, Basle.

McKinnon, R. (1963) 'Optimum Currency Areas', *American Economic Review* 53: 717–25.

McKinnon, R. (1993) 'The Rules of the Game, International Money in Historical Perspective', *Journal of Economic Literature* 31: 1–44.

Mundell, R. A. (1961) 'A Theory of Optimum Currency Areas', *American Economic Review* 51: 657–65.

Tschoegl, A. (1996) 'Country and Firms Sources of International Competitiveness: The Case of the Foreign Exchange Market', Wharton School.

White, W. (1998) 'The Coming Transformation of Continental European Banking?', *BIS Working Paper no. 54*, Bank for International Settlements, Basle.

8 Are financial conglomerates and universal banks efficient?

Evidence from European banking

Rudi Vander Vennet

Introduction

In contrast to the USA, where universal banking is still legally prohibited, the Second Banking Directive allows European banks to form financial conglomerates and to hold equity stakes in non-financial firms. Financial conglomerates are defined here as financial institutions that combine the conduct of traditional banking activities with insurance- and securities-related activities. These activities can be carried out via integrated in-house departments or through subsidiaries. The directive permits unlimited reciprocal ownership links between commercial banks, insurance companies and investment banks. Moreover the directive also allows universal banking, more or less following the example of German banking. The distinguishing feature is that universal banks may hold equity stakes in non-financial firms. They may vote the shares they own and, if proxy provisions exist, also those they hold in trust for other agents. Holding equity participations in non-financial firms is, however, subject to certain limits. Individual stakes in industrial and commercial firms should not exceed 15 per cent of the bank's capital, while the sum of these holdings must remain below 60 per cent of the capital.

Within this legal framework, universal banking is allowed in all EU member states, and it has also been present historically in other countries such as Switzerland. As a result of worldwide deregulation and intensified international competition, the debate about conglomeration and universality is also high on the agenda in the US. The debate on the repeal of the Glass–Steagall (1933) provisions separating commercial and investment banking has been intensified in recent years. An US Treasury Report of 1991 advocated the abolition of the barriers between banking and commerce, and supported the establishment of financial service holding companies with insurance and investment banking subsidiaries next to commercial banking subsidiaries. Recently, a number of academic studies have produced evidence in favour of universal banking in the US. Benston (1994) and Saunders and Walter (1994) argue that a move to universal banking would enhance the operational efficiency of the financial services sector, without increasing the risks to financial system stability. Yet until now Congress has opposed such an evolution, although the Federal Reserve has used its powers under Glass–Steagall to increase the ceiling on the proportion of total revenue a commercial bank can earn from brokering from 10 per cent to 25 per cent. The merger between Citicorp and Travelers may speed up the decision process.

The regulatory choices concerning the functional scope of banking institutions may have implications for the evolution of the structure of world banking, since the strategic options for banks in terms of functional diversification depend to a large extent on the regulatory environment in which they operate. Within the deregulated EU institutional setting, the EMU and the introduction of the euro are prompting banks with varying degrees of functional and geographic specialization to restructure. The number and the total value of mergers and acquisitions, mostly domestic, have increased steadily over the last few years. In many cases banks have acquired dominant stakes in insurance firms or investment houses, or vice versa. The question is whether a generalized shift to universal banking and the formation of financial conglomerates would benefit the EMU economies in terms of the efficiency and risk of the financial system. For individual financial institutions, the strategic trade-off is whether becoming diversified and/or universal is necessary in order to remain competitively viable. In this respect the actual behaviour of EU banks displays marked differences. A number of banks are refocusing towards greater specialization (e.g. several UK banks). Others are opting for a strategy of diversification, often through a merger with, or the acquisition of, insurance companies and/or investment firms. A number of recent (mega)mergers in Benelux, Switzerland and Scandinavia are examples of the ongoing bancassurance conglomeration trend (Fortis–Générale Bank, Crédit Suisse–Winterthur). Throughout the 1990s large continental European banks have acquired a series of (often London-based) securities brokers and investment banks. The takeover of Bankers Trust by Deutsche Bank in 1998 has put the issue in a global context. On the universal banking scene, a number of gradual shifts can also be discerned. The big German banks, led by Deutsche Bank, have announced that they will reconsider the organizational form in which they hold equity stakes in industrial firms. Undoubtedly, shareholder pressure and other corporate governance considerations are contributing to this phenomenon.

The main arguments in the debate over universal banking have been well documented (see Saunders 1994). On the positive side, it is argued that universal banks provide discipline to corporate management, actively intervene in the restructuring of corporations, often more efficiently than stock markets, and allow the realization of economies of scale and scope across various financial services. Moreover, due to the diversification of their income streams, financial conglomerates are viewed as inherently stable institutions, which in turn promote systemic financial stability and economic development. Opponents raise serious doubts about the alleged cost advantages, and invoke conflicts of interest and concentration of power as the main drawbacks. Unfortunately, the issue has received only limited attention from the empirical research community. As a result, a number of authors have stressed the need for a structural examination of the gains from the activities of universal banks (Benston 1994, Saunders 1994). This paper therefore investigates the cost and profit efficiency of banks characterized by various degrees of diversification, conglomeration and universality. For that purpose the EU constitutes an ideal setting, because financial conglomerates and universal banks operate in all member states. A few previous studies have examined universal banking on a country-by-country basis (Saunders and Walter 1994, Allen and Rai 1996). However, even in countries where universal banking is allowed, financial conglomerates, universal banks and specialized banks coexist. Therefore, our approach is to analyse EU banks based on their degree of diversification and universality, as revealed by their institutional structure and by their operational and financial characteristics, instead of referring solely to the country in which they are headquartered.

In what follows, the sub-samples of European financial conglomerates, universal banks and specialized institutions are analysed in terms of their relative cost and profit efficiency. Stochastic cost and profit functions are estimated for different classes of European banks. The main findings are that financial conglomerates are more revenue efficient than their more specialized competitors, and that the degree of both cost and profit efficiency is higher in universal banks than in non-universal banks. These results indicate that the current trend towards further despecialization may lead to a more efficient banking system. Since competition is expected to increase in the euro environment, the customer should in theory be one of the main beneficiaries of the enhanced operational efficiency of financial institutions.

The rest of this paper is organized as follows. The next section discusses the economics of non-specialized banking, and reviews some of the existing empirical evidence. This is followed by an attempt to offer an operational definition of diversified banks, financial conglomerates and universal banks, and a description of the data. A further section outlines the econometric methodology used to test the hypotheses relating to cost and profit efficiency. Then there is a presentation of the main empirical results. and the final section contains some conclusions.

The comparative advantages of financial conglomerates and universal banks

Economically, the formation of financial conglomerates would be beneficial if there were positive cost and/or revenue effects from combining various financial service activities. Consolidated revenues would be improved if the income-generating capacity of the combined institutions were enhanced, for example through diversification and cross-selling. Similarly, the operating costs of financial conglomerates would be lower relative to specialized banks if integration allowed the realization of operational synergy, for example through economies of scale and scope. Funding costs might also be lowered due to reputation effects or market power. Universal banks might exhibit superior performance if informational or other advantages associated with equity holdings produced positive spill-overs to the traditional and non-traditional banking activities they undertake.

Economies of scale exist if, assuming a constant product mix, a bank faces declining average costs as its size expands. Pure scale economies cannot be invoked as a reason for the formation of financial conglomerates, but they may explain the growth of these financial firms. In fact, since conglomerates and universal banks tend to be relatively large institutions, the scale argument has intuitive appeal as an explanation for growth. Moreover, technological advances may be an obvious catalyst for increased size. Economies of scope capture the effect of a change in a bank's product mix on aggregate costs. If an expanded set of products and services is produced in a more efficient way by financial conglomerates, cost may be lowered. The sharing of inputs such as labour, technology and information across multiple outputs constitutes the major source of such potential cost savings.

The presence of economies of scale and scope in banking remains a controversial subject. The early US studies found that economies of scale were exhausted at relatively small output levels (see Clark 1988 for a review). More recently, studies including larger banks have found evidence of scale economies up to the US\$ 2–6 billion asset range (Noulas, Ray and Miller 1990, Hunter, Timme and Yang 1990). Apparently, regulatory and technological changes have shifted the optimal scale in banking. Shaffer (1988) found evidence of scale economies up to the US\$ 60 billion size range for the hundred largest US banks. Berger and Mester (1997) found substantial unexploited cost scale economies for fairly large sizes of bank in the 1990s, suggesting a change from the 1980s. However, studies of US banks cannot provide evidence on the cost dynamics in non-specialized financial institutions, because regulatory constraints prohibit conglomeration and universal banking. In a study based on non-US data, Saunders and Walter (1994) found economies of scale up to US\$ 25 billion in loans for the world's 200 largest banks. Vander Vennet (1994a) found similar results for a sample of 1,500 EU banks. Lang and Welzel (1995, 1996) found scale economies among German universal banks up to a size of DM 5 billion, and significant scale economies for a sample of relatively small Bavarian cooperative banks.

Based on similar methods, the bulk of US studies conclude that economies of scope in banking, if at all present, are exhausted at very low levels of output (see Berger, Hanweck and Humphrey 1987, Mester 1992,

Berger, Hunter and Timme 1993). However, Clark (1988) noted that some studies do find evidence of cost complementarities between certain product pairs. Recent studies tend to support this finding (Hughes and Mester 1994). One exception is a study by Kolari and Zardkoohi (1987) in which economies of scope between 10 and 50 per cent for all size ranges and output pairings are reported. In Europe, Muldur (1991) concludes that cost complementarities exist between certain product pairs, but they tend to compensate for each other, resulting in near zero net benefits. For British building societies, diseconomies of scope are the prevalent outcome in Hardwick (1990) and Drake (1992). Lang and Welzel (1995, 1996) report the absence of scope economies in German universal banks, but they do find such economies in small cooperative banks. Saunders and Walter (1994) find important diseconomies of scope between loans and fee-earning business for the world's largest banks, many of which are universal.

Scale and scope economies, however, refer only to the static effect of size and activity mix on costs. Faced with a rapidly changing competitive and regulatory environment, the improvement of operational or X-efficiency may be even more important for ensuring the competitive viability of banks, especially since a number of studies have documented that technical inefficiencies (excess use of inputs) and allocative inefficiencies (suboptimal input mix) may be large, and even dominate scale and product mix economies (Berger and Humphrey 1991). Increasing competitive pressure and technological advances will force banks to shift to an institutional form that allows maximum X-efficiency. The question is whether financial conglomeration or universal banking offers a sustainable advantage over specialist suppliers.

One argument relates to corporate governance and the working of the takeover market. If specialized financial firms (banking, insurance, securities business) are sheltered from acquisition, for example because there are legal barriers to takeover, inefficient managers are protected and agency costs are high. If cross-activity mergers are allowed, managers of financial firms incur stronger monitoring by the takeover market. Saunders (1994) argues that allowing banks to be acquired by other financial companies or even commercial firms would impose monitoring and create incentives for efficiency and value-maximizing behaviour. It would also reduce expense-preference behavior, which has been found to be present in banking (Arnould 1985, Akella and Greenbaum 1988). Often, the formation of a financial conglomerate constitutes an occasion for focused rationalization programmes, a phenomenon that has also been observed in EU bank mergers by Vander Vennet (1996).

Over the past several years, substantial effort has gone into the measurement of X-efficiency of financial institutions. Berger and Humphrey (1997) survey 130 studies on efficiency, using data from twenty-one countries, from multiple time periods, from various types of institution including banks, savings institutions, and insurance companies, and using various efficiency concepts and measurement methods. It appears that the average inefficiency in banking ranges between 20 and 25 per cent of total costs. Berger, Hancock and Humphrey (1993) find that larger banks are more efficient. However, since there are large disparities between banks of similar size, they indicate that the way individual banks are run is much more important than their form of organization or size as such. These data, however, mostly cover US banks and make no explicit distinction between universal and non-universal banks. One of the few European studies compares the efficiency of banks in Norway, Sweden and Finland. Berg *et al.* (1993) find that Swedish banks are generally more efficient than Norwegian and Finnish banks. All of these countries have universal banking. Allen and Rai (1996) document wide variations in country-specific efficiency for 194 banks in fifteen countries. They also find that large banks in separated banking countries (that is, countries that prohibit the integration of commercial and investment banking) are significantly less efficient than other bank groups for the period 1988–92. In a review article, Benston (1994) concludes that the data on economies of scale and scope and X-efficiency indicate some advantage for universal banks over specialized banks. However, considering that specialized banks are able to survive in direct competition with universal banks, the author concedes that the efficiency advantages of neither form of banking appear to be overwhelming. Clearly, a more direct assessment of efficiency in universal versus non-universal banks is needed.

Next to potential cost advantages, a more efficient combination of financial products and services may also entail revenue gains. The ability for conglomerate financial services providers to market and distribute the full range of banking, securities and insurance services may increase their earnings potential. On the demand side, customers may value a bundled supply of financial services more highly than dispersed offers by separate firms for reasons of transaction and information costs. Canals (1993) finds that the increased revenues obtained from new business units have contributed significantly to improving bank performance in recent times. Gallo, Apilado and Kolari (1996) find that mutual fund activities also increase the profitability of banks. Moreover, the combination of banking, insurance and securities activities may lead to a more stable profit stream, since the revenues stemming from different products in a conglomerate organization are usually imperfectly correlated. Saunders and Walter (1994) find that expanding banks' activities reduces risk, with the main risk-reduction gains arising from insurance rather than securities activities. Boyd, Graham and Hewitt (1993) find that simulated mergers of bank holding companies (BHCs) with life insurance or property/casualty insurance firms may reduce risk, but that mergers of BHCs with securities firms would likely increase risk. Benston (1989) reports that returns for combined commercial and investment banking would be significantly higher, without a compensating increase in overall risk.

A full universal bank may also optimize the efficiency of the information exchange with corporate customers. Financial intermediaries deal with incomplete and asymmetric information by becoming delegated monitors (Diamond 1984). In a bank-based corporate finance system, the information flowing from firms to banks is often produced through multiple contacts within the framework of a long-term lender–borrower relationship. Hence, relationship banks should have an informational advantage in the monitoring of moral hazard. Empirically, it has been observed that companies may benefit because bank monitoring may overcome problems of financial constraints and asymmetric information (see James 1987, James and Wier 1990, Lummer and McConnell 1990). In a universal bank system, the bank–firm relationship can be enhanced by adding finance-related services (issuing and placement of securities, advisory services, risk management facilities, guarantees and contingent credit lines). Once the banker also becomes a shareholder, sometimes including a presence on the board of directors, the full insider status should perfect information flows even further. Monitoring then becomes a variable cost to the bank (Steinherr and Huveneers 1994). Using data for banks in eight countries (including German, Dutch and Swiss universal banks), Dewenter and Hess (1998) find evidence that the equity market risk of transactional banks relative to relationship banks rises during economic contractions. These results support the notion that relationship banks monitor moral hazard more effectively than transactional banks.

Definition of conglomerates and universal banks

Based on the previous discussion, it is necessary to classify European banks into more or less homogeneous categories in order to allow meaningful comparisons between specialized financial institutions and their more diversified competitors. However, banks have not been classified as universal based on their country of origin, because even in countries permitting universality, many banks opt to remain (or become) specialized. As an alternative, the basic sample of European banks has been regrouped according to three criteria:

1   the degree of diversification (diversified versus specialized banks)
2   the degree of conglomeration (financial conglomerates versus specialized banks)
3   the degree of universality (universal versus specialized banks).

The actual classification of each bank depends on its type of corporate organization, and on a number of financial indicators derived from its annual statement.

Obviously, the legal environment in which banks operate determines the organizational forms which they can adopt. The liberalization of the range of activities in which banks can engage, either directly or through ownership stakes, has been most fully achieved in the EU. Both the remaining legal distinctions between various types of credit institutions (such as commercial banks, savings banks and credit unions) and the legal demarcations between commercial banking, securities business and insurance have been abolished by the Second Banking Directive enacted in 1989. As a result, banks can perform securities and insurance activities directly or through subsidiaries. The directive also regulates the holding of equity stakes in non-financial enterprises. Yet despite regulatory harmonization, the corporate structure of financial services companies still differs across countries, mainly reflecting historical differences (Borio and Filosa 1994).[1] There are roughly three organizational ways of combining commercial banking, investment banking and insurance:

1   in house, via a department of the bank
2   via a separately capitalized subsidiary of the bank
3   via a separately capitalized affiliate of the bank holding company (see Saunders and Walter 1994).

A fully-fledged financial conglomerate would combine banking, insurance and securities activities as in-house departments. Contrary to conventional wisdom, German universal banks do not conform to this type. They conduct only their merchant banking and securities operations in-house, while insurance, mortgage banking and investment funds are usually supplied through affiliate companies. Moreover, many German banks do not in practice carry out the full range of universal banking business (Edwards and Fischer 1994). The same is true for other countries in which universal banking is legally allowed.

As a result, the classification of banks should not be based on their country of origin or their institutional type. The preferred approach in this research was to delineate banks by their revealed degree of functional diversification and universality, based on observed organizational and financial characteristics. Three major areas of financial services were distinguished: traditional banking, insurance, and securities-related activities. Specialized banks were defined as those mainly engaged in traditional intermediation activities. Financial conglomerates were defined as financial services firms which conduct at least two of the three activities. While some operations may be exercised through a subsidiary, the criterion was that the parent institution should consolidate non-traditional bank activities in its annual statement. Conglomeration is thus associated with the potential conduct of a range of financial services comprising deposit-taking and lending, trading of financial instruments and their derivatives, underwriting of new debt and equity issues, brokerage, investment management, and insurance. Universal banks were defined as diversified banking institutions that also hold equity stakes in non-financial companies. This definition follows Steinherr and Huveneers (1994) who assert that the key feature of universal banking is the range of activities and, in particular, the holding of equity shares large enough to monitor corporations as an equity owner.[2]

Operationally, a bank was classified as diversified (DB) when the ratio of non-interest income to total revenues exceeded 15 per cent. In the European setting, this threshold effectively disentangles structurally diversified banks from specialized ones, those that engage occasionally in non-traditional banking activities, and those that have undertaken diversification efforts only recently. It is argued that the proportion of non-interest income in total revenues is a useful indicator of relative diversification, because the fee-income earned on non-traditional banking activities such as insurance and securities trading is registered as non-interest income in the annual statements.

A financial institution was labelled a financial conglomerate (FC) when two conditions were met. First, the bank is engaged in non-traditional banking through an in-house department, or consolidates at least one subsidiary active in investment banking and/or insurance. For this type of bank, the existence of a group structure, fully integrated or not, is the main feature. This condition was checked for each bank, based on an in-depth analysis of its organizational structure in the annual statement. Second, the ratio of non-interest income in total revenues should exceed 20 per cent. This diversification threshold was added to ensure that the non-traditional banking activities are considered by the management as strategically important. Because of the strictness of these criteria, only 176 banks fulfilled both and were classified as conglomerates.[3]

Finally, universal banks (UB) were defined as those institutions in which equity stakes in non-financial companies account for more than 1 per cent of total assets.[4] Moreover, it was a criterion that universal banks should have a ratio of non-interest income in total revenues higher than 5 per cent. This minimum diversification threshold was chosen to ensure that activities for which information advantages are expected to be present (underwriting, risk management, and other fee business) were effectively undertaken by the bank. Consistent with regulatory practice, no distinction was made according to institutional type. Hence, all subsamples could consist of a mixture of commercial banks, cooperative banks, savings institutions, and government-owned banks. Table 8.1 lists the various samples subdivided by country.

The full sample consisted of 2,375 EU banks from seventeen countries, for which all the variables were available from their published annual statements for the years 1995 and 1996.[5] Together, these banks cover more than

Table 8.1 European banks subdivided according to their degree of diversification, conglomeration and universality. Number of banks in each category and their country of origin

	Degree of diversification			Degree of conglomeration		Degree of universality	
	Total	Diversified banks	Specialized banks	Financial conglomerates	Specialized banks	Universal banks	Specialized banks
Austria	71	24	47	14	57	62	9
Belgium	99	13	86	7	92	28	71
Denmark	95	22	73	13	82	83	12
Finland	9	6	3	4	5	4	5
France	269	141	228	31	338	166	203
Germany	586	42	544	23	563	436	150
Greece	17	3	14	5	12	4	13
Ireland	21	5	16	2	19	2	19
Italy	236	75	161	22	214	85	151
Luxembourg	118	19	99	4	114	8	110
Netherlands	55	13	42	10	45	14	41
Norway	32	3	29	2	30	6	26
Portugal	41	12	29	2	39	6	35
Spain	168	32	136	16	152	48	120
Sweden	25	7	18	3	22	2	23
Switzerland	298	151	147	4	294	82	216
UK	135	65	70	14	121	30	105
Totals	2,375	633	1,742	176	2,199	1,066	1,309

85 per cent of aggregated bank assets in their countries. Average values for 1995–6 were used in order to alleviate the effect of idiosyncratic events. All nominal amounts were converted into ECUs.[6] The choice of the time period was motivated by the fact that universal banking has been allowed at least since 1993 onwards in all EU countries. In many member states, however, conglomeration and/or universal banking have a longer tradition. As a consequence, if a bank was identified as a conglomerate or a universal bank in 1995–6, this should reflect a deliberate strategic choice for which sufficient financial and managerial resources have been mobilized. The 1995–6 period was also relatively neutral with respect to the macroeconomic environment, since banks were facing more or less similar business cycle and monetary policy conditions across all countries. The bank crises that occurred in a number of countries at the beginning of the 1990s were also largely resolved.[7] This is important because loan quality and loan losses may affect observed efficiency and profit levels, but the data did not permit us to control for the bank's asset quality.

Methodology

The aim of this contribution is to investigate whether or not it is possible to find structural efficiency differences between universal banks, financial conglomerates, diversified banks, and their more specialized competitors in the EU. The theoretical considerations elaborated in both previous sections suggest a number of testable hypotheses related to cost and revenue effects of conglomeration, and the competitive viability of specialized versus universal banks. Hence revenue and profit dynamics were analysed, based on an estimation of stochastic cost and profit functions.

First, it was postulated that there might be differences between specialized and non-specialized banks with respect to production technology and operational efficiency. To test this conjecture a cost function was estimated for the different types of banks, and examined to discover whether there were systematic differences in terms of operational efficiency.

Cost efficiency provides a measure of how close a bank's actual cost is to what a best-practice institution's cost would be for producing an identical output bundle under comparable conditions. The measure is usually derived from a cost function in which costs depend on the prices of inputs (p), the quantities of outputs (y), risk or other factors that may affect performance (z), and an error term (ε). The function can be written as $C = f(p,y,z) + \varepsilon$, in which ε is treated as a composite error term $\varepsilon = u+v$, where v represents standard statistical noise and u captures inefficiency. In the parametric methods, a bank is labelled inefficient if its costs are higher than a best-practice bank after removing random error. The methods differ in the way u is disentangled from the composite error term ε. This research used the stochastic cost frontier as proposed by Aigner, Lovell and Schmidt (1977). In general, the non-parametric methods are less suitable because they assume away noise in the data and luck. But for this purpose, the most important drawback was that these methods generally ignore prices, and thus can only account for technical inefficiency related to using excessive inputs or producing sub-optimal output levels. As Berger and Mester (1997) observe, these methods cannot compare firms that tend to specialize in different inputs or outputs, because it is impossible to compare input and output configurations without the benefit of relative prices. Moreover, Berger and Mester (1997) use the distribution-free approach as well as the stochastic frontier approach for both the translog and the Fourier specification of the cost and profit function. They conclude that the choices made concerning efficiency measurement make very little difference to the empirical findings, in terms of either average industry efficiency or ranking of individual banks, the topics of the exercise described here.

The random error term (v) is assumed to be normally distributed and the inefficiency term (u) is assumed to be one-sided. Both the half-normal and the exponential distribution were tried, but since the results were similar, only those based on the half-normal distribution are reported. The inefficiency factor (u) incorporates both allocative inefficiencies from failure to react optimally to changes in relative input prices, and technical inefficiencies from employing too much of the inputs to produce the observed output bundle.

The log-likelihood function is given by

$$InL = \frac{N}{2}\ln\frac{2}{\pi} - N\ln\sigma - \frac{1}{2\sigma^2}\sum_{i=1}^{N}\varepsilon_i^2 + \sum_{i=1}^{N}\ln\left[\phi\left(\frac{\varepsilon_i\lambda}{\sigma}\right)\right] \qquad (1)$$

where

$$\varepsilon_i = u_i + v_i, \sigma^2 = \sigma_u^2 + \sigma_v^2, \lambda = \sigma_u/\sigma_v \qquad (2)$$

N is the number of banks and $\phi(.)$ is the standard normal cumulative distribution function. Jondrow *et al.* (1982) show that bank-specific estimates of inefficiency can be obtained as the mean of the conditional distribution:[8]

$$E(u_i\varepsilon_i) = \left(\frac{\sigma_u\sigma_v}{\sigma}\right)\left[\frac{\phi\left(\frac{\varepsilon_i\lambda}{\sigma}\right)}{\Phi\left(\frac{\varepsilon i\lambda}{\sigma}\right)} + \frac{\varepsilon_i\lambda}{\sigma}\right] \qquad (3)$$

A Farrell-type measure of operational efficiency can be calculated as:

$$CEFF = e^{-u_i} \qquad (4)$$

A CEFF score of 0.8 would mean that the bank is using 80 per cent of its resources efficiently, or alternatively wastes 20 per cent of its costs relative to a best-practice bank.

For the functional form of f(p,y,z) both the standard translog and the Fourier-flexible specification were tried (see McAllister and McManus 1992, Mitchell and Onvural 1996, Berger and Mester 1997). The Fourier functional form augments the translog by including Fourier trigonometric terms. It is a global approximation because the sin and cos terms are mutually orthogonal, so that each term aids in fitting the function closer to the true path of the data. But while formal tests indicate that the Fourier terms are jointly significant, the statistical fit, the average level and dispersion of efficiency, and the bank rankings are very similar for both functional forms. Hence, the results reported here are those for the following translog specification:

$$\ln C = a_o + \sum_i a_i \ln y_i + \sum_j b_j \ln p_j + \frac{1}{2}\sum_i\sum_j c_{ij}\ln y_i\ln y_j + \frac{1}{2}\sum_i\sum_j d_{ij}\ln p_i\ln p_j \qquad (5)$$

$$+ \sum_i\sum_j g_{ij}\ln y_i\ln p_j + f_z\ln z + \frac{1}{2}h_{zz}\ln z\ln z + \sum_j k_{zj}\ln z\ln y_j + \sum_j m_{zj}\ln z\ln p_j$$

where C is total costs, y_i the output quantities, p_j the input prices and z is financial capital. Consistent with the research topic two specifications were examained with a different set of outputs. The first specification is based on the intermediation approach and uses two traditional banking outputs (loans and securities) and three input prices (the cost of labour, physical capital and deposits). The price of labour is obtained by dividing salaries and other personnel expenses by the number of employees. The cost of fixed capital is calculated as depreciation and occupancy expenses divided by net fixed assets. The price of deposits is the ratio of interest expenses over interest-bearing liabilities. However, since the study concerned financial institutions that have expanded their scope beyond commercial bank activities, an estimate was also made for a specification where traditional and non-traditional banking activities were treated as outputs, measured, respectively, as total interest income and total non-interest revenues. In this estimation output quantities were replaced by revenue flows. Although this treatment is not standard in the literature, there is no known better alternative for adequately including non-banking activities in the cost function. In both specifications financial capital was included, to capture default risk and the risk preferences of bank management (see Mester 1996, Berger and Mester 1997). In all estimations the usual symmetry and linear homogeneity restrictions were imposed a priori.

The next step was to analyse the behaviour of the various bank types with respect to potential scale and scope economies. Scale economies were computed as:

$$\text{SCALE} = \sum_{i=1}^{2} \frac{\delta \ln C}{\delta \ln y_i} + \frac{\delta \ln C}{\delta \ln z} \tag{6}$$

This measure was calculated with the mean values of inputs and outputs in various size classes. An estimate of SCALE less than, equal to or greater than 1 indicates, respectively, scale economies, no economies or diseconomies of scale.

The conventional measures of scope economies consider the cost differential associated with a division of a given output mix into specialist banks. However, a more realistic scenario is that a large financial firm faces competition from smaller ones with a different product mix, although none of the outputs is actually equal to zero. Since this research focused on competitive viability, the approach of Berger, Hanweck and Humphrey (1987) was adopted. They call a bank competitively viable if no other set of banks with different scales and/or output mixes could jointly produce the same product mix at lower, scale-adjusted, costs. They limit their comparison to 'representative firms' located at the means of a number of size classes. In this research two measures were calculated for scope economies. The first one was an indicator of within-sample scope economies calculated as (see Mester 1996):

$$\text{SCOPE} = (C(y_1 - y_1^m, y_2^m) + C(y_1^m, y_2 - y_2^m) - C(y_1, y_2))/C(y_1, y_2) \qquad (7)$$

where y^m is the minimum value of y_i in the sample and $C(.)$ is the predicted cost of producing an output bundle at the average input prices. Thus, SCOPE measures the percentage cost increase (decrease) of dividing up the outputs into relatively specialized institutions, but none more specialized than the most specialized in the sample. This procedure avoids having to extrapolate outside the sample (in fact, none of the banks in the sample was fully specialized). A positive SCOPE estimate would indicate the existence of within-sample scope economies.

Another possibility for investigating the existence of diversification effects is the cost subadditivity measure introduced by Berger, Hanweck and Humphrey (1987). Assume that bank A has the choice between increasing its business to B along a given expansion path, expanding its activities through an existing network, or setting up a new branch, C. Expansion path subadditivity (EPSUB) can be measured as:

$$\text{EPSUB}(B) = (C(y^A) + C(y^C) - C(y^B))/C(y^B) \qquad (8)$$

where $y^A(y^B)$ is the output bundle produced by bank A(B), and the output of the hypothetical bank C is the difference of the output vectors of banks B and A. The measure gives the relative cost increase or decrease from producing bank B's outputs in bank A and the complementary bank C. Positive (negative) values of EPSUB suggest the presence of potential economies (diseconomies) of scope. If EPSUB >0 it would be more cost effective for bank A to expand through the establishment of a new office C (or acquire C).

A complementary type of analysis focuses on the alleged superiority of financial conglomerates and universal banks in terms of revenue efficiency. As was argued earlier, diversification into non-traditional bank activities may increase the revenue-generating capacity of conglomerates, while relationship-specific advantages could increase both the interest and non-interest revenues of universal banks. These conjectures were analysed by estimating a profit function for the various types of banks. As in the parametric cost function approach, a bank is labelled inefficient if its profits are lower than the best-practice bank after removing random error. In other words, profit efficiency measures how close a bank comes to generating the maximum obtainable profit, given input prices and outputs. This research used the concept of alternative profit efficiency introduced by Berger and Mester (1997), which relates profit to input prices and output quantities instead of output prices. This specification was chosen for modelling European bank profitability because:

1   output prices cannot be measured accurately because of data unavailability
2   there may be differences in the quality of banking services

3 output markets may not be perfectly competitive, so that banks can
   exercise some degree of market power.

Condition 2 is particularly relevant to the research topic of this paper,
because service quality may be one of the means by which specialized and
non-specialized banks try to distinguish themselves from each other. If
customers are willing to pay for high-quality services, these banks should
be able to earn higher revenues that compensate for any excess expenditures, and still remain competitively viable. The occurrence of condition 3
cannot be ruled out, because there is empirical evidence indicating that a
number of European banking markets may be characterized by less than
perfect competition (Vander Vennet 1994b).

Consequently, the profit function is specified in a similar way as the cost
function. The dependent variable is $\ln(\pi + |\pi^{min}| + 1)$, where $|\pi^{min}|$ is the
absolute value of the minimum level of π in the appropriate subsample.
Since a constant term $|\pi^{min}| + 1$ is added to every bank's profits, the natural
log is taken of a positive number. This adjustment is necessary since a
number of banks in the sample exhibited negative profits in the sample
period. The dependent variable is $\ln(1) = 0$ for the bank with the lowest
value of π. Profits π are calculated as all interest and non-interest earnings
minus interest and operating costs, excluding any extraordinary items.
The explanatory variables remain unaltered. Consistent with the research
topic, the results for the specification are reported based on the output
mix combining traditional and non-traditional bank activities. This
produces a measure of profit efficiency for all banks in the sample. A PEFF
of 0.8 means that a bank is actually earning 80 per cent of best-practice
profits, or that the bank is losing 20 per cent of possible profits owing to
excessive costs, deficient revenues, or both.

Results

The cost and profit functions were estimated for the whole sample and for
the various subgroups. Both the translog and the Fourier-flexible versions
were estimated for the two specifications of the cost function (intermediation approach and traditional/non-traditional banking activities) and for
the alternative profit function. In most cases, test statistics indicated that
the Fourier terms were jointly significant, but both the statistical fit and the
calculated levels of inefficiency were very similar for both functional forms.
Hence, only cost indicators derived from the translog stochastic frontier
are reported here.

For both the cost and profit function, the linear homogeneity
conditions were imposed during estimation by normalizing the costs and
inputs by the last input price (deposits).[9] For the stochastic frontier
approach to yield meaningful estimates of efficiency, the residuals must
have the appropriate skew. This turned out to be the case, with a positive

skew for costs and a negative one for profits. The R^2 values were larger for the cost functions (between 0.85 and 0.93) than for the profit functions (between 0.30 to 0.45). Berger and Mester (1997) report similar differences. Apparently, there are factors beyond input prices, output composition and the level of financial capital that systematically affect bank profits.

Cost and profit efficiency were calculated for the specialized and non-specialized samples relative to a common efficient frontier. This allowed a comparison of average efficiency scores for the various subgroups based on t-tests. The estimated coefficients of the frontiers were used to compare efficiency across size classes within each subsample. The actual delimitation of the size classes, while inherently arbitrary, was chosen to ensure a reasonable distribution of the banks across size categories. Nine size classes were considered for the specialized banks, and seven categories for the non-specialized ones, because of the relatively small numbers of observations in the smallest size classes.

The average cost inefficiency for the entire sample of European banks turned out to be on the order of 30 per cent for the functional specification including traditional intermediation outputs. It was somewhat lower, around 20 per cent, when bank outputs were defined as interest and non-interest revenues. The inefficiency levels found in this study are broadly consistent with inefficiencies of 20 per cent or more of total banking industry costs that were reported in surveys by Berger and Humphrey (1997) and by Molyneux, Altunbas and Gardener (1996) for several European bank markets. Hence, the consensus seems to be that, if the average European bank were to use its inputs as efficiently as the best practice institutions, it would be able to reduce its production costs by a non-negligible fraction. However, whereas Berger and Mester (1997) found that average cost inefficiency in US banks tended to decrease in the early 1990s (to about 13 per cent), the results here failed to reveal a similar trend in European banking. Hence, the ongoing restructuring in European banking will need to focus further on improvements of operational efficiency levels. The recent wave of – often large – mergers in preparation for changing working conditions in an EMU environment may accelerate this trend. In the case of revenues, this research found inefficiency levels to be around 30 per cent. This suggests that European banks have less performance slack than the profit inefficiency of 50 per cent of profits reported by Berger and Mester (1997) for US banks in the 1990s. However, differences in the allowable functional scope of banks and different functional specifications may preclude a meaningful comparison.

Table 8.2 reports the average values of cost and profit efficiency for the different bank types, relative to a common frontier. The mean efficiency levels are calculated against a common benchmark, allowing statistical tests of cross-type differences. First, the efficiency of specialized versus non-specialized banks was examined for each of the three classifications. For the

Table 8.2 Cost efficiency of European banks subdivided according to their degree of diversification, conglomeration, and universality. The efficiency estimates are based on a stochastic cost function, assuming a common technology for all banks. Data are 1995–6 averages

	Degree of diversification			Degree of conglomeration			Degree of universality		
	DB	SB	DB–SB*	FC	SB	FC–SB*	UB	SB	UB–SB*
Cost function with traditional banking activities as outputs									
Average cost									
efficiency	65.5	70.2	-4.7	68.2	70.8	-2.6	73.6	68.0	5.6
Std. dev'n	15.50	10.70	7.04	13.00	15.10	2.52	11.20	16.90	9.66
Cost function with traditional and non-traditional banking activities as outputs									
Average cost									
efficiency	78.1	76.2	1.9	82.1	78.4	3.7	82.4	79.1	3.3
Std. dev'n	13.30	12.80	3.11	12.50	15.80	3.69	14.30	15.70	5.35
Profit function									
Average profit									
efficiency	67.9	68.8	-0.9	68.7	67.1	1.6	70.1	67.9	2.2
Std. dev'n	11.50	14.20	1.54	11.20	14.60	1.77	11.30	15.30	4.02
N	633	1,742		176	2,199		1,066	1,309	

Note: * Difference between specialized and non-specialized banks, standard deviations values are t-statistics assuming unequal variances

criterion of diversification, the numbers suggest that specialized banks are relatively more efficient in traditional intermediation (efficiency score of 71.5 versus 65.5, with a t-value of 7.04). On the other hand, diversified banks appear to be slightly more cost efficient for the combination of traditional interest-dependent bank activities and fee-business (the efficiency differential is 1.9 with a t-statistic of 3.11). For the criterion of conglomeration, the results are qualitatively similar. Specialized banks are more efficient in traditional intermediation activities (a significant difference of 2.6 points), while conglomerates appear to be better managed when non-traditional activities are also included. In terms of profit efficiency, financial conglomerates achieve a slightly higher average efficiency level than their specialized peers, and the difference is marginally significant (1.6 with a t-value of 1.77). For the criterion of universality, the evidence clearly points to an efficiency advantage for universal banks. For both specifications of the cost function, universal banks exhibit significantly higher average operational efficiency levels. They are also superior in terms of profit efficiency (the difference with specialized banks is 2.2 with a t-value of 4.02).

A number of cross-type comparisons also deserve some comment. First, the degree of dispersion of efficiency levels, measured as the standard deviation of individual bank efficiency scores, is usually lower for the non-specialized banks. This indicates that the non-specialized banks behave more similarly than the specialized ones. For the traditional intermediation activities, universal banks appear to possess a distinct cost advantage: their average efficiency level of 73.6 per cent is higher than that of the other subgroups. For the non-traditional banking activities, conglomerates and universal banks attain the highest average cost efficiency levels. This may indicate that technology spill-overs, cost synergies and managerial skill transfers are best achieved by a high degree of organizational integration. The diversified banks, defined as banks with reasonable levels of non-interest income but obtained in a loosely organized corporate structure, perform less well in this respect. On the other hand, it could be hypothesized that revenue synergies do not require full integration. The cross-selling and marketing of inter-company products might enhance the revenue-generating capacity of the banks, irrespective of the level of integration of the various departments. However, superior profit efficiency can be observed for universal banks and financial conglomerates, but not for diversified banks. Apparently, the organizational and managerial integration and the common strategic focus in financial conglomerates is a distinct advantage in the realization of revenue synergies. In the case of universal banks, the closer relationships they maintain with their corporate customers allow them to reap both cost and profit benefits.

The size distribution of efficiency was also examined for each subsample, again measured against a common frontier. The results are reported in Tables 8.3 to 8.5 for the different functional specifications. For the cost function with traditional bank outputs, Table 8.3 shows that cost

Table 8.3 Cost efficiency of European banks subdivided according to their degree of diversification, conglomeration, and universality. The estimates are based on a cost function with traditional banking activities as outputs, assuming a common technology for all banks. Data are 1995–6 averages

Size class (ECU bn)	Degree of diversification		Degree of conglomeration		Degree of universality	
	Diversified banks	Specialized banks	Financial conglomerates	Specialized banks	Universal banks	Specialized banks
>100	73.5	72.0	73.9	69.4	72.0	75.5
20–100	70.6	70.1	68.8	71.0	71.3	68.9
5–20	68.5	67.7	68.0	67.9	70.5	65.8
3–5	63.1	69.2	62.1	68.7	71.2	65.0
1–3	62.0	71.9	62.2	71.4	74.8	66.2
0.5–1	61.7	71.6	66.7	70.5	74.9	65.8
<0.5	62.5		69.3		75.2	
0.1–0.5		71.7		70.8		69.6
<0.1		78.3		77.8		77.7
Average	65.5	70.2	68.2	70.8	73.6	68.0
Std. devn.	10.7	15.5	13.0	15.1	11.2	16.9
N	633	1,742	176	2,199	1,066	1,309

Table 8.4 Cost efficiency of European banks subdivided according to their degree of diversification, conglomeration, and universality. The estimates are based on a cost function with traditional and non-traditional banking activities as outputs, assuming a common technology for all banks. Data are 1995–6 averages

Size class (ECU bn)	Degree of diversification		Degree of conglomeration		Degree of universality	
	Diversified banks	Specialized banks	Financial conglomerates	Specialized banks	Universal banks	Specialized banks
>100	84.3	78.5	85.9	78.6	80.6	79.0
20–100	80.0	83.3	81.6	81.8	82.1	81.0
5–20	81.0	80.4	81.9	80.0	83.2	80.5
3–5	82.1	76.0	82.5	74.2	83.5	80.3
1–3	83.5	77.8	84.1	79.4	85.6	81.8
0.5–1	81.7	80.1	82.4	80.5	85.0	79.9
<0.5	68.8		78.8		73.8	
0.1–0.5		74.2		76.5		78.5
<0.1		69.0		72.7		69.4
Average	78.1	76.2	82.1	78.4	82.4	79.1
Std. devn.	10.2	17.8	12.5	15.8	14.3	15.7

efficiency is largely unrelated to size for the specialized banks. In the group of diversified banks, the larger banks seems to be more efficient than their smaller competitors. Taken as a whole, the different size classes of universal banks appear to outperform their peers. A striking result is that in all three classifications, the very small specialized banks are relatively cost efficient. Hence, it can be predicted that small but efficient incumbent banks or new entrants will remain competitively viable from the point of view of cost

Table 8.5 Profit efficiency of European banks subdivided according to their degree of diversification, conglomeration, and universality. The estimates are based on a profit function with traditional and non-traditional banking activities as outputs, assuming a common technology for all banks. Data are 1995–6 averages

Size class (ECU bn)	Degree of diversification		Degree of conglomeration		Degree of universality	
	Diversified banks	Specialized banks	Financial conglomerates	Specialized banks	Universal banks	Specialized banks
>100	80.3	82.6	80.2	82.2	80.6	80.6
20–100	71.3	73.1	73.2	70.4	71.1	74.2
5–20	69.8	67.9	64.9	67.4	67.0	68.7
3–5	66.1	66.0	63.3	65.9	66.3	66.7
1–3	67.9	67.4	63.0	66.1	68.9	67.1
0.5–1	66.0	67.0	64.1	63.8	69.8	66.2
<0.5	66.1		62.5		65.8	
0.1–0.5		67.5		64.8		66.8
<0.1		63.3		64.1		63.4
Average	67.9	68.8	68.7	67.1	70.1	67.9
Std. devn.	11.5	14.2	11.2	14.6	11.3	15.3

efficiency in traditional intermediation. In the case of non-traditional bank activities (Table 8.4), it is clear that size does matter. The largest banks usually outperform their smaller competitors in terms of efficiency. In all cases, the smallest group of specialized banks turns out to be relatively inefficient. For universal banks, size appears to be relatively unimportant (except for the smallest size class), hence the way individual banks are managed dominates. Table 8.5 presents the results for the profit function. Here again, the results indicate that the quality of management may be closely related to size, for both specialized and non-specialized banks. Especially the megabanks (assets over 100 billion ECU) appear to be relatively profit efficient.

The results on cost efficiency can be compared with those reported by Allen and Rai (1996). They find an average cost inefficiency based on a stochastic frontier for banks in separated banking countries of 21.1 per cent. For large banks inefficiency amounted to 27.5 per cent, while for small banks the corresponding number is 15.6 per cent. Inefficiencies in universal banks were found to be around 15 per cent, for both large and small banks. The results here for universal versus specialized banks suggest somewhat larger cost inefficiencies for both universal and specialized banks, but the results depend on the specification of the cost function (intermediation versus non-traditional banking activities, see Table 8.2). It was also found in this research that the difference in terms of cost efficiency between small and large universal banks was relatively low, while it was somewhat more pronounced for specialized banks, but not as high as reported by Allen and Rai. The differences are probably due to the use of different samples.

Tables 8.6 and 8.7 report the scale economies, scope economies and cost subadditivity measure evaluated at the mean output, input price and financial capital levels for the different bank types. The cost frontier parameters are used to measure output efficiency net of any input inefficiencies. The cost measures indicate whether a bank could lower costs proportionately by changing its output level, its input mix, or both. SCALE measures the relative cost increase caused by a proportionate increase of the output vector for the different size classes. The results should be interpreted with care, because the scale measures are based on different cost function estimates.

The results on scale economies are similar for the two specifications of the cost function and across the various bank types. In general, fairly large unexploited scale economies were identified for the small banks, especially the specialized ones. For universal banks and financial conglomerates, there were neither scale benefits nor disadvantages, except for the very large ones. This is consistent with the results of Allen and Rai (1996). The translog produces a symmetric U-shape for the cost frontier, possibly causing measured scale diseconomies on the large banks. However, re-estimation with the more flexible Fourier function

Table 8.6 Scale economies, within-sample scope economies and expansion path subadditivity for European banks subdivided according to their degree of diversification, conglomeration and universality. The estimates are based on a cost function with traditional banking activities as outputs

Banks subdivided according to the degree of diversification

Size class***	Diversified banks			Specialized banks		
	Scale	Scope	EPSUB	Scale	Scope	EPSUB
> 100	1.12	-10.2 *	-7.8 *	1.07 *	-9.5 *	-7.5 *
20–100	1.03	-6.4 *	-4.7	1.01	-3.4 -	4.7
10–20	0.99	0.1 -	1.8	0.98	-0.2	-3.6
5–10	0.96	1.5	-1.4	0.98	1.1	-0.8
3–5	0.95	4.8 -	1.1	0.98	3.1	0.2
1–3	0.92	6.9 *	1.3	0.97 *	4.8 *	1.9
0.5–1	0.84	9.8 *	4.3 *	0.95 *	6.5 *	5.7 *
< 0.5	0.81	—				
0.1–0.5				0.95 *	7.1 *	14.2 **
< 0.1				0.95 *	—	—

Banks subdivided according to the degree of conglomeration

Size class***	Financial conglomerates			Specialized banks		
	Scale	Scope	EPSUB	Scale	Scope	EPSUB
> 100	1.09	6.5 *	4.8	1.07	-10.1 *	-7.2*
20–100	1.06	2.8	0.3	1.00	-4.8	-3.5
10–20	1.02	0.6	-1.7	0.98	-1.3	-1.5
5–10	1.03	-0.3	-3.7	0.99	1.2	-2.8
3–5	1.01	-1.6	-1.3	0.97	2.7	0.5
1–3	1.01	-0.5	0.4	0.96 *	5.2 *	1.9
0.5–1	1.00	1.8	0.1 *	0.96 *	7.0 *	10.4**
< 0.5	1.00	— —				
0.1–0.5				0.95 *	11.1 **	17.8**
< 0.1				0.93 *	—	—

Banks subdivided according to the degree of universality

Size class***	Universal banks			Specialized banks		
	Scale	Scope	EPSUB	Scale	Scope	EPSUB
> 100	1.09	25.1 **	-7.8	1.06 *	-1.7	-8.1 *
20–100	1.03	13.8 *	-5.0	0.99	-0.4	-4.4
10–20	0.99	6.3 *	-3.6	0.98	3.5	-3.8
5–10	1.00	3.7	-3.1	0.97	2.6	-0.6
3–5	0.98	2.1	-0.2	0.96 *	7.5 *	-0.2
1–3	0.98	1.1	1.6	0.94 *	10.7 *	2.5
0.5–1	0.98	4.3	3.8	0.93 *	17.7 **	7.2 *
< 0.5	0.96	—	—			
0.1–0.5				0.92 *	25.3 **	15.2 **
< 0.1				0.91 *	—	—

Notes:
*, **   indicate significance at the 5% or 1% level
***   billions of 1996 ECU, total assets

Table 8.7 Scale economies, within-sample scope economies and expansion path subadditivity for European banks subdivided according to their degree of diversification, conglomeration and universality. The estimates are based on a cost function with traditional and non-traditional banking activities as outputs

Banks subdivided according to the degree of diversification

Size class***	Diversified banks			Specialized banks		
	Scale	Scope	EPSUB	Scale	Scope	EPSUB
> 100	1.10	10.2*	5.6	1.08 *	5.6	-6.8
20–100	1.03	4.9	10.2 *	1.04	-4.3	-12.3 *
10–20	0.99	-2.3	4.8	1.02	-4.9	-7.2
5–10	0.96	-5.6	-1.3	1.00	-4.1	-4.3
3–5	0.95	-3.5	-3.5	0.99	-3.6	-6.5
1–3	0.94	2.1	-8.9	0.99	-0.2	-5.1
0.5–1	0.93 **	8.8*	-1.3	0.98	1.5	-3.1
< 0.5	0.91	—	—			
0.1–0.5				0.96 *	3.1	6.5 *
< 0.1				0.95 *	—	—

Banks subdivided according to the degree of conglomeration

Size class***	Financial conglomerates			Specialized banks		
	Scale	Scope	EPSUB	Scale	Scope	EPSUB
> 100	1.10	15.2 *	-6.9	1.06	7.2*	4.8
20–100	1.06	8.9 *	-5.4	1.01	1.7	3.1
10–20	1.04	5.3	-4.1	0.99	-0.7	1.2
5–10	1.04	2.1	-1.8	0.99	-4.8	-2.5
3–5	1.02	2.8	-4.2	0.97	-6.8	-5.3
1–3	1.01	-2.7	-3.1	0.97	-7.0	-4.9
0.5–1	1.00	-7.3 *	-2.7	0.96 *	-4.6	-9.2 *
< 0.5	0.99	—	—			
0.1–0.5				0.94 *	6.7 *	-6.1
< 0.1				0.94 *	—	—

Banks subdivided according to the degree of universality

Size class***	Universal banks			Specialized banks		
	Scale	Scope	EPSUB	Scale	Scope	EPSUB
> 100	1.09	6.8*	-4.9	1.02	11.8 *	-6.9 *
20–100	1.06	1.5	-5.4	0.99	3.5	-4.9
10–20	1.04	-1.2	-2.2	0.99	-0.6	-2.1
5–10	1.02	-1.8	2.8	0.99	-2.2	-1.3
3–5	1.00	-2.3	-3.9	0.98	-5.7	-3.5
1–3	0.99	-1.5	-2.1	0.98	-1.4	2.3
0.5–1	1.00	6.5*	5.4 *	0.96 *	1.6	7.6 *
< 0.5	0.98	—	—	0.94 *	—	—
0.1–0.5						
< 0.1						

Notes:
*, **   indicate significance at the 5% or 1% level
***   billions of 1996 ECU, total assets

reduced the estimated scale diseconomies for the largest size class towards unity, but did not eliminate them. For both specialized and non-specialized banks, the size for which the scale estimate does not exceed unity extends to the ECU 10–100 billion range. This finding would suggest that the bank sizes for which no diseconomies are found are higher than in the 1980s, a finding that was also reported for US banks by Berger and Mester (1997).

The scope economy estimates measure cost efficiency gains to be made by a bank's changing its output mix. The spreading of fixed costs such as branch offices, computer equipment and customer information across several financial products and services would constitute the most likely rationale for such gains, if any. The approximate standard errors for scope and expansion path subadditivity (EPSUB) are based on Fuller (1962). The results should be interpreted with great caution in view of the inherent drawbacks of the translog function. In general unexploited scope economies were found for the smallest size categories, which are larger and more often significant for specialized than for non-specialized banks. This is consistent with Lang and Welzel (1996) who found scope economies for small German cooperative banks. For financial conglomerates, and even more so for universal banks, the scope results point to non-negligible possibilities for cost decreases due to joint production in the highest size classes. However, the scope results are only weakly supported by the expansion path subadditivity measure. An attempt was made to check the robustness of this finding by substituting lower values for y_m in the scope estimates for the size categories above 20 billion ECU. This produced somewhat lower estimates of scope economies but did not eliminate them. These results differ from those reported by Allen and Rai (1996) who found no scope economies for universal and separated banks.

Conclusions

Non-specialized banking involves a highly complex set of interrelated costs and benefits. This paper focuses on the alleged superiority of financial conglomerates and universal banks in terms of cost and profit efficiency. For financial conglomerates, the potential advantage is hypothesized to originate in the operational integration of banking, insurance and securities-related activities under one roof. In the case of universal banks, the higher degree of efficiency may be related to positive externalities associated with the combination of equity investments and banking and corporate finance activities. Therefore European banks were subdivided according to their degree of diversification, conglomeration and universality. This classification was based not on the banks' country affiliation but on their organizational structure and the observed mix of income sources. The empirical analysis presents new evidence on cost and profit efficiency for a large sample of European banks covering the period 1995–6. This period is well suited for this investigation because the Second Banking

Directive has allowed European banks to pursue a strategy of conglomeration or universality, and because the macroeconomic environment was relatively neutral in these years.

The main findings can be summarized as follows. In terms of cost efficiency, specialized banks appear to exhibit no disadvantage relative to diversified banks or financial conglomerates in traditional intermediation activities. However, the latter are more cost efficient when non-traditional banking activities are taken into account. Universal banks are characterized by significantly higher average levels of operational efficiency relative to specialized banks. They also dominate their non-universal competitors in terms of profit efficiency. Part of the superior profit efficiency in universal banks is probably related to the comparative information advantage acquired through their corporate insider status. Both for cost and profit efficiency, size does seem to matter. Especially, the very large banks appear to outperform their smaller competitors in terms of revenue efficiency. In general, fairly large unexploited scale economies were found for the small banks, especially the specialized ones. For universal banks and financial conglomerates neither scale benefits nor disadvantages were found, except for the very large ones. The bank sizes for which no diseconomies were found are higher than reported for the 1980s. As a consequence, the continued expansion of financial conglomerates and universal banks in Europe, partly as a response to EMU, should lead to a more efficient financial system. The increasing competition should induce these banks to strengthen further their cost and profit efficiency. It is up to further research to determine the sources of the efficiency differences between various types of banks, and assess the impact of universality on bank-specific and systemic risk.

Notes

1   In most European countries, the ability to perform investment banking functions has been broadened since the mid-1980s. In Germany and several Nordic countries, few if any restrictions have existed. The deregulation of banking and insurance combinations has usually proceeded more slowly. The rules governing the production or the in-house provision of insurance services have usually been less flexible than those related to the distribution of insurance products, or ownership linkages between banks and insurance companies.

2   Allen and Gale (1995) distinguish between transactional and relationship banks. Relationship banks, such as the German, Dutch and Swiss main banks, provide both debt and equity financing to firms, have long-lasting ties with them, serve on corporate boards and remain committed in periods of financial distress.

3   Note that only bank-initiated conglomeration is considered, not insurance firms or investment banks expanding into banking. Borio and Filosa (1994) mention the existence of some 200 banking/insurance groups operating within the EU.

4   Universal banks have no incentive to hold all the shares of a company because of the potential loss in the case of bankruptcy. Moreover, equity investments

are counted as risk assets and are subject to capital adequacy rules. Equity stakes in the 5–20 per cent range seem to be optimal and, indeed, are observed in Japan and Germany (Steinherr and Huveneers 1994). Hence, using a threshold of total participations of more than 1 per cent of assets is a reasonable cut-off.

5 The countries are the EU member states (Austria, Belgium, Denmark, Finland, France, Germany, Greece, Ireland, Italy, Luxemburg, Netherlands, Portugal, Spain, Sweden, UK) plus Norway and Switzerland. Data for the variables described below are subject to error. All observations from the original sample in which one of the variables was more than 2.5 standard errors away from its mean value in that year were eliminated. This produced a sample of 2,375 financial institutions.

6 The exchange rates of the European countries *vis-à-vis* the ECU is traditionally much more stable than the US$ exchange rate. Over the period 1995–6 the average $/ECU rate was 1.27.

7 Except in a number of individual cases such as Crédit Lyonnais.

8 As Mester (1996) observes, the conditional mean is an unbiased but inconsistent estimator of u_i, since regardless of the number of observations, the variance of the estimator remains nonzero.

9 All quantity variables were also expressed as ratios of the capital variable z to control for heteroscedasticity. The efficiency results remained qualitatively unaltered.

Bibliography

Aigner, D., Lovell, K. and Schmidt, P. (1977) 'Formulation and Estimation of Stochastic Frontier Production Function Models', *Journal of Econometrics* 21–37.

Akella, S. R. and Greenbaum, S. I. (1988) 'Savings and Loan Ownership Structure and Expense-Preference', *Journal of Banking and Finance* (September): 419–37.

Allen, F. and Gale, D. (1995) 'A Welfare Comparison of Intermediaries and Financial Markets in Germany and the US', *European Economic Review* 39 (February): 179–209.

Allen, L. and Rai, A. (1996) 'Operational Efficiency in Banking: An International Comparison', *Journal of Banking and Finance* (May): 655–72.

Arnould, R. J. (1985) 'Agency Costs in Banking Firms: An Analysis of Expense Preference Behaviour', *Journal of Economics and Business* (May): 103–12.

Benston, G. J. (1989) 'The Federal Safety Net and the Repeal of the Glass–Steagall Act's Separation of Commercial and Investment Banking', *Journal of Financial Services Research* (October): 2: 287–306.

Benston, G. J. (1994) 'Universal Banking', *Journal of Economic Perspectives* (Summer): 8.3: 121–43.

Berg, S. A., Forsund, F. R., Hjalmarsson, L. and Suominen, M. (1993) 'Banking Efficiency in the Nordic Countries', *Journal of Banking and Finance* (April): 17: 371–88.

Berger, A. N., Hancock, D. and Humphrey, D. B. (1993) 'Bank Efficiency Derived from the Profit Function', *Journal of Banking and Finance* 17: 317–47.

Berger, A. N., Hanweck, G. A. and Humphrey, D. B. (1987) 'Competitive Viability in Banking. Scale, Scope, and Product Mix Economies', *Journal of Monetary Economics* (December): 501–20.

Berger, A. N. and Humphrey, D. B. (1991) 'The Dominance of Inefficiencies over Scale and Product Mix Economies in Banking', *Journal of Monetary Economics* 28: 117–48.

Berger, A. N. and Humphrey, D. B. (1997) 'Efficiency of Financial Institutions:

International Survey and Directions for Future Research', *European Journal of Operational Research* 98: 178–212.

Berger, A. N., Hunter, W. C. and Timme, S. G. (1993) 'The Efficiency of Financial Institutions: A Review of Research Past, Present and Future', *Journal of Banking and Finance* (April): 17: 221–49.

Berger, A. N. and Mester, L. J. (1997) 'Inside the Black Box: What Explains Differences in the Efficiencies of Financial Institutions', *Journal of Banking and Finance* (July): 21(7): 895–947.

Borio, C. E. V. and Filosa, R. (1994) 'The Changing Borders of Banking: Trends and Implications', *SUERF Papers on Monetary Policy and Financial Systems no. 19*, Société Universitaire Européenne de Recherches Financières .

Boyd, J. H., Graham, S. L. and Hewitt, R. S. (1993) 'Bank Holding Company Mergers with Nonbank Financial Firms: Effects on the Risk of Failure', *Journal of Banking and Finance* (February): 43–63.

Canals, J. (1993) *Competitive Strategies in European Banking*, Oxford University Press, Oxford.

Clark, J. A. (1988) 'Economies of Scale and Scope at Depository Financial Institutions: A Review of the Literature', *Federal Reserve Bank of Kansas City Economic Review* (September/October): 16–33.

Dewenter, K. L. and Hess, A. C. (1998) 'An International Comparison of Banks' Equity Returns', *Journal of Money, Credit, and Banking* (August): 2: 473–92.

Diamond, D. (1984) 'Financial Intermediation and Delegated Monitoring', *Review of Economic Studies* 51: 393–414.

Drake, L. (1992) 'Economies of Scale and Scope in UK Building Societies: An Application of the Translog Multiproduct Cost Function', *Applied Financial Economics* (December): 211–19.

Edwards, J. and Fischer, K. (1994) *Banks, Finance and Investment in Germany*, Cambridge University Press, Cambridge.

Fuller, W. A. (1962) 'Estimating the Reliability of Quantities Derived from Empirical Production Functions', *Journal of Farm Economics* (August): 82–99.

Gallo, J. G., Apilado, V. P. and Kolari, J. W. (1996) 'Commercial Bank Mutual Fund Activities: Implications for Bank Risk and Profitability', *Journal of Banking and Finance* (December): 1775–91.

Hardwick, P. (1990) 'Multi-Product Cost Attributes: A Study of UK Building Societies', *Oxford Economic Papers* (April): 446–61.

Hughes, J. P. and Mester, L. J. (1994) 'Accounting for the Demand for Financial Capital and Risk-taking in Bank Cost Functions', *Federal Reserve Bank of Philadelphia*, working paper.

Hunter, W. C., Timme, S. G. and Yang, W. K. (1990) 'An Examination of Cost Subadditivity and Multiproduct Production in Large US Banks', *Journal of Money, Credit, and Banking* (November): 504–25.

James, C. (1987) 'Some Evidence on the Uniqueness of Bank Loans', *Journal of Financial Economics* 19: 217–35.

James, C. and Wier, P. (1990) 'Borrowing Relationships, Intermediation and the Cost of Issuing Public Securities', *Journal of Financial Economics* 28: 149–71.

Jondrow, J., Lovell, C. A. K., Materov, I. S. and Schmidt, P. (1982) 'On the Estimation of Technical Inefficiency in the Stochastic Frontier Production Model', *Journal of Econometrics* 19: 233–8.

Kolari, J. and Zardkoohi, A. (1987) *Bank Costs, Structure and Performance*, D. C.

Heath, Lexington.

Lang, G. and Welzel, P. (1995) 'Technology and Cost Efficiency in Banking: A Thick Frontier Analysis of the German Banking Industry', *Discussion Paper no. 130*, University of Augsburg.

Lang, G. and Welzel, P. (1996) 'Efficiency and Technical Progress in Banking. Empirical Results for a Panel of German Cooperative Banks', *Journal of Banking and Finance* (July): 1003–23.

Lummer, S. L. and McConnell, J. J. (1990) 'Further Evidence on the Bank Lending Process and the Capital-Market Response to Bank Loan Agreements', *Journal of Financial Economics* 25: 99–122.

McAllister, P. H. and McManus, D. (1992) 'Resolving the Scale Efficiency Puzzle in Banking', *Journal of Banking and Finance* 17: 389–405.

Mester, L. J. (1992) 'Traditional and Nontraditional Banking: An Information-Theoretic Approach', *Journal of Banking and Finance* (June): 16: 545–66.

Mester, L. J. (1996) 'A Study of Bank Efficiency Taking into Account Risk-Preferences', *Journal of Banking and Finance* (July): 1025–45.

Mitchell, K. and Onvural, N.-M. (1996) 'Economies of Scale and Scope at Large Commercial Banks: Evidence from the Fourier Flexible Functional Form', *Journal of Money, Credit, and Banking* (May) 28(2): 178–99.

Molyneux, P., Altunbas, Y. and Gardener, E. (1996) *Efficiency in European Banking*, Wiley, Chichester.

Muldur, U. (1991) 'Echelle et gamme dans les marchés bancaires nationaux et globaux', *Revue d'Economie Financière* 17: 167–96.

Noulas, A. G., Ray, S. C. and Miller, S. M. (1990) 'Returns to Scale and Input Substitution for Large US Banks', *Journal of Money, Credit, and Banking* (February): 94–108.

Saunders, A. (1994) 'Banking and Commerce: An Overview of the Public Policy Issues, *Journal of Banking and Finance* 18 (January): 231–54.

Saunders, A. and Walter, I. (1994) *Universal Banking in the United States*, Oxford University Press, Oxford.

Shaffer, S. (1988) 'A Revenue-Restricted Cost Study of 100 Large Banks', mimeo, Federal Reserve Bank of New York.

Steinherr, A. and Huveneers, C. (1994) 'On the Performance of Differently Regulated Financial Institutions: Some Empirical Evidence', *Journal of Banking and Finance* 18 (March): 271–306.

Vander Vennet, R. (1994a) 'Economies of Scale and Scope in EC Credit Institutions', *Cahiers Economiques de Bruxelles* no. 144: 507–48.

Vander Vennet, R. (1994b) 'Concentration, Efficiency, and Entry Barriers as Determinants of EC Bank Profitability', *Journal of International Financial Markets, Institutions, and Money* 3/4: 21–46.

Vander Vennet, R. (1996) 'The Effect of Mergers and Acquisitions on the Efficiency and Profitability of EC Credit Institutions', *Journal of Banking and Finance* (November): 1531–58.

Commission 2

Challenges to monetary and supervisory authorities

9 Managing the euro in a tri-polar world

John Arrowsmith, Ray Barrell and Christopher Taylor

Introduction

Contrary to policymakers' ambitions for the euro, the widespread view among economists is that the new currency is likely to be less stable than its main national predecessors; see, for example, Kenen (1995), Alogoskoufis and Portes (1997), Bergsten (1997), and Begg, Giavazzi and Wyplosz (1998). (There is less agreement whether the euro will be an inherently strong or weak currency.) A number of factors are expected to contribute to euro instability, principally: the large size and relatively closed nature of the euro area, which suggests that, *ceteris paribus*, exchange rate variations will have a smaller impact on participating economies than before EMU, and so will matter less to them; the emphasis, enshrined in the treaty, on internal price stability as the ECB's primary objective, which suggests that monetary policy will give little weight to exchange-rate stability; and the non-availability of national exchange-rate adjustment for buffering shocks which have differential effects on participants' economies, implying that a heavy onus for coping with shocks will fall on the euro interest rate, with uncomfortable consequences for the exchange rate. Subsuming all these arguments is the worry that, if and when the euro develops into a global currency, it will prove to be at least as unstable as the dollar and yen have been, and further polarization might add to those instabilities.

Although these concerns appear widely shared, the arguments are not entirely clear-cut. As Bénassy-Quéré, Mojon and Pisani-Ferry (1997) have pointed out, it is important when discussing prospects for the euro to distinguish between transitional and long-run stages of EMU, between currency instability within Europe and externally, and between alternative régimes against which to compare EMU. The present paper focuses on exchange rate stability between EU currencies and the key non-European currencies, mainly in a long-run context (assuming that the euro is successfully established as a credible low-inflation currency). The relevant comparator is taken to be the status quo of the ERM, namely a system of pegged but adjustable rates with very broad bands, within which a core group of currencies pursue close *de facto* stability against the anchor currency, the Deutschmark, while a peripheral group maintain relatively loose commitments, amounting to quasi-floating in some cases.

With these reference points in mind, the paper addresses three topics:

1   The likely causes of euro instability and the implications for exchange-rate variability in the new régime. As a way into these questions, the next section of this paper reviews the experience of major currencies during the era of generalized floating since the end of Bretton Woods, drawing on some new estimates of long-period exchange rate variability. Attention then turns to particular sources of euro instability, including the much-discussed 'overhang' of dollar reserves in the EMU area and the potential role of private international capital flows, which could be a crucial factor in due course if the euro develops as an investment currency with global appeal.

2   The economic implications of exchange-rate volatility in the EMU area, and the possibility that they will be uneven as between participating economies. This topic is explored in the next section with the help of some new simulations using the NIGEM model, a large multi-country model developed and operated at the National Institute of Economic and Social Research (NIESR). The simulations examine the impact of exogenous exchange rate disturbances on individual economies, under the assumption of a single monetary policy aimed exclusively at price stability in the medium term; attention is paid to differences in national monetary transmission mechanisms and labour market responses.

3   The implications for the management of the new currency by its policymaking authorities. The next part of the paper argues that EMU's policymakers would be unwise to ignore the euro exchange rate, but should instead aim systematically to limit euro instability, so far as this can be done without jeopardizing the ECB's price-stability objective. In a world where strong commitments to nominal exchange-rate stability among major currencies are out of favour, this points towards a unilateral strategy of managing the *real* euro exchange rate, along the lines of the flexible 'target zone' approach suggested by Williamson (1993) and others. Such a policy would not only offer the best available prospect of external stability for the euro, but also facilitate the development of a regional euro-centric zone embracing currencies in the expanding EU and its vicinity, which will be among those to suffer most if the euro proves unstable. It would also leave open the door for initiatives at the G3/G7 level, or bilaterally with the US authorities in an increasingly 'bipolar' currency world.

Lessons from the past thirty years

The record of exchange rate behaviour in the thirty or so years since the Bretton Woods system began to break down does not encourage the view that stability is a natural state of affairs for the main floating currencies. There is much evidence that the adoption of generalized floating after the end of Bretton Woods led to a large increase in volatility among major currencies, in both nominal and real terms, and it is generally accepted that this instability developed into sustained misalignment of the US dollar, yen, DM, pound and other floating currencies in the subsequent period of 'benign neglect' in the late 1970s and early 1980s.[1] Efforts to stabilize the major currencies through concertation among the G7 monetary authorities, orchestrated by the United States government around the Plaza agreement of 1985 and Louvre accord of 1987, appear to have been effective in promoting their immediate objective for a time, as Catte, Galli and Rebecchini (1992) have shown, but they gave way to, and may have encouraged, monetary and fiscal policy mistakes which in due course created the conditions for new instabilities (Funabashi 1988, Poole 1992). In consequence, volatility has re-emerged between the major currencies in the 1990s and, despite a remarkable degree of downward inflation convergence among them, it has shown little sign of diminishing. An inescapable lesson from this experience – illustrated yet again in the current East Asian crisis – is that international convergence towards low inflation by no means guarantees exchange-rate stability.

Skeptical about the merits of floating exchange rates, especially for an integrating group of small and medium-sized open economies, the member states of the European Community have long striven to reduce global currency volatility through formal stabilization arrangements at the European level. Their first attempt, the European currency 'snake' initiated in 1972, failed to survive the inflationary tensions of the mid-1970's, except in the case of the DM and its close satellites, but its successor – the European Monetary System and its multilateral exchange-rate mechanism (ERM), set up in 1979 – has survived successfully, at least to the extent of reducing instability among its core currencies and in due course promoting the preconditions for monetary union. There is considerable evidence that, despite recurrent turbulence and the major crisis of 1992–3, the ERM has largely achieved its original objective of creating a zone of monetary stability within the Community, although it appears to have been less successful in protecting its participants from instability against third currencies.

Most studies of exchange-rate volatility in an ERM context have concentrated on short-period volatility – essentially, fluctuations with a frequency of less than a year – and they suggest fairly unequivocally that the ERM has reduced intra-area volatility of both nominal and real exchange rates. However, they also suggest that greater intra-ERM stability has been at the expense of greater volatility against non-ERM currencies. This is a widely-found result (Barr 1984, Rogoff 1985, Ungerer *et al.* 1986, Taylor and Artis 1988), and it holds whether the measure of volatility is 'unconditional' (inclusive of all short period variations, whether or not anticipated by agents) or 'conditional' (modified to exclude anticipated variations, estimated using various statistical techniques).[2] Accordingly, there is doubt that the EMS has reduced the *total* (that is, effective-rate) volatility of its member currencies, as compared either with the pre-EMS period or with that of non-ERM currencies; the evidence on this issue appears at best inconclusive (see Haldane 1991, in a wide-ranging review of the EMS literature).

In contrast, the evidence relating to long-period variability, and especially 'misalignment', is rather sparse. When addressing this question in 1988, M. P. Taylor and M. Artis found that the ERM did not appear to have halted the tendency of participating currencies to become mutually misaligned, although they also noted that it might have been successful in reducing the speed at which those misalignments developed, so that 'the ERM appears to have increased exchange rate predictability' (Taylor and Artis 1988: 23). A recent exercise by C. Taylor, assessing long-period variability (fluctuations lasting more than a year) among ERM currencies and comparing it with that of the major floating currencies, reaches conclusions which parallel those on short-period volatility (Taylor 1998). The evidence from this study is that although ERM membership has reduced long-period instability *between* participants, there has been no reduction in their *overall* variability (that is, in their effective rates), and indeed this appears to have increased in the run-up to EMU. In other words, as with the studies of short-run volatility mentioned, greater ERM stability appears to have been delivered at the expense of greater variability against third currencies. A related conclusion, partially implicit in the former, is that the two dominant 'closed economy' floating currencies, the dollar and yen, have experienced much greater long-period instability than the main 'open economy' currencies through most of the period since the collapse of Bretton Woods.

Figures 9.1 and 9.2, taken from this study, show deviations of annual real effective exchange rates from their long-run trends for five currencies that have mainly or wholly floated since the end of Bretton Woods, and five currencies that have participated in the ERM since its start.[3] According to this measure of long-period variability, the major floating currencies, particularly the dollar and yen, have been markedly less stable than the ERM currencies, and although there was some improvement among the floaters during the phase of post-Plaza concertation, this has not been maintained through the current period. It also appears on this measure that there has been little if any improvement in overall (effective-rate) stability for the currencies that joined the ERM, even though the system has assisted intra-group stability. The latter conclusion emerges more clearly in Table 9.1, from the same study, which reports a standard measure of variability in real effective exchange rates for the same currencies, through the succession of some five principal policy régimes since the Bretton Woods system began to break down. Although the ERM currencies have experienced markedly less long-period instability against the DM

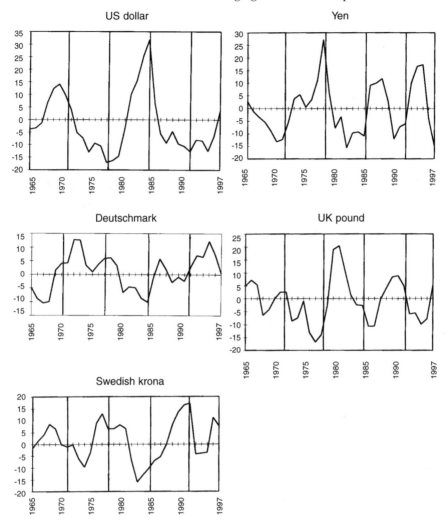

Figure 9.1 Real effective exchange rates 1966–97: deviations from fifteen-year
moving averages: five floating currencies (%)

Note: Uses European Commission's measure of relative unit labour costs

Source: Taylor 1998

since the system's formation, there has been little improvement in their
overall stability since then; indeed it seems to have deteriorated during the
current period, in part because of greater external variability of the DM.[4]

The conclusion that ERM participation has tended to augment the
variability of most EU currencies against the dollar, whether in terms of
nominal or real rates or of short- or long-run fluctuations, does not
necessarily conflict with the more optimistic view, sometimes expressed,

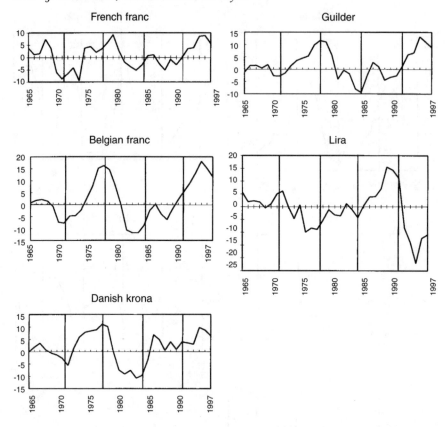

Figure 9.2 Real effective exchange rates 1966–97: deviations from fifteen-year
        moving averages: five ERM currencies (%)

Note: Uses European Commission's measure of relative unit labour costs

Source: Taylor 1998

that ERM participation has tended to damp down fluctuations between the
DM and the dollar, by mitigating speculative capital flows between the two
'polar' currencies and by inducing the German authorities at times to
attenuate the ERM links. However the results of the various studies cited
here suggest that the latter tendency has been less marked overall than the
former.

    If these conclusions hold, the omens for external stability of the euro
are not reassuring. There must be a high expectation that the new
currency will behave in due course like a major floating currency, and on
the past record, co-operative efforts at currency stabilization at the global
level are unlikely to meet with sustained success. Strong formal commitments to an adjustable-rate ERM appear to have been comparatively
successful in promoting regional exchange-rate stability, but they have not
managed to shield participants from external currency instability; if

Table 9.1 Long-run variability of real exchange rates: major floating and ERM
currencies (%)

	1965–71	1972–8	1979–85	1986–92	1993–7
Five floating currencies					
Based on real effective exchange rates:					
US dollar	8.7	10.4	18.8	8.8	8.3
Japanese yen	8.1	11.7	9.6	8.9	13.5
Deutschmark	7	7.5	6.7	2.9	7.6
UK pound	4.9	10.6	11.4	7.7	7.1
Swedish krona	4.4	7.8	10.2	11.3	6.7
Average of above	6.6	9.6	11.4	7.9	8.7
Five ERM currencies					
Based on real effective exchange rate:					
French franc	5.3	5.4	5.1	2.5	6.5
Italian lira	3.2	6.6	3.3	9.6	14.3
Belgian franc	4.3	9.3	10.4	3.8	13.8
Netherlands guilder	1.9	6.5	6.8	2.8	9.5
Danish krona	1.9	7.5	8.5	4.1	6.8
Average of above	3.3	7.1	6.8	4.6	10.2
Average of above excluding lira	3.4	7.2	7.7	3.3	9.2
Based on real exchange rate against DM:					
French franc	9.5	8.8	4.6	2.2	2.9
Italian lira	6.6	10.7	6.2	9	18.5
Belgian franc	8	9.2	6.7	3.6	7.2
Netherlands guilder	9.5	5.6	3.7	1.5	3.5
Danish kroner	7.3	6.3	3.1	3.8	3.1
Average of above	8.2	8.1	4.9	4.1	7
Average of above excluding lira	8.6	7.5	4.5	2.8	4.2

Note: Root mean squared percentage deviations of annual real exchange rates (relative
unit labour costs) from 15-year moving averages. Averages for groups of currencies
are unweighted.

Source: Taylor 1998

anything they may have exacerbated it, particularly latterly. Only if the
euro proves to be more stable against third currencies than the DM has
been can it be predicted with reasonable confidence that monetary union
will improve the *total* exchange rate stability experienced by most participating economies. Some economists have argued that such a result may
indeed be possible, essentially on the ground that the single monetary
policy for the euro should be designed to suit average conditions in the
Eurozone whereas, under the ERM, national monetary policies tended to
emulate German policy, which has led to unnecessary instability in their
external exchange rates (see for example Bénassy-Quéré *et al.* 1997).
However, the more likely risk is that the euro will turn out to be at least as
unstable against third currencies as the DM has been and, in that case,
exporters in most EMU-area states can expect little or no overall
improvement in their trading conditions. The situation could be worse if

the euro turns out to be less stable externally than the DM and franc have been, which might happen for various reasons: for example, the greater vulnerability of a widely-held global currency to shifts in international investor sentiment (reflecting 'safe haven' factors) and the possibility that the single monetary policy may have uneven national effects in the large-group EMU, so the ECB may have to work particularly hard to achieve price stability among them. It is to these questions that the discussion now turns.

International asset holdings after EMU and the balance of payments of the euro area

It is widely expected, by academic and financial market economists alike, that EMU – by eliminating the exchange risk between the eleven partici-pating countries through the replacement of their national currencies with the euro – will result in a significant shift in the currency composition of both private and official foreign asset holdings in favour of the euro, primarily at the expense of the US dollar. We examine here the size of the potential 'dollar overhang', the immediate (negative) arithmetic impact that EMU will have on international holdings of assets denominated in EMU-area domestic currencies, the possible scale of any subsequent re-adjustments in private and official foreign asset stocks, and the implications these might have for the balance of payments of the EMU area and the exchange rate of the euro.

The 'dollar overhang'

An important concern addressed in many recent studies has been whether EMU might result in a net excess supply of foreign exchange reserves within the European System of Central Banks (ESCB) and, if so, what implications this might have for the dollar and its exchange rate against the euro. EMU will automatically result in a reduction in the supply of foreign exchange reserves available to EMU countries: any reserves held by an EMU participant which are denominated in other participants' currencies will automatically cease to be foreign exchange. There will also be a reduction in the demand for reserves, because of economies of scale in pooled reserve holdings, the redenomination of intra-EMU trade and financial flows, and the elimination of ERM intervention obligations among EMU participants. Much less certain is whether the net result will be an overall excess supply or excess demand. Estimates range from a large excess supply of (predominantly dollar) reserves of up to US\$ 200–230 billion (European Commission 1990) to a possible excess in demand of up to US\$ 55 billion (Leahy 1996).[5] The differences in these various estimates reflect differences in methodologies and assumptions about central bank behaviour as well as deficiencies in publicly available data of official reserve holdings.

Arrowsmith (1998) uses EMI and national sources for EU countries' holdings of official ECUs in 1996, in conjunction with 1995 benchmark data of the currency composition of EU countries' reserves presented in Masson and Turtelboom (1997) from internal IMF sources, to improve the timeliness and accuracy of estimates of the dollar and other components of the EU central banks' reserves. This approach has the additional advantage of yielding fairly precise estimates of the dollar and gold components of individual EU member states' reserve holdings in 1996, broad estimates of their holdings of individual EU currencies and, hence, the portion of their reserves which will be redenominated as euros when EMU starts.[6] These estimates (see Table 9.2) show that, as a result of redenomination, the foreign exchange reserves of the eleven countries entering EMU in 1999 will fall by about a third (US$ 85 billion in 1996 terms) to US$ 180 billion; for an EMU of all fifteen member states, the corresponding figures would be US$ 137 billion and US$ 220 billion. The Maastricht Treaty provides for the pooling of up to ECU 50 billion (US$ 63 billion at end-1996 exchange rates) of these reserves at the European Central Bank (ECB), with individual countries contributing according to a key based on population and GDP. If the reserve pool is scaled down to reflect the participation of only eleven rather than fifteen member states, US$ 132 billion of foreign exchange would be left in the reserves of the participating national central banks (NCBs).[7]

It would be misleading to regard this figure as a measure of the surplus of foreign exchange (the so-called 'dollar overhang') which NCBs might be tempted to dispose of when EMU takes place. Two Council Decisions are in preparation which will entitle the ECB to call up further reserves from NCBs and will place restrictions on the use to which reserves held by NCBs may be put. As Table 9.2 shows, the residual reserve holdings are also very unevenly distributed, with some countries (notably France) probably facing a need to acquire foreign exchange if the ECB were to make a further call. Furthermore, if allowance were made for the sizeable foreign (non-EMU) currency debt of some of the participating countries, the net stock of 'free' reserves within the ESCB would be a relatively modest US$ 42 billion – only two thirds the size of the reserves of Germany when it was underpinning the ERM – and the net position of six countries would be negative.

A number of commentators have pointed to the practical difficulties and exchange rate consequences that would be a deterrent to any large-scale off-loading of excess reserves by the EMU members; Manzocchi and Padoan (1997) even give detailed consideration to alternative deployment of the excess to facilitate Central and Eastern European countries' preparations for EU membership. The above analysis suggests that in practice, however, the problem of a foreign exchange overhang is unlikely to arise; indeed, of greater concern might be the gold overhang. ECB President Duisenberg (1998) has stated that 15 per cent of national contributions to

Table 9.2 EU countries' gold and foreign exchange reserves after EMU: US$ billion, end-1996 data

	Total FX reserves in 1996	of which: in US dollars	in EU currencies	non-EU (total)	Non-EU excluding pooled*	Residual net of FX borrowing	Non-EU excluding pooled**	Residual gold and FX	of which: gold (%)
Austria	20.6	12.5	7.4	13.2	11.8	-1.8	12.0	17.1	29.8
Belgium	14.7	6.4	7.0	7.8	6.0	-6.5	6.3	13.3	52.9
Denmark	14.1	3.4	9.0	5.2	4.1	2.4	4.3	4.9	13.0
Finland	6.4	2.0	3.7	2.7	1.7	-8.5	1.9	2.5	26.0
France	15.3	10.3	4.1	11.2	0.5	0.5	2.1	40.1	94.8
Germany	69.1	62.0	7.0	62.1	48.0	48.0	50.1	94.6	47.0
Greece	17.6	5.2	10.4	7.2	5.9	5.3	6.1	7.7	20.8
Ireland	9.8	3.0	5.8	4.1	3.6	-2.8	3.7	3.8	3.3
Italy	43.0	22.6	17.2	25.8	15.9	-19.9	17.4	48.1	63.9
Luxembourg	—	—	—	—	-0.1	-0.1	-0.1	0.1	185.0
Netherlands	22.1	6.1	13.4	8.7	6.0	6.0	6.4	22.8	71.9
Portugal	13.7	3.7	8.4	5.3	4.1	0.6	4.3	11.9	64.0
Spain	50.6	37.9	10.7	39.9	34.4	26.8	35.2	42.5	17.1
Sweden	23.6	5.4	15.3	8.3	6.5	-5.1	6.8	8.9	23.9
UK	36.1	14.7	17.6	18.4	8.8	3.4	10.2	17.9	42.8
EU-15	356.7	195.2	137.0	219.9	157.2	48.3	166.6	336.2	50.4
EMU-11	265.3	166.5	84.7	180.8	131.9	42.3	139.2	296.8	53.1
Non-EMU 4	91.4	28.7	52.3	39.1	25.3	6.0	27.4	39.4	30.5

Note: 'Non-EU excluding pooled*' assumes contributions to ECB reserve pool consist solely of foreign exchange
'Non-EU excluding pooled**' assumes 15% of each country's contribution is in gold
Key for ECB reserve contributions as for national contributions to the EMI's financial resources

Sources: IMF; EMI; national central bank balance sheets; Masson and Turtleboom 1997; Paribas Capital Markets; authors' calculations

the reserve pool will be in the form of gold but, as the final column of Table 9.2 shows, this would still leave EMU NCBs with more than 50 per cent (and France 95 per cent) of their marketable reserves in gold.

Two other questions arising from this analysis, which merit attention but are not discussed here, are whether the participating countries and their NCBs will dispose of those official foreign currency liabilities and reserve assets which automatically become redenominated in euros at the start of EMU; and whether it would be legally admissible for national governments to use any of the residual non-euro foreign exchange reserves, held by their NCBs within the ESCB, to extinguish their own non-euro foreign currency debt.[8] Either or both of these steps might be attractive to participating governments as a means of reducing their debt/GDP ratios and so giving more headroom to national fiscal policies under the Stability and Growth Pact.

Global shifts into euro assets

Potentially much more likely sources of euro exchange rate volatility than the residual dollar holdings of the EMU countries are shifts in the currency composition of other countries' official reserves and of international investors' portfolios. Table 9.3 shows the amount of EU currencies held internationally, in non-EU countries' official reserves and by investors outside the EU. As a result of the redenomination of the EU-11 countries' own reserve holdings of EU currencies, the world total of official foreign currency reserves held in the currencies of the eleven EMU countries will fall by about US$ 80 billion, from 16 per cent to 11 per cent of total world reserves. If the attraction of the euro as a reserve currency to official holders outside EMU were sufficient to restore its share of world reserves to that taken at present by the currencies of the eleven participating members of EMU, their euro holdings would rise by US$ 66 billion; for the euro, over time, to achieve a share equal to that of the US dollar in non-EU countries' reserves would require (assuming other currencies' shares are unchanged) a switch from the dollar to the euro of US$ 260 billion (in 1996 terms); and, similarly, equality with the dollar in total world reserves would entail a switch to the euro of US$ 360 billion.[9]

While these figures give some indication of the potential scale of future shifts of official holdings towards the euro, there is no presumption that movements on such a scale will take place or, if they were to do so, over what period of time. Certainly some European politicians publicly express a desire to see this happen.[10] For it actually to happen will require reserve managers to perceive positive advantages in holding euro assets that they have not seen so far in assets denominated in the individual national currencies of the EU. This will depend on a number of factors. The credibility of the euro as a store of value over the longer term – and its attractiveness as an anchor currency for countries outside EMU – will be

Table 9.3 Use of EU currencies in international financial markets (as at end-1996)

	Amount ($ bns)	As % of all currencies	As % of US$ holdings	As % of EU GDP
All countries' official reserve holdings of EU currencies	276.4	19.0	31.9	3.2
holdings of EMU-11 currencies	*228.6*	*15.8*	*26.4*	*3.3*
of which:				
Non-EU countries' official reserve holdings of EU currencies	155.2	14.1	23.1	1.8
holdings of EMU-11 currencies	*118.5*	*10.8*	*17.6*	*1.7*
EU currency deposits held as foreign currency (all sectors)	1,856.0	31.7	70.3	21.6
EMU-11 currencies	*1,574.1*	*26.9*	*59.6*	*22.9*
of which:				
EU currency deposits held by non-banks as foreign currency	561.1	40.5	109.1	6.5
EMU-11 currencies	*449.1*	*32.4*	*87.3*	*6.5*
of which:				
EU currency deposits held by non-EU non-banks	239.2	17.3	46.5	2.8
EMU-11 currencies	*150.3*	*10.9*	*29.2*	*2.2*
International debt securities denominated in EU currencies	1,124.3	34.9	90.2	13.1
EMU-11 currencies	*873.0*	*27.1*	*70.1*	*12.7*
of which:				
held by non-EU residents (guesstimate)	(479)	(15)	(38)	(6)
EMU-11 currencies	*(293)*	*(9)*	*(24)*	*(4)*

Sources: IMF; BIS; EMI; Masson and Turtleboom (1997); McCauley (1997); authors' calculations (for assumptions, see text)

determined not only by the monetary policy pursued by the ECB but also by the fiscal policies of the participating countries and the exchange rate policy (if any) which they collectively adopt. It will also depend on the extent to which EMU results in a single homogeneous market in government securities (including short-term instruments) across the Eurozone, rather than one which remains segmented by national differences in issuing terms or tax treatment. The euro's value to reserve managers as a currency hedge will also depend on whether its exchange rate shows greater variability (as we suggested earlier might happen) than the national currencies it replaces have shown collectively.

Much the same set of considerations will determine the extent to which international asset holders – including institutional investors and corporate treasurers – respond to EMU by altering the currency composition of their portfolios. From published BIS statistics it is possible to derive data for non-banks' holdings of the EU-11 currencies as foreign currency deposits (excluding EU residents' offshore holdings of their own domestic currencies). In 1996 these amounted to US$ 450 billion: some

32 per cent of the total for all currencies and not far short of the US dollar's 37 per cent share (see Table 9.3). This figure, however, includes EU-11 residents' holdings of each other's currencies, for which official data are not publicly available. According to McCauley (1997), presumably drawing on internal BIS information, such cross-holdings amounted in 1996 to about US$ 300 billion. As these will become domestic currency in EMU, the share of the euro in total world foreign currency deposits will fall from 32 per cent to 11 per cent. For this fall in share to be offset, a switch of US$ 250 billion into euro deposits would be required, while to achieve an equal share with the dollar would entail a switch of US$ 180 billion (to give a 27 per cent share in total foreign currency deposits after EMU).

Greater still would be the potential scale of portfolio shifts in the international debt market. Since there is no published information on the nationality of holders of international debt securities, only a very rough estimate of non-EU holdings of international securities denominated in EU currencies is presented in Table 9.3, by assuming that EU countries' cross-holdings of such debt constitute the same proportion of the total as that of their cross-holdings of deposits to total foreign currency deposits denominated in EU currencies, and also that a quarter of all dollar-denominated international securities are held by US residents. On this crude reckoning, a movement of US$ 410 billion would restore the euro's share in the international debt market to that presently held by the EU-11 currencies, while reaching parity with the dollar would require a shift of US$ 320 billion.

The purpose of the above estimates – which together total some US$ 720–860 billion (see Table 9. 4) – is to illustrate the potential scale of international asset flows if the euro were to acquire the status of a major international currency.[11] Given the many uncertainties about the extent to which this might be achieved and the speed at which it might take place, they also highlight the potential for exchange rate and interest rate volatility and the caution with which one should view any predictions about the future value of the euro.

Table 9.4 Potential increases in international holdings of euro assets: some illustrative figures (US$ billion, end-1996 data)

	With an EMU of 11		With an EMU of 15	
	To restore present EU-11 share	*To achieve equal share with dollar*	*To restore present EU-15 share*	*To achieve equal share with dollar*
Official currency reserves	66	358	111	364
Foreign currency deposits	250	182	225	138
International debt securities	408	321	397	228
Total	724	861	733	730

Sources: see Tables 9.2 and 9.3; authors' calculations (for assumptions see text)

A further dimension is added to this uncertainty by the possibility that international *borrowers* may be attracted to the euro by much the same qualities that might appeal to *investors*: broader, deeper and more liquid markets, with scope for lower issuing and transactions costs, as well as larger-scale individual issues, than in the present national markets of the EU could result in an increase in the supply of, as well as the demand for, euro assets. To the extent that increased foreign borrowing in euros is forthcoming, the potential exchange rate effects of a shift into euro assets could be mitigated or even offset. On the other hand, there can be no assurance that the relative scale and timing of such inflows and outflows will match. The European Commission (1990) and Alogoskoufis and Portes (1997), for example, assume that the supply of euro assets will be relatively inelastic in the short to medium term, so that the increase in demand will initially cause the euro to appreciate and the balance of payments of the euro area as a whole to move into current account deficit in order to accommodate the postulated net inflows on capital account. In contrast, Cooper (1998) suggests that the inflows might not be very large and that low interest rates in Europe could lead EU residents to seek higher-yielding claims on the rest of the world, obviating the need for a current account deficit.[12] These conflicting conclusions suggest the need for a more detailed study of the possible implications that international use of the euro might have for the structure of the balance of payments of the monetary union.

Balance of payments implications

The European Commission (1998) forecasts that, with Germany returning to surplus this year, the EU-11 will have a collective current account surplus in 1998 and 1999 equivalent to 1.9 per cent of GDP (while the US deficit will continue rising, to 2.4 per cent of GDP in 1999). Longer-term projections by the National Institute of Economic and Social Research (NIESR), based on its July 1998 forecast using the NIESR's large world model, indicate the EU-11 surplus growing from US$ 102 billion this year to US$ 200 billion by the year 2006 (when the US deficit is projected to be US$ 230 billion), a turn-around of US$ 240 billion from the deficits recorded in 1991 and 1992 in the aftermath of German reunification. It is necessary to consider whether and how such *surpluses* on current accounts, implying continuing net acquisition of external assets by EU residents, can be reconciled with additional gross *inflows* of foreign capital on the scale implied by the illustrative figures of the potential demand for euro assets presented earlier. Even if such a shift into euro assets were spread over a ten-year adjustment period, representing an annual capital inflow of some US$ 70–86 billion, with the annual current account on average over the next ten years some US$ 50 billion higher that in 1998, equivalent additional outflows (or reduced inflows) amounting to US$ 120–136 billion per annum would have to take place elsewhere in the capital account.

There is no economic law or accounting rule that requires a country to run a deficit on current accounts if its currency is to acquire international status, although that might in practice be slower and more difficult to achieve if the country is running a large current account surplus. On average over the eleven years from 1980 to 1990 the annual current deficit of the United States amounted to US$ 76 billion and the annual increase in the volume of other countries' official reserves held in dollars (excluding valuation changes) was US$ 17 billion. Over the same period, Germany and Japan had current account surpluses averaging US$ 23 billion and 38 billion respectively, while the annual average increase in the volume of official holdings of DMs and of yen was US$ 6 billion and 3 billion. During the six years following German reunification (1991–6), this apparently negative association between current account balances and reserve currency status was even more pronounced: the US deficit averaged US$ 106 billion, Germany recorded deficits averaging US$ 18 billion and Japan ran surpluses of US$ 103 billion, while the respective annual increases in official holdings of their currencies were US$ 72 billion, 10 billion and 2 billion. While this negative relationship appears

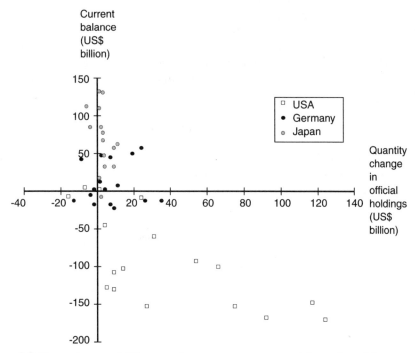

Figure 9.3 Current account balances of reserve currency countries and world reserve holdings of their currencies (average 1980–96)

broadly to hold from year to year for the US dollar (see Figure 9.3), however, it is far from evident in the annual data for Germany and Japan.[13] It may therefore be instructive to examine more closely the structure of the external payment flows of these three reserve currency countries.

During the Bretton Woods era, the conventional view of the role of the principal reserve currency country was that, on a sound platform of current account balance (that is, with a modest and sustainable surplus or deficit) it should act as banker to the world by transforming short-term capital inflows into long-term investment outflows.[14] The United States clearly did not conform to this model during the 1980s and early 1990s (see Table 9.5a): an annual current deficit of 1.7 per cent of GDP (US$ 78 billion) was associated with sizeable net inflows not only of short-term but also of long-term capital.[15] The German balance of payments was almost the mirror image of this until reunification: a large current surplus (US$ 24 billion per annum, 2.6 per cent of GDP) and net outflows of both short and long-term capital. With its subsequent abrupt move into deficit, Germany became a net recipient of long-term capital, while net short-term outflows were halved. Only Japan corresponded (loosely) to the Bretton Woods model, despite its large current surplus (US$ 55 billion, 2.4 per cent of GDP), as net recipient of short-term capital and a (very much larger) net supplier of long-term direct and (especially) portfolio investment to the rest of the world.

From these examples it is apparent that various patterns of capital account may be compatible with a given (surplus or deficit) current account position. A change in the net flow in one capital account category may be accommodated by an opposite change in the net flow in another category. Furthermore, an increase in the gross inflow in one part of the capital account may be compensated by a reduction in gross inflows in other parts, or by an increase in gross outflows on the same or on other parts of the account. In the context of EMU, consideration needs to be given to whether such compensating capital movements are plausible, in relation to the scale of the projected increase in the current account surplus of the EU-11 and the postulated shift by non-residents into euro financial assets.

Table 9.5b presents a summary of the aggregate balance of payments of the EU-11 immediately prior to German reunification and subsequently. Despite the sizeable shift in Germany's current account and the reduction in the overall EU-11 surplus, the basic pattern of the aggregated capital account of the EMU area has been maintained, with net portfolio inflows but net outflows of direct investment and 'other' investments (a major part of which consists of bank deposits and loans). While these net flows are modest in relation to the postulated US$ 70–85 billion additional annual inflow that might need to be accommodated as a result of EMU, the underlying gross flows in both directions are considerably larger than the net positions, total gross capital inflows and outflows each averaging about US$ 400 billion per annum between 1991 and 1996.[16]

Table 9.5a Balance of payments flows and reserve currency status: three reserve currency countries, 1980–93 (annual averages, % of GDP)

	US 1980–93	Japan 1980–93	Germany 1980–90	Germany 1991–3
Current account	-1.7	2.4	2.6	-1.1
Direct investment	0.2	-0.8	-0.8	-0.7
Portfolio and other long-term capital	0.4	-1.7	-0.4	3.1
Short-term capital	0.8	0.3	-1.7	-0.9
o.w. non-resident official	0.5	0.1	0.2	-0.3
Change in official reserves (increase(-))	-0.1	-0.2	-0.1	-0.3
Net errors and omissions	0.3	-0.1	0.3	-0.1

Table 9.5b Balance of payments flows and reserve currency status: Germany and the EU-11, 1988–96 (annual averages, US$ billion)

	Germany 1988–90	Germany 1991–6	EU-11 1988–90	EU-11 1991–6
Current and capital account	51.3	-18.2	27.9	15.3
Direct investment	-13.6	-20.5	-21.6	-26.3
Portfolio investment	-13.6	39.1	23.4	51.7
Other capital	-33.3	8.6	-3.5	-16.1
Change in official reserves (increase(-))	1.8	-3.5	-22.9	-3.6
Net errors and omissions	7.5	-5.5	-3.3	-21.0

Note for both tables: inflows (+)/outflows (-)

Sources for both tables: IMF, *Balance of Payments Yearbooks,* various years

The potential effects of such capital inflows on the exchange rate, current balance and economic activity of the euro area would be neutralized if EMU were also to induce an equivalent upward shift in the total supply of euro-denominated assets (an increase in euro borrowing by EU and/or non-EU residents) or an upward shift in EU residents' demand for non-euro assets (accompanied by a downward shift in their demand for euro assets). In principle this could take place through a number of channels. As was pointed out earlier, some of the factors which might attract non-residents to invest in euro assets could also prove an attraction for foreign borrowers. For the same reason, residents of the EMU area who currently borrow in US dollars or other foreign currencies in order to attract international investors might find they can achieve the same global reach by issuing debt (or raising bank credits) denominated in euros. In both cases this seems likely to take place over a number of years, predominantly through a combination of a shift towards the euro in the stream of net new borrowing and a stock adjustment as existing debt matures, with quite a rapid transformation in the denomination of short-term debt but a more gradual transformation of longer maturities. Less likely, because of contractual penalties, is an abrupt re-denomination of outstanding debt from non-EMU currencies to euros.

It is also conceivable that EMU might induce an upward shift in EU residents' demand for foreign assets. As Anderton, Arrowsmith and Wlodek (1997) show, the likely convergence and increased correlation of asset returns within the euro area could provide a strong incentive for resident investors to diversify their portfolios out of EMU-area currencies into other currencies. The scale of such diversification could be enhanced if, faced with the alternative of a large appreciation of the euro, governments in the EMU area were to remove the present restrictions on the currency composition and asset location of institutional portfolios. Similar reasoning might also lead the authorities to intervene in the foreign exchange market, selling euros and thus accumulating additional foreign reserves, rather than (as discussed earlier) liquidating any dollar overhang. This and other aspects of exchange rate policy for the euro are discussed later in this paper.

The European Commission (1990) has suggested that an increase in outward direct investment would be another means by which inflows into euro assets might be offset. It could be argued that unaccommodated portfolio inflows would bring about a real appreciation of the euro and a slowing of activity within the euro area, and that this would in turn create an incentive for companies to seek investment opportunities abroad. It is less plausible that monetary union of itself would simultaneously induce a spontaneous direct investment outflow which negated these economic effects. Indeed, to the extent that EMU is a success, enhancing efficiency and economic growth, it should encourage both domestic and inward direct investment rather than increased net outward investment.

To what degree these various responses to the advent of the euro, by resident and non-resident borrowers and investors, will prove to be offsetting, must be highly uncertain. It is possible, however, to put forward with rather more confidence two other propositions: the full adjustment of inflows as well as outflows is unlikely to be immediate (or very sudden) or to take place smoothly over a longer period; and it is also unlikely that the timing of capital outflows, even if they have the potential to be fully offsetting, will always be synchronous with the inflows. Furthermore, any significant increase over time in the outstanding stock of euro assets relative to those denominated in dollars would make the euro and dollar markets (for borrowers and lenders) closer substitutes, with greater capital flows and reflows in response to varying yield differentials and exchange rate expectations. These arguments lend additional support to the view that the euro exchange rate (and the current account of the euro area) could be subject to periods of considerable shorter and longer-term volatility.

Will volatility matter?

We have argued that there may be reasons for the euro to become a strong currency over the next few years, but our arguments suggest that the timing and scale of any changes are very uncertain. Volatility seems quite likely for several reasons: as a new central bank, the ECB may decide to bolster its credibility by tightening monetary policy; there may be a net demand for the euro as a reserve currency in excess of the current supply; or the financial markets may have a significantly increased demand for euro assets.[17] It is clear that exchange rate volatility has real effects on open economies, especially when it involves significant and sustained, but uncertain, movements in exchange rates. The effects on EU economies will obviously depend upon their characteristics and their economic institutions. It can be argued, as in Frankel and Rose (1997), that institutions will change in response to the new currency and, in particular, that trade patterns will evolve in response to the removal of currency-related barriers. Such changes may be inevitable, and some have already been seen in Europe, but it will be a number of years before they have an impact.

Whatever the changing pattern of responses in Europe, it is clear that a strong euro would have a significant and, at least in the short to medium term, deleterious effect on the level of activity in the Eurozone. An announcement of a tightening of monetary policy would, if believed, lead to an initial rise in interest rates, an appreciation of the currency and a slowdown in activity, followed by a fall in interest rates and a decline in consumer prices compared with their previously expected trajectory. It is useful to have a framework for analysing these effects, and we utilize for this purpose the NIESR's large, rational expectations model of the world economy. The model is widely used by European finance ministries and central banks, and has a fully adumbrated model of each of the European (and OECD) economies.[18]

In contrast, a strengthening of the demand for the euro independently of the fundamentals of monetary policy would have different effects, as interest rates would not rise as much as they would if monetary policy were tightened. We would expect that a rise in the demand for the currency in this way would not keep its exchange rate permanently away from what was warranted by the fundamentals, but rather that any deviation would gradually disappear.

In this section we analyse these two possible scenarios in a variety of ways. We first look briefly at the effects of an announcement of a cut in the monetary target, tightening policy with the intention of achieving an annual inflation rate which is 1 per cent lower (or thereabouts) for ten years. This policy shift, as compared to our baseline, might be justified on the ground that it would enhance the credibility of the monetary authorities, but it would do so at some cost. We then look at the effects of an autonomously strengthened euro, with euro assets trading at a premium because of a positive shift in demand that emerges immediately and slowly disappears. We look at both scenarios with the UK alternatively in and out of EMU.

An analysis of the effects of an announced change in the money stock target helps to illustrate both the effects of a strong euro and the properties of the model. We have assumed that the target for the money stock is cut by 10 per cent, and that financial market operators are fully aware of this. Financial markets recognize the tightening, interest rates rise, and the exchange rate appreciates. As we assume financial markets are forward-looking, the exchange rate 'jumps' toward the new equilibrium in the first period of the run, and long-term interest rates also rise sharply, representing as they do the forward combination of expected successive short rates. Figure 9.4 plots the resulting differences from baseline for the exchange rate and for short and long-term interest rates, in a scenario where the UK is outside the euro block. A shift in the money target will eventually reduce the price level by roughly the same proportion, and in the process Eurozone GDP will grow less rapidly than it would otherwise have done. This is apparent from Figure 9.5, where it can be seen that one factor driving GDP is a temporary appreciation of the Eurozone's real effective exchange rate (shown with an inverse sign to the nominal rate). In the long run output returns to its baseline, as does the real exchange rate, but nominal inertia in the EMU economies means that the tightening is associated with slow growth for five years or more, much as in the early to mid 1980s.[19]

The effects of the change in the money target differ between countries, as can be seen from Table 9.6, which compares the situation over the first few years of the simulation for the major European countries (with the UK remaining outside EMU).[20] The effects of the tightening build up more quickly in Germany than in say France, but both countries return more quickly to the baseline than the smaller European economies. France adjusts slowly because of its rather sluggish labour market, which is affected by strong employment protection. The speed of response in Germany may well reflect the effects of the habitual use of tight monetary

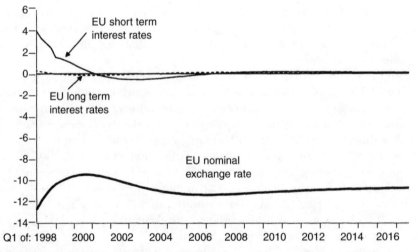

Figure 9.4 Effects of a permanent 10% fall in EU money stock: percentage difference from base forecast

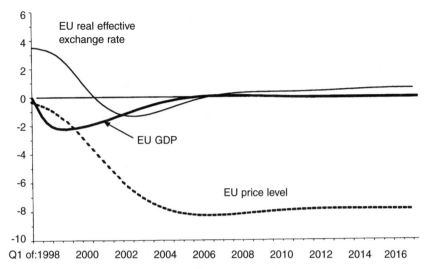

Figure 9.5 Effects of a permanent 10% fall in EU money stock on EU GDP and prices: percentage difference from base forecast

Table 9.6 Effects of a 10% monetary shock on EU GDP

	1998	1999	2000	2001	2002	2003	2004	2005	2006
EU	-1.44	-2.20	-2.03	-1.65	-1.17	-0.71	-0.34	-0.09	0.04
US	0.01	-0.02	-0.07	-0.16	-0.20	-0.20	-0.15	-0.10	-0.06
Japan	-0.21	0.19	0.36	0.27	0.10	-0.04	-0.13	-0.15	-0.13
Germany	-2.27	-3.15	-2.54	-1.78	-1.07	-0.54	-0.22	-0.05	0.03
France	-1.33	-2.45	-2.48	-2.06	-1.38	-0.60	0.07	0.51	0.69
Italy	-1.20	-2.16	-2.01	-1.46	-0.77	-0.15	0.26	0.42	0.38
Spain	-2.19	-3.50	-3.30	-2.53	-1.59	-0.75	-0.16	0.14	0.24
Belgium	-2.52	-2.32	-1.92	-1.80	-1.68	-1.47	-1.19	-0.88	-0.58
Netherlands	-2.75	-3.28	-2.72	-2.11	-1.56	-1.10	-0.75	-0.50	-0.31
Austria	-2.41	-2.38	-2.19	-2.04	-1.82	-1.53	-1.20	-0.83	-0.50
Denmark	-1.75	-2.21	-2.05	-1.99	-1.99	-1.93	-1.77	-1.53	-1.23
Finland	-1.68	-2.48	-2.38	-2.07	-1.74	-1.43	-1.15	-0.90	-0.66
Ireland	-2.19	-2.61	-1.70	-1.01	-0.68	-0.59	-0.56	-0.47	-0.29
Portugal	-1.92	-2.43	-2.44	-2.39	-2.26	-2.02	-1.70	-1.33	-0.92
Sweden	1.00	0.84	0.24	-0.31	-0.56	-0.57	-0.47	-0.33	-0.19
UK	0.39	0.11	-0.24	-0.56	-0.72	-0.74	-0.65	-0.50	-0.35
UK in	-1.46	-2.92	-3.39	-3.46	-3.19	-2.70	-2.12	-1.53	-1.01

Note: assumes UK and Sweden are outside EMU. Denmark is also assumed to be outside, but to follow the ECB's monetary policy closely

policy on the construction of bargaining and other institutions in the German economy. A number of the smaller, more open, economies suffer a more protracted reduction of activity (notably Austria, Belgium, Finland, Ireland and Portugal). We do not, however, expect the ECB to adopt such a contractionary policy, especially in the light of the problems in the financial markets currently being experienced; and we would advise it not to do so.

If the UK were to remain outside EMU, its monetary authorities would be able to use interest rates and the exchange rate as a buffer against the contractionary policy in the rest of Europe. The pattern for UK GDP in Table 9.6 is significantly different from that of the rest of Europe. Initially the effects are slightly expansionary for the UK, because there is a significant gain in competitiveness, at least against its European partners. However, the slowdown in activity in continental Europe, along with the slower inflation there, reduces demand for UK exports and erodes the gain in competitiveness. Hence in the medium term the sharp slowdown in the rest of Europe leads to a slight slowdown in the UK, despite the benefits of an independent, and less contractionary, monetary policy.

The last row in Table 9.6 shows the effects for the UK on the assumption that it will be inside EMU. The UK is then much more affected in the early years than are the majority of EU countries. This is partly because of the greater orientation of UK trade towards the non-EU world, but also because of the UK's greater sensitivity to changes in short-term interest rates, due mainly to the structure of its system of housing finance. In addition, wealth effects have a greater impact on consumption in the UK than in, say, Germany. Hence a rise in long rates, which reduces wealth through its effects on bond and equity prices, would have greater effects in the UK than in other countries in the Eurozone.

Although we do not expect the ECB to pursue an aggressively contractionary policy, it may be unable to avoid the effects of a sharp appreciation of the euro around the time when EMU commences. Figure 9.6 plots the potential path for the euro/dollar exchange rate if demand for the euro were to strengthen in 1998, by assumption raising the rate by 10 per cent in the first period of our scenario. The appreciation is caused by an exogenous shift in investor preferences rather than by a rise in interest rates. In our exercise this is contrived by inserting a declining wedge between the interest differential against US rates, and the prospective change in the euro/dollar exchange rate. The existence of this 'premium' changes the impact of the appreciation, as its deflationary effects are neither permanent, nor accompanied by the rise in short and long-term interest rates we saw in the previous scenarios. Indeed, short-term (and long-term) interest rates initially fall in the Eurozone as the ECB relaxes policy in response to the fall in inflation and the slowdown in activity engendered by the appreciation.

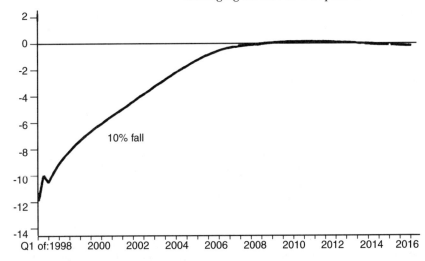

Figure 9.6 Temporary 10% exchange rate appreciation: percentage difference from base forecast

The effects of the temporary appreciation eventually disappear both from the price level and from the level of GDP but, as Figure 9.7 shows, they are initially contractionary for the Eurozone as a whole. Moreover, as with the first simulation, analysis of the autonomous appreciation of the euro leads to some interesting conclusions about the differences between the individual EU economies. Table 9.7 shows the effects of the 10 per cent euro appreciation for each economy, with the UK outside EMU. Again the last row shows the effects for the UK if it was inside EMU, and clearly within the first five years the cumulated output losses are lower if the UK stays out. After

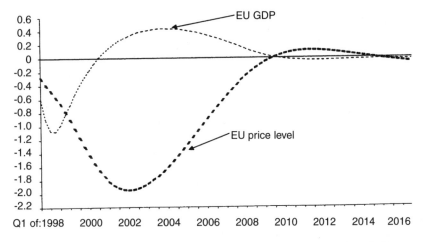

Figure 9.7 Effects of a temporary 10% exchange rate appreciation on EU GDP and prices: percentage difference from base forecast

Table 9.7 Effects of a 10% appreciation of the euro on EU GDP

	1998	1999	2000	2001	2002	2003	2004	2005	2006
EU	-0.92	-0.75	-0.23	0.11	0.30	0.40	0.43	0.41	0.35
US	0.01	0.05	0.01	-0.10	-0.18	-0.20	-0.18	-0.13	-0.09
Japan	-0.17	0.31	0.53	0.43	0.22	0.03	-0.11	-0.17	-0.19
Germany	-1.46	-1.11	-0.26	0.25	0.49	0.57	0.58	0.54	0.48
France	-0.89	-0.98	-0.34	0.27	0.71	0.95	0.98	0.84	0.58
Italy	-0.67	-0.49	0.06	0.34	0.44	0.45	0.42	0.37	0.32
Spain	-1.45	-1.47	-0.67	0.04	0.51	0.74	0.77	0.68	0.50
Belgium	-2.10	-1.16	-0.32	0.01	0.22	0.42	0.58	0.68	0.70
Netherlands	-1.87	-1.34	-0.50	0.03	0.36	0.57	0.70	0.75	0.72
Austria	-1.78	-1.00	-0.55	-0.27	0.00	0.29	0.55	0.70	0.74
Denmark	-1.32	-1.12	-0.59	-0.32	-0.16	0.02	0.23	0.43	0.57
Finland	-1.02	-0.78	-0.22	0.15	0.36	0.47	0.53	0.55	0.53
Ireland	-1.76	-1.25	0.03	0.67	0.79	0.68	0.53	0.45	0.43
Portugal	-1.18	-0.68	-0.35	-0.24	-0.16	-0.05	0.10	0.26	0.39
Sweden	1.05	1.12	0.58	0.02	-0.29	-0.41	-0.42	-0.37	-0.31
UK	0.39	0.29	0.06	-0.20	-0.39	-0.49	-0.51	-0.48	-0.40
UK in	-0.80	-0.90	-0.55	-0.18	0.18	0.48	0.70	0.83	0.86

Note: assumes UK and Sweden are outside EMU. Denmark is also assumed to be outside, but to follow the ECB's monetary policy closely

five years the appreciation has essentially disappeared, but has left the Eurozone with a cumulative loss of output of 1.5 per cent.

The small open economies are, in general more influenced by this exchange rate change than are the larger more closed economies, although Germany's reliance on trade is clearly a factor in this scenario. If the UK were inside EMU then initially, at least, it would be less affected by the appreciation than Germany or, especially, Belgium and the Netherlands. This is largely because of the differential effects of lower interest rates which help offset the deflationary effects of the appreciation. If the UK were outside the EMU, GDP would initially rise, as sterling would not appreciate and there would be a gain in UK competitiveness. Here we can see the potential benefits of an independent exchange rate in an uncertain world, suggesting that perhaps the UK might benefit from its decision to stand aside from the formation of the euro area for a few years.[21]

These simple scenarios illustrate the difficulties to be faced by the ECB when it operates monetary policy. Eventually the EU economies may all converge, and may well develop institutions and trade patterns much closer to each other than they are currently. This would make the Eurozone resemble the traditional paradigm of an optimal currency area much more closely, but we have not approached that situation yet. In France, the sluggish labour market may induce the French monetary authorities to press for a moderate monetary stance. The history of

German monetary policy success could mean that the German authorities push for the use of monetary instruments rather than fiscal ones. On the other hand, the vulnerability of the smaller countries, each of which has the same vote in ECB policy-making as the large countries, and which collectively command a significant weighted vote in the ECOFIN Council, could argue for some moderation of the overall policy stance. In the UK, if it were to become a member of EMU, the importance of wealth effects could make the UK authorities much more concerned than their partners about autonomous developments in financial markets. The very diversity of structures within the euro area, depending upon legal institutions as well as on history, may make consensus difficult to achieve in all but the most desperate of situations.

Implications for euro management

Potential policy conflicts within EMU

The foregoing considerations suggest that it would be inadvisable for the EMU area's policymaking authorities to ignore the euro exchange rate, even though political guidance on these matters has so far been relatively cautious.[22] Although the euro area will be comparatively 'closed', persistent exchange-rate movements may have significant effects on its aggregate inflation rate and GDP, and these effects are likely to be uneven between states, depending on their labour market flexibility and industrial structure. Moreover, countries with the greatest sensitivity to exchange rate changes may not necessarily be those with the greatest sensitivity to interest rates.[23] Unevenness in country impacts, when combined with more familiar market asymmetries (the downward nominal stickiness often found in imperfectly competitive markets) may exacerbate the ratcheting up of wages and prices associated with exchange rate fluctuations in EMU, making this aspect of the ECB's task harder than that, until now, of the national central banks.

In some respects, a moderate degree of aggregate domestic sensitivity to the euro exchange rate should be helpful, since it means that the monetary transmission mechanism in EMU will not be confined totally to internal linkages. Consistently with this the ECB, even if it concentrates exclusively on internal price stability, will have an interest in discouraging exchange rate changes which are clearly contrary to 'the fundamentals'. And the governments of vulnerable states, with local employment/output and inflation objectives in mind, will clearly have a special interest in avoiding euro misalignment. If only for these reasons, the ECB will have to take careful account of the euro in formulating monetary policy, and it should be able to count on sympathetic support from finance ministers in such cases.

Even though the sensitivity of the aggregate price level to the euro exchange rate displayed in the foregoing model simulations (see Figure

9.7) is fairly muted compared with that of most open economies, it would seem clearly in the ECB's interest to resist 'pure' exchange-rate shocks (those bearing no relation to the fundamentals) which unambiguously conflict with internal price stability. It was suggested in earlier sections that such shocks may not be uncommon in EMU. Admittedly, exchange rate instability does not appear to have impeded global inflation convergence but there is evidence that, in particular, long-period exchange-rate variability has damaged the trade performance of EU economies (see Sekkat 1998 for a review of previous empirical studies, and some new results supporting this conclusion). Substantial foreign exchange market intervention by the ECB may therefore be needed from time to time, either to counter unwarranted nominal swings in the euro/dollar rate, or to correct slower-emerging misalignments.[24] In addition the ECB should not refrain from complementary action on short-term interest rates as well, if necessary to counter 'pure' exchange rate instability, given that such actions should assist its primary objective, even when current domestic monetary conditions within its jurisdiction do not appear to call for such action.

The ECB could face more complicated policy choices in the event of an exchange rate shock which, while offering temporary assistance to price stability, threatens to induce structural imbalances in participants' real economies. A potential scenario of that type was depicted earlier in this paper, namely the development of upward pressure on the euro in EMU's early years through a combination of substantial current account surpluses and capital inflows from euro asset seekers. Especially given that the ECB is likely to be keen to establish a strong anti-inflationary reputation in the phase after EMU starts, it might well be tempted to take advantage of the extra disinflationary effects of a gratuitous euro appreciation to get inflation down to a very low rate, despite the unwelcome effects of an emerging and possibly persistent exchange rate misalignment. In these circumstances, and assuming aggregate fiscal policy in the euro area were close to its collective medium-term target, an optimal monetary policy would counteract some of the upward pressure on the euro by encouraging a (temporary) reduction in short-term interest rates such that, in conjunction with the temporarily higher euro, there would be a zero net effect on inflation during the appreciation phase. The case for such a policy relaxation would be particularly strong if the prospective pressure on the euro were to be caused in part by continuing financial and goods market crises in Russia and East Asia.

The ECB could face harder policy choices if disturbances occurred that called for a major exchange rate adjustment which itself conflicted with internal price stability, at least in the short to medium term. Examples are a marked global terms-of-trade shift against the euro area, or a structural increase in its aggregate domestic savings–investment balance, either of which would arguably require a fall in the real euro exchange rate in order to restore internal equilibrium. The ECB would then have to weigh the case for encouraging a downward adjustment in the nominal euro rate, as a means of reducing the real rate, against any temporary departure from internal price stability that such an adjustment might cause. Its judgements would be further complicated if the developments in question threatened to affect some member states more than others, either because of inherent asymmetries in the shocks themselves, or because of asymmetric national responses of the kind discussed in the previous section. An example of a shock with asymmetric effects would be an oil-price shock (more likely to be troublesome after the UK, a net oil exporter, joins EMU, since some EU states are heavy net energy importers). A more imminent example might be sizeable increases in some states' domestic savings ratios, such as would result from previously high-deficit states adopting medium-term targets of zero fiscal balance, as required under the Stability and Growth Pact.

However, the most difficult dilemmas with an exchange-rate dimension facing the ECB may arise not from exogenous shocks, so much as from an inappropriate domestic macro-policy mix. EMU may be more prone than previous regimes to such problems because of the unusually sharp division of responsibility for monetary and fiscal policies adopted for the new regime, which may lead to policy conflicts associated with the 'assignment problem' (see Meade and Weale 1995 for a theoretical discussion and Hughes-Hallett and Yue Ma 1996 for quantitative simulations using a small numerical model). Policy errors could occur if the ECB Council, in control of the single monetary policy, and the eleven national finance ministers, each controlling their own national fiscal policy – albeit subject to constraints under the Stability and Growth Pact – fail to anticipate each others' responses to demand and supply shocks confronting the EMU area (Taylor 1997).

Exchange-rate instability could both induce and feed on such developments. For example, starting from a situation of equilibrium in EMU, consider the implications of a persistent positive exchange-rate shock, reflecting (say) a major net reallocation of global investment portfolios in the euro's favour, such as was discussed earlier in this paper. *Ceteris paribus*, the EMU economies would be likely to experience a temporary GDP deflation, affecting some states more than others. The optimal response by EMU authorities would be a joint temporary relaxation of monetary and fiscal policy, sufficient to maintain aggregate GDP near its equilibrium level, with interest rate reductions at least partially countering the euro rise. The danger is that national finance ministers, acting without adequate consultation either with each other or the ECB, would over-relax fiscal policies, especially in states disproportionately affected by the euro's strength, whereas the ECB might hesitate to relax monetary policy because of its commitment to price stability. With the burden of combating the deflationary effects of an overvalued euro falling on fiscal policy, aggregate government debt/GDP ratios would rise in the euro area, preventing the adjustment in long-term interest differentials which should otherwise help to stem the capital inflows and the euro's appreciation. A sub-optimal mix of monetary and fiscal policies could emerge, which in the worst non-co-operative scenario could develop into an unstable and highly damaging 'tit-for-tat' cycle of policy adjustments.

The clear message is that there will need to be regular consultation and effective co-operation between the ECB and euro-area finance ministers if policy errors of this kind are to be avoided. Unfortunately, the Maastricht blueprint is not well designed in this respect: the extreme emphasis on policy independence for the ECB, and the absence of an effective central authority to conduct fiscal policy, threaten to leave an important institutional lacuna in the area of monetary-fiscal co-operation, not addressed in the Stability and Growth Pact. Similarly, there is a risk of confusion arising from the separation of responsibility for exchange-rate policy, which falls to the Ministers' Council, from day-to-day exchange-rate management, which falls to the ECB. Ways will surely have to be found of remedying these institutional weaknesses if the euro is to be managed successfully.[25]

A strategy for the euro

In contemplating any strategy for managing the euro in a world where increased polarization brings a risk of greater long-period instability between a few key currencies, the EMU authorities' task would be much assisted if they could count on effective co-operation at global level, particularly by the US and Japanese authorities. Unfortunately the prospects at this level are not immediately very bright. Earlier in this paper we recalled the evidence from the Plaza/Louvre period that exchange market intervention at the G7 level can be effective if it is carefully concerted among the major central banks, widely publicized, and accompanied by supportive monetary policy action, but we also noted the criticism of policy actions undertaken by the major countries in the post-Plaza and Louvre period and the subsequent re-emergence of instability among the main floating currencies. Partly for those reasons, and partly because governments' attention has been absorbed by regional initiatives like EMU and NAFTA in the past decade, efforts at global policy co-operation have been under a cloud. Hardly surprisingly, the economic literature on international monetary co-ordination has also acquired a negative tinge in recent years (see the review by Nolan and Schaling 1996, and the references there). The message from this literature seems now to be that the largest errors in the policy mix between major economies tend to come about through defective internal policy design rather than myopic national objectives, and the most that can be expected from international collaboration is that policymakers will be able to avoid internal policy mistakes through being better informed about other countries' intentions (Nolan and Schaling 1996: 415).

Against this unpropitious background, Europe's more optimistic policy-makers have looked to EMU to usher in a more productive era of international monetary co-operation, at least from a European viewpoint. In principle, the amalgamation of national policy interests, across an economic area as large as EMU will be, should enhance EU representatives' bargaining power at the global level, because their policy actions will have spillover effects which other major blocs will no longer be able to ignore. Yet, as was hinted in Tables 9.6 and 9.7, simulations of large multi-country models suggest that the spillovers from EMU policy actions may not be large enough to matter vitally to US and Japanese policymakers.[26] Furthermore, the institutional design of EMU does not appear helpful for exploiting EMU's collective influence at global level, as a number of transatlantic observers have pointed out (Williamson 1992, Kenen 1995, Henning 1997). Although the merging of responsibility for monetary policy in a single body should assist EU influence in G7 discussions, fiscal policies will still be under the control of national finance ministers, who may not speak with one voice; although responsibility for the euro exchange rate will be amalgamated via the Euro-11 Council, they may not easily reach agreement on 'general orientations', much less on a formal exchange rate regime, given the likely need for unanimity, informally if not formally.[27]

Accordingly, without a more coherent system of macroeconomic policy formation in EMU, and related changes of representation in the main international fora – the G7 and the IMF – it will be hard fully to exploit the advantages of size that should accrue if and when the euro becomes a global currency (see Henning 1997 for a discussion of feasible reforms and obstacles to be overcome). Such reforms may materialize eventually, if and when a full appreciation of the benefits both to EMU states and to the other global players shows them to outweigh the inertia and narrow pursuit of national interest that keep the existing arrangements in place. Eventual UK participation could also affect the equation. So far, however, there is little indication that the newly-established ECB or the EMU Ministers' Council will be ready to tackle these institutional problems soon.

The most that might be hoped for in this field in the foreseeable future, therefore, is that EMU's twin policy-making authorities will be prepared to adopt jointly a unilateral and relatively informal approach to stabilizing the euro, at least to the extent of systematically discouraging what can clearly be judged to be excessive real exchange-rate fluctuations. Given the manifest vulnerability of inflexibly pegged exchange-rate commitments in a world with liberalized capital markets and a few major players, each pursuing independent monetary policies, this might most feasibly follow a flexible 'target zone' approach, somewhat along the lines suggested by Williamson (1993), building on his proposals of ten years earlier (Williamson 1983), namely a relatively broad band with 'soft' edges, temporary enlargements of band width or suspensions of limits to partially accommodate large shocks, and the possibility of frequent small realignments to cope with permanent changes in fundamentals. Given also the ECB's virtually certain opposition to any strategy that would conflict with its freedom to select and pursue its price stability objective, the focus of the strategy should be the euro's real exchange rate (preferably in effective terms, but bilaterally against the dollar if transparency is at a premium). This focus would permit the ECB to pursue, with a modest degree of short-term flexibility, an internal inflation objective independently of the other major blocs; and it would be entirely consistent with the strategy's objective, namely to lean against exchange-rate misalignment rather than to provide a (redundant) nominal anchor for the euro area. The strategy would mean *inter alia* that if, for example, the US economy became gripped by inflation at the prevailing exchange rate, the EMU authorities should encourage an appreciation of the euro, thereby avoiding the importation of inflation and the depreciation of Europe's real exchange rate otherwise implied.

In time, if not immediately (since it may be difficult to identify a sustainable level for the euro in its first few years), a flexible approach of this kind could be made to fit the unique institutional arrangements of EMU more easily than a more formal stabilization scheme.[28] If designed and operated with care, it could carry more conviction with the financial markets, and therefore achieve a larger stabilization payoff, than the most likely alternative, namely a strategy of *ad hoc* discretion by the ECB, under loose and unsystematic guidance from the Euro-11 Council. (The analytics of a flexible approach along these lines are set out in a recent paper by Artis, Gallo and Salmon (1998).) Instead, the Euro-11 Council should declare a general intention, with ECB co-operation, to resist excessive fluctuations in the euro, and perhaps back this up by announcing an indicative range for the euro's real exchange rate, which might however be amended or suspended without prior warning. It would then be left to the ECB to select (but not publish) its degree of commitment to the Council's target range, balancing the gains to *external* stability from actions that demonstrated a close adherence to the indicated range, against the losses to *internal* stability from departing temporarily from the monetary action implied by strict adherence to the inflation target. If a properly articulated institutional framework for policy co-operation between the Euro-11 Council and the ECB Governing Council were introduced, the ECB could keep finance ministers properly informed of the reasons for taking such action.

Such a strategy could and should be employed to moderate the costs of excessive currency instability which may threaten the euro area from time to time, without running major risks with internal price stability in the medium and long term. It seems a fair presumption that useful, although lesser, benefits would also be felt in the dollar and yen areas without risks to inflation there.[29] Furthermore, a strategy that brought a measure of global stability to the euro would also be of benefit to economies that border the euro area and have, or are developing, extensive trade and investment links with it, and may well consider stabilizing their currencies against the euro. Clearly, the advantages of targeting the euro for the EU's neighbours and for its newer trading partners to the east and south, whether aimed at acquiring a nominal anchor via a large, low-inflation, economy like the EMU area or at achieving stable competitive conditions against the Single European Market, would be much enhanced if the euro's real exchange rate were stable against the other key currencies.

A notable implication from the model simulations discussed in the previous section, in particular the results for the UK (and Sweden to a lesser extent) outside EMU, is that pan-European exchange rate stability would considerably benefit the euro's neighbours as well as the euro area proper. Indeed, for this reason, the most promising avenue of international monetary co-operation involving the euro may lie, in the near term, mainly in the development of exchange rate links with the remaining Western and Central European currencies. The instrument is already to hand in the form of the proposed 'ERM2', which by virtue of the flexibility built into it (the width of fluctuation bands and adjustability of central rates) should be capable of catering for a variety of national circumstances, while giving primacy to the euro as the system's nominal anchor for those who want one.

In principle, given the size of the euro area and its dedication to price stability, the reformed ERM in tandem with an externally stable euro should be able to offer, at least on a continental scale, as stable a trade environment as was available globally in the heyday of Bretton Woods. However, if the euro's zone of stability is to develop in this way, the EMU authorities, and especially the ECB given its influence at the heart of the new regime, must not only maintain price and output stability inside the euro area and assist partners in the new ERM to achieve stability against the euro (in return for adopting convergent economic policies) but also be prepared to give some weight to minimizing euro instability against third currencies, principally the US dollar. Accordingly, advocacy of the above rather unilateral and regional strategy for the euro does not diminish the case for multilateral co-operation at G3/G7 level. Despite the fairly discouraging omens, global co-operation to minimize fluctuations between the key currencies of the tripolar, or more probably bipolar, post-EMU world would also be worth trying to revive, if only for the familiar reason that, in the past, DM/US dollar fluctuations have periodically created tensions between currencies in the old ERM, and could pose similar problems for the euro and its prospective partners in the new one.

Notes

1 See Williamson 1983 and Shafer and Loopesko 1983, among others. The increase in volatility occurred despite sporadic 'smoothing' intervention by some central banks, acting alone or in tactical concert.

2 See the discussions in Barr 1984: 3–4, and Taylor and Artis 1988: 10–11.

3 The DM is classed here as a floating currency because, unlike the other ERM currencies, the German authorities have consistently given a high weight to domestic monetary/inflation objectives and have only occasionally and briefly allowed ERM links to dominate their policies.

4 As in any study of exchange rate variability, the results cited here depend somewhat on the precise measure of the real effective exchange rate and method of trend extraction used (see Taylor 1998 for details) However, although alternative methods may produce significantly different point estimates of misalignment, they are thought unlikely to lead to substantially different conclusions regarding the timing and extent of long-period variations in the currencies studied. The indicator of real effective exchange rates used here is the European Commission's measure of relative unit labour costs.

5 Other studies offer a variety of intermediate estimates, for example: Brookes 1996, US$ 143 billion; Masson and Turtelboom 1997, US$ 105 billion; Gros and Thygesen 1992, US$ 100 billion; Kenen 1995, adjusting the Commission's estimate, US$ 40–70 billion. For a summary of other estimates published in 1996 and 1997, see McCauley 1997.

6 Since each EU country's official ECU holdings represent three-month revolving swaps against 20 per cent of both its US dollar reserves and its gold reserves, the size of its total dollar holdings can be calculated from its residual gold reserves and its total holdings of official ECUs. Data on these last two items is typically published in national central banks' balance sheets or financial statements. In the case of the UK, for which there is no public information about the stock of ECUs held, similar calculations can be applied to the announced quarterly revaluation adjustments applied in respect of successive ECU swaps.

7 The ECB has recently announced that EUR 40 billion will be pooled in the first instance: see Duisenberg 1998.

8 In accordance with Article 105.2 of the Treaty and Articles 3.1 and 3.2 of the ESCB/ECB Protocol, the official foreign exchange reserves of the participating member states, with the exception of governments' 'working balances', are to be held and managed by the ESCB, that is, by the ECB and the participating NCBs. In a number of countries, however, governments have undertaken foreign currency borrowing for the express purpose of boosting official reserves. The advent of EMU threatens to deprive participating governments of the use of their national reserves as a hedge against exchange risk on their foreign currency borrowings and as a ready source of foreign exchange for meeting their repayment obligations. If they are obliged, in EMU, to purchase foreign exchange in the market to meet these non-euro obligations (which total around US$ 90 billion for the EU-11), it could have a sizeable negative impact on the euro exchange rate.

9 There is no particular economic rationale for any of these alternative, but equally arbitrary, representations of the euro as a major reserve currency. Their purpose is to illustrate the orders of magnitude that might be involved if, for the reasons discussed later, the euro were to prove more attractive to reserve managers than existing EU currencies

10 Thus, French finance minister Strauss-Kahn has claimed on several occasions that 'the euro will be the equal of the dollar' and 'one of the two international currencies': see, for example, speeches in Bonn (9 Dec. 1997), France (14 May 1998) and Frankfurt (23 June 1998). At the Council on Foreign Relations in New York (11 Nov. 1997) he added, diplomatically, 'I do not envisage, and moreover do not wish, that [the euro] replace the dollar'. European Commissioner de Silguy (1998) has expressed either the presumption or the

wish that 'the euro should account for a greater share of central bank reserves than that currently taken by European currencies'.

11 Comparable calculations by Henning 1997 and by Bergsten 1997 indicate that a shift of US\$ 795 billion and US\$ 1,000 billion respectively would achieve equality between euro and dollar in international financial markets.

12 Cooper points to the self-reinforcing network externalities that currently favour the dollar, the poorly-developed market in short-term securities in Europe and the fragmentation of European markets by differences in tax treatment. Portes and Rey 1998 also recognize the importance of network externalities and the associated possibility of multiple equilibria, but argue that the expected fall in transactions costs in euro financial markets will result in a switch from the dollar to the euro for financial transactions between Europe and Asia.

13 The absence of such a relationship in the case of the DM and the yen could reflect both their regional and their residual nature as reserve currencies. Whether the euro will share these restricting characteristics remains an open question.

14 For a summary of the extensive debate about the appropriate balance of payments categorization and configuration for a reserve currency country in the context of the dollar 'shortage' in the 1950s and dollar 'glut' in the 1960s, see Yeager 1966 and Cohen 1969. Similar questions have surfaced recently in the debate about current account targeting (see, for example and for references, Williamson and Mahar 1998).

15 The IMF introduced major changes in its balance of payments classification scheme w.e.f. 1994. Under the new scheme, foreign official flows are not identified and short-term flows are no longer shown as a distinct category.

16 These figures will include flows between the EU-11 countries and therefore overstate the size of flows between the euro area and the rest of the world.

17 The effects of a change in monetary policy are discussed in Barrell and Pain 1998a.

18 Further details of the model can be found in NIESR 1998 and in Barrell and Sefton 1997.

19 Our models of the labour market, which are based on Anderton and Barrell 1995, allow for forward-looking behaviour, but we regard the degree of rational expectations effects in this market as an empirical matter, and reactions to shocks are inevitably slow.

20 We have assumed that Sweden remains outside EMU in both scenarios.

21 We do not think that these small gains are a convincing reason in themselves for enduring the political costs of staying outside. Barrell and Pain (1998b and 1998c) argue that the sterling effective rate is significantly overvalued at present (perhaps some 15 per cent above its long-run sustainable level) and that this overvaluation, if sustained into EMU, would have long-run deleterious effects, potentially reducing the size of UK manufacturing permanently by 3 to 5 per cent.

22 In a formal Resolution, the European Council (1997) has instructed ECOFIN to monitor the exchange rate and to exchange views on it with the ECB, but it has also laid down that only in 'exceptional circumstances, for example in the case of a clear misalignment' should ECOFIN 'formulate general orientations for exchange rate policy in relation to non-EC currencies', which are to be consistent with the ECB's primary objective of price stability.

23 It is hard to judge a priori whether asymmetry in this respect would help or hinder the operation of the single monetary policy.

24 Bearing in mind the orders of magnitude of potential capital flows posited earlier, if the ECB is to contemplate an active policy of foreign exchange market

intervention soon after EMU starts, it will probably need to exercise its prospective power to call for a larger reserve pool from member central banks than the maximum of EUR 50 billion initially earmarked under the treaty. In due course, the ECB may find that it accumulates substantial reserves through market intervention, if the current account surpluses and capital inflows envisaged earlier in this paper materialize.

25 The only formal Treaty provisions for policy co-operation between the ECB and the ECOFIN Councils, that their respective presidents may participate (without the right to vote) in meetings of the other, seem quite inadequate for this purpose. With similar reservations in mind, the House of Commons Treasury Committee (1998) have questioned the non-voting role of the UK Treasury representative on the Bank of England's Monetary Policy Committee.

26 Admittedly, other approaches suggest that there may be useful global benefits from policy co-ordination; see for example Masson and Turtelboom 1997: 27 *passim* for estimates of benefits to the EU, USA and Japan from lower short-run exchange-rate and interest-rate volatility.

27 As Henning (1997: 60) points out, although under Article 109 of the Treaty, 'general orientations' on exchange rate policy could be adopted by a qualified majority (of the Euro-11 Council), whereas a decision to include the euro in a formal exchange rate regime would require unanimity, experience of consensus decision-making in the field of multilateral trade negotiations such as the Uruguay Round suggests that, even where unanimity of the Council is not a formal requirement, one large member state may still effectively block agreement at EU level on national grounds. It is perhaps significant that the only pronouncement so far on exchange rate policy for EMU has been by the Heads of State and Government in a Resolution of the European Council (1997); such Resolutions are conventionally made 'by common accord', that is, unanimously.

28 Even as staunch an advocate of target zones and FEERs as Bergsten (1997: 30) argues that EMU will be such a far-reaching shock that there may be no sound basis for estimating a fundamental equilibrium exchange rate for the euro in its early years.

29 This assumes that the EMU authorities would select a range for the euro exchange rate (probably an effective rate) that would be acceptable to its partners in the G3. Should the putative range be unacceptable to the US and Japanese authorities, it would be a lever for getting them to switch from 'benign neglect' to positive co-operation on exchange rate stabilization.

Bibliography

Alogoskoufis, G. and Portes, R. (1997) 'The Euro, the Dollar and the International Monetary System', paper for a seminar on EMU and the International Monetary System, Fondation Camille Gutt/International Monetary Fund, Washington, D.C., 17–18 March.

Anderton, R., Arrowsmith, J. and Wlodek, K. (1997) 'Optimal Portfolios for Institutional Investors in Europe Following Deregulation and Monetary Union', paper presented to the European Financial Markets Advisory Panel, National Institute for Economic and Social Research, London (October).

Anderton, R. and Barrell, R. (1995) 'The ERM and Structural Change in European Labour Markets: A Study of 10 Countries', *Weltwirtschaftliches Archiv*, Band 131, Heft 1.

Arrowsmith, J. (1998) 'Official Reserve Portfolios and International Capital Movements in EMU', draft in mimeo.

Artis, M., Gallo, G. and Salmon, M. (1998) 'What Exchange Rate Policy Should be Adopted for the Euro?', draft in mimeo.

Barr, D. G. (1984) 'Exchange Rate Variability: Evidence for the Period 1973–82', *Bank of England Discussion Papers (Technical Series) no. 11* (November).

Barrell, R. and Pain, N. (1998a) 'EMU: the UK National Context', in J. Bradley (ed.), 'Regional Economic and Policy Impacts of EMU: The Case of Northern Ireland', *Northern Ireland Economic Council Research Monograph no. 6.*

Barrell, R. and Pain, N. (1998b) 'Real Exchange Rates, Agglomerations and Irreversibilities: FDI and Macro Policy in EMU', *Oxford Review of Economic Policy.*

Barrell, R. and Pain, N. (1998c) 'Choosing the Rate Again', *New Economy* (July).

Barrell, R. and Sefton, J. (1997) 'Fiscal Policy and the Maastricht Solvency Criteria', *Manchester School* (June).

Begg, D., Giavazzi, F. and Wyplosz, C. (1998) 'Options for Exchange Rate Policy of the EMU', *Centre for Economic Policy Research Occasional Paper no. 17.*

Bénassy-Quéré, A., Mojon, B. and Pisani-Ferry, J. (1997) 'The Euro and Exchange Rate Stability', *Centre d'études prospectives et d'informations internationales, Working Paper 97–12.*

Bergsten, F. (1997) 'The Impact of the Euro on Exchange Rates and International Policy Co-operation', paper for a seminar on EMU and the International Monetary System, Fondation Camille Gutt/International Monetary Fund, Washington, D.C., 17–18 March.

Brookes, M. (1996) 'EMU's Excess Foreign Reserves', *EMU Briefing* no. 6, Goldman Sachs, London (September).

Catte, P., Galli, G. and Rebecchini, S. (1992) 'Concerted Interventions and the Dollar: An Analysis of Daily Data', paper prepared for the Ossola Memorial Conference, Banca d'Italia, Perugia, 9–10 July.

Cohen, B. J. (1969), *Balance of Payments Policy*, Penguin Modern Economics Texts.

Cooper, R. N. (1998) 'Key Currencies after the Euro', *ICMB Occasional Papers no.11*, International Centre for Monetary and Banking Studies, Geneva (May).

De Silguy, Y.-T. (1998) 'The Impact of the Creation of the Euro on Financial Markets and the International Monetary System', speech at the Institute of International Finance, Washington, D.C., 29 April, European Commission, Speech /97/102.

Duisenberg, W. (1998) 'President's Inroductory Statement' to Press Conference on 8 July, Frankfurt, ECB, available on www.ecb.int/key/sg980708.htm.

European Commission (1990) *One Market, One Money*, European Economy no. 44, Brussels (October).

European Commission (1998) 'The Community Economy in 1997–99: Spring 1998 Economic Forecasts', European Community, Brussels.

European Council (1997) 'Resolution of the European Council on Policy Co-ordi-nation in Stage 3 of EMU and on Treaty Articles 109 and 109b', Presidency Conclusions (Annex 1), Luxembourg European Council, 12–13 December, DOC/97/24.

Frankel, J. and Rose, A. (1997) 'Endogeneity of the Optimum Currency Area Criteria', *Economic Journal* (July) vol. 108.

Funabashi, Y. (1988) *Managing the Dollar: from the Plaza to the Louvre*, Institute for International Economics, Washington, D.C.

Gros, D. and Thygesen, N. (1992) *European Monetary Integration*, St Martin's Press, New York.

Haldane, A. (1991) 'The Exchange Rate Mechanism of the European Monetary System: a Review of the Literature', *Bank of England Quarterly Bulletin* (February).

Henning, C. R. (1997) 'Co-operating with Europe's Monetary Union', *Policy Analyses in International Economics no. 49*, Institute for International Economics, Washington, D.C.

House of Commons Treasury Committee (1998) *Bank of England: Operation of Accountability – One Year On*, Session 1997–98, Seventh Report, The Stationery Office, London (July).

Hughes Hallett, A. and Yue Ma (1996) 'Changing Partners: The Importance of Co-ordinating Fiscal and Monetary Policies Within a Monetary Union', *Manchester School* 64(2) (June).

Kenen, P. B. (1995) *Economic and Monetary Union: Moving Beyond Maastricht*, Cambridge University Press, Cambridge and New York.

Leahy, M. P. (1996) 'The Dollar as an Official Reserve Currency Under EMU', *Open Economies Review* 7: 371–390 (January).

McCauley, R. (1997) 'The Euro and the Dollar', *Essays in International Finance no. 205*, Princeton University, International Finance Section, Princeton, N.J. (November).

Manzocchi, S. and Padoan, P. C. (1997) 'Alternative Uses of Excess Reserves after the Introduction of the Euro', *CIDEI Working Paper no. 44*, CIDEI, Università di Roma 'La Sapienza' (December).

Masson, P. R. and Turtelboom, B.G. (1997) 'Characteristics of the Euro, the Demand for Reserves, and Policy Co–ordination Under EMU', *IMF Working Paper*, WP/97/58, International Monetary Fund, Washington, D.C. (May).

Meade, J. and Weale, M. (1995) 'Monetary Union and the Assignment Problem', *Scandinavian Journal of Economics* 2 (May).

NIESR (1998) *The National Institute World Model Users Manual* (July).

Nolan, C. and Schaling, E. (1996) 'International Monetary Policy Co-ordination: Some Lessons from the Literature', *Bank of England Quarterly Bulletin* (November).

Poole, W. (1992) 'Exchange-Rate Management and Monetary-Policy Misalignment: A Study of Germany, Japan, United Kingdom and United States after Plaza', *Carnegie-Rochester Conference Series on Public Policy 36*.

Portes, R. and Rey, H. (1998) 'The Emergence of the Euro as an International Currency', in D. Begg, J. von Hagen, C. Wyplosz and K. F. Zimmermann (eds), *EMU: Prospects and Challenges for the Euro*, Blackwell, Oxford.

Rogoff, K. (1985) 'Can International Monetary Co-operation be Counter-Productive?', *Journal of International Economics* 18.

Sekkat, K. (1998) 'Exchange Rate Variability and EU Trade', *European Commission Economic Papers no. 127* (February).

Shafer, J. R. and Loopesko, B. E. (1983) 'Floating Exchange Rates After Ten Years', *Brookings Papers on Economic Activity*, Brookings Institution, Washington, D.C.

Taylor, C. T. (1997) 'Potential Monetary/Fiscal Policy Conflicts in EMU: Simple Analytics and Some Model-based Estimates', paper presented at a conference on The Monetary, Fiscal and Financial Implications of European Monetary Union, European University Institute, Florence, 27/28 June.

Taylor, C. T. (1998) 'Long-Run Exchange Rate Instability Among Major Currencies:

Some Unsophisticated Estimates', draft in mimeo available from author.

Taylor, M. P. and Artis, M. (1988) 'What has the European Monetary System Achieved?', *Bank of England Discussion Papers no. 31* (March).

Ungerer, H., Evans, O., Mayer, T. and Young, P. (1986) 'The European Monetary System: Recent Developments', *IMF Occasional Papers no. 48*, International Monetary Fund,

Williamson, J. (1983, rev. 1985) 'The Exchange Rate System', *Policy Analyses in International Economics no. 5*, Institute for International Economics, Washington, D.C.

Williamson, J. (1992) 'External Implications of EMU', in R. Barrell (ed.), *Economic Convergence and Monetary Union in Europe*, Sage for the National Institute of Economic and Social Research.

Williamson, J. (1993) 'Exchange Rate Management', *Economic Journal* 103 (January).

Williamson, J. and Mahar, M. (1998) 'Current Account Targets', Appendix 1 in S. Wren-Lewis and R. Driver, *Real Exchange Rates for the Year 2000*, Policy Analyses in International Economics, Institute for International Economics, Washington, D.C. (May).

Yeager, L. B. (1966) *International Monetary Relations*, Harper and Row, New York.

10 Are European central banks over-capitalized?

Daniel Gros and Franziska Schobert

Introduction: are European central banks over-capitalized?

In textbooks central banks have a very simple balance sheet: their liabilities consist of the monetary base. On the asset side one finds either domestic assets, that is, claims on domestic banks or the government, or foreign assets, that is, foreign exchange reserves. Some authors add that capital also appears on the liability side and that the accounting for losses and gains on foreign assets due to exchange rate changes is difficult. Overall, however, the impression one gets from textbooks is that the balance sheet of a central bank should be simple. This is not the case in reality.

The job of central banks is to conduct monetary policy, not to maximize profits. The job of the European System of Central Banks (ESCB) is to maintain price stability. Thus the details of the balance sheets of the constituent national central banks and their profit and loss accounts should be irrelevant. But this is unlikely to be the case for several reasons.

A first reason is that central banks care about the profitability of their financial position in defining their day-to-day policies. Sometimes great importance is attributed to losses or gains that appear negligible in a macroeconomic context, for example if expressed as a percentage of GDP. It is understandable that central banks try to avoid losses. This is indispensable if they want to maintain their financial independence. Moreover, if a central bank makes large losses in some operations, others, presumably some private market operators (often called 'speculators'), make correspondingly large profits. Loss-making operations imply thus a subsidy for the private sector.

A second reason is that the balance sheet of the European Central Bank (ECB) is negligible as practically all operations are implemented by the national central banks. One has to concentrate on the balance of the system, that is, of the ESCB, which in turn is made up of the consolidated sum of the balance sheets of the component national central banks. This is different from the situation even in very federally organized countries. In Germany the Landeszentralbanken do not have their own balance sheets. In the US each Federal Reserve Bank publishes its financial statement individually as well, but these regional balance sheets are irrelevant as they reflect only the policy of the system (decided by the Board of Governors of the Federal Reserve System), whereas the balance sheets of the national central banks of the Eurozone reflect many other activities as shown below. A further difference from the US is that the ESCB as such is not even a legal entity.

One thus has to aggregate the national balance sheets if one wants to analyse the position of the system. Moreover, the balance sheets of national central banks differ greatly in their structure, so that aggregation is not straightforward, and there are great differences in their exposure to foreign exchange losses.

The combination of these elements is potentially troublesome because the allocation of profits and losses within the ESCB is governed by different principles from that of the determination of the common monetary policy. The monetary policy is the same for everybody, but there is no solidarity in financial terms. Decisions on monetary policy are taken by the Governing Council in which all members have one vote. Financial matters are discussed only by the governors alone, so that the six members of the Executive Board are excluded, and decisions are taken with weighted voting (capital shares constitute the weights). There is thus a risk that there are different majorities for the setting of monetary policy and for decisions concerning financial matters, including distributing the profits of the system.

The fact that the common monetary policy is not reflected in a common balance sheet means also that the system has no automatic mechanism for ensuring financial solidarity in a case where a particular national central bank makes large losses. The Treaty recognizes this when it leaves this matter to *ad hoc* decisions by the Governing Council of the ECB as foreseen in Article 32.4 of the Statutes of the ESCB:

> The Governing Council may decide that national central banks shall be indemnified for costs incurred in connection with the issuance of bank notes or *in exceptional circumstances for specific losses arising from monetary policy operations* undertaken for the ESCB. The indemnification shall be in the form deemed appropriate in the judgement of the Governing Council.

The inadequacy of the ESCB statute regarding the financing of losses is not uncommon in central banking laws.[1] But as losses within the ESCB imply transfers across countries, it is more important to provide clear guidelines for this eventuality in the case of the ESCB than in the case of a normal (national) central bank.

Central bank losses can be separated into current losses and capital losses. Current losses arise from imbalances in current revenues and expenditures; but they are rare for industrialized countries. Central banks

make large losses only when domestic interest rates are much above international ones and the central bank attempts to sterilize large capital
inflows. This is unlikely to happen under the European Monetary Union
(EMU). Capital losses result from differential changes in the value of assets
and liabilities, mainly from exchange rate changes, which affect the value
of the central bank's foreign exchange reserves. This has been a problem
for some national central banks with very large foreign exchange reserves
(for example Portugal). It might also be a problem for the ECB, whose
balance sheet on the asset side will be dominated by the approximately 40
billion euro in foreign exchange reserves it has called up from the national
central banks so far. However, most losses arising from unrealized valuation changes on the asset side are not visible, as they are usually excluded
from the profit and loss account. Instead, they are matched by corresponding changes in a revaluation account on the liability side. The ESCB
is likely to follow this practice. According to the approved accounting principles for the ESCB, the balance sheet will mainly reflect market values.
Unrealized gains from revaluations will not be recognized as income.
Unrealized losses will be taken to the profit and loss account if they exceed
previous revaluation gains registered in the revaluation account (EMI
1997: 77).

One can argue that central bank losses do not matter at all. For
example, Robinson and Stella argue that 'unlike commercial banks, there
is no reason why a central bank cannot continually make losses and have a
persistently negative net worth. Therefore, unlike other public sector
entities, central bank losses need not be "funded"' (Robinson and Stella
1988: 23). However this position does not take into consideration the
possible negative impact of losses on a central banks' prestige and
authority (Vaez-Zadeh 1991: 76). Moreover, the power to create money to
finance losses is soon likely to run into conflict with the goal of protecting
domestic price stability. A sterilization of this outcome either has an
adverse effect on the domestic financial system, or demands an interaction
between the central bank and the treasury. Thus, although central banks
need not have capital to function in a technical sense, a deterioration of
their balance sheets might be followed by a loss of control over inflation,
by a repression on the domestic financial system or by a threat to its institutional independence (Stella 1997: 10–12).

Apart from some important general reasons for analysing the balance
sheets of central banks, there is also a specific reason to look closer at the
structure of European central banks on the eve of EMU, which has
attracted much public attention.[2] It is the fact that in EMU, national
central banks will no longer need all the foreign exchange reserves that
they accumulated in the past. Some politicians have even proposed to use
these excess foreign exchange reserves to fund large-scale European initiatives.[3] But foreign exchange reserves are just part of the overall
asset–liabilities management of central banks. The question of excess

reserves is just part of the general issue of why central banks should own large amounts of assets, whether foreign exchange reserves or claims on commercial banks. The issue of excess foreign exchange reserves liberated by EMU is thus implicit in the entire discussion of this paper. However, as foreign exchange reserves are only part of the general problem of over-capitalization of European central banks, we have preferred discussing this deeper issue instead of concentrating only on the one part that has attracted most public attention.

The remainder of this paper is organized as follows. The next section analyses the balance sheet of the ESCB and compares it with that of the US Federal Reserve and of the Bank of Japan. It also shows that more independent central banks had a 'cleaner' balance sheet (in the sense defined later). The third section tries to aggregate national balance sheets to establish how that of the ESCB will look like at the start of EMU. The fourth section then turns to the future and presents a model balance sheet for a lean ESCB. The fifth section asks what kind of asset mix (domestic versus foreign) the ESCB should hold. The paper concludes by stressing that it is in the interest of the national central banks and the ECB to be much more transparent in their financial accounting, because otherwise serious problems could arise with the Treaty provisions on the distribution of seigniorage, and because financial transparency is part of accountability.

Central bank balance sheets: a comparative perspective

What do the balance sheets of central banks in Europe look like? We will discuss this separately for liabilities and assets.

Liabilities

Table 10.1 gives the standard broad items on the liability side for the eleven participants in EMU. In this table all items were simply added (after converting them into euro) without any attempt to consolidate claims within this group. For comparison, we also include the same data for the US and Japan. The data refer to the end of 1997.

The starting point is also interesting in a longer-run perspective, because once EMU starts, national central banks will lose any residual control over the evolution of their balance sheets, at least if they only implement the common monetary policy and do not engage in any other transactions.

The first row of Table 10.1 shows that the central banks of the EU-11 countries, Japan and the US have a monetary base of a similar size.[4] The more important lesson that emerges from this table is that the euro area balance sheet is much longer than the standard textbook central bank balance sheet. Total liabilities and capital accounts are, at 753 billion euro, more than one and a half times as big as the monetary base. We will show

Table 10.1 Liabilities of central banks (end 1997) in billion euro

	Sum of EU-11 national central banks	US Federal Reserve	Bank of Japan
Monetary base	429	442	405
o/w banknotes in circulation	335	414	381
o/w deposits of financial institutions	94	28	24
Other liabilities and capital accounts	324	86	98
Total liabilities and capital accounts	753	528	503

Source: Financial statements of national central banks, 1997 (details may not add up to totals because of rounding)

that the initial ESCB monetary base will amount to only about 400 billion euro if one takes into account that the minimum required reserves decided by the ECB are much lower than that of the Banca d'Italia as of end-1997. The data for the US and Japan show that such a large difference between monetary base and total assets is not a feature of other large central banks.[5]

The aggregate data in Table 10.1 hide the large differences among national central banks. Table 10.2 therefore gives the percentage share of liabilities and capital accounted for by the monetary base for the EU-11 countries, the US and Japan. Gold and foreign assets are valued at market prices, and the monetary base has been harmonized in order to avoid differences in the monetary base resulting from national discrepancies in minimum reserve holdings.[6] The Bundesbank with 69.4 per cent, while still far from the US or the Japanese values, has one of the cleanest balances in the EU-11. The case of Portugal stands out because the total liabilities of the Banco do Portugal are over four times larger than the monetary base. The reason is that when reserve requirements were reduced from about 16 per cent the Bank of Portugal did not allow commercial banks to dispose of the deposits they had, but transformed them into medium-term liabilities which will mature in 2004. When they mature, the balance sheet of the Bank of Portugal will shrink considerably.

Assets

A first problem, which is common to all analyses of the asset side of central bank balance sheets, is that of valuing gold. As gold is no longer actively used for monetary policy purposes we simply value gold at market prices. We would argue however that one should no longer count it among foreign exchange reserves. We will return to this proposal later.

The positions of national central banks at the International Monetary Fund (IMF), including holdings of Special Drawing Rights (SDRs), are also part of foreign exchange reserves, but should be treated differently

Table 10.2 The monetary base of central banks as a percentage of total liabilities and capital accounts

Germany	France	Italy	Spain	Austria	Belgium	Ireland
69.4	55.8	37.5	66.5	53.7	52.7	53.2

Luxembourg	Netherlands	Portugal	Finland	EU-11	USA	Japan
64.2	56.0	25.8	38.8	55.4	85.2	82.3

Source: Financial statements of national central banks, 1997 and own calculations assuming a minimum reserve ratio of 2%

because in general they will not be liquidated. EMU will not change the fact that countries, not currencies, are members of the IMF, so that the introduction of the euro does not affect the legal positions of national central banks *vis-à-vis* the IMF. However, it is clear that from an economic point of view all countries of the Eurozone should now be treated equally, in the sense that when the IMF needs liquidity in euro it should go to the national central banks in fixed proportions. In a longer-term perspective it would make sense to use capital shares in the ECB as the key. The corresponding claims on the IMF that will appear on the books of the national central banks should thus be proportional to their share in the ECB, which would facilitate the eventual complete pooling of foreign exchange reserves. This line of reasoning would also suggest (but of course does not imply as a logical corollary) that over time, the relative quotas of member countries in the IMF should also be proportional to their capital shares.

A more radical solution would be for the IMF to deal directly with the ECB from the start of EMU, so that the use of the euro by the IMF would lead to claims by the ECB on the IMF. This is explicitly foreseen in Article 30.5: 'The ECB may hold and manage IMF reserve positions and SDRs and provide for the pooling of such assets.' National central banks would still be the ultimate beneficiaries of these claims because they own the shares of the ECB. This solution would also pave the way for a re-arrangement (and probably also reduction) of the quotas of EMU countries.[7]

Why would central banks accumulate so many items on their balance sheet that have little to do with the execution of monetary policy? The main reason must be that most national central banks were, over the last decades, in a quite different position from that in which they are today. During the 1970s and 1980s most were not independent, inflation was much higher, and the national banking systems were often highly distorted. Until capital market liberalization was imposed through the internal market programme, national central banks in a number of member countries had special relations with certain groups of banks, and gave the public sector privileged access to financing. During this period they thus accumulated large stocks of assets that did not result from monetary policy operations. The more distorted the banking system, and the higher inflation, the stronger in general was the incentive for governments to lean on central banks in order to provide cheap financing or somehow to offset the high implicit taxation on the banking sector, which resulted from the combination of high nominal interest rates and high required reserve ratios. After about 1992 all this had to stop, partially because of the liberalization of banking under the Internal Market Programme, and ultimately because the Maastricht Treaty forced governments to make central banks independent and allow them to concentrate on monetary policy in their role as guardians of price stability. However, the stocks that they had accumulated were there; they were frozen, but no national central bank showed much inclination to get rid of them. If this conjecture about the genesis of the excess assets on central bank balance sheets is true, their size should be correlated with central bank independence and inflation. This is indeed the case as is shown in Figures 10.1 and 10.2.

Indicators of the 'cleanliness' of the balance sheets of a central bank (the share of the monetary base in total liabilities and capital accounts) are directly calculated from central bank balance sheet data, and from data from International Financial Statistics (IFS). The countries included are participants of the EMU. The data from the balance sheets are adjusted for

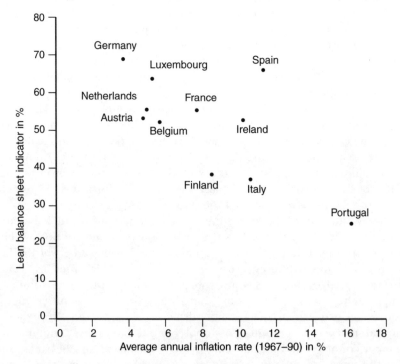

Figure 10.1 Average inflation and lean balance sheet indicator for central banks

Source: Annual reports of national central banks 1997, IFS 1997; authors' calculations assuming a minimum reserve ratio of 2%

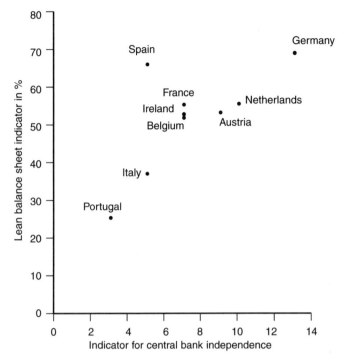

Figure 10.2 Indicators for central bank independence and lean balance sheets

Source: Annual reports of national central banks 1997, 1FS 1998, Grilli, Masciandarro and Tabellini 1991, authors' calculations assuming a minimum reserve ratio of 2%

differences in minimum reserves, and valued at market rates. Both lean balance sheet indicators are indeed highly correlated with the average inflation rate during the pre-Maastricht period (1967–90). Countries with higher inflation typically had balance sheets in which the monetary base was only a small part of total liabilities and capital accounts. The correlation coefficient is about -0.7 and -0.6 for the indicator calculated directly from balance sheet data and calculated from IFS data. Assuming a normal distribution, it is statistically significant at the usual confidence levels.

The correlation with central bank independence is strong as well. More independent central banks had clearly cleaner balance sheets. The correlation coefficients are between 0.7 and 0.8 depending on the two lean balance sheet indicators. They are again statistically significant. For central bank independence we use here the most popular indicator by Grilli, Masciandarro and Tabellini (1991).[8]

The balance sheets of national central banks today are thus an indicator of their past in terms of independence and price stability. Adjusting balance sheets today cannot change this. However, the excess assets and liabilities that central banks still carry on their balance sheets constitute a nuisance and, in some cases, even a potential threat for the financial independence of certain national central banks.

Portugal represents an extreme case (see also Stella 1997: 23–7). The Banco do Portugal is really a hedge fund. It has levered its capital by a factor of almost five to invest in mainly foreign assets, and is thus taking enormous risks. Until not so long ago, investing in foreign assets was a better investment than investing in domestic Portuguese assets because the currency was depreciating and domestic interest rates were controlled. This will be completely different under EMU. With non-euro (presumably mostly US dollar) assets larger than its monetary base, the Banco do Portugal runs the risk of making large losses if the US dollar depreciates suddenly.

Taking stock: the balance sheet of the ESCB

Constructing a detailed balance sheet for the ESCB from national data should in principle be easy. It should be sufficient to add all assets and liabilities in different categories and then account for the limited pooling of reserves of 39.5 billion euro that has been decided so far. In reality, however, we found out that constructing the balance sheet of the ESCB is very difficult, because the balance sheets of most national central banks are so opaque that it is very difficult to find out exactly what kind of assets and liabilities are behind the various items recorded on them. Accounting rules vary from country to country, so it is not straightforward to compare balance sheets across countries.

For example, the Bank of Italy carries a security on its balance sheet which is a residual of its past activities with the treasury before the Bank of Italy gained more independence. This claim on the government has a book value of 39 billion euro, about 20 per cent of its published total asset value. But considering its nominal interest rate of 1 per cent and its long time till maturity (the last tranche will become due in 2044), the market value of this asset is only about 30 per cent of its nominal value.

Another example is Finland. In accord with the Act on the Bank of Finland, fixed assets, shareholdings and long-term expenditures are entered in full as expenditures in the year of acquisition, and thus do not appear on the balance sheet. Although the absolute amount of these items is not so important in relation to total assets, it is just one more reason why central bank balance sheets are not easily comparable.

The most egregious case of accounting rules that hide the true value of assets concerns the 'lower of cost or market value' used until recently by the Bundesbank. Under this approach the foreign exchange reserves are valued at the lowest value ever recorded. For example, at the end of 1996 the Bundesbank valued its US dollars in foreign exchange reserves at 1.36 (this rate was reached briefly during a period of exceptional dollar weakness in early 1995) whereas the end-year exchange rate was 1.55. At the end of 1997 the Bundesbank adjusted its accounting principles and valued its dollar reserves at 1.54 (compared with a market rate of 1.79), the main reason for the extraordinary high profit in 1997.

This 'lower of cost or market value' is in contrast to the principle 'mark to market' that is widely used in the private financial sector. Understating systematically the true value of assets might be useful for enterprises that want to be careful not to overstate their financial wealth (and thereby save taxes), but there is no reason for adopting this principle for a central bank. In Germany it is sometimes argued that if the Bundesbank abandoned conservative accounting principles other institutions would follow and that this would not be desirable, but this argument is not convincing. If valuing assets below the market value allows firms to save on taxes they will continue to do so even if the Bundesbank changes its practice. But as US accounting principles, which in any case are being adopted almost every-where, embody the principle of 'mark to market', it is not likely that the behaviour of the Bundesbank will have a strong impact. Moreover, the ESCB will also adopt this principle.

The case of gold is another example. Given that there is no prospect that gold will ever again be used actively in the international monetary system, it may actually make sense to avoid the continuous revaluation gains and losses that valuing at market prices would imply. But if gold is no longer to be used one may ask why central banks should still carry it on their balance sheets. The decision by the ECB to use gold for 15 per cent of the total call-up of reserves is difficult to understand from this point of view. The amount thus obtained would anyway be insufficient if gold ever returned to occupy an important role.

The ECB has decided to present its balance sheet and that of the ESCB according to the 'mark to market' principle. However, it is impossible to deduce from the aggregate ESCB figures how the national components would look if they all followed the common accounting rules.

The only point about the balance sheet of the ESCB that is clear at present is that it has no financial implications, as Article 26.3 makes clear: 'For analytical and operational purposes, the Executive Board shall draw up a consolidated balance sheet of the ESCB, comprising those assets and liabilities of the national central banks that fall within the ESCB.' The second half of this statement could be taken to mean that the balance sheet of the system would comprise, on a consolidated basis, only the monetary base on the book of national central banks. If the ECB were to choose this interpretation it could simply consider the other liabilities on the balance sheets of national central banks as being irrelevant for monetary policy. This is explicitly foreseen in Article 14.4 of the statute of the ECB, which says that national central banks may perform functions 'other than those specified in this Statute', unless a majority of two-thirds in the Governing Council finds that they interfere with the monetary policy of the system. However, first indications are that the ECB will not follow this route, since this would require national central banks also to choose which assets they would consider as the counterpart to the monetary base. The choice of the assets would, in turn, have implications for the distribution of seigniorage.

Table 10.3 shows our best guess of what the initial balance sheet of the ESCB would look like. Foreign assets are valued at market prices, deposits of financial institutions have been adjusted for a minimum reserve ratio of 2 per cent, the rolling swap operations creating ecu for the European Monetary Cooperation Fund have been unwound and an estimated amount of intra EMU currencies, which used to be counted as foreign assets, will become counted as domestic assets. We assumed 60 billion euro to be intra EMU currencies in foreign assets. The estimation of intra-EMU currencies is based on end of 1995 figures (Masson and Turtelboom 1997: 16). Assuming a proportional increase of the value of intra-EMU currencies and total foreign exchange reserves in the EU-11 countries, the figure could be about 25 per cent higher. However as these adjustments have only a limited impact this consolidated balance sheet is not much different from the simple sum of balance sheets for the national central banks presented earlier.[9]

The figure 'Other liabilities and capital accounts' amounting to 324 billion euro includes the items which could be disposed of as counterparts to a reduction on the asset side. We identified almost 250 billion euro. This consists of about 112 billion euro of revaluation reserves, 26 billion euro of capital and reserves, 32 billion euro of provisions, 28 billion euro of debt certificates issued by national central banks and 50 billion euro of public sector accounts. The biggest share, the revaluation reserves, will appear on a revaluation account after foreign exchange reserves and gold have been marked to market.

Table 10.3 The initial balance sheet of the ESCB (in billion euro)

Assets			Liabilities and capital accounts		
Foreign		325	Monetary base		402
of which: gold	108		of which: banknotes in circulation	335	
			of which: deposits of financial institutions	66	
Domestic assets		401	Other liabilities and capital accounts		324
Total assets		725	Total liabilities and capital accounts		725

Source: Own elaboration on data from financial statements of national central banks and other national sources, International Monetary Fund, International Financial Statistics, and Masson and Turtelboom 1997: 16 (details may not add up to totals because of rounding)

A comparison of the ESCB and the US Federal Reserve System

An example of simplicity: the allocation of assets and returns across Federal Reserve Banks in the US

Formally the US Federal Reserve System is much more federally structured than the Bundesbank in that it is based on twelve Federal Reserve Banks which are all legally separate and independent entities with their own balance sheets, and presidents that are elected by local representatives. However, in most respects the system is *de facto* completely unified, even more than the German system in which the *Landeszentralbanken* have no separate balance sheets because they are *de jure* only departments (*Hauptverwaltungen*) of the Bundesbank.

The regional accounting is based on two keys: a capital key that is relevant for foreign assets and a note issue key that is relevant for domestic assets.

Foreign assets and the capital key

The capital of the System is based on contributions from member commercial banks. Any federally chartered (commercial) bank in the US must buy a part of the capital of the Federal Reserve System (on which it obtains a fixed dividend yield of 6 per cent). The participation of each commercial bank is based on its own capital. The share of any Reserve Banks in the total capital of the Federal Reserve System is thus proportional to the sum of the capital of the commercial banks located in its district. (It is surprising that despite the concentration of banking activity in Manhattan, the New York Federal Reserve has only about 20 per cent of the aggregate capital of the system. The reason is that although many large banks are headquartered in New York, their subsidiaries in different states are formally incorporated as independent banks because of the restrictions on inter-state banking. This might now change as all the remaining restrictions on inter-state banking are lifted. One consequence of this could be seen in 1997, when a bank headquartered in the Federal Reserve District of Richmond acquired another large bank from a different area. As a result the share of the Richmond Federal Reserve in the overall capital doubled in one year.)

The New York Fed has a special role in the system in that it manages all foreign exchange interventions for the system. However, the New York Fed does not intervene on its own account. All foreign exchange interventions are booked directly to an account of the System; the role of the New York Fed is only to provide the personnel that manages this account of the System. The New York Fed acts under instruction from the Board in Washington (and under a special authorization which has to be formally renewed every year).

The foreign exchange position of the System that results from any interventions is then distributed on the accounts of all Federal Reserve Banks according to the capital key. As foreign exchange positions carry the risk of losses, they are distributed on the basis of the 'ability to bear losses' principle, which is supposed to be represented by capital. (Foreign exchange swaps remain on the books of the New York Federal Reserve and thus constitute the only significant exception to the rule that foreign exchange related operations are distributed according to the capital key.)

Domestic assets and the note issue key

All dollar bank notes have to carry an identifier, which marks them as the liability of a particular Reserve Bank. This was needed at the start of the Federal Reserve System, when the dollar was convertible into gold and all the constituent Reserve Banks had their own separate gold holdings. At the beginning of each year the printing department decides how many notes to print for each of the twelve District Reserve Banks. (Once a note has the New York identifier it is considered issued by the Federal Reserve of New York even if it is handed out to the public by the San Francisco Federal Reserve.)

By law the issue of currency has to be backed by assets. Each individual Reserve Bank has therefore to have on its book Treasury Bills, or other securities, equivalent to the amount of bank notes with its identifier. However, individual Federal Reserve Banks do not engage directly in purchases and sales of securities. Instead, the New York Federal Reserve Bank executes open market transactions on behalf of the system and holds the resulting securities in the so-called System Open Market Account (SOMA). The balance on this account is then distributed over the balance sheets of the individual Reserve Banks according to the note issue key, ensuring that the domestic assets of the entire system are allocated across the individual Federal Reserve Banks according the amounts of currency that they have issued. The same applies to the returns; there is thus an (almost) perfect correspondence between the allocation of note issue and the allocation of the income from domestic assets. As almost 40 per cent of all notes are issued by the New York Federal Reserve it is also credited with a similar percentage of the total return on domestic assets, but this is independent of its role as the manager of the open market operations of the system.

Adjusting to EMU I: a proposal for a lean ESCB

We have showed that the balance sheets of national central banks are much more complicated and opaque than is necessary. The example of the US shows that even a federally structured central bank can be transparent in its accounting.[10] There is therefore no reason why the national central banks in the Eurozone should not aim at the 'clean' balance sheet of the textbook central bank that is only concerned with conducting monetary policy. This would imply that they simply pay off all their liabilities except the monetary base plus a minimum capital base.

The balance sheet of the ESCB would then become much shorter (and simpler) as illustrated in Table 10.4. The total of assets and liabilities would shrink by about 300 billion euro, from about 720 billion euro to 420 billion euro. The liability side, which in our view should determine the size of the overall balance sheet, would be composed of a euro-area monetary base of 402 billion euro (unchanged) and capital and revaluation reserves of 18 billion euro. The monetary base would consist mostly of cash in circulation, as the ECB will use a reserve coefficient of 2 per cent. The amount foreseen for capital was set at about 4 per cent of the total monetary base using the Bundesbank and the Federal Reserve as examples.[11] This sum is also several times the capital of the ECB, which is only 5 billion euro.

The amount of the revaluation reserve could be estimated by a value-at-risk (VaR) approach. As the volatility of the euro against other major reserve currencies is unknown yet, the sample calculation is based on a portfolio worth of DM 100 billion at the end of 1997. The portfolio consists of US dollars and Japanese yen, the US dollar is the primary reserve currency and the Japanese yen the third most important reserve currency at present. The procedure chosen for computing the VaR is based on a standard variance–covariance model, a most simple model as it is assumed that all asset price changes can be modelled as conditionally normally distributed. The VaR of the portfolio (VaR_P) consisting of asset 1 and 2 would be:

$$VaR_P = \sqrt{(VaR_1)^2 + (VaR_2)^2 + 2VaR_1 VaR_2 \rho_{12}}$$

where ρ is the correlation between the two assets and the individual VaR_j of each position is calculated:

$$VaR_j = E_j \times b \times \sigma_j$$

E is the exposure of the individual position, b is a parameter depending on the desired confidence interval and σ_j is the standard deviation of the individual position. The computation chosen for calculating the VaR_P for the foreign assets of the model central bank focuses only on the foreign exchange risk and is nondiversified. Blejer and Schumacher (1998: 23) argue that the calculation of a diversified VaR could be favourable for stable conditions, but in scenarios of crises or contagion, correlations tend to be very high. Thus, it is a more cautious option not to consider effects of diversification. Data for calculating the VaR are taken from the Regulatory Data Set (J. P. Morgan 1998a) and are adjusted to comply with the volatilities suggested by the Basel Committee on Banking Supervision of the Bank for International Settlements (BIS). The BIS rules require market risk estimates to be calculated over a ten-day holding period and a 99 per cent confidence interval.

The VaR$_P$ of the foreign exchange portfolio ranges from DM 4.3 billion to 6.6 billion depending on the composition of the portfolio (a higher US dollar share implying a lower VaR$_P$ in this case). The interpretation of the VaR$_P$ is that, given a foreign exchange portfolio of DM 100 billion at the end of 1997, the forecasted amount that may be lost given an adverse market move ranges between about DM 4.3–6.6 billion in 99 per cent of all outcomes over the next ten days. However, the procedure chosen has several disadvantages. For example, it cannot be applied to nonlinear positions and it requires the assumption of normal distributions. Distributions of changes in asset prices have been found to have 'thicker tails' than are predicted by a normal distribution. This means that extreme movements seem to occur more frequently than are predicted by a normal distribution (J. P. Morgan, *RiskMetrics*, 1996: 64, 65). Thus, especially in times of pressure on the exchange rate, the risk might be underestimated by this method.

For the proposed ESCB balance sheet we have chosen a revaluation reserve of about 5 per cent, which would be suitable for the above sample portfolio and for the method chosen to calculate the VaR$_P$ given equal weighing of US dollar and yen positions in the portfolio. However, the proposed amount of the revaluation reserve could be quite different depending on the future volatility of the euro exchange rate. (See Table 10.4.)

The asset side of the model ESCB balance sheet would consist, as usual, of foreign exchange reserves plus domestic assets. Ideally domestic assets should consist only of claims on the private sector. There is no reason why national central banks, which are part of a system which has been barred

Table 10.4 A proposal for a lean ESCB balance sheet (in billion euro)

Assets		Liabilities		
Foreign exchange	100	Monetary base		402
o/w gold	0	o/w banknotes in circulation	335	
		o/w deposits of financial institutions	66	
Domestic assets	320	Capital and reserves		18
Total assets	420	Total liabilities and capital accounts		420

Source: see Table 10.3

from financing governments either directly or indirectly, should keep any claims on governments. (Foreign exchange reserves consist usually of government paper, but on governments outside the area.) However, as markets in private debt are usually not as deep and liquid as markets in government debt, this proposal might not be feasible. It is also apparent that all non-marketable assets should disappear. As far as possible, national central banks should also realize claims they have of a similar nature on private sector institutions. The counterparts on the liability side can be everything apart from the recommended items mentioned earlier. One obvious item will be the excessive revaluation reserve. On the proposed ESCB balance sheet it is much lower than on the initial balance sheet of the ESCB. One reason is that gold is not kept on the accounts of the central banks any more, and so the high difference between the former book value and the market value of gold disappears from the revaluation reserve. Another reason is that the risk the ESCB faces will possibly never be so great as to justify a revaluation reserve of its initial size. The exact value depends on the overall risk of the asset portfolio. Even if a more advanced method is chosen to calculate the VaR_P of the ESCB, the absolute amount should not be nearly as high as the present revaluation reserve. (For an assessment of central bank risk see Blejer and Schumacher 1998.) Other items on the liability side could also be used as counterparts. For example, the various kinds of provisions national central banks keep on their balance sheets could be scrutinized in more detail for this purpose. Even after all this is done, however, one is left with the issue of what mix of foreign and domestic assets should be kept.

Adjusting to EMU II: the composition of the asset side, or what to do with excess foreign exchange reserves

Even after the balance sheets of the national central banks have been cut down to a reasonable size, one is still left with the question what mixture of asset should remain. The main choice here is between domestic and foreign assets. The sum of the total foreign assets of the eleven national central banks is almost the same size as the monetary base of the system. It follows that, even if one subtracts from the sum of foreign assets the part that is held in intra-Eurozone currencies, some foreign exchange reserves should be disposed of; unless one accepts that the ESCB starts off virtually without any domestic assets.

The level of reserves in most industrial countries is determined primarily by the perceived need for reserves for very short-term exchange rate management. Wealth or portfolio considerations do not generally influence the level of foreign exchange reserves held by the central bank, but rather its composition (Roger 1993: 13). It is thus difficult to estimate the optimum level of foreign exchange reserves for countries or areas such as the Eurozone which tend to have very open capital markets. They might desire a certain level of reserves, not for actually using it in interventions, but rather to have a 'war chest' for potential speculative attacks. This demand is highly subjective, and thus cannot easily be transformed into an operational figure to measure the level of optimum reserves.

The issue of excess foreign exchange reserves arises, however, whether or not our proposal of reducing the balance sheet of the ESCB is adopted. The general question that arises in this context is why central banks, which are after all part of the public sector, should hold large amounts of low-yielding assets when the government at the same time pays more on its debt.

A related argument applies to the case of gold. As it does not play a role in the international monetary system there is no reason why it should be held by central banks; the current holdings of national central banks could thus be transferred to national ministries of finance. The question whether or not gold should be sold is a different issue, and depends mainly on expectations about future gold prices. A common argument for not selling the gold reserves of central banks is that if major central banks start selling gold, other central banks will follow in order to avoid losses. This will put further pressure on the gold price and thus will create instability in the gold market.

National central banks have been extremely reluctant to divest themselves of any assets. The main reason for this attitude is that every bureaucracy instinctively wants to hold on to any control over resources it has. The reason adduced by central banks is naturally different. They argue that transferring any assets to governments will only lead to more wasteful expenditure, as most governments and parliaments would probably not resist the temptation to use at least part of these assets to finance their deficits instead of simply reducing public debt. This view betrays a particular view of democracy, but it is probably also realistic.

We would argue that stripping their role as investment managers from central banks allows them to concentrate on their role as guardians of price stability, and can only increase their independence. Otherwise they would have to be held accountable not only for price stability, but also for their performance as managers of a large portfolio of foreign investments.

The decisions taken so far by the ECB imply that national central banks will keep all their assets, but distinguish between their investment portfolios and the rest, which they want to keep liquid in case there is a further call on reserves by the ECB. Our position would be that there is no reason why central banks should manage a sizeable investment portfolio on behalf of the country. Even if they perform better than in the past, they are unlikely to outperform the market. An asset swap operation would be particularly appropriate in countries where foreign exchange reserves are large relative to public debt. Portugal represents the extreme in this respect, as foreign assets held by the central bank amount to about 10 per cent of GDP, compared to an overall gross public debt ratio of slightly above 60 per cent of GDP.

Conclusions

We would argue that a monetary union and the creation of the ESCB constitute a good occasion to simplify and streamline the balance sheets of national central banks, which in many cases contain items that are only of historical interest. Moreover, the ESCB should stop the tendency for central banks to hide the true state of their balance sheets from public view. There is no reason why the ESCB should not be completely open about the financial situation of its constituent national central banks.

As this area belongs formally to the responsibility of national central banks, it is up to them to act and dispose of parts of their assets and liabilities until the remainder is equal to the monetary base plus a small capital and an appropriate revaluation reserve. Of the approximately 300 billion euro excess balance sheet items, the excess assets that represent net wealth amount probably to about 100 billion euro, mostly in the form of the excess foreign exchange reserves. The counterparts on the liability side are excess revaluation reserves. These excess assets belong to the governments, and represent real wealth that was accumulated before EMU started. They should be used to reduce public debt.

The direct financial gain from this operation would be modest. There would be an immediate reduction in public debt ratios, as measured under the gross concept of the Maastricht Treaty. The reduction would be modest, however. The 100 billion euro correspond to about 1.5 per cent of GDP on average for the EU-11, compared to public debt of about 70 per cent of GDP now. Moreover, while the reduction in public debt should lead to lower interest expenditure, it will also imply lower transfers of profits from national central banks. The gain for governments lies in the difference between the low returns central banks usually earn on their assets and the cost of public debt. Even if this difference is equal to two full percentage points, the total gain for public sector budgets would be only 0.03 per cent of GDP for the EU-11. For individual countries, for example Portugal or Spain, the gain might be much larger, but it would still remain modest in relation to overall public debt.

Would this reduction in balance sheets impair the ability of the ESCB to conduct its tasks? This cannot be the case. Monetary policy is conducted through asset transactions at the margin, which, provided there is no need to intervene on foreign exchange markets, involve even during exceptional times at most a fraction of the total a central bank has at its disposal.

Over the longer run, central banks should consider further reductions of excess assets and liabilities which do not reflect the conduct of monetary policy. Gold might be put in a special account with national ministries of finance, as there is no prospect that it will ever have a role in the international monetary system.

Our proposal would also make it easier to resolve the controversy concerning the distribution of seigniorage which arises from the discrepancy in the distribution of capital shares and currency (and hence interest income) between France and Germany. The US Federal Reserve System contains a very close analogy. The position of the New York Federal Reserve Bank is similar to that of the Bundesbank. Its share in the capital of the System is about 20 per cent, whereas its share in currency outstanding is much larger at about 36 per cent. The position of the Federal Reserve Bank of San Francisco resembles that of the Banque de France, in that its share in the capital is not far below that of the New York Fed (about 18 per cent); but its share in currency is only one-third, namely about 12 per cent. The New York Fed therefore contributes almost three times as much (as the San Francisco Fed) to the net current income of the System (36 per cent versus 12 per cent)

However, the disproportionately large contribution of the New York Fed to the overall seigniorage (or net current income as it is called) is not an issue in the US. The allocation of the net income across different Federal Reserve Districts is regarded as an arbitrary accounting exercise of no economic significance, because anyway all the surplus of the Federal Reserve System is immediately transferred to the US Treasury. In Europe, seigniorage is distributed to national governments according to the capital shares in the ECB. The distribution of the overall seigniorage revenue thus matters. But if central banks had cleaner balance sheets they could at least avoid one problem, which arises from the Treaty provisions concerning the measurement of the national contributions to the overall sum. Article 32.2 of the Statutes stipulates that each contribution of each national central bank to the overall monetary income of the system should be equal to the income from the assets that each national central bank has earmarked as being held as the counterpart to its monetary base. If the entire balance sheet is not much longer than the monetary base there is not much to choose. However, for a national central bank whose balance sheet is twice as long as its monetary base the temptation will be strong to earmark the returns of only the half of its assets that yield a low income for the ESCB. This will of course be resisted by other national central banks. It would be even better if one could avoid this conflict of interest entirely by cleaning up the balance sheets of European central banks and making them more transparent. The seigniorage problem has been postponed by the decision of the ESCB to apply an alternative method for the initial years. This time should be used for the clean-up operations we have described.

Notes

1 See Vaez-Zadeh (1991: 70) who mentions a review of the central banking laws in some sixty countries; it revealed that almost one-third did not have any specific provisions regarding the treatment of losses.
2 For a discussion of EMU's excess foreign reserves see Brookes 1996; for a broader discussion of the management of ESCB assets under EMU see J. P. Morgan 1998b.

3 The Italian Minister of Defence, Andreatta, proposed this in early 1998. See Andreatta 1998.

4 Gold and foreign assets are valued at market prices.

5 The size of the asset holdings of EU-11 national central banks has implications for their profits, and hence for the distribution of seigniorage. See Gros 1998.

6 Deposits of financial institutions at the central bank are assumed to be 2 per cent of a broad monetary aggregate minus currency held outside depository institutions.

7 Quotas in the IMF are based, *inter alia*, on the importance of external trade; with the introduction of the euro only the trade outside the EMU area counts as foreign trade. As the ratio of intra- to extra-EU trade is approximately 2 : 1 for most member countries, this implies that EMU would justify on this count a considerable reduction in their IMF quotas.

8 The indicator for legal independence which is used is the sum of the indices for political and economic independence by Grilli, Masciandarro and Tabellini 1991. The political independence indicator focuses on appointment procedures for board members, the length of members' terms in office, and the existence of the statutory requirement to pursue monetary stability. The economic-independence indicator considers the extent to which the central bank is free from government influence implementing monetary policy (Eijffinger and Haan 1996: 23).

9 See Chapter 9 this volume for an estimate of the composition of foreign exchange reserves in the EU countries at the end of 1996.

10 The Reserve Bank of Australia has set another example in transparency, in disclosing not only how it manages its external reserves but also the return it makes on them. See Pringle 1995, and the annual reports of the Reserve Bank of Australia.

11 The only reason why central banks might want to keep a larger capital base is that they might need it in their function as lenders of last resort. However, the lender of last resort function is not a reason to over-capitalize central banks. The only danger that central banks might run as lenders of last resort is to create additional money, but this they can always do without limits, independently of their capital. Of course, if a central bank lends big amounts to banks in trouble during a financial crisis, it might have difficulties collecting the loans when the crisis is over. These losses should, of course, not be covered through additional money creation, but they are anyway normally a responsibility of national ministries of finance, which would have to make up any losses national central banks incur as lenders of last resort.

Bibliography

Andreatta, B. (1998) 'Ecco il dividendo l'euro', *I Sole*, 24 Ore, 4 May.

Blejer, M. I. and Schumacher, L. (1998) 'Central Bank Vulnerability and the Credibility of Commitments: A Value-at-Risk Approach to Currency Crises', *International Monetary Fund Working Paper no. 65.*

Brookes, M. (1996) 'EMU's Excess Foreign Reserves', *EMU Briefing Issue no. 6,* Goldman Sachs.

Eijffinger, S. C. W. and de Haan, J. (1996) 'The Political Economy of Central-Bank Independence', International Finance Section, *Special Papers in International Economics no. 19.*

EMI (1997) *Annual Report 1996,* European Monetary Institute, Frankfurt.

Financial Statements of national central banks, *Annual Reports,* 1997.

Grilli, V., Masciandarro, D. and Tabellini, G. (1991) 'Political and Monetary Institutions and Public Financial Policies in the Industrial Countries', *Economic Policy* 13: 341–92.

Gros, D. (1998) 'Distributing Seigniorage under EMU', *CEPS Working Document no. 118*, Centre for European Policy Studies, Brussels.

International Financial Statistics, *Yearbook* 1997 and May 1998, International Monetary Fund, Washington, D.C.

J. P Morgan (1996) *RiskMetrics*™ Technical Document, J. P. Morgan Bank, New York, 4th edn.

J. P. Morgan (1998a) *RiskMetrics*™ datasets, http://www.riskmetrics.com/rm/index_datasets.html.

J. P. Morgan (1998b) *EMU and Euro-Central Bank Assets*, J. P. Morgan Securities Ltd., London (May).

Masson, P. R. and Turtelboom, B. G. (1997) 'Characteristics of the Euro, The Demand for Reserves and Policy Coordination Under EMU', *International Monetary Fund Working Paper no. 58*.

Pringle, R. (1995) 'How the Reserve Bank Manages Australia's Reserves', *Central Banking* 6: 2.

Robinson, D. J. and Stella, P. (1988) 'Amalgamating Central Banking and Fiscal Deficits', *International Monetary Fund Occasional Paper no. 59*.

Roger, S. (1993) 'The Management of Foreign Exchange Reserve', Bank for International Settlements, *Economic Papers no. 38*, Basle.

Stella, P. (1997) 'Do Central Banks Need Capital?' *International Monetary Fund Working Paper no. 83*.

Vaez-Zadeh, R. (1991) 'Implications and Remedies of Central Bank Losses', in P. Downes and R. Vaez-Zadeh (eds), *The Evolving Role of Central Banks*, International Monetary Fund, Washington, D.C.

11 Will the European Central Bank be the lender of last resort in EMU?

Alessandro Prati and Garry Schinasi

In my opinion, banking supervision is a central bank function. The combination, within the central bank, of banking supervision with lender of last resort, oversight and monetary policy functions offers distinct advantages. These advantages should not be ignored, considering the significance of financial stability – especially within an open and liberalized economy – and the contribution which banking supervision makes in this respect.

(W. F. Duisenberg, president of the Netherlands Bank and of the Bank for International Settlements, in a speech at the symposium Monetary Policy in an Open Economy, organized by the Bank of Korea in Seoul, 19 June 1995)

Introduction

The decentralized approach to financial policy making embedded in the Maastricht Treaty and other EU official documents creates considerable ambiguity within European Economic and Monetary Union (EMU) about important aspects of the broader responsibilities for financial crisis management, including the supervision of pan-European banks, surveillance of pan-European financial markets, pan-European financial systemic risk management, and lender-of-last-resort (LOLR) responsibilities. In particular, the treaty does not provide clear delineations of responsibilities to the European Central bank (ECB), eleven national central banks (NCBs), eleven national supervisors, and eleven national treasuries for crisis management and for the provision of liquidity support to pan-European financial institutions. Nor does the Treaty foresee a centralized authority within EMU to ensure European-wide financial market stability.

As pan-European banking groups emerge, national supervisors are likely to become less able to assess adequately bank soundness and the risks of systemic contagion, because of their national orientations toward supervision and regulation. For similar reasons, cross-border coordination is unlikely to fill these gaps as well. Indeed, the sharing of responsibilities between home and host supervisors has proved to be difficult among Group of Ten countries, and is unlikely to improve quickly within EMU.

Most importantly, the Treaty does not assign LOLR responsibilities, and the *de facto* decentralization of LOLR responsibilities could create an uneven playing field by introducing different levels of moral hazard across the countries within EMU, cause delays, and increase the cost of resolving financial crises. Moreover, the lack of ECB independent access to supervisory information essentially leaves the new central bank at the centre of European financial markets without the tools necessary for independently assessing the creditworthiness of counterparties or for providing liquidity support directly to solvent but illiquid institutions. From the perspective of industrial-country practices and experiences, and because of the strong bond between monetary stability and financial stability, EMU arrangements appear to be suboptimal if not risky, and this could affect ECB and EMU credibility (see Prati and Schinasi 1999).

Against this background, it is reasonable to wonder who will step forward to manage a fast-breaking EMU-wide (cross-border) financial problem involving pan-European financial institutions. Are national authorities capable of successful EMU-wide financial surveillance? Are national supervisors capable of monitoring risk taking by pan-European financial institutions? Are national authorities capable of deciding who will provide liquidity assistance to individual illiquid institutions quickly enough to prevent pan-European financial contagion? Or will the ECB become the lender of last resort in EMU?

This paper attempts to formalize this last question by examining the feasibility of some of the options for assigning LOLR responsibilities within EMU. The next section briefly examines the proposed EMU framework for financial policy making, and concludes that the arrangements between the ECB, NCBs, national supervisory authorities, and national treasuries for managing a bank crisis are unclear, and there is considerable, and not necessarily constructive, ambiguity about the roles of the ECB and/or the NCBs in crisis management. Following this are a discussion of Bagehot's principles of LOLR responsibilities, and two alternative concepts of the potential role of central banks in implementing LOLR responsibilities. Because the Deutsche Bundesbank is the model on which the ESCB is designed, the next section examines the existing crisis management framework within Germany, and concludes that in practice the Bundesbank has played a more active role in banking supervision, crisis management, and LOLR than is generally understood.

The core of the paper examines options for crisis management within EMU, and in particular the options for assigning LOLR responsibilities for pan-European financial crises.[1] This section concludes that if the existing framework is strictly implemented, LOLR practices in EMU would deviate in important ways from country experiences among industrial countries, including those of Germany and other EMU member countries. From a pragmatic crisis-management perspective, it appears to be a risky strategy to maintain the existing ambiguous division of responsibilities between the

ECB, the NCBs, and the numerous national authorities, in part because attempts to overcome ambiguities and coordination problems during a fast-breaking pan-European financial crises in EMU could cause delays, raise the cost of resolutions, and damage EMU's credibility. This is especially relevant in the early years of EMU, a period in which rapid market integration and accelerating banking system consolidation and restructuring might require faster policy responses than have been necessary historically in the pre-EMU European financial environment, characterized by nationally-segmented markets and public-sector ownership and support of financial institutions. This core section of the paper also discusses alternatives for eliminating existing ambiguities. A concluding section suggests ways in which the EMU framework may evolve in the future.

The ambiguity of LOLR responsibilities in EMU

The structure of European financial policy making, and that of the European System of Central Banks, is set down in the Maastricht Treaty. The framework for banking supervision and regulation is laid down in EU Directives, including the Second Banking Directive, the Capital Adequacy and Solvency Directives, and the BCCI Directive, with the competence for banking supervision and regulation remaining with the national author-ities, which in the EU may be NCBs, non-central bank bodies, or both, depending on the country (See IMF 1997: 177–80.) The basic EU prin-ciple of 'home country control' coupled with cross-border cooperation among supervisors will not be modified in EMU. The ESCB Statute (Article 25(1)) and the Maastricht Treaty (Article 105(4,5,6)) together assign some relatively ambiguous responsibilities to the ESCB in the areas of prudential supervision and financial stability.[2] The 1997 Annual Report of the EMI (EMI 1998: 61–3) indicates how the EMI and the Banking Supervisory Sub-Committee expect these provisions to be imple-mented in EMU. This report indicates that any transfer of supervisory powers to the ECB is, at this time, considered to be premature. Despite these other ambiguities, the ESCB is given an explicit role in promoting the smooth functioning of the payment system (Article 22 of the Statute and Article 105(2) of the Treaty).

It is clear from the ambiguous assignment of responsibilities in the Treaty and other EU official documents that the framers of EMU did not envision a centralized mechanism for dealing with European financial and banking problems, and did not foresee the need for a centralized crisis-management mechanism. The absence of a well defined and centralized EMU crisis-management mechanism reflects, in part, the 'narrow' concept of central banking envisioned in the Maastricht Treaty.[3] The ECB has a mandate to focus almost exclusively on monetary policy. Although it has been given some regulatory functions related to the operation of the TARGET payment systems, the ECB has only a limited, peripheral, and ambiguous role in banking supervision, and no explicit mandate at all for providing emergency liquidity support directly to individual financial institutions. A 'broad' concept of central banking would include other financial policy functions such as a mandate for ensuring financial stability, for providing liquidity support to financial institutions, and for the supervision of systemically important financial institutions (with access to the payments system). In implementing the vision of the Treaty, the ECB is continuing to make the necessary preparations for the functioning of TARGET and ESCB monetary policy operations. The broader decisions about crisis management, and in particular LOLR responsibilities, have deliberately been left ambiguous. Neither the ECB, the NCBs or any other EMU institution has been assigned the role of lender of last resort. Thus there is, at present, uncertainty whether in the event of a banking crisis across pan-European markets there will be a central provider or coordinator of emergency liquidity, or whether these functions will remain decentralized.

Within this institutional framework, it is unclear how a fast-breaking liquidity crisis would be handled, especially if it involves a pan-European financial institution for which supervisory, regulatory, and LOLR responsibilities would be shared to some extent. The issue is what the ESCB or NCBs will do if it becomes apparent that a financial institution is unable to meet its financial obligations because it does not have enough eligible assets to obtain the necessary liquidity from the ESCB and its failure may have systemic implications across EMU.

Crisis management: two views of the role of central banks

The provision of central bank liquidity to individual institutions in emergency situations can have implications for both monetary stability and financial stability. Moreover, the manner in, and conditions under, which such funds are provided to individual institutions can also have implications for moral hazard and fiscal policy. Because of the complexity of these matters, there is no conceptual framework for the provision of liquidity assistance during emergency situations (that is, financial crises) that is uniformly viewed as appropriate by practitioners and academics, and there is a wide range of industrial-country practices. In most countries, financial safety nets have two key elements, namely, a lender of last resort (LOLR), whose responsibility is usually – but not always – assigned to the central bank, and a deposit insurance scheme.[4] Although they are common practice, central bank LOLR interventions have been frequently criticized because they might, one, have moral hazard implications; two, affect the central bank's financial condition; and three, conflict with monetary (price) stability objectives.

To minimize the risks of moral hazard, financial losses, and compromising monetary stability, possibly associated with LOLR operations, central banks can follow a set of best practices. Bagehot set the benchmark over a century ago (Bagehot 1873). The application of his doctrine would require a central bank to:

1   make LOLR facilities available to the whole financial system, but lend only to illiquid institutions that are solvent
2   let insolvent institutions fail
3   lend speedily
4   lend only for the short term
5   charge penalty interest rates
6   require good collateral
7   announce these conditions well in advance of any crisis, so that the market would know exactly what to expect.

These best practices are generally still considered to be valid.[5]

In principle, strict adherence to Bagehot's rules would alleviate most, if not all, concerns about central bank involvement in LOLR operations. Lending only to solvent institutions, at penalty rates, would eliminate the risk of moral hazard; and lending against good collateral would insure against losses. Moreover, lending only for the short term would limit the inflationary consequences of LOLR intervention.

In practice, three factors complicate the implementation of Bagehot's guidelines. First, in the midst of a crisis, the information available is generally insufficient to distinguish unambiguously illiquid institutions that are solvent from those that are insolvent (as well as 'bad' from 'good' collateral). Second, if a crisis has systemic implications, authorities might tend to bail out insolvent banks to prevent the failure of other, potentially solvent, banks or the collapse of the financial system. Third, if a part of the banking system is allowed to fail, the authorities may find it even more difficult to achieve macroeconomic objectives, including monetary, price, and fiscal stability, in part because a loss of confidence could alter private sector behavior (see Goodhart and Huang 1999).

These three factors can interact, worsen a crisis, and complicate crisis management. If imperfect information forestalls a clear delineation of insolvent from solvent institutions, a local crisis can become systemic as market participants fail to distinguish 'good' from 'bad' institutions and 'good' from 'bad' collateral, and assume all are 'bad'. At the same time, asymmetric information and asset mispricing could make it difficult to limit moral hazard by providing LOLR assistance only to illiquid and systemically-important institutions. Moreover, if liquidity assistance is provided to insolvent institutions against 'bad' collateral – in order to contain the systemic implications of the crisis – then the central bank could endanger its own financial position. Finally, if the confidence effects of a crisis were miscalculated, the central bank could risk choosing a monetary policy that may be too tight – as in the 1930s – or too loose, as in the period after the 1987 stock market crash.

Thus the moral hazard and monetary stability outcomes associated with LOLR interventions (to maintain financial stability) mainly reflect the (increased) degree of imperfect information available to central banks in emergency situations. If central banks had access to perfect information and were equipped to evaluate it rapidly, they could limit and manage the systemic consequences of a crisis with limited moral hazard. In cases of payments systems crises, for example, central banks could rescue banks selectively by providing temporary liquidity assistance only to solvent lending banks, and by refusing such assistance to insolvent debtor banks and letting them fail, so that bank management and shareholders bear the full consequences of the bank's financial condition (see Rochet and Tirole 1996). Similarly, perfect information about the confidence effects of bank failures would allow central banks to fine-tune their monetary policies and achieve their macro objectives.

Realistically, central banks do not have access to perfect information, and there are very high and costly informational requirements for distinguishing between solvent and insolvent institutions and for selecting the appropriate monetary policy in a crisis situation. These costly requirements raise the issue of whether central banks can justify their LOLR role, not only by showing that they have better information than market participants, but also because LOLR interventions yield benefits in excess of several costs: first, the costs of the supervision and regulation necessary to acquire superior information; second, the costs of moral hazard, which remain as long as the supervisory information in the hands of central banks is imperfect; third, the costs of reduced peer monitoring among market participants due to the central banks' LOLR role (see Rochet and Tirole 1996); and fourth, the costs of potential monetary policy errors resulting from LOLR intervention.

In practice, the pivotal issue is whether a central bank should distribute liquidity by screening strong from weak banks and assessing the systemic implications of bank failures, or whether it should only provide liquidity to the market (and leave the allocation of liquidity to market participants) and focus exclusively on providing liquidity to the system against well-defined collateral, for example government paper. There are two clearly distinct views in the academic and policy literatures on this issue. At one extreme there is the 'market-operations' approach. According to this approach, in order to avoid moral hazard, a central bank should supply emergency liquidity to financial markets (not individual institutions) through its open market operations, with government securities as underlying assets.[6] A simple interpretation of this approach is that central banks should only be concerned with monetary stability, and financial stability will naturally follow.

At the other extreme is the 'banking policy' approach, which favours a more interventionist financial stability role for central banks, on the assumption there is a strong relationship between achieving and maintaining monetary and financial stability.[7] This approach rests on three main arguments. First, market failures may preclude the fast and reliable channelling of liquidity to illiquid, solvent institutions. Second, widespread failures of financial institutions could affect the confidence and the behaviour of the private sector in such an unpredictable way that the conduct of monetary policy by means only of open market operations would become extremely difficult; to continue basing monetary policy on predictable relationships, central banks might then follow some sort of 'too-big-to-fail' policy and bail out sufficiently large illiquid institutions regardless of their financial condition and viability (see Goodhart and Huang 1999). Third, central banks can reasonably contain the moral hazard implications of such policies by following the practice of 'constructive ambiguity.'[8] An additional point often made by those favouring a 'banking policy' approach is that central banks are likely to be involved in most instances of banking crises, including those regarding insolvent institutions, because they generally are the only source of *immediate* funds. Whether central banks will be the *ultimate* source of funds depends on arrangements between them and treasuries, deposit insurance schemes, and regulatory agencies.[9] Although central banks may be indemnified, initially they might have to provide funds to insolvent institutions, and possibly even to institutions that are not systemically important (as occurred in Japan in November 1997), if the responsible authorities decide that there should be intervention. It is evident that the faster a crisis occurs, the more likely this scenario becomes.

Although the banking policy approach seems to be more consistent with the historical experiences of many, if not most, industrial countries, the market-operations approach provides a conceptual benchmark for examining the EMU framework, because the ECSB has a 'narrow' monetary stability mandate. In many respects, the EMU framework seems to reflect the market-operations approach of providing liquidity to the economy by using only open market operations to smooth interest rate movements and a Lombard (strictly defined collateralized) facility to provide emergency liquidity assistance at a 'penalty' rate. This approach contrasts with the discount window policy of the US Federal Reserve System, which gives considerable leeway to the Fed in selecting eligible collateral and counterparties, and which enables loans to be made at a subsidized rate.

An important reservation about the market operations view is that it does not address systemic or contagion risk, defined as the risk that financial difficulties at one or more bank(s) spill over to a large number of other banks or the financial system as a whole. If the failure of a troubled institution has systemic implications, then a central bank might want to provide funds to this institution even if solvency is an issue, and even if it does not have adequate collateral. Bagehot was concerned about systemic risk: 'In wild periods of alarm, one failure makes many, and the best way to prevent the derivative failures is to arrest the primary failure which causes them' (Bagehot 1873: 51–2). The pre-Fed period in the United States is instructive because it offers a rare opportunity to test hypotheses using data that are not distorted by the presence of a public safety net. According to the market-operations view, the successful functioning of clearing houses in this period provides evidence that, as long as the overall supply of currency can be increased in the event of a crisis, the role of distributing the additional liquidity to individual institutions can be left to the private sector. The evidence is mixed, however. On the one hand, simple descriptive statistics on failure rates suggest that allowing private clearing houses to perform LOLR functions did not increase systemic risk, but on the contrary reduced it: the average annual failure rate of banks over the 1870–1913 pre-Fed period was 0.91 per cent compared with one of 1.01 per cent for nonbanks; conversely, in the 1914–94 period, the average annual failure rate of banks was 1.09 per cent against one of 0.65 per cent of nonbanks.[10] On the other hand, recent econometric studies that control for macro-economic factors find evidence of contagion risk in the pre-Fed period.[11]

On balance, the issues are mainly whether, central banks can, one, assess the solvency of illiquid institutions better than the market in crisis situations in which there is the potential for far-reaching systemic implications, and two, contribute to an orderly resolution of such crises with a limited and tolerable impact on moral hazard and monetary (price) stability. In recent years, the clearest example of the markets' inability to distinguish between illiquidity and insolvency has been the Bank of New York episode in 1985. In this instance, the Bank of New York became unable to borrow from the money market to meet its liquidity needs, although its difficulties were entirely temporary and owing to a computer breakdown. To prevent its failure and the related systemic implications, the Fed provided collateralized overnight credit equivalent to more than 10 per cent of the US monetary base (see Folkerts-Landau and Garber 1992). In other instances, central banks – usually the only immediate providers of liquidity – might have to inject liquidity into undercapitalized and perhaps even insolvent financial institutions that are too big to fail in order to ensure an orderly resolution of financial problems or crises before they become systemic (that is, in order to maintain or restore financial stability). In such cases, while central banks usually are the only immediate source of liquidity, other public institutions, or consortia of private banks, can and should bear the ultimate costs of the bail-out.

Crisis management in Germany

Because the ESCB statute is similar to that of the Bundesbank in many respects, the German system is a useful benchmark for examining how crisis management might be structured within EMU. The Bundesbank is widely perceived as the central bank that has been involved in crisis management to the least possible extent. It is generally believed that no

Bundesbank funds have been used *directly* to bail out troubled institutions in the post-war period. In addition, eligibility criteria for the use of collateral in refinancing operations are strict. The range of eligible assets for Lombard loans and open market operations is the same, including both public and high-quality private securities.[12] An even more limited range of assets, comprising only shorter-term private and public bills, is accepted at the discount window.[13] Although the Bundesbank is allowed, on the basis of its Statute, to make some additions to the list of eligible *debt* securities for open market operations and the Lombard facility, its leeway is limited compared to that of other major central banks (including the Bank of England, the Banque de France, the Bank of Japan, and the Federal Reserve System, which has flexibility in determining eligible collateral for discounting).[14] As such, the Bundesbank is probably the central bank that seems best to fulfil the market-operations prescription of sticking to monetary policy goals and avoiding involvement in banking policy.

Conceptually, the German framework for dealing with banking and financial crises appears to be constructed so as to ensure that the Bundesbank focuses exclusively on price stability and to avoid a direct role in providing funds for bank rescue operations. The crisis management framework in Germany appears to embody three lines of defence aimed at preventing any direct use of Bundesbank funds:

1   banking supervision and regulation by an independent body, the Federal Banking Supervisory Office
2   deposit insurance schemes, and public guarantees for the publicly owned segment of the banking system, to prevent a run by depositors
3   brokered market solutions combined with short-term emergency liquidity assistance provided by the Liquidity Consortium Bank (*Liquiditäts-Konsortialbank GmbH, LCB*), and, if the liquid resources of the LCB are insufficient, short-term emergency liquidity assistance provided directly by the Bundesbank but only if the LCB guarantees the troubled institution.

The LCB is a specialized financial institution that has the objective of ensuring the due settlement of domestic and external payments among banks. It grants short-term liquidity assistance in the event of temporary illiquidity faced by financial institutions that are judged to be in sound financial condition. The identity of the intervened institution is publicly revealed neither at the time of the crisis nor *ex post*. The LCB was established in 1974 in the wake of the failure of Herstatt Bank. The Bundesbank holds 30 per cent of the LCB's capital (DM 372 million at end-1997); the rest is held by private banks (31.5 per cent), savings banks (26.5 per cent), cooperative banks (11.0 per cent), and instalment-credit financing institutions (1 per cent). The four-member Credit Committee of the LCB (one Bundesbank member plus one member for each association of credit institutions) decides on the granting of liquidity support. Banks in need of such support, but with no solvency problems, may borrow from the LCB by rediscounting three-month promissory notes (*Banksola-wechsel*).[15] The LCB's partners are obliged – if necessary – to make supplementary payments of up to five times their equity stakes, but this option thus far has not been used in the midst of a crisis. If the liquid resources of the LCB are insufficient, troubled banks can instead use a special rediscount facility at the Bundesbank, which allows them to discount – exceeding, if necessary, normal rediscount quotas – promissory notes that they themselves have issued but on which the LCB has provided the 'second good signature' required by law. New arrangements will have to be made in relation to the discounting of promissory notes in EMU, because the discount window of the Bundesbank will cease to exist and banks' promissory notes may not be considered eligible collateral by the ECB.

In principle, these lines of defence appear to limit considerably the involvement of the Bundesbank, in judging the solvency of individual financial institutions, in decisions concerning the provision of liquidity assistance to illiquid institutions, and in banking supervision. In practice, however, the Bundesbank must be involved in all these situations, all of which go far beyond open-market and monetary policy operations. First, the Bundesbank owns 30 per cent of the capital of the LCB and the remainder is owned by a large number of the different categories of banks within Germany. When the LCB has played a role in providing liquidity assistance, its decisions to provide liquidity have required the unanimous agreement of its Credit Committee, and it is difficult to imagine that a 30 per cent shareholder would not be intimately involved in the judgements and the decisions of the Consortium. Second, and perhaps more importantly, the success of the Bundesbank in finding alternative solutions to the use of central bank funds requires it to have direct access to supervisory information. Section 7 of the German Banking Act requires that 'The Deutsche Bundesbank and the Federal Banking Supervisory Office shall communicate to each other any observations and findings which may be of significance for the performance of their respective functions.' Indeed, as the Bundesbank itself specifies in one of its publications:

> the Supervisory Office, which has no branches of its own, takes advantage of the Bundesbank's familiarity with local conditions and its relevant expertise. There is a mutual exchange of information, which may be significant for the discharge of the duties each institution has to perform.
> (Deutsche Bundesbank 1995: 3: 'The Monetary Policy of the Bundesbank')

Third, the very existence of the LCB indicates that German policy makers recognize that liquidity problems cannot be tackled satisfactorily exclusively with normal market-based monetary policy operations, implying that German financial policy making does not wholly subscribe to the monetary-operations view of LOLR responsibilities and contains aspects of the banking-policy approach.

Options for crisis management in EMU

The ECB – like the Bundesbank – has no *explicit* responsibility for crisis management beyond an advisory role for safeguarding the stability of the EMU financial system, and it does not have a mandate as a LOLR. In some respects, EMU's institutional arrangements – in particular the ECB's dependent and limited access to supervisory information – allow the ECB less scope and flexibility than the Bundesbank to play a role in market surveillance, the detection of financial problems, crisis management, and liquidity support to single illiquid institutions, although the ECB seems to have greater leeway than the Bundesbank in altering the list of eligible collateral.[16] Because of these differences, the EMU and ESCB frameworks imply that the LOLR function within EMU resembles the market-operations view of LOLR responsibilities more closely than the German framework (or any other the authors are familiar with) (see IMF 1997: 174–7).

In particular, in EMU, an illiquid bank would use the same eligible assets to obtain intraday credit in the payments system, bid aggressively for funds in open market operations, and access the marginal lending facility. In the event of a liquidity crisis, the ECB would not have the mandate to assess the solvency of the illiquid bank. The ECB might keep access to the marginal lending facility unrestricted, but it would then have to decide whether to sterilize the liquidity impact of any lending, depending on whether the liquidity crisis were local or EMU-wide. Under the current ESCB structure, there is no obvious way by which the ESCB could *quickly and unilaterally* provide liquidity to a financial institution that does not have eligible assets.[17]

Assuming it was a deliberate decision of the EU framers of EMU to conform closely to implementing the market-operations approach to LOLR responsibilities (or something like it), EMU is unlikely to achieve the main benefits of this approach, even though EMU will most likely bear the costs of the reduced ability to cope with a banking crisis. First, according to the market-operations approach, one key advantage of having a central bank that focuses exclusively on monetary policy is that it could eliminate, or considerably reduce, supervisory and regulatory costs. This is unlikely in EMU. On the contrary, pan-European banking institutions will have to deal with eleven different supervisory and regulatory agencies, whose practices and regulations are still not fully harmonized (see IMF 1997: 174–87). Second, the potential reduction in moral hazard from not having the ESCB involved in resolving banking crises is also unlikely to be realized, because the exclusion of the ESCB from crisis resolution might be viewed as not credible given the degree of ambiguity in the current institutional set-up. One reason for this is that the exclusion of the ECB itself might be seen as an unusual departure from current practices in most industrial countries, including those of participating countries in EMU, including Germany. To achieve the desired reduction in moral hazard, banks operating in EU banking systems where there is a clearly defined LOLR must change their expectations of assistance within the new EMU LOLR regime. However, this requires that the transition to the new EMU LOLR regime be adequately publicized and clarified. Otherwise, banks will continue to rely on central banks' assistance. This would pose the strong risk that excluding the ECB from providing central bank funds in the management of banking crises would create a time-inconsistent policy.[18]

The foregoing analysis raises the question whether there are viable substitutes to central banks for fulfilling LOLR responsibilities, and whether these alternatives are feasible within EMU. In particular, is it pragmatic to manage fast-breaking financial or banking crises within EMU without involving either the ECB, the NCBs, or both? The feasibility of two possible approaches is now considered: first, an approach based on a lender of penultimate resort, in which neither the ECB nor the NCBs would use central bank funds to provide liquidity to individual institutions; and second, a decentralized approach, in which LOLR assistance is left entirely to NCBs without involvement of the ECB. The important implications of the following analysis are:

- Because only central banks can provide unlimited and *immediate* liquidity assistance in the form of 'good' (central bank) funds, it is difficult to conceive a financial safety net that excludes them completely in the midst of a fast-breaking crisis.
- The lender-of-penultimate-resort approach would be impractical during a fast-breaking, EMU-wide financial or banking problem.
- The decentralized approach would necessarily involve ECB decisions about system-wide liquidity and what the NCBs should be allowed to do.

Lenders of penultimate resort: LOLR responsibilities without central bank funds

Lenders of penultimate resort can reduce the need for central bank funds. Provided that the necessary political consensus is achieved, relationships can be established between other agencies and the ESCB to limit recourse to the ESCB as the *ultimate* source of funds. The possibilities for lenders of penultimate resort include deposit insurance schemes, liquidity consortia, pools of solvent banks, and national treasuries.[19]

There are several reasons why deposit insurance schemes alone might not be effective in managing a liquidity crisis in an EMU banking system.

First, the coverage of most deposit insurance schemes in EMU would be enough to protect small depositors but not to ensure financial stability (see IMF 1997: 180–1). Second, payouts from deposit insurance funds generally are very slow so there would still be a need for an immediate provider of liquidity assistance.[20] Finally, in an integrated EMU banking system with several EMU-wide institutions, there is the risk that the use of deposit insurance schemes would mean that considerable time was taken to determine how the financial responsibilities would be shared among national authorities, and could delay the resolution of a problem bank.[21]

The concept of a liquidity consortium is a natural candidate for EMU, because of Germany's approach in minimizing the use of central bank funds and the analogies between the ESCB and the Bundesbank statutes. Nevertheless, there are several reasons why the German approach (three lines of defence, with use of central bank funds only if the consortium guarantees the discounted debt instruments of the troubled bank) might not work within EMU. First, there is no analogue of the Liquidity Consortium Bank in other EMU countries, nor is one planned at the EMU level. Second, even if such an institution existed in each EMU country, or an EMU-wide consortium were created, it would seem inadequate in relation to the size and the cross-border systemic implications of a liquidity crisis involving a major pan-European banking group, unless such institutions were endowed with considerable resources and could with their guarantees transform ineligible into eligible collateral. Third, the German liquidity consortium never had to face a systemic crisis as large or as complicated as could occur in pan-European markets involving pan-European institutions. The German system worked well in an environment with a large share of public ownership in the banking system, and capital markets less developed than those that are likely to emerge in EMU. In this environment, crises took place 'in slow motion' and most likely did not have the same liquidity and systemic implications that a sudden correction in asset prices, or the insolvency of a major financial institution, would have in integrated EMU-wide capital markets. Fourth, the success of the German consortium may have reflected the presence of the Bundesbank – providing 30 per cent of its capital and a special rediscount facility – along with its credibility and its commitment to make it work with its moral suasion. The arrangements of such consortium, or of any other that could be created in other EMU countries, would have to be adapted to make it compatible with the transference of monetary policy responsibilities to the ECB. Finally, and perhaps more importantly, an EMU-wide liquidity consortium would need to have much greater access to supervisory information than national supervisors seem willing to provide to the ECB.[22] Close cooperation between the Bundesbank and the Federal Banking Supervisory Office (discussed earlier) was certainly essential in identifying illiquid but solvent institutions and convincing banks to provide emergency liquidity assistance.

In sum, although liquidity consortia could be an important lender of penultimate-resort in EMU, it is unlikely that, even if they were created in each EMU country, they could address a pan-European crisis without access to supervisory information and new arrangements for obtaining central bank resources should their liquid assets be exhausted.

Could pools of commercial banks resolve a banking crisis in EMU without central bank funds, and with or without the brokering role of the ECB or NCBs? This kind of solution has several precedents from the pre-Fed clearing-house experience mentioned earlier, to the more recent cases, documented by Goodhart and Schoenmaker (1995), of takeovers of troubled institutions. Many of the latter required the central bank to play a brokering role, often based on its ability to gauge better the systemic implications of the crisis, as well as moral suasion and access to supervisory information. In the case of the near collapse and private rescue of Long-Term Capital Management in September 1998, the Federal Reserve Bank of New York 'facilitated' the creation of a private consortium of creditors. Within EMU, such solutions might be difficult to arrange for several reasons. First, the increased banking competition and the greater size of the institutions that are likely to emerge from the ongoing consolidation process at the EMU level could make it unlikely that commercial banks would have enough solidarity and resources to orchestrate bank rescues like those observed in the past (see Goodhart and Schoenmaker 1995). Second, increased competition could also reduce the ability of central banks to organize and coordinate such rescues. Third, in organizing brokering solutions, NCBs would probably lose most of their power of moral suasion with the transfer of monetary policy responsibilities to the ECB, although the Banque de France may maintain the organizing power that it has on the basis of Article 52.2 of the banking law. Fourth, the current agreement about sharing information between the ECB and the national supervisors – which can be summarized by the formula 'no real obligation, no real obstacle, and some understanding' – does not provide the ECB with the same authority as the Bundesbank, or any of the pre-EMU central banks, in brokering a solution to a banking crisis at the EMU level. The ECB could probably still try to play this role if it were perceived to have the same access to supervisory information at the EMU level as the Bundesbank has at the German level, or if it had independent authority to inspect counterparties in order to assess creditworthiness.

The last option is to have national treasuries play a greater role in EMU than they have played so far in the management of banking crises. One possibility would be to transfer the LOLR function to the treasury, which would then create and fully finance an emergency fund. Given Maastricht Treaty limits on monetary financing of the public sector, any pool of liquidity set aside by treasuries to deal with banking crises *cannot* be provided by the ESCB or by NCBs. An emergency fund would need to be created *ex ante*, before using its resources for providing liquidity assistance or for bailing out a troubled institution, by raising taxes or issuing bonds.

There are several problems with this solution. First, although the liquid resources of treasuries can be sizeable (the Italian Treasury, for example, had a balance of some US$ 30 billion in its account at the Bank of Italy at end 1997), they would always be limited and have a sizeable opportunity cost. Second, especially if the use of these funds is subject to Parliamentary approval, there would be an obvious risk of delays in the management of crises, and it would certainly be more difficult to provide liquidity assistance in a discreet way and without political interference. Third, it may take too much time before national governments agree on the distribution of responsibility for bailing out an institution with EMU-wide interests.[23] Fourth, the mere existence of such a fund could create at least as much moral hazard as leaving the LOLR function with the central bank. These considerations suggest it is unlikely that treasuries could become the immediate providers of funds for bank rescues.

Another option would render the ESCB the *immediate* provider of liquidity for LOLR operations, and treasuries the *ultimate* providers of funds. In practice, this solution would amount to a treasury guarantee on LOLR operations of the central bank. Although such an arrangement is possible, it would need to be structured so that the independence of the central bank was maintained, and the central bank itself and the supervisors were not subject to moral hazard in distinguishing between solvency and illiquidity. That this incentive problem is serious is clear from the amendment of the Federal Reserve Act that was introduced with section 142 of the FDIC Improvement Act of 1991. This amendment severely limited the Fed's discretion to lend to undercapitalized institutions, and specified that if the Fed did so lend, and that lending caused losses to the FDIC, the Fed would have to reimburse the FDIC.[24] Finally, it is likely that, if the Treasury had to provide funds, it would also want to control how the ESCB would use them, with all the potentially negative implications discussed above in terms of delays and political interference. As Goodhart and Schoenmaker (1995) put it: 'he who pays the piper calls the tune.'

NCBs as lenders of last resort

In the current institutional framework – composed of the Maastricht Treaty, the Statute of the ESCB, and the regulations and guidelines proposed by the EMI (and approved by the ECB Council) – considerable uncertainty remains about the scope that NCBs have in providing emergency liquidity assistance to troubled banks. To identify this uncertainty it is necessary to distinguish between two types of crisis: a general liquidity crisis affecting the entire EMU, and a local liquidity crisis affecting a large institution within an EMU country.

Consider the case of a general liquidity crisis reflecting, for example, gridlock in the payment system or a sudden drop of prices across European equity markets, for which the ECB might relax temporarily the overall monetary policy stance and increase EMU-wide liquidity. In some instances, collateralized intraday credit and extraordinary open market operations might be sufficient to inject the required liquidity. In other instances these operations might not suffice, because of a shortage of eligible collateral on the part of some financial institutions. The latter situation could arise, for example, because of a sudden increase in the volume of payments in RTGS systems, such as occurred in CHAPS (the UK large-value payment system during the pound sterling crisis of September 1992), which caused foreign exchange transactions to double (Schoenmaker 1995: 7). The 1987 stock market crash is another example of general liquidity crisis in which the Fed made clear that banks would have unrestricted access to the discount window so that they could keep their credit lines open to brokers and securities houses. If banks did not have enough eligible collateral to obtain intraday credit, gridlock could occur within TARGET and force the ESCB to accept non-eligible paper as collateral for payments system overdrafts or open market operations.

It remains to be seen whether, in the instance of a general liquidity crisis, the ECB would stick to a policy of accepting only 'good' collateral at the Lombard facility and in open market operations. In principle, the Governing Council of the ECB has some leeway in changing the list of eligible collateral that NCBs can accept, because the ECB Statute is vague on what collateral is eligible and only indicates that it should be 'adequate' (Article 18). In practice, in the midst of a crisis the seventeen-member Council of the ECB would have to decide rapidly whether or not to change the list of eligible collateral, most likely without independent access to supervisory information. The Council would have to rely exclusively on the information that national supervisors (only in some cases the NCBs) provided via the national central bank governors on the Council or, if willing, directly to the ECB Board members (also in the Council). This procedure could prove to be laborious during a fast-breaking, pan-European liquidity problem, and would seem to require communication channels between several authorities at national and supranational level to work extremely well. In addition, it seems to require the staff of the ECB (or of some other central agency) to have the expertise and the infrastructure needed to aggregate quickly the parcelled information provided by the national authorities, and to assess the systemic implications of the crisis.

Coordination problems would most likely be even greater in cases of local liquidity crises that have potentially systemic implications. In these cases an excessive degree of decentralization at the NCB level would complicate the assessment of the systemic implications of the crisis and risk transforming a local liquidity crisis into one that cut across national borders or across the entire EMU financial system.

The critical questions seem to be whether or not a NCB can provide liquidity assistance to a troubled institution without violating the ESCB statute or guidelines, and whether the ECB needs to be informed of such operations, is required to authorize them, or can require NCBs to conduct them. The first uncertainty is whether a NCB can provide liquidity support, as one of those functions not explicitly specified in the ESCB Statute that can be 'performed on the responsibility and liability of national central banks', unless prohibited by the Governing Council of the ECB (Article 14.4 of the ESCB Statute).[25] The question is whether this article provides enough leeway to NCBs to provide liquidity to a bank in trouble by purchasing some of its non-eligible assets (for example, commercial paper or loans) and letting the ESCB sterilize the 'macro' liquidity effects of this operation. The specific language in the Statute suggests that NCBs will be able to perform these operations unless the Governing Council of the ECB decides to prohibit the provision of liquidity against non-eligible assets either with a qualified majority vote – because this operation 'interferes with the objectives and tasks of the ESCB' (Article 14.4) – or through guidelines and instructions issued according to Articles 12.1 and 14.3 of the Statute.[26] The ECB has not yet publicly clarified this issue, but the existence of secret understandings between the ECB and the NCBs cannot be ruled out.

It is possible to invent ways for the NCBs to assist banks having liquidity problems. For example, an NCB can provide liquid assets in return for a bank's illiquid assets and assume the credit, market, and liquidity risks. Similarly, an NCB could guarantee the obligations of the troubled institution (or undertake other similar off-balance-sheet activities), as the Bank of England did in 1984 and 1991. If this were done, the Governing Council could argue on the basis of Article 14.4 that these NCB operations 'interfere with the objectives and tasks of the ESCB' even if such operations do not affect EMU liquidity. Accordingly, the Council could issue guidelines prohibiting certain types of on- and off-balance-sheet operations of the NCBs or specify that its prior authorization is required. Once more, it remains to be seen whether the Council will remove these ambiguities or maintain them.

If ECB guidelines are going to be strict enough to prevent NCBs from providing any form of direct or indirect liquidity assistance to a bank in trouble, there may be remaining leeway for NCBs through the definition of eligible Tier 2 collateral within the monetary policy framework of the ESCB. NCBs have some flexibility in redefining the list of eligible paper, and can propose additions of assets to the list of eligible Tier 2 collateral.[27] But because eligible collateral must be accepted by all NCBs, the Governing Council would have to approve these proposed additions. How quickly the approval process could work is unknown, and probably will not be known until it is used for the first time. If it became necessary to provide liquidity assistance, the tendency probably would be to consider problems on a case-by-case basis rather than to allow NCBs to propose, and the Council to approve, the inclusion of additional assets in the list of Tier 2 eligible collateral on a permanent basis.

Is it prudent and practical to delegate the management of local liquidity crises entirely to NCBs? Decentralized crisis management poses risks, in part because it might not permit the proper assessment of the systemic implications of a local liquidity crisis. The more integrated the EMU financial market becomes, the greater is this risk. By contrast, *centralizing* decisions on LOLR operations at the ECB level would allow for the possibility – if the ECB has adequate access to supervisory information – of a correct assessment of the systemic implications of a crisis. This benefit could more than counterbalance the risk that the ECB – in light of the higher threshold of systemic failures associated with EMU-wide money and capital markets – might refuse to assist important national institutions that single NCBs would save. With centralization of these decisions, national considerations would inevitably lose importance as financial integration proceeds. Moreover, in the short run, local governments might ask the ECB to provide emergency liquidity assistance to a troubled bank, under the understanding that they would refund the ECB any losses incurred. To limit the associated moral hazard and maintain it at a uniform level across EMU, it would be necessary to establish rules and procedures for obtaining such temporary liquidity assistance from the ECB. (Similar rules and procedures would actually be necessary for the same purpose in a decentralized system.) Of course, in a centralized system, LOLR decisions might not need to be taken by the ECB alone, but as in the UK model discussed later, they might involve the approval of independent EMU-wide supervisory and political institutions once those were created.

Some have argued (for example, Schoenmaker 1995) that as long as bank supervision remains decentralized, LOLR operations should also be decentralized so that national supervisors have the incentive to avoid problems in their national financial systems because their country would bear the related costs. This argument is valid only as long as bank supervision remains at the national level. As is discussed below, there are reasons for greater centralization in this area as well. In addition it is not obvious that even with decentralized supervision, centralizing LOLR decisions requires all EMU countries to share the costs of LOLR operations. On the contrary, national authorities could be considered responsible for any costs that the system would ultimately incur, because it is on the basis of the information they provide that centralized LOLR intervention would be based. Indeed, the 'indirect method' for distributing EMU monetary income – which is going to be used during the first five years of EMU – implies that any loss incurred by an NCB would not be shared by the others (unless the Governing Council decides otherwise on the basis of Article 33.2 of the ECB Statute).[28]

Finally, another reason for centralizing LOLR decisions is that, in the current situation, the ESCB balance sheet is equal to the consolidated balance sheet of the eleven NCBs. It is difficult to imagine that the ECB would not be involved in deciding inherently risky LOLR operations that might adversely affect the balance sheet of the ESCB, and the strength and stability of the euro.

The adequacy of the ECB's access to supervisory information

In all relevant cases discussed in the previous section, the ECB appears to have to either make a decision about injecting funds into the system in the event of a general liquidity crisis, or allow NCBs to intervene in a local liquidity crisis. These decisions require access to information on the financial condition of counterparty institutions. Supervisory information would be necessary to assess the systemic implications of a crisis, as well as the credit risk that any lender of last resort would incur in the event that non-eligible collateral needed to be accepted. In both cases, the ECB would probably be unable to rely only on market assessments.

Thus, even if the ECB is only minimally involved in the management of liquidity crises – possibly only to authorize or deny LOLR operations of NCBs – the current information-sharing arrangements between national supervisors and the ECB seem to be too limited to allow well-informed decisions. An arrangement in which the ECB does not have access to supervisory information on a systematic basis, and in which banking supervisors 'will be prepared to inform the ESCB on a case-by-case basis should a banking crisis arise', means the ECB is dependent on national supervisory authorities for the information required to make decisions, in some cases about EMU-wide financial markets and pan-European institutions. By contrast, the German Banking Act contemplates a much wider sharing of information between the Bundesbank and the Federal Banking Supervisory Office. Other European countries also have more explicit sharing arrangements. For example, the recent Memorandum of Understanding (MoU) between the UK Treasury, the Bank of England and the FSA is a case in point. After attributing the responsibility of banking supervision to the FSA (a non-central bank), the MoU introduces sharing-of-information provisions. The MoU (paragraph 9) stipulates, for example, that:

> the FSA and the Bank will establish information sharing arrangements, to ensure that all information which is or may be relevant to the discharge of their respective responsibilities will be shared fully and freely. Each will seek to provide the other with relevant information as requested.

The Bank of England also has 'free and open access' to supervisory records (MoU paragaph 21). While these arrangements do not rule out possible conflicts among the three institutions involved in crisis management, they are more explicit than the current understanding between the ECB, the eleven

NCBs, the eleven supervisory authorities, and possibly the eleven Treasuries in EMU. In the event of a crisis involving a European banking group, these multiple understandings between EMU national authorities are bound to raise problems in sharing information and in coordinating roles.

It may be argued that no new arrangements will be needed to ensure adequate ECB access to supervisory information, because Governors of all NCBs are represented in the decision-making body of the ECB (the Governing Council) and MoUs (and an established network of contacts) among supervisors, and between them and the respective NCBs, have been in place for many years. By encouraging the development of pan-European markets and institutions, the introduction of the euro will create an environment in which speed will increasingly become a critical factor in the handling of systemic crises, and in which bilateral agreements and channels of communication based on the large number and permutations of *bilateral* MoUs may prove too complicated and slow to allow a rapid assessment of the systemic implications of a crisis.[29] As a minimum, if the ECB is to discharge even its limited obligations in this area, it would seem to require access to supervisory information and developing expertise in aggregating this information at the EMU level.

In case of disagreements among NCB governors on the appropriate course of action, an independent ECB assessment of the systemic implications of a crisis could be helpful in resolving conflicts and in avoiding risky delays. Ultimately, the ECB Executive Board's responsibilities in this area could evolve into a leading and coordinating role within the Council.

In this respect, the historical evolution of the US Federal Reserve System is an interesting example of how decision-making power and authority shifted out of necessity from the district banks to the Board of Governors. It is generally believed that the conflicts in the late 1920s and early 1930s between the centre (the Federal Reserve Board) and the periphery (the Federal Reserve Banks, especially New York) contributed to the mismanagement of the great depression (see Friedman and Schwartz 1963). These conflicts led to the creation in 1935 of the Federal Open-Market Committee, composed of seven members of the Board and five Federal Reserve Banks (rotating but always including New York), which shifted the balance of power to the centre. In the United States, Federal Reserve District Banks administer discount window lending, but before granting any advances they need to have the consent of not less than five members of the Board.[30] In addition, either the chairman of the Board or the head of the appropriate *federal* banking agency needs to certify the viability of a borrowing institution, which is a precondition for obtaining advances for a period longer than five days.[31]

By contrast, in EMU the balance of power is at the periphery, not only because national supervisors assess the viability of each institution and NCBs may grant emergency liquidity assistance, but also because in the Governing Council of the ECB, the eleven NCB Governors outnumber the six members of the Executive Board. Against this background, if decentralized crisis management in EMU proved to be ineffective, serious consideration could be given to using Article 12.1 of the ECB Statute to delegate certain powers to the Executive Board in the event of a crisis.[32]

Is the ambiguity of EMU crisis management mechanisms 'constructive'?

The existing uncertainty about how liquidity crises will be managed in EMU raises a natural question: is this ambiguity intentional? And if so, is there any rationale for maintaining it? In practice, central banks often have kept their involvement in financial safety-net operations secret, arguing that such 'constructive' ambiguity was reducing moral hazard and that, to avoid a panic and maintain confidence in the banking system, LOLR intervention had to be 'discreet'. In recent years, however, there has been a tendency towards greater disclosure, reflecting growing concerns that ambiguity reduces the accountability of supervisors and encourages regulatory forbearance, and may not therefore be 'constructive' (see e.g. Kane 1998). In many ways, the current debate parallels the debate on rules versus discretion in monetary policy.[33]

The focus, in theory and in practice, has been on rule-based exit policies that guarantee prompt and orderly closures of insolvent institutions and ensure that at least part of the costs of a bank failure are borne by managers, owners/shareholders, and perhaps creditors.[34] The provisions for prompt corrective action (PCA), introduced by the 1991 FDICIA in the United States, and recently implemented in Japan, are an example of a rule which requires supervisors to take prompt action when an institution's capital ratio falls below a specified level. A more radical example is the market-based regulation in New Zealand in 1996, by which banks are required to disclose publicly information that in other countries is normally viewed as the 'proprietary' information of the authorities. The objective of the reforms is to limit regulatory forbearance by passing some of the responsibility for supervizing the banking system to the markets, and to reduce moral hazard by changing the incentives of bank managers. Together with full disclosure, these reforms increase the frequency of external audits and credit ratings, eliminate official deposit insurance, and make financial institutions' managers *personally* liable and accountable.

In the United Kingdom, the clear attribution of responsibilities and the high degree of accountability signed into the recent MU between the Treasury, the Bank of England, and the FSA is another example of rules. The explicit attribution of LOLR responsibilities to the Bank of England may actually have made the FSA more willing to share supervisory information. The arrangement still maintains some ambiguity on the *means* that will be employed in dealing with an emergency situation ('The form of the response would depend on the nature of the event and would be determined at the time', paragraph 12 of the MoU) and on *whether* support will be granted ('the Bank and the FSA would need to work together very closely and they would immediately inform the Treasury, in order to give the Chancellor of the Exchequer the option of refusing support action', paragraph 13 of the MoU). The UK example shows that a clear attribution of LOLR responsibilities is not an obstacle to maintaining some 'constructive' ambiguity on how and whether emergency liquidity assistance would be granted.

By contrast, in EMU the limited agreement on information sharing reflects the fact that no clear LOLR function has been attributed to the ECB. Current understandings seem to imply that crises would be managed in a decentralized fashion and through *ad hoc* arrangements by which to assess and avert systemic problems. The idea may be that in the event of a crisis, a NCB or a national authority would find a way to provide liquidity support, and then central banks and supervisors would quietly pursue longer-lasting solutions, including finding buyers. While this ambiguity and lack of transparency may be interpreted as 'constructive ambiguity' aimed at reducing moral hazard, the current understandings and arrangements within EMU would need to be developed significantly further before they could be workable in an environment in which speed is increasingly becoming a critical factor in the handling of systemic crises. In other words, although constructive ambiguity about the conditions under which lender-of-last-resort facilities will be available is a necessary element in preventing moral hazard, prudence would require that there should be no ambiguity among policymakers about the mechanisms that can be used to manage crisis situations.[35]

The current approach to crisis management in EMU risks delaying the prompt resolution of banking problems and other financial difficulties that might occur across the pan-European financial markets and in pan-European financial institutions. It also risks not fully realizing the considerable potential benefits of reductions in moral hazard that might accompany a well designed strategy of 'constructive ambiguity'. A rigorous application of the Maastricht Treaty that excludes the use of central bank funds in the management of banking crises – at the ECB or at the NCB levels – would represent a significant departure from current practices in many countries. Such a change in regime might be more credible if it were more transparent, and it would then possibly bring about the desirable reduction in moral hazard, if this is the overriding objective.[36] If not, European banks might expect to be bailed out and take excessive risks. That is, one way to commit to having the ESCB not be involved in the EMU safety net is to publicize a credible mechanism for crisis management. Otherwise the policy of granting the ECB only monetary functions would turn out to be time-inconsistent.

Concluding remarks

The situation in EMU might evolve in two possible directions. The first direction would be the development of more ambitious, and novel, solutions to the problem of crisis management. As has been observed in this paper, the 'narrow' concept of a central bank that inspired the Treaty and the Statute of the ESCB led to the creation of an institutional framework that may completely preclude the involvement of the ECB, and even of NCBs, from crisis management. If the Governing Council of the ECB decides to move in this direction, this would represent a departure from current practices for most EMU central banks, including the Bundesbank. Given that the potential for crises would not simultaneously diminish, and on the contrary might increase in the short and medium run, it would become necessary to develop other mechanisms for crisis management that do not involve the central bank, such as a privately-funded liquidity consortium that also has natinoal authorities as shareholders.

This study has considered whether such mechanisms, including deposit insurance schemes, German-style liquidity consortia, pools of solvent banks, and emergency liquidity funds of national treasuries, would permit the management of banking crises without central bank funds. The conclusion reached is that, given that all non-central bank institutions can set aside *ex ante* only a limited amount of resources, and that speed is increasingly becoming a critical factor in the handling of systemic crises, the ECSB, or the NCBs, will have to remain, at least in the case of pan-European crises, the *immediate* providers of liquidity, while other entities would become the *ultimate* providers of funds. Any arrangement of this kind would require changes to existing plans. In addition, the effective resolution of crises involving pan-European financial institutions would appear to require the involvement of the ECB, and eleven NCBs, supervisory agencies, national treasuries, and deposit insurance schemes. Although this is technically feasible, it would appear to require a significantly higher degree of political consensus and coordination than is currently present, or is likely to be present in the near term, in EMU. Such consensus and coordination is more likely in the long run, however, especially if progress towards political union is made. The EMU framework for crisis management may evolve in this direction, but it seems at this point to be unrealistic for it to occur soon after the start of EMU.

Another possible direction in which the framework might change is that the ECB might evolve into an institution that would assume a leading and coordinating role in crisis management. If no other institution can satisfactorily take up LOLR responsibilities at the EMU level, then it might devolve to the ESCB, or to the NCBs. It could evolve to the NCBs, but the ECB would, at a minimum, need to be able to assess the systemic implications of a crisis rapidly, especially if it involves pan-European institutions. This implies that the ECB would have greater access to supervisory information on an independent and regular basis than is currently foreseen. Although the ECB may end up not assuming any supervisory function directly, extensive information-sharing agreements, such as the one recently agreed between the Bank of England and the FSA, and the existing one between the

Bundesbank and the Federal Banking Supervisory Office, would be desirable.

The ECB and the other relevant authorities might be tempted to maintain ambiguity about crisis-management mechanisms, on the principle that some ambiguity would be 'constructive' and would reduce moral hazard. It may be desirable to maintain ambiguity about the conditions under which liquidity and LOLR support would be considered and granted. However it is quite a different matter, and would be risky and even counterproductive, not to clarify in advance, and perhaps even make public, the channels of communications and the division of responsibilities between the ECB and the several national authorities and central banks.

Greater transparency about the mechanisms (not about their application) is justifiable for three main reasons. First, in the event of a crisis, the coordination problems faced by EMU authorities would be orders of magnitude greater than have been faced before in similar situations. In practice, it would be difficult and potentially costly to work out ambiguities of responsibilities and coordination problems in the midst of a crisis and on an *ad hoc* basis. Second, because of the greater integration of financial markets and banking systems within EMU, crises may develop more rapidly and less transparently than in smaller, national markets. It is a reasonable assumption that faster response times would be required to detect and assess problems and to contain the consequences of crises compared to what has been necessary during past crises in European countries, where financial markets have remained segmented, protected, and insulated (until recently), and where there are still large segments of the banking system in which public sectors are large shareholders. Third, if the intention is to control tightly the conditions under which central bank funds are provided to institutions experiencing problems, then it would be desirable adequately to clarify and to announce the change in regime, so that the desired reductions in moral hazard could be achieved. It would be desirable to avoid situations in which 'constructive ambiguity' encourages financial institutions to expect liquidity assistance in crisis situation, while at the same time the ECB has no authority or intention to grant it. In this case, the risk of widespread insolvency could force the ECB to renege on its commitment and reveal the time-inconsistency of its stated policy.

Notes

The views expressed in this paper are solely those of the authors and should not be attributed to the International Monetary Fund or its staff. The paper is adapted from the authors' longer paper, 'Financial Stability in EMU'. The authors acknowledge discussions on related technical issues with the staffs of the Bank of England, the Banque de France, the Bundesbank, and the UK Financial Services Authority, and the comments and suggestions of conference participants in Milan on the longer paper. The authors would also like to thank John Arrowsmith, Christian de

Boissieu, Michael Dooley, Daniel Gros, Gerhard Illing, Alain Vienney, and Axel Weber for the comments and suggestions they made during the SUERF Colloquia.

1 This paper *does not* consider national or local financial problems that are of no immediate threat to national or European financial markets. Such localized problems would include, for example, the recapitalization of small local retail banking institutions in the towns and villages of individual countries. In general, these local problems are relatively slow moving and involve decisions by local or national fiscal authorities rather than EMU-wide monetary authorities. In cases where a national problem entails considerable ambiguity about the EMU cross-border monetary and financial implications, the involvement of the ESCB and a number of national supervisory authorities and national treasuries could warrant the involvement of a pan-European LOLR if and when one is put in place.

2 Article 25(1) envisions a specific advisory function for the ECB in the field of Community legislation relating to the prudential supervision of credit institutions and the stability of the financial system. Article 105(4) contemplates a somewhat stronger role for the ECB, by stipulating that it must be consulted on draft Community and national legislation falling within its field of competence. Article 105(5) makes clear that the role of the ESCB is subordinate to that of the competent supervisory authorities, by indicating that the ESCB is expected 'to contribute to the smooth conduct of policies pursued by the competent authorities relating to the prudential supervision of credit institutions and the stability of the financial system.' Article 105(6) limits the role of the ECB in the area of prudential supervision to 'specific tasks' that the EU Council may confer to it on a proposal of the European Commission.

3 See Folkerts-Landau and Garber 1994, Mishkin 1993, Monticelli and Viñals 1993.

4 In IMF 1998, LOLR policies are described as having typically three primary objectives: (1) to protect the integrity of the payments system; (2) to avoid runs that spill over from bank to bank and develop into a systemic crisis; (3) to prevent illiquidity at an individual bank from leading unnecessarily to its insolvency. By contrast, the primary objective of a deposit insurance scheme is to prevent self-fulfilling runs on deposits and to provide a safe asset to small savers.

5 See Box 2 in IMF 1998: 28.

6 Goodfriend and King 1988 argue that control only of high-powered money is sufficient to deal with liquidity crises.

7 Goodfriend and King 1988 define a central bank's *banking policy* – in contrast to monetary policy – as involving: (1) changes in the composition of the asset side of the central bank's balance sheet, holding the total fixed, or (2) its regulatory and supervisory actions.

8 The practice of 'constructive ambiguity' is discussed later in this paper. Goodhart and Huang 1999 provide a rationale for it, whereas Giannini 1999 emphasizes its key role in controlling moral hazard when central banks cannot easily separate illiquid from insolvent banks.

9 Goodhart and Schoenmaker 1995 make this point based on a sample of 104 major bank failures in several industrial countries.

10 See Table 2 of Kaufman 1996. See also Temzelides 1997.

11 See Grossman 1993, Hasan and Dwyer 1994, and Schoenmaker 1996.

12 See sections 19.3 and 21 of the Bundesbank Act.

13 This is probably owing to the fact that the discount window is subsidized. See sections 19.1 and 19.2 of the Bundesbank Act for a definition of the eligible assets.

14 See point e) in section 19.3 and section 21.4 of the Bundesbank Act. No bank loans or equity can, in any case, be accepted as collateral.

15 To determine solvency, the LCB Credit Committee uses information from various sources, including supervisory information to which the Bundesbank

representative has easy access given that the Bundesbank (in particular the Landeszentralbanken) often acts as an agent for the Bank Supervisory Office in collecting supervisory data.

16 In the existing framework, there is no straightforward way, for example, to accept noneligible assets from an institution in trouble without making that typology of assets eligible for credit operations with the entire system.

As already discussed, in Germany, the Bundesbank Statute specifies the eligibility characteristics of collateral. This implies that, to accept ineligible collateral, it would be necessary to go through the lengthy process of changing the Bundesbank Statute. The Liquidity Consortium Bank is probably a way to reintroduce some flexibility in the management of liquidity crises. By contrast, the ECB Statute only specifies that ECB's lending should be based on 'adequate' collateral, leaving the exact definition of 'adequate' to the Governing Council of the ECB (Article 18). In EMU, a decision of the Governing Council of the ECB would then be enough to change the assets included in the Tier 1 and Tier 2 lists of collateral.

17 The options available are further discussed later in this paper. The list of eligible assets includes government paper, and, especially in the case of Tier 2 collateral, assets whose quality needs to be assessed by NCBs.

18 Goodfriend and King consider this the worst possible case:

> the government would have to precommit itself not to provide emergency liquidity assistance. The worst possible case would be one where the government announced its intention not to provide emergency credit assistance in the future, but the banks believed that in fact it would. Then, if a liquidity problem arose, banks would not have prepared for it by holding sufficient capital and by arranging lines of credit. If the government remained true to its policy, widespread insolvency could prevail.
>
> (Goodfriend and King 1988: 15)

19 In the past, public banks and public financial institutions were lenders of penultimate resort, but this role will diminish with the number of public banks.

20 In the United Kingdom, for example, payouts on BCCI deposits began in April 1992, well after the liquidation of the bank on 5 July 1991 (see Schoenmaker 1992).

21 For example, under the Directive on Deposit-Guarantee schemes (see IMF 1997: 180–1), foreign branches can join a host country scheme so that foreign branches obtain 'insurance coverage in a country even though that country has no authority to regulate the risk-taking behavior of those branches because of mutual recognition' (Barth, Nolle and Rice 1997: 25). In cases of supervisory oversight, these provisions are likely to generate disputes between supervisors and deposit insurance schemes.

22 The 1997 EMI *Annual Report* indicates that the ESCB will not systematically receive supervisory information. ESCB requests for information will be considered by banking supervisors, who will inform it on a case-by-case basis in the event of a banking crisis with systemic implications. This common understanding among EU supervisors is, however, intended to cover the specific needs of the ESCB in its capacity as monetary authority. It remains possible that another, perhaps wider, understanding might be sought (or agreed but not publicly announced) for the provision of emergency liquidity assistance.

23 An independent EMU-wide emergency fund might overcome some of these problems.

24 The applicability of this norm is limited, because it is extremely difficult to identify precisely the point in time when the Fed's lending allows a troubled institution not to be liquidated and increases its losses.

25 This article may have been adopted to provide NCBs leeway in performing functions with limited liquidity impact, such as paying employee salaries or purchasing assets for employee pension funds. Nevertheless, there is uncertainty about its broader interpretations.
26 Article 12.1 stipulates, 'The Governing Council shall adopt the guidelines and take the decisions necessary to ensure the performance of the tasks entrusted to the ESCB under this Treaty and this Statute.' Article 14.3 stipulates that:

> The national central banks are an integral part of the ESCB and shall act in accordance with the guidelines and instructions of the ECB. The Governing Council shall take the necessary steps to ensure compliance with the guidelines and instructions of the ECB, and shall require that any necessary information be given to it.

Article 18.1 of the Statute does not prohibit these operations even though it requires that lending should be based on 'adequate collateral,' because this article refers to the ESCB – not NCBs – and is in the chapter 'Monetary functions and operations of the ESCB.' On this ambiguity see Schoenmaker 1995: 8–9.
27 Tier 2 assets are eligible as collateral EMU wide. Losses on Tier 2 collateral will be borne by the NCB that proposes it. Losses on Tier 1 collateral will be shared within the ESCB.
28 This is the 'indirect method' as opposed to the 'direct method,' see EMI 1997b: 77.
29 Bini Smaghi 1999 lists several reasons why decentralized bank regulation and supervision in EMU is 'not only inefficient but also potentially dangerous for financial stability'.
30 See Section 10A of the Federal Reserve Act and Sections 201.4 and 201.5 of Regulation A ('Extension of Credit by Federal Reserve Banks').
31 See Section 201.4 of Regulation A ('Extension of Credit by Federal Reserve Banks').
32 Article 12.1 of the Statute of the ESCB foresees that 'the Executive Board may have certain powers delegated to it where the Governing Council so decides'.
33 See Quinn 1996 and Cordella and Levy-Yeyati 1997 on the risks of excessive information disclosure.
34 See IMF 1998, chap. 5. See also Aghion, Bolton, and Fries 1998.
35 This observation was first made in IMF 1997: 55.
36 IMF (1998: 27) warns in the context of financial safety nets that any 'abrupt changes in public policies may have adverse effects. Such changes would need to be accompanied by transparent public explanations of the new policy.'

Bibliography

Aghion P., Bolton, P. and Fries, S. (1998) 'Optimal Bank Bailouts,' IMF Research Department Seminar (April).
Bagehot, W. (1873) *Lombard Street*, Kegan Paul, London.
Barth, J. R., Nolle, D. E. and Rice, T. N. (1997) 'Commercial Banking Structure, Regulation and Performance: An International Comparison,' *Contemporary Banking Issues* 23(11).
Bini Smaghi, L. (1999) 'Who Takes Care of Financial Stability in Europe?' in L. Bini Smaghi and D. Gros (eds), *Open Issues in European Central Banking*, Macmillan, London.
Bishop, G. (1997) 'The European Central Bank and the Prudential Regulation of the Financial System,' paper presented at a conference on the Monetary, Fiscal

and Financial Implications of European Monetary Union, European University Institute, Florence, June.

Cordella, T. and Levy-Yeyati, E. (1997) 'Public Disclosures and Bank Failures,' *IMF Working Paper 97/96* , International Monetary Fund, Washington, D.C.

Cordella, T. and Levy-Yeyati, E. (1998) 'Financial Opening, Deposit Insurance, and Risk in a Model of Banking Competition,' International Monetary Fund, Washington, D.C., mimeo.

Crockett, A. (1996) 'The Theory and Practice of Financial Stability,' *De Economist* 144(4).

Deutsche Bundesbank (1995) *The Monetary Policy of the Bundesbank*, Frankfurt.

Dooley, M. P. (1997) 'Profitable Speculation and Monetary Unions,' paper presented at a conference on the Monetary, Fiscal and Financial Implications of European Monetary Union, European University Institute, Florence (June).

EMI (1997a) *The Single Monetary Policy in Stage Three: Specification of the Operational Framework*, European Monetary Institute, Frankfurt (January).

EMI (1997b) *Annual Report 1996*, European Monetary Institute, Frankfurt (April).

EMI (1997c) *The Single Monetary Policy in Stage Three: General Documentation on ESCB Monetary Policy Instruments and Procedures*, European Monetary Institute, Frankfurt (September).

EMI (1997d) *Second Progress Report on the Target Project*, European Monetary Institute, Frankfurt (September).

EMI (1997e) *Technical Annexes to the Second Progress Report on the Target Project*, European Monetary Institute, Frankfurt (September).

EMI (1998) *Annual Report 1997*, European Monetary Institute, Frankfurt (May).

Federal Reserve Bank of New York (1988) 'Federal Reserve Security Loans to Dealers', *Fedpoints 37*, Federal Reserve Bank of New York.

Federal Reserve System (1994) *Federal Reserve Discount Window*.

Folkerts-Landau, D. and Garber, P. (1991) *The Microeconomic Impact of the European System of Central Banks*, Report of a Conference organized by the CEPR and the Paolo Baffi Centre for Monetary and Financial Economics, Milan.

Folkerts-Landau, D., and Garber, P. (1992) 'The European Central Bank: A Bank or a Monetary Policy Rule,' *NBER Working Paper no. 4016*, National Bureau of Economic Research, Cambridge, Mass.: 1–33.

Folkerts-Landau, D. and Garber, P. (1994) 'What Role for the ECB in Europe's Financial Markets?', in A. Steinherr (ed.), *30 Years of European Monetary Integration from the Werner Plan to EMU*, Longman, London.

FRB (1997) 'Testimony of Chairman Alan Greenspan before the Subcommittee on Banking and Financial Services' Federal Reserve Board, Washington, D.C. (March).

FRB (1997) 'Remarks by Governor Susan M. Phillips at The Exchequer Club', Federal Reserve Board, Washington, D.C. (June).

Friedman, M. and Schwartz, A. J. (1963) *A Monetary History of the United States, 1867–1960*, Princeton University Press, Princeton, N. J.

Friedman M. and Schwartz, A. J. (1986) 'Has Government Any Role in Money?', *Journal of Monetary Economics* 17(1) (January): 37–62.

FSA (1997) 'Memorandum of Understanding between HM Treasury, the Bank of England and the Financial Services Authority', in *Financial Services Authority: An Outline*, Financial Services Authority, London: 34–39.

Giannini, C. (1999) '"Enemy of None but a Common Friend of All?" An

International Perspective on the Lender-of-Last-Resort Function', *Essays in International Finance no. 214,* International Finance Section, Princeton University, Princeton, N. J. (June).

Goodfriend, M. and King, R. G. (1988) 'Financial Deregulation, Monetary Policy, and Central Banking', *Economic Review,* Federal Reserve Bank of Richmond (May/June).

Goodhart, C. (1986) 'The Draft Statute of the European System of Central Banks: A Commentary', *LSE Financial Markets Group, Special Paper no. 37,* London School of Economics, London.

Goodhart, C. (1987) 'Why Do Banks Need a Central Bank?' *Oxford Economic Papers* no. 39: 75–89, Oxford University Press, Oxford.

Goodhart, C. (1992) 'The ESCB After Maastricht,' *LSE Financial Markets Group, Special Paper no. 44,* London School of Economics, London.

Goodhart, C. (1993) 'Can We Improve the Structure of Financial Systems?' *European Economic Review* 37: 269–91.

Goodhart, C. (1995) 'Should the Functions of Monetary Policy and Banking Supervision be Separated?' *Oxford Economic Papers* no. 47: 539–60, Oxford University Press, Oxford.

Goodhart, C. and Huang, H. (1999) 'A Model of the Lender of Last Resort', *IMF Working Paper no. 99/39,* International Monetary Fund, Washington, D.C. (March).

Goodhart, C. and Schoenmaker, D. (1993) 'Institutional Separation Between Supervisory and Monetary Agencies,' *LSE Financial Markets Group, Special Paper no. 52,* London School of Economics, London.

Grossman, R. (1993) 'The Macroeconomic Consequences of Bank Failures under the National Banking System', *Explorations in Economic History* 30: 294–320.

Hasan, I. and Dwyer, G. (1994) 'Bank Runs in the Free Banking Period,' *Journal of Money, Credit, and Banking* 26: 271–88.

Holmström, B. and Tirole, J. (1998) 'Private and Public Supply of Liquidity,' *Journal of Political Economy* 1(106) (February).

IMF (1997) *International Capital Markets, Developments, Prospects and Key Policy Issues,* World Economic and Financial Surveys, International Monetary Fund, Washington, D.C.

IMF (1998) *Towards a Framework for Financial Stability, World Economic and Financial Surveys,* International Monetary Fund, Washington, D.C.

Kane, E. (1998) 'Banking Crises and Offshore Financial Regulatory Competition', IMF Research Department Seminar, International Monetary Fund, Washington, D.C.

Kaufman, G. G. (1996) 'Bank Fragility: Perception and Historical Evidence', paper presented at the Federal Reserve Bank of Chicago and the Western Economic Association meetings.

Mishkin, F. S. (1993) 'Comments to "European Monetary Pol;icy in Stage Three: What Are the Issues?"' in C. Monticelli and J. Viñals, 'European Monetary Policy in Stage Three: What Are the Issues?', *CEPR Occasional Paper no. 12,* Centre for Economic Policy Research,

Monticelli, C. and Viñals, J. (1993) 'European Monetary Policy in Stage Three: What Are the Issues?', CEPR Occasional Paper no. 12, Centre for Economic Policy Research,

Padoa-Schioppa, T. (1996) 'Retail Payments: Recent Developments and Central Banks,' paper presented at the Fifth JCB World Conference.

Prati, A. and Schinasi, G. (1997) 'European Monetary Union and International Capital Markets: Structural Implications and Risks,' in P. Masson, T. H. Krueger and B. G. Turtelboom (eds), *EMU and the International Monetary System*, International Monetary Fund, Washington, D.C.: 263–319.

Prati, A. and Schinasi, G. (1999) 'Financial Stability in European Economic and Monetary Union,' *Princeton Studies in International Finance no. 86*, International Finance Section, Princeton University, Princeton, N. J. (August).

Quinn, B. (1996) 'Rules v. Discretion: The Case of Banking Supervision in the Light of Debate on Monetary Policy,' *LSE Financial Markets Group and ESRC Research Centre, Special Paper no. 85*, London School of Economics, London.

Rochet, J.-C. and Tirole, J. (1996) 'Interbank Lending and Systemic Risk', *Journal of Money, Credit and Banking* 28(November): 733–62.

Schoenmaker, D. (1992) 'A Note on the Proposal for a Council Directive on Deposit Guarantee Schemes', *LSE Financial Markets Group, Special Paper no. 48*, London School of Economics, London.

Schoenmaker, D. (1995) 'Banking Supervision in Stage Three of EMU,' *LSE Financial Markets Group and ESRC Research Centre, Special Paper no. 72*, London School of Economics, London.

Schoenmaker, D. (1996) 'Contagion Risk in Banking,' *LSE Financial Markets Group and ESRC Research Center, Discussion Paper no. 239*, London School of Economics, London.

Temzelides, E. (1997) 'Are Bank Runs Contagious?' *Business Review*, Federal Reserve Bank of Philadelphia (November/December).

Thygesen, N. (1989) 'Propositions pour une banque centrale européenne,' *Revue Francaise d'Economie*, 4(1): 3–38.

Toma, M. (1995) 'The Compatibility of Central Bank Price Rules with Financial Stability,' *Temple University*.

Vittas, D. (1992) 'Thrift Regulation in the United Kingdom and the United States: A Historical Perspective,' World Bank, Washington, D.C.

Vives, X. (1992) 'The Supervisory Function of the European System of Central Banks,' *Giornale degli Economisti e Annali di Economia* 51: 523–32.

Commission 3
Issues for portfolio management and corporate finance

12 The effects of the euro on portfolio allocation

Andrea Beltratti

Introduction

What will be the effects of the introduction of the euro on economic and financial markets? Standard economic models suggest that in an ideal world with competitive markets, a change in the numeraire should not affect the general equilibrium of the system. In practice this may not be true. First, actual economies are not completely competitive. The disappearance of exchange rates among European currencies will eliminate a way to readjust relative prices after asymmetric shocks. Without perfect mobility of labour and perfect flexibility of relative prices, such a loss may affect the equilibrium. Second, the process of convergence towards the euro has carried with it a number of macroeconomic readjustments in order to comply with the Maastricht criteria on inflation, deficit and debt. Limitations to the instruments of national economic policy are supposed to be permanent and are likely to affect the allocation of resources.

Will the introduction of the euro also affect the process of asset allocation and risk management? If one adopts the simple framework of static mean–variance maximization it is easy to identify in theory the determinants of portfolio choice, which are preferences and market opportunities. Preferences are described by the risk aversion coefficient, while market opportunities are represented by the first two moments of the joint distribution of returns. According to this theoretical model, the factors which may trigger modifications in global asset allocations will above all be new market opportunities associated with the introduction of the euro.

In practice the distinction between preferences and market opportunities is much less clear than it is in theory. Actual asset allocation choices represent the result of interactions among preferences, opportunities and regulations. Existing regulations prevent many investors from freely allocating their wealth among available securities. Various currency-matching rules, for example, force long-term investors such as insurance companies and pension funds to limit their exposure to securities denominated in foreign currency. Currently a German insurance company regards a Spanish stock as an investment denominated in foreign currency.

This immediately brings out a relevant impact of the euro, since in the future the European securities will all become domestic securities from the point of view of the currency of denomination. A German insurance company will be able to purchase a euro-denominated Spanish stock without assuming any currency risk. Therefore a very important element of the asset-allocation process of individuals and institutional investors will change. The enlargement of the domestic market will allow European investors to choose among a richer set of securities, with a possible impact also on the demand for non-euro and non-EMU assets.

This paper considers an empirical application of the mean–variance model to broad asset classes of stocks and bonds, to study the modifications caused by the change in the currency of denomination. At first minimal assumptions are made about the changes in the financial opportunity set, in order to evaluate the effects of the introduction of the euro on portfolio choice. In particular, the existence of only one European short-term and long-term interest rate is assumed, therefore the model ignores all the dimensions related to credit risk. Next, the importance of a sort of currency matching constraint is analysed, imposing the condition that the share of the securities denominated in foreign currencies cannot exceed a certain upper bound. Optimal portfolios are computed for before and after the euro, in order to evaluate the most relevant factors causing modifications in the structure of the portfolio and in the return–risk trade-off available to international investors. The plan of the paper is as follows. The second section looks at the mean–variance optimization problem, the third section presents the empirical results, and the fourth section is a conclusion.

The mean–variance allocation model

The theory of asset allocation is in general very complex. In the presence of a stochastically-evolving investment opportunity set, the investor should modify the optimal allocation depending on the evolution of the state variables, as suggested by Merton (1990). Implementation of such an approach is technically difficult. In this paper a very simple static mean–variance framework is considered. There are two reasons for this choice. First, the efficient frontier derived under such a framework is widely adopted in practice; changes in asset allocations identified by means of the mean–variance model are likely to be of interest to practitioners. Second, this paper is not concerned with 'the' optimal asset allocation before and after the euro: its more modest interest is in studying some of the modifications of the asset allocation process connected with the introduction of the European common currency. The mean–variance framework is sufficiently simple and specific to enable it to highlight a few factors which may be of practical relevance, and it should not bias the comparison in any meaningful way.

On the negative side, one should acknowledge that from the beginning the deficiencies of the mean–variance approach in terms of excess sensitivity to the assumptions made about the vector of expected returns. This sensitivity often produces efficient frontiers with large positive and negative positions in the various assets. Such extreme asset allocations are disliked by practitioners because they eliminate the very element that is looked for in the model, that is diversification. In this paper the problem is handled by imposing non-negativity constraints on the share of the assets. Such an approach is certainly *ad hoc*, but it should be sufficient to provide an initial look at the problem of the change in asset allocation after the introduction of the euro.

The description of the optimization problem that will be solved in the empirical section of the paper is the following:

$$\min_w w'\Sigma w \tag{1}$$

$$w'Er - Er_B = r_T \tag{2}$$

$$w^U \geq w \geq 0 \tag{3}$$

$$\sum_{f \in F} w_f \leq U \tag{4}$$

where w is the (N,1) vector to be optimized, Er_B is the expected rate of return of the benchmark, Er is the vector of expected returns, $i = (1...1)'$, r_T is the target rate of return and Σ is the covariance matrix of the returns relative to the benchmark. Equation (1) shows that the objective is to minimize the variance of relative returns of the portfolio. Equation (2) imposes the constraint that the expected excess return of the portfolio is equal to a target return. Equation (3) is the set of non-negativity constraints on the assets, which are also required to be lower than a vector of upper bounds w^U. It is well known that the solution of problem (1) is extremely sensitive to the vector of expected returns. In many cases the solutions involve large long and short positions in the different assets included in the efficient frontier. Extreme positions are unacceptable to practitioners for many reasons, among which are the implied lack of diversification of a portfolio composed of few securities, and institutional constraints preventing negative holdings. In order to prevent the emergence of such solutions, the problem is solved here by considering constraints of the form (3). As was shown by Best and Grauer (1991), non-negativity constraints are also helpful to stabilize the return–risk characteristics of the efficient portfolios in the face of modifications to expected returns.

Finally, (4) is the currency matching constraint, according to which the sum of the shares in the securities denominated in foreign currencies, belonging to the set F, must be lower than an upper bound U. Equation

(4) realistically describes the asset allocation problem of an investor who is constrained in diversification possibilities because of the attempt of regulators to limit the foreign exchange risk. Dickenson (1998) reports data on such requirements for European insurance companies, which in most cases need to maintain the share of assets denominated in foreign currency below 20 per cent. The same is true of many pension funds.

It is unclear to what extent this constraint is really binding, given that many investors set their target with respect to the return of a benchmark denominated in domestic currency. Indeed, the inclusion of a benchmark in (1) is aimed at reinforcing the realism of the model and its relevance for the problem at hand. It increases realism from several points of view. It may help, for example, to consider the problem of a fund manager whose performance is evaluated against the performance obtained by other managers of similar funds. Alternatively it may describe the case of a pension fund or an insurance company with a long-run horizon, whose benchmark is represented by the rate of return offered by a long-term bond. It may also be used to describe the problem of a final investor who evaluates the returns in the light of the domestic short-term nominal interest rate, because of a target set with respect to the purchasing power of the value of the investment.

The choice of the benchmark is relevant to the problem because from the point of view of a global investor based in one currency, for example Italian lire, it is very likely that the benchmark will be composed of a portfolio denominated in the same currency. Global investors based in different countries will therefore target different benchmarks. In the extreme case where the benchmark is composed of domestic short-term bonds, the benchmarks in different countries are represented by the different short-term interest rates. This may bias the optimal portfolios towards domestic assets, to the extent that foreign assets include an extra element of risk associated with foreign exchange. It follows that the currency-matching constraint may not necessarily be binding, because of the attempt to compare the returns to those of a benchmark denominated in domestic currency.

The existence of a domestic benchmark may also be connected to the home-country bias. As was noted initially by French and Poterba (1991), investors hold an excess proportion of portfolios in assets denominated in domestic currency. There are currently no convincing general explanations of the home-country bias. In particular it is unclear whether it represents a bias against foreign currency risk, which would disappear with the euro, or against securities issued in foreign countries, which would not disappear with the euro. Griffin (1997) suggests that the existence of a benchmark represented by the return of a long-term bond goes some way towards explaining the bias in favour of domestic assets.

How general is the problem described? It is general for its ability to describe investors interested in different benchmarks and looking at different currencies. On the other hand, it is mainly a short horizon problem, which can meaningfully be applied to an horizon of six months or one year. Even though practitioners often apply it also for long-run horizon problems, I am skeptical of this possibility. One could in principle use the historical evidence, plus some assumptions about the stochastic process followed by prices, in order to estimate the moments of the long-run distribution of returns. However there is considerable uncertainty about the description of stock returns, and this uncertainty makes the application of the static mean–variance framework to a long-run horizon problem less relevant.

Before this section is concluded, it is worth emphasizing one fundamental point characterizing this paper: its results are only valid from the point of view of the single investor. Specifically, the empirical exercise carried out in what follows ignores the possible changes of expected returns, covariances and variances which may follow the introduction of the euro. Indeed the actual problem of the investor will be different from the present one in two aspects, that it will not involve such a limited number of assets, and that there are modifications in the joint distribution function of returns. Here the first element is considered, but not the second. The relevance of the results therefore revolves essentially around the assumption that the various moments of the distributions do not change. In order to consider also the second element of the problem it would be necessary to make assumptions about a model for the determination of stock prices. This task is considerably more complicated than the one pursued here, and it is left to future research.

Empirical analyses

The optimization problem

The assets considered in the exercises are the short-term interest rates, the indices of long-term government bonds and the stock markets indices (produced by Morgan Stanley) of the following countries: Germany, Italy, the US, Britain, Japan, Switzerland, France, Holland, Spain and Sweden. The choice of the countries is motivated by the need to consider a set of assets which may represent a significant sub-set of the investable universe of global international investors. Moreover the sample includes countries which will immediately join the EMU, countries that are likely to join in the short run (Britain) or might join in the medium run (Switzerland), and countries that will not join the EMU block.

Assets such as commodities, derivatives, and emerging markets are not considered here. Even a simple stock/bond case is however of practical interest to many individuals and institutions which restrict themselves (or are restricted) to investing in primary securities. Also, the assumption of normal distributions implicit in the use of the efficient frontier is more likely to be satisfied by stocks and bonds, especially at the monthly frequency considered in this paper. It is important to notice that in the empirical exercise, bonds are not managed separately on the basis of measures such as duration and convexity. They are an integral part of the Markowitz asset allocation problem, so that their covariance with stocks and exchange rates is a fundamental element that drives portfolio composition.

In order to stress the importance of changing benchmarks, the optimization problem is considered in terms of excess returns rather than absolute returns. This means, for example, that larger changes should be apparent in the solution for the Italian investor if one believes that the euro will inherit the statistical distribution of the Deutschmark in a context of European interest rates equal to the average German interest rates. In such a case, in fact, the Italian investor would switch from a current situation where the benchmark is represented by a high domestic nominal interest rate to one where the benchmark is represented by a low nominal domestic interest rate.

The modifications in the financial environment which are considered to describe the changes connected with the euro cannot be chosen in a simplistic way. For example one cannot use historical data for, say, Italian long-term interest rates and simply assume that after the euro such rates will be equal to the historical average. Such a scenario would probably lead to long-term Italian assets being the most profitable because of the historically high interest rates associated with the expected lira depreciation and with the lira risk. On the other hand it is impossible, without a structural model, to determine the joint distribution of asset returns after the euro. As a reasonable solution, the historical data are used only to represent the current pre-euro situation. To describe the post-euro situation the following assumptions have been made:

- There is no exchange rate between the countries joining EMU.
- There is only one short-term European nominal interest rate, taken to be equal to German short-term interest rates.
- There is only one long-term bond, taken to be equal to the German long-term bond.
- The translation of non-euro asset returns into euro asset returns takes account of two possibilities. The first is that the euro is equal to the DM; the second is that the euro is equal to the Italian lira.

The consequences of these assumptions for a European investor are the following:

- The excess return on any euro-country stock market is equal to its historical value.
- The uncovered excess return on any non-euro stock market equals its historical stock return in foreign currency minus the historical nominal German short-term interest rate, plus the rate of change of

the exchange rate against the mark (lira) if the euro is strong (weak).
* The covered excess return on any non-euro stock market equals its historical stock return in the foreign currency minus the historical nominal short-term interest rate in that country.

Overall, the changes considered to describe the post-euro situation take mainly the form of exclusion of assets. This may introduce a bias towards believing that the future will be similar to the past. The next section looks at a few descriptive statistics about the distribution of stock and bond returns and exchange rates.

Optimization inputs

Tables 12.1 to 12.3 report values for the average and standard deviations of returns for different sample periods, from the points of view of Italian and German investors. Such values represent the basis for the optimization problem to be solved next. The tables report excess returns, both covered and uncovered from exchange rate risk. Uncovered excess returns are defined as $r_t^* + \Delta e_{t+1} - i_t$ where r_t^* is the nominal rate of return denominated in the foreign currency, Δe_{t+1} is the rate of change of the nominal exchange rate and i_t is the domestic short term interest rate. Covered excess returns are defined as $r_t^* - i_t^*$ where i_t^* is the foreign short term interest rate. All the data in the tables refer to continuously compounded annualized returns.

Table 12.1 contains data on stocks. It shows the great attractiveness of stocks in general in the most recent sample period, particularly of some European stocks, from the point of view of both Italian and German investors. Such an increased attractiveness holds regardless of whether one is considering hedged or unhedged returns. Hedging exchange rate risk has some impact in terms of reducing the standard deviations of stock returns, even though the reduction is often minimal. There are, for example, substantial reductions in the volatility of US and Spanish stocks from the point of view of the German investor.

The table also suggests that the returns to complete hedging depend heavily on the sample period. From the point of view of the Italian investor, for example, it was advantageous to hedge foreign exchange fluctuations in 1995–7, because of the revaluation of the Italian lira, while over the longer sample period the average hedged return is not far from the average unhedged return. This confirms a result which is common knowledge in the financial literature, that is that the optimality of hedging depends on the sample period: see Abken and Shrikhande (1997) for a survey and an empirical analysis.

It is also worth commenting on the huge differences in average stock returns for a given sample period. If one considers the 1985–97 period as a better indicator of future returns than the 1995–7 period (owing to the number of observations contained in each period), it can be seen that there

Table 12.1 Average and standard deviations of returns for different sample periods, for Italian and German investors (stocks)

	Italian investor				German investor			
	1987–97		1995–7		1987–97		1995–7	
	mean	vol.	mean	vol.	mean	vol.	mean	vol.
Uncovered returns:								
Germany	2.86	21.22	10.56	16.92	3.89	21.33	23.65	17.16
Italy	-3.62	23.42	12.99	23.27	-2.58	26.60	26.07	26.00
Japan	-6.52	24.94	-21.37	20.11	-5.48	25.26	-8.28	22.14
Switzerland	8.16	19.11	17.27	16.84	9.20	18.44	30.36	16.09
UK	6.64	19.82	14.33	11.28	7.68	20.01	27.41	12.16
US	7.33	19.75	20.27	16.15	8.37	20.31	33.35	18.01
France	2.03	26.17	5.16	18.77	3.07	25.80	18.25	21.02
Netherlands	8.81	22.87	16.01	17.42	9.85	22.56	29.10	18.89
Spain	4.96	27.44	23.99	19.57	6.00	28.64	37.07	22.55
Sweden	6.48	28.48	19.71	20.79	7.52	29.70	32.79	22.24
Returns covered from exchange rate risk:								
Germany	3.90	21.33	23.65	17.16	3.89	21.33	23.65	17.16
Italy	-3.62	23.42	12.99	23.27	-3.62	23.42	12.99	23.27
Japan	-3.51	22.02	-0.46	17.50	-3.51	22.02	-0.46	17.50
Switzerland	10.30	18.65	31.33	15.47	10.30	18.65	31.33	15.47
UK	5.11	17.88	14.25	10.06	5.11	17.88	14.25	10.06
US	9.54	14.97	21.40	11.77	9.54	14.97	21.40	11.77
France	2.58	20.57	16.01	17.12	2.58	20.57	16.01	17.12
Netherlands	10.60	16.86	29.92	16.34	10.60	16.86	29.92	16.34
Spain	4.16	22.57	30.90	17.93	4.16	22.57	30.90	17.93
Sweden	7.66	24.42	23.53	17.73	7.66	24.41	23.53	17.73

Note: vol. = volatility

is about a 15 per cent difference between the best performer and the worst performer. Both Italy and Japan were bad performers with a negative average return.

Table 12.2 analyses bond returns. This table suggests, contrary to what has been observed for stocks, the essential importance of hedging for determining overall returns, especially over the most recent sample periods. In 1995–7 the unhedged return for a German investor from investing in US bonds was equal to 14 per cent, which was reduced to 2.5 per cent when hedging was pursued by assuming debt in high-rate short-term US liquidity in order to invest in low-rate short-term German liquidity. This clearly reflects the well-known failure of uncovered interest rate parity. Historically, the high returns provided by liquidity have very often not been compensated by a devaluation of the currency. On the contrary, hedging was a key element of success for an Italian investor buying Japanese and Swiss bonds over the 1995–7 period.

The table also shows the very good performance of Italian long-term bonds for a German investor, especially when no systematic hedging is

Table 12.2 Average and standard deviations of returns for different sample
periods, for Italian and German investors (bonds)

| | Italian investor | | | | German investor | | | |
| | 1987–97 | | 1995–7 | | 1987–97 | | 1995–7 | |
	mean	vol.	mean	vol.	mean	vol.	mean	vol.
Uncovered returns:								
Germany	0.31	8.22	-7.89	5.70	1.35	3.22	5.19	2.86
Italy	3.30	4.42	10.38	4.80	4.34	9.83	23.46	10.13
Japan	-0.51	13.51	-15.63	11.53	0.53	11.01	-2.55	11.16
Switzerland	-1.54	9.60	-8.89	8.60	-0.50	5.05	4.20	4.63
UK	2.53	10.17	3.76	7.66	3.57	9.89	16.84	8.11
US	-0.30	11.38	1.44	8.68	0.74	11.28	14.53	10.49
France	0.77	14.66	-5.14	8.00	1.81	13.17	7.94	9.48
Returns covered from exchange rate risk:								
Netherlands	-0.27	14.54	-8.67	8.05	0.77	12.27	4.41	9.02
Germany	1.35	3.22	5.19	2.86	1.35	3.22	5.19	2.86
Italy	3.30	4.42	10.38	4.80	3.30	4.42	10.38	4.80
Japan	2.50	4.36	5.27	3.70	2.50	4.36	5.27	3.70
Switzerland	0.59	3.01	5.17	2.56	0.59	3.01	5.17	2.56
UK	0.99	5.47	3.68	3.32	0.99	5.47	3.68	3.32
US	1.91	4.17	2.58	3.52	1.91	4.17	2.58	3.52
France	1.32	3.73	5.70	2.81	1.32	3.73	5.70	2.81
Netherlands	1.52	3.19	5.23	2.73	1.52	3.19	5.23	2.73

Note: vol. = volatility

Table 12.3 Average and standard deviations of returns for different sample
periods, for Italian and German investors (liquid currency)

| | Italian investor | | | | German investor | | | |
| | 1987–97 | | 1995–7 | | 1987–97 | | 1995–7 | |
	mean	vol.	mean	vol.	mean	vol.	mean	vol.
Germany	-1.04	7.21	-13.08	6.35	0	0	0	0
Italy	0	0	0	0	1.04	7.21	13.08	6.35
Japan	-3.01	12.25	-20.90	11.13	-1.97	9.95	-7.82	10.78
Switzerland	-2.14	8.83	-14.05	8.28	-1.10	4.43	-0.97	3.96
UK	1.54	7.52	0.07	8.23	2.57	7.81	13.16	7.44
US	-2.21	11.08	-1.13	7.66	-1.17	11.24	11.95	9.12
France	-0.55	13.73	-10.85	7.80	0.49	11.90	2.23	8.18
Netherlands	-1.79	13.65	-13.91	7.96	-0.75	11.50	-0.82	7.82
Spain	0.80	13.20	-6.91	7.84	1.84	12.67	6.17	9.65
Sweden	-1.17	13.66	-3.83	9.31	-0.13	13.82	9.26	11.12

Note: vol. = volatility

carried out. This is because of the high yield paid by Italian bonds over the sample, together with the appreciation of the Italian lira against the DM. This suggests that the emergence of the euro could make some difference to European investors by eliminating such high-yield assets from the investable universe.

Finally, Table 12.3 reports the excess return in domestic currency from investing in liquid currency of different countries. Only unhedged results are reported, since hedging amounts to achieving a null excess return. For the Italian case, the table shows that investing in foreign liquidity was in general not profitable, owing to high Italian interest rates. Such assets were particularly unattractive (*ex post*) in the most recent period 1995–7 because of the strength of the Italian lira. For the German investor there are a few successful examples, such as Italian, British and American liquid assets.

Co-movements between exchange rates and stock markets

These results are interesting in themselves, but they do not offer much information about the key issue of whether eliminating exchange rates among European countries will affect stock returns in a substantial manner. Many European countries have been trying for years to peg their nominal exchange rate to that of Germany, with varying degrees of success. In general this pegging, and the process of economic convergence associated with it, have produced important effects on the co-movements between European financial markets. The convergence of short-term interest rates is well known. There has also been convergence from the point of view of the increase in the correlation between stock markets.

Figure 12.1 shows estimates of the correlation coefficients for stock returns of various pairs of countries. In each case the estimate has been computed on the basis of monthly data for the previous sixty months, for the period 1986–97. The figure clearly shows that the progressive increase in the correlation coefficients has been peculiar to European countries. Other major stock markets do not seem to show any definite trend over the period 1986–97. Particularly noticeable are the positive trend between Spain and Germany, and the high levels of correlation between Germany and Holland, whose correlation coefficient is equal to 0.84 at the end of 1997, and Germany and France. These trends can be contrasted with the dynamics of the correlation coefficients between the US and Japan, Switzerland and Germany, the US and Germany.

Of course there are many caveats to the figure, connected with the instability of the correlation coefficients between stock markets, a fact already noted by Solnik, Boucrelle and Le Fur (1996) and by Erb, Harvey and Viskanta (1994). A formal structural model would be needed in order to test possible hypotheses about the effects of convergence and, most of all, to discover whether the increase in the correlation coefficients reflects an increase in the correlation between fundamentals.

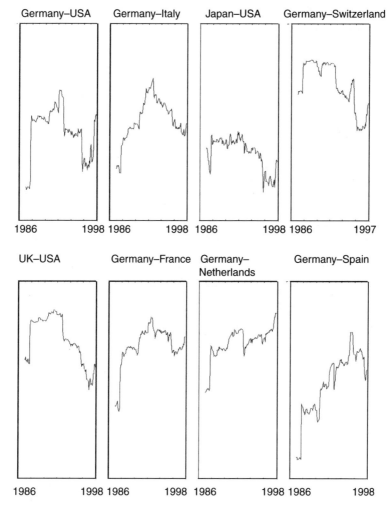

Figure 12.1 Correlations between excess stock returns for various pairs of countries

One way to understand the implications of the move to the euro is to consider the relation between the exchange rate and stock returns. The correlation coefficient has been computed for the rate of change of the nominal exchange rate and the rate of return on the national stock index. The results also hold for the excess rate of return on the stock market rather than the rate of return. All the data are monthly for the period 1986–97. They are reported in Figure 12.2.

Looking at the dynamics over time of the correlation coefficients, the results may be subdivided into three groups. The first group is composed of Britain, Italy and Spain, for which there is an increase in the correlation

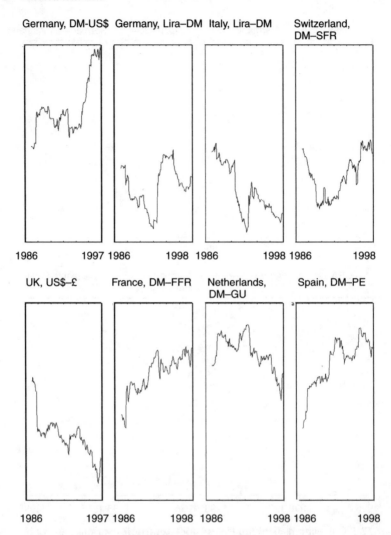

Figure 12.2 Correlations between stock returns and exchange rates for various
           countries

between the stock market and the exchange rate. The trend in such
correlation coefficients is clear from Figure 12.2. In all three cases, an
appreciation of the domestic currency tends to be more and more
correlated with a positive rate of return in the domestic stock market.
These countries all had a difficult macroeconomic situation at the
beginning of the 1990s which markedly improved during the 1990s,
although for different reasons. The interpretation of these results is
therefore that an improvement in the state of the domestic economy has
been connected with an increased demand for stocks.

A second group of European countries show some increase in the correlation coefficient over the sample period. However for Holland the correlation is close to 0, and for France the increase in the correlation coefficient took place in the early part of the sample period. Holland, France and Germany represent a more homogeneous set of countries which seem well integrated from the point of view of the stock markets.

As far as non-euro countries are concerned, there are a wide variety of outcomes. There is no trend in the correlation coefficient between the Japanese stock market and the yen–dollar rate (not reported in Figure 12.2), an unstable but driftless coefficient for the Swiss market and the DM–Swiss franc, and a high and increasing correlation coefficient between the German stock market and the DM–US$ rate.

Table 12.4 gives the correlation coefficients between the nominal stock return and the rate of change of the reported nominal exchange rate, estimated over the whole sample period. It shows, first, that there is no difference between nominal and real exchange rates. Second, it shows that the correlation coefficients are not particularly high among European countries, even though the evidence reported in the previous figures showed a positive dynamic.

Finally, a few coefficients have been computed for correlations between stock returns and exchange rate volatility, measured as the absolute value of the change in the exchange rate. The numbers are all slightly negative, confirming the pictorial evidence presented by the Deutsche Bundesbank (in Deutsche Bundesbank 1998). This implies that integration between stock markets falls during periods of high volatility.

This evidence raises two issues. First, if there is a correlation, what, if any, is the direction of causality? Second, is such evidence relevant?

As to the direction of causality, without a structural model it is impossible to evaluate the causality of the relation and the possible origins of the various situations. In cases where the exchange rate is determined by the market both stock returns and exchange rates are endogenous. Regarding relevant evidence, it is perhaps surprising that the correlation

Table 12.4 Nominal and real exchange rates

	Nominal exchange rate	*Real exchange rate*
German stock, DM/US$	0.49	0.47
German stock, Lira/DM	-0.17	-0.14
Italian stock, Lira/DM	-0.35	-0.31
Japanese stock, Yen/US$	0.03	-0.01
Swiss stock, SFr/DM	-0.05	0.04
British stock, US$/£	-0.29	-0.27
French stock, FFr/DM	0.28	0.27
Dutch stock, Guilder/DM	0.15	0.14
Spanish stock, Peseta/DM	0.27	0.29

between stock markets and exchange rates is not larger than has been reported. A larger correlation could be expected on the basis of the argument that the nominal exchange rate is a key element in determining the level of competitiveness of a country, which in turn seems to be an important element of stock market valuation.

As to the relevance of the evidence, the issue is very difficult and would deserve a study of its own. Here I simply consider one specific case study and make some comments.

Figure 12.3 reports the level of the Italian stock market in real terms, and the level of the exchange rate against the DM, also in real terms. It shows that the relation between the two variables is fairly complex. Between 1982 and 1992 there was a continuous and gradual depreciation of the lira, which does not seem to be particularly connected with the behaviour of the stock market. The jump in the price of stocks in 1985 must be attributed to domestic factors, mainly the introduction of Italian mutual funds. There seems however to be a strong correlation between the depreciation of the currency and the rise in stock prices after September 1992, although this does not hold for the whole of 1994 and early 1995, when the currency depreciated strongly in a period of continuously falling

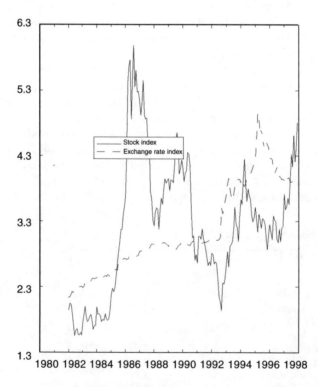

Figure 12.3 The real index of the Italian stock market and real level of the lira/DM exchange rate

stock prices. In 1996 and 1997 the currency then appreciated in a period which showed a strongly rising stock market.

The lesson to be drawn from this figure is that the connection between stock returns and exchange rates is unlikely to be stable. Given the lack of applied models that can convincingly explain nominal and real exchange rates, such a connection is likely to be on the research agenda for the future.

The empirical evidence presented in this section seems to show that an increase in the economic integration between two countries tends to bring with it an increase in the correlation between stock markets and a stabilization of exchange rates, even though a theoretical and empirical explanation for such co-movements has still to be found.

Results on portfolio composition

Figures 12.4, 12.5, 12.6 and 12.7 report the optimal share of various assets for portfolios yielding varying expected returns. The vertical axis reports the expected return from the various portfolios, while the horizontal axis reports the standard deviation of the return, which is connected to the portfolios promising the various returns. Portfolios to the right of the figures are those implying lower degrees of risk aversion.

All the analyses have been carried out in terms of returns relative to the benchmark. In each case the optimization has been carried out by

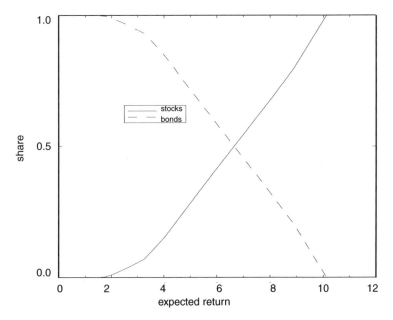

Figure 12.4 Returns for portfolios of various assets: stocks and bonds before introduction of the euro

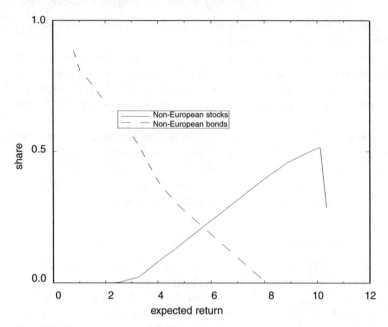

Figure 12.5 Returns for portfolios of various assets: non-European stocks and bonds before introduction of the euro

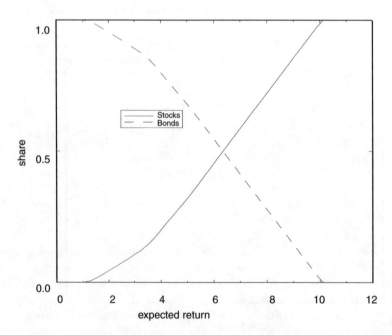

Figure 12.6 Returns for portfolios of various assets: stocks and bonds after introduction of the euro

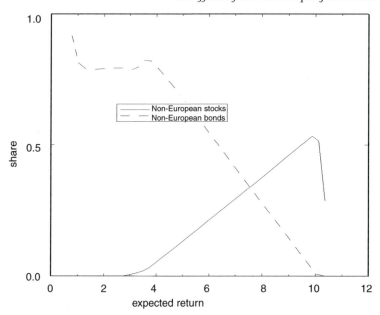

Figure 12.7 Returns for portfolios of various assets: non-European stocks and
bonds after introduction of the euro

imposing a constraint that the share of each asset is non-negative. The
following results are based on a portfolio which includes thirty-six assets
before the euro and twenty-three assets after the euro. In both cases liquid
currency is excluded from the portfolio, which includes only covered and
uncovered stocks and bonds.

Figures 12.4 to 12.7 show results for a German investor (the benchmark
is the short-term German interest rate), but the results are very similar for
an Italian investor. Figure 12.4 reports the optimal shares of stocks and
bonds for various levels of the target return. It shows quite naturally that
stocks take a larger proportion of the portfolio as the expected return
increases. Figure 12.5 shows that non-European stocks amount to about
50 per cent of a portfolio aiming at a high expected return. The sudden
drop in the proportion of non-European stocks is due to the mechanics of
the efficient frontier construction. The frontiers are in fact built in such a
way as to represent portfolios which at the highest expected return are
largely invested in one asset. Therefore moving towards high levels of
expected returns implies a decrease in the diversification of the portfolio.
Figure 12.5 shows that at the highest expected return the share of a
European stock increases suddenly.

Figures 12.6 and 12.7 represent what happens in the post-euro situation.
The figures are stikingly similar to their pre-euro counterparts. A
comparison of the results before EMU and after EMU reveals that there
are no effects on the overall portfolio composition. However, such a

stability in the optimal structure hides large changes in the sub-asset composition of euro and non-euro assets. The share of non-euro bonds increases substantially to compensate for European unification, while the share of non-euro stocks increases as well, but less dramatically.

To be more specific about the portfolio composition, at high levels of risk aversion (target expected excess return of about 2 per cent) the portfolio of a German investor before the euro is composed 100 per cent of bonds with the following composition: 1 per cent uncovered Italian, 20 per cent uncovered Spanish, 15 per cent uncovered Swedish, 40 per cent covered Italian, 17 per cent covered Swiss and 6 per cent covered US. There is not much change when expectations and standard deviations are computed on the basis of the most recent period, except for the fact that Italian bonds increase to 51 per cent and are not covered from exchange rate risk any more. This result is explainable in terms of the high return offered in the last five years by Italian bonds, and by the strong Italian lira.

At low levels of risk aversion (target expected excess return of about 10 per cent) there is 10 per cent in bonds (mainly covered Japanese) and 80 per cent in stocks, of which about half is in uncovered Swiss stock and 20 per cent in uncovered Dutch. In the most recent period, Italian uncovered bonds would have replaced Japanese bonds, and US stocks would have formed half the portfolio, replacing Swiss stocks.

After the euro there is a large movement towards non-euro bonds: covered Swiss amount to 63 per cent of the portfolio and Japanese bonds to almost 20 per cent. Euro bonds are limited to 10 per cent. This structure holds true regardless of whether one assumes a weak or a strong euro. In the high-risk portfolio, euro bonds take 15 per cent of the portfolio while the stock part is almost equally divided between Dutch and covered US, again regardless of the strength of the euro. If the most recent period is used to estimate the relevant moments, bonds decrease to 7 per cent and the rest of the portfolio comprises 18 per cent uncovered Swiss stocks, 30 per cent Dutch stocks, 28 per cent covered Swiss stocks and 14 per cent covered US stocks.

Therefore when expected returns and covariances are estimated on the basis of the 1993–7 data, the share of stocks in the optimal portfolios increases substantially. This is to be expected given the large sensitivity of the efficient frontier to the data on mean returns, and given the excellent performance of stock markets in this sample period.

Figures 12.8 and 12.9 show details of the composition of stocks and bonds in the various portfolios. The share of non-European stocks in high-return portfolios increases substantially, amounting to about 70 per cent (versus 50 per cent before).

Figure 12.10 reports the whole efficient frontiers (in the space of mean-standard deviation excess returns) before and after the euro in the scenario of a strong euro. The result is consistent with those reported in the previous figures. The overall effect is far from dramatic. There is a

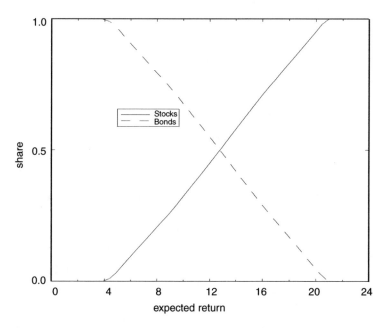

Figure 12.8 Portfolio composition of stocks and bonds before introduction of the euro

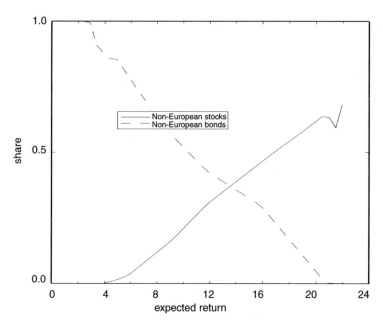

Figure 12.9 Portfolio composition of stocks and bonds after introduction of the euro

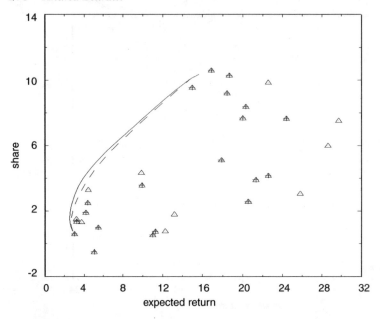

Figure 12.10 Efficient frontiers before and after introduction of the euro

slight movement to the right of the frontier, implying a deterioration of the risk–return trade-off. At a mechanical level this is to be expected, to the extent that some assets are eliminated from the post-euro situation, which becomes a particular case of the pre-euro situation.

Finally, the exercises were repeated with the constraint that the share of assets denominated in foreign currency should be lower than 20 per cent. In the pre-euro case, this means that the bond and stock indices of the various European countries are among the constrained assets for a German investor. After the euro, however, all the European stock indices are denominated in the same currency and become domestic securities from the point of view of the currency of denomination. Figures 12.11 and 12.12 report the shares respectively of stocks and bonds, and non-European stocks and bonds, before the euro with currency constraints. These figures should be compared with Figures 12.13 and 12.14 for the after euro case.

The comparison clearly shows the impact of the euro in the case of currency constraints. The elimination of such a constraint for the European stocks has a large impact on the portfolio. Notice in particular the increase in non-European stocks and bonds. The efficient frontiers are a synthetic way of comparing the situations (see Figure 12.15).

The figures show that the efficient frontier post-euro is much more favourable to an investor who is constrained in terms of allocation to foreign assets. The elimination of the currency-matching constraint for a

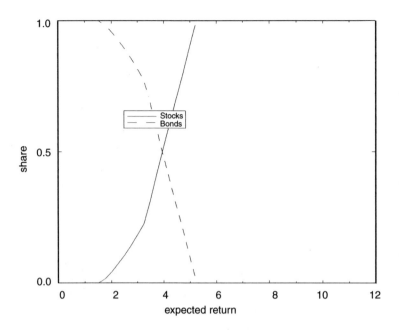

Figure 12.11 Portfolio composition of stocks and bonds given currency
constraints: before introduction of the euro

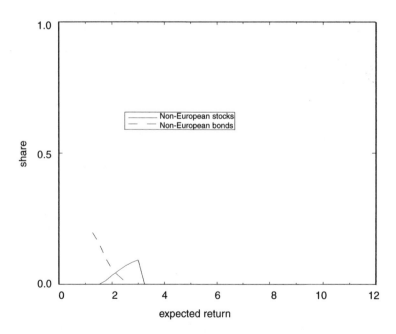

Figure 12.12 Portfolio composition of non-European stocks and bonds given
currency constraints: before introduction of the euro

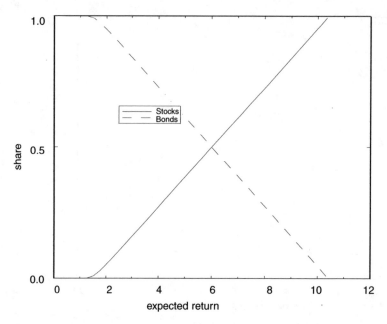

Figure 12.13 Portfolio composition of stocks and bonds given currency
constraints: after introduction of the euro

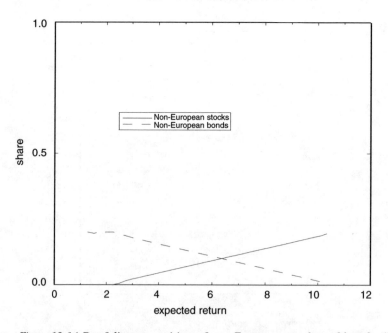

Figure 12.14 Portfolio composition of non-European stocks and bonds given
currency constraints: after introduction of the euro

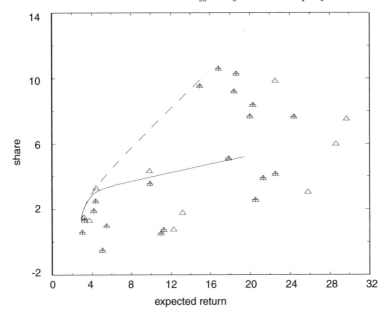

Figure 12.15 Efficient frontiers before and after introduction of the euro given currency constraints

large number of securities improves considerably the return–risk trade-off which is perceived by a single investor. (Again, it should be recalled that the change in moments of returns following the introduction of the euro has been ignored.)

Conclusions

There are many theoretical reasons for believing that the introduction of the euro will change the optimal asset allocation of European investors. Given the increase in the covariances between stock markets and between bond markets, one may expect an increase in the share of non-European securities. In this paper a prudential methodology has been adopted, and it has simply considered the effects on the optimal asset allocation of eliminating a few of the assets which are now traded.

Even under such minimal assumptions it is possible to notice some modification in the structure of portfolios. The simulations conducted on the basis of historical data reveal that by itself, the cancellation of a few securities does not alter significantly the optimal asset allocation between stocks and bonds. There is some switch towards non-European stocks, and a general increase in the demand for non-euro bonds. The solution is sensitive to the assumptions about the sample period used for estimating the relevant inputs of the efficient frontier calculations, but the general message remains unaltered.

Of course much more work remains to be done on the subject of asset allocation after the euro. Among the possible areas of interest, I want to point out four. The first is solving the optimal portfolio on the basis of different assumptions about the changes introduced by the euro on expected returns, variances and covariances of returns. One could for example decompose the covariances of returns by using the method of Ammer and Mei (1996) and make hypotheses about the various components in order to derive the new covariance in the euro scenario.

The second refers to a more careful sensitivity analysis of the optimal asset allocation to the different assumptions about mean returns. In order to take into account the structural break provided by the euro, it may be of interest to mix historical data and a priori opinions with the model of Black and Litterman (1992). There are various reasons why relying too much on historical data may be dangerous.

The third refers to a more detailed analysis of various European markets. Here only two countries have been considered. It would be interesting to analyse whether the results hold true also for investors based in different currencies. Finally, it is of interest to study in detail the issue connected with sectoral rather than national allocation.

The data used in this study are of a very aggregate nature. Looking at data for single companies may be much more revealing about the process of stock picking on the part of future investors. I believe that such a study would give very interesting indications in terms of which stocks would be included in optimal portfolios.

Note

A previous version of this paper was presented at the Centre for European Policy Studies seminar on Capital Markets and EMU, Brussels, 19 January 1998, and at the 21st SUERF Colloquium, Frankfurt, 17 October 1998. I thank Daniel Gros and Karel Lannoo, as well as all the participants at the meetings, for useful comments. I am grateful to Fabiano Cavadini for help with the data set.

Bibliography

Abken, P. A. and Shrikhande, M. M. (1997) 'The Role of Currency Derivatives in Internationally Diversified Portfolios', *Federal Reserve Bank of Atlanta Economic Review*, (Third Quarter): 34–59.

Ammer, J. and Mei, J. (1996) 'Measuring International Economic Linkages with Stock Market Data', *Journal of Finance* 51: 1743–63.

Best, M. J. and Grauer, R. G. (1991) 'On the Sensitivity of Mean–Variance-Efficient Portfolios to Changes in Asset Means: Some Analytical and Computational Results', *Review of Financial Studies* 4(2): 315–42.

Black, F. and Litterman, R. (1992) 'Global Portfolio Optimization', *Financial Analysts Journal* 9: 28–43.

Campbell, J. Y. and Shiller, R. J. (1988) 'The Dividend–Price Ratio and Expectations of Future Dividends and Discount Factors', *Review of Financial Studies* 1: 195–228.

Cooper, I. and Kaplanis, E. (1994) 'Home Bias in Equity Portfolios, Inflation Hedging, and International Capital Market Equilibrium', *Review of Financial Studies* 7(1): 45–60.

Deutsche Bundesbank (1998) *Structural Changes in the German Capital Market in the Run-up to European Monetary Union* (April): 55–69.

Dickenson, G. (1998) 'The Impact of the Euro on the Investment and Treasury Management Policies of European Insurance Companies', 21st SUERF Colloquium, Frankfurt, 17 October.

Erb, C. B., Harvey, C. R. and Viskanta, T. E. (1994) 'Forecasting International Equity Correlations', *Financial Analysts Journal* (November–December): 32–45.

French, K. and Poterba, J. (1991) 'Investor Diversification and International Equity Markets', *American Economic Review* 81: 222–6.

Griffin, M. W. (1997) 'Why Do Pension and Insurance Portfolios Hold So Few International Assets?', *Journal of Portfolio Management* (Summer): 45–50.

Merton, R. (1990) *Continuous-Time Finance*, Blackwell, Cambridge, Mass.

Solnik, B., Boucrelle, C. and Le Fur, Y. (1996) 'International Market Correlation and Volatility', *Financial Analysts Journal* (September–October):17–34.

13 Delivering the benefits of EMU: securitization

Graham Bishop

What does 'securitization' mean?

Securitization is defined in the broadest sense, for this analysis. It means connecting the suppliers of funds directly with the users: via a market for securities, rather than through an intermediary bank. That market only has to be sufficiently organized to give investors confidence that they will be able to turn their financial asset into a liquid form when they wish, rather than having to adopt a 'buy and hold to maturity' policy which would require a continuous, and close, involvement with the issuer.

The term is often applied to the specific process of turning small loans – perhaps on residential mortgages or even credit cards – into bonds which can be issued on the capital markets and purchased by large investment institutions. More generally, it can include the process of governments transforming their non-marketable debts into highly liquid bonds that command a lower interest rate, and thus cost saving.

One result of this process is that there is a clear market price for assets and, as recent experience shows all too vividly, the price can change rapidly in response to a reassessment of the economic worth of the assets. The mark-to-market process shows the change in value, giving all investors a fair view of their holdings.

Background

It is a commonplace that Europe's financial markets are about to undergo a profound change. The scale of the resultant markets means that this has a global significance. Moreover, the driving forces are so deep-seated and strong that there can be no question of escaping from the recent turmoil by reverting to the 'old' markets of yesteryear.

The scale of the Eurozone

The euro eleven countries have a bigger population than that of the USA, and the GDP of the eleven is a little smaller than the US currently. But if the Eurozone eventually covers the whole of the EU, it will have a bigger economy than the US. (See Figure 13.1.) If all Eastern and Central European applicants eventually enter the EU, its population will be roughly twice that of the US.

Government bond markets are the foundation of modern fixed income markets. Many international investors use the family of Salomon Smith Barney Bond Indexes as their performance benchmark for the universe of bonds that are sufficiently liquid to be 'investible'. Also, the term 'bond' has a specific definition in our indexes, of fixed rate securities with more than one year of remaining life, thus excluding much Italian debt. On 4 January 1999 the European governments' bond market will be denominated entirely in one currency – euro – and be roughly 20 per cent larger than the corresponding US Treasury market. If the UK joins, with Denmark, Sweden and Greece, then the European market will be another 20 per cent bigger.

Therefore the birth of the Eurozone is a big event for the world's financial system, because a new global market is coming into existence. The preparations are intense: for example, the Bank of England (perhaps surprisingly for an 'out' central bank) has been pursuing a very active policy of ensuring that the City of London, a cornerstone of the European financial system, is fully involved with the preparations.

The sheer scale of preparations is unreported by the media, but the intention is to turn the European Union's capital market, in the remaining business days, into a simple, transparent, harmonized market. This market will be seen as a straightforward competitor to the US Treasury market. Initially, the preparations were at the conceptual level of agreeing harmonized 'conventions' for the markets. Now the focus is on the mechanics –

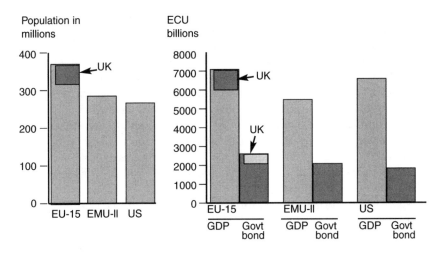

Figure 13.1 Population, GDP and government 'bonds'

Source: Eurostat, Salomon Smith Barney 1998a, 1998b

the detailed IT aspects of the changeover – and contingency planning for any unexpected difficulties.

At the time of writing, there is no evidence that the changeover will create any serious difficulties. So, in the early part of 1999, the euro-denominated government bond market will surpass the size of the US Treasury market. It could even approach its liquidity, despite the eleven separate issuers, even though they are of the highest credit quality.

Driving forces for EMU

EMU is often cited as *the* driving force for changes in the financial system, and by itself it certainly will create change. But it would be a mistake to view EMU as the sole driving force, and perhaps one whose economic effects may be muted because of the political motivation. Three key driving forces should be considered. Their interaction over the next decade could easily change the face of Europe's financial system, creating opportunities for both providers and users of Europe's savings.

- *European integration* is an obvious 'driver' because EMU is a political event, but one with profound economic consequences which must, by themselves, be beneficial to society if the project is to command general support. The desire for peace and prosperity triggered the creation of a process in 1946 that has led on to the European Union of today. That desire is an extraordinarily powerful motor to keep Europe rolling along its current path, whatever the short-run difficulties. The practical outcome of this political process is the creation of the Single European Market (SEM), of which the financial services component is especially relevant. But the SEM is not yet complete and the European Commission has been requested to report back to the European Council Summit in Vienna in December 1998 with proposals to achieve that completion, a result that should maximize the efficiency of the financial markets and benefit all users, whether they are savers or borrowers.
- *Demographic trends* are now set for the next twenty to thirty years. Increasing sophistication plus rising retirement savings opens new opportunities to intermediate these savings. An ageing electorate may also have a different political priority, namely preserving the purchasing power of its assets. As a side effect, that rising tide of liquid savings will also increase the political influence of the financial markets on public policy.
- *Technology* is a global driving force which will have a profound impact, whether EMU exists or not. Information technology (IT) covers both computing and communications. During the last quarter century, IT performance has multiplied a hundred thousand times. Suddenly, this has brought a key part of the users of the financial system to the dawn of 'cybersociety'. That will re-shape the mechanics of securities markets.

Securitization in the US

Factors indicating that the US experience is a good analogy for Europe

When analysing the possible development of the European financial system, a number of parallels can be drawn with the US, particularly its banking system. The share of credit extended by it, as a percentage of GDP, over the past twenty years has remained essentially unchanged. But the striking feature of the US financial system is the rise in total bonds outstanding as a percentage of GDP, a measure of the securitization of the US economy. (See Figure 13.2.)

The most interesting aspect for Europe is that the growth of the US bond market has not been driven by the size of the government's deficit but by the non-Federal government sector. This enormous surge in non-government activity has included agencies, mortgage-backed bonds, corporate bonds, and Yankee (that is, foreign issuer) bonds – the latter reflecting the role of the dollar as a global reserve currency – as well as bonds backed by all sorts of financial assets, including credit cards, and even loans to small companies. In practice, virtually any financial asset which produces a predictable inflow of cash – a 'receivable' – can now be 'securitized'. This means that a bond can be issued, via the capital markets, that gives the lender the right to receive those cash items, or a proportion thereof.

Today, the dollar debt markets offer a broad range of products, ranked by maturity and credit quality. They range from treasury bills to thirty-year

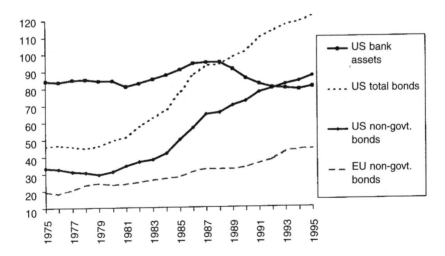

Figure 13.2 Securitization versus bank credit, as a percentage of GDP, 1975–95

Sources: Federal Reserve Board 1997, Salomon Smith Barney

government bonds, and all the way through the spectrum of credit-worthiness from 'risk-free' to highly risky bonds where the expected default rate is explicitly factored into the required yield. (See Figure 13.3.)

However, two decades ago the US market was much more straight-forward, with three comparable segments: government and agency (see Table 13.1 for a description of their functions), municipal and corporate bonds. But, the Eurodollar market was already gaining in significance and other sectors became significant in the 1980s:

1984	non-agency mortgage backed bonds
1986	high-yield corporate bonds
	foreign bonds (Yankee bonds)
1989	asset-backed bonds (other than mortgage backed).

Table 13.2 shows the build-up of these extra components, as well as the agency market that was the raw material for the mortgage bond market. Many of these securities might well have been bank assets but, for example, the high-yield issuers were often trying to escape from onerous debt amor-tization provisions or the restrictive covenants that banks would have required.

One significant factor in boosting the US bond market in the mid-1980s was the banking system's capital adequacy problems. In particular, banks like Citibank (now part of Citigroup, the parent of Salomon Smith Barney) decided that the problems of capital inadequacy were so great that they needed to sell off some of the assets on their balance sheet. The chosen mechanism was to securitize them, thereby removing them from the balance sheet while retaining customer relationships by servicing the credit cards and so on. That opened the door to new competitors such as speciality credit card companies, where economies of scale became a key competitive advantage, non-banks such as the automobile finance companies, and even mutual funds that invest in bank loans. NationsBank has now securitized a portfolio of loans to small and medium-sized companies, hitherto seen as the last bastion of bank lending.

In effect, investors can now extend credit directly to virtually all the sectors of the US economy that were formerly the preserve of the banks.

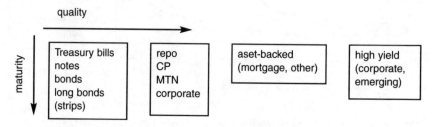

Figure 13.3 The quality/maturity matrix in US dollar security markets

Table 13.1 Agencies in the US security market

Fannie Mae *(formerly Federal National Mortgage Association or FNMA)*	This Government-sponsored, but shareholder-owned, enterprise is regulated by the US Federal Government. The Secretary of the Treasury must authorize issuance of debt obligations, and the Treasury has the authority to purchase US$ 2.25 billion of its obligations, as a credit support. As a result, it has a AAA/Aaa credit rating. Created in 1938 by Congress, it became entirely shareholder-owned in 1969 with the public purpose of promoting mortgage credit through increasing the liquidity of mortgages. At year-end 1997, it had US$ 1,287 billion of mortgage assets in its own portfolio or backing Mortgage Backed Securities (MBS).
Freddie Mac *(Federal Home Loan Mortgage Corporation)*	This Government-sponsored, but shareholder-owned, enterprise is regulated by the US Federal Government and the Secretary of the Treasury must authorize issuance of debt obligations. There is no legal obligation on the Government to support Freddie Mac, but the implied support is sufficient for a AAA/Aaa credit rating. It was founded in 1970 and given a statutory mission that includes promoting access to mortgage credit throughout the US by increasing the liquidity of mortgage investments to facilitate home ownership. At year-end 1997, it had US$ 773 billion of mortgage assets in its own portfolio or backing MBS.
GNMA *(Government National Mortgage Association)*	In 1968, the US Government restructured its role in housing finance and GNMA was spun off from FNMA as a separate agency. Its most important activity is its mortgage pass-through programme whereby it guarantees (with the full faith and credit of the Federal Government) pools of Federal Housing Administration insured and Veterans Administration guaranteed mortgages. At year-end 1997, it had guaranteed US$ 536.9 billion of mortgages (MBS only).

This could only happen, however, with the new-found technology: first, to do the underlying customer transaction and second, to turn a pool of these into a set of cash flows that could be sold as securities. Europe has the technology and can import these tried and tested techniques, so there are some grounds for regarding the US experience as a leading indicator for Europe. But this does require investors to build up the capacity to do detailed investigation of the underlying assets. However, there are some other factors that point in a different direction.

Factors that indicate the US experience is a poor analogy for Europe

The political structure of the European Union is designed to achieve 'ever closer union' but the Maastricht Treaty explicitly ruled out any sharing of

Table 13.2 US bond market components: dollar bonds outstanding, 1970–96 (nominal value, US$ billion)

Year-end	Total publicly issued	Governments Total	Governments Held outside U.S. govt.[3]	Federal agency[1] Total	Federal agency[1] Mortgage pass-throughs	Federal agency[1] Non-agency mortgage securities[4]	Municipals	Corporate[5]	International bonds[2] Foreign bonds (Yankees)	International bonds[2] Eurodollar bonds[6]
1970	485.4	159.8	105.7	77.4	0.4	–	131.1	117.1	n/a	n/a
1975	750.0	205.7	136.6	120.6	17.8	–	224.1	199.6	n/a	n/a
1976	850.7	257.3	185.6	135.6	28.4	–	239.5	218.3	n/a	n/a
1977	928.9	298.8	224.4	157.8	49.7	–	236.6	235.7	n/a	n/a
1978	1,025.2	325.8	245.9	182.5	65.0	–	265.6	251.3	n/a	n/a
1979	1,176.0	358.1	274.9	235.2	91.1	–	279.7	303.0	n/a	n/a
1980	1,377.0	407.1	320.2	278.3	114.0	–	288.0	339.8	n/a	63.8
1981	1,597.0	475.3	385.3	323.5	129.0	–	347.2	370.7	n/a	80.3
1982	1,870.3	569.6	n/a	387.2	178.5	–	381.2	418.9	n/a	113.4
1983	2,193.7	707.1	n/a	455.0	244.9	–	429.0	457.5	n/a	145.1
1984	2,626.9	873.0	778.4	529.4	289.0	11.0	477.4	540.2	n/a	195.9
1985	3,236.5	1,037.8	915.4	629.9	368.9	24.0	630.6	647.0	n/a	267.2
1986	3,860.6	1,192.3	1,067.6	808.2	531.6	16.6	703.7	737.7	51.5	350.6
1987	4,363.0	1,335.2	1,202.3	978.8	670.4	28.5	798.0	779.1	56.0	387.4
1988	4,732.9	1,425.8	1,281.8	1,116.0	745.3	37.3	866.5	804.7	62.0	420.6
1989	5,323.0	1,532.9	1,374.8	1,267.1	869.5	48.3	914.5	997.3	66.3	496.6
1990	5,816.5	1,668.4	1,512.5	1,445.9	1,019.9	61.3	957.3	1,083.9	75.6	524.1
1991	6,466.6	1,881.3	1,716.6	1,577.9	1,156.5	106.4	1,031.7	1,241.5	86.1	541.8
1992	7,062.9	2,096.5	1,918.7	1,734.0	1,272.0	168.6	1,054.0	1,352.5	103.7	553.7
1993	7,657.8	2,274.8	2,074.9	1,907.0	1,356.8	213.9	1,115.1	1,463.3	125.8	557.9
1994	8,232.0	2,422.1	2,183.4	2,199.5	1,472.1	254.7	1,078.6	1,515.0	137.7	624.5
1995	8,845.6	2,546.5	2,326.2	2,405.1	1,570.3	291.6	1,039.9	1,728.7	155.6	678.2
1996	9,583.4	2,682.3	2,446.5	2,634.5	1,711.0	346.9	1,049.6	1,910.0	175.9	784.3

Notes to Table 13.2:

1   includes budgeted and sponsored Federal agencies
2   includes straight, convertible and floating-rate debt
3   includes domestic holdings outside of the US Government and US Federal Reserve banks, and all foreign holdings
4   consists of non-government agency pass-throughs and collaterized mortgage obligations (CMOs). Includes single-family, residential, multi-family and commercial mortgages
5   includes straight convertible and floating-rate debt, tax-exempt corporate bonds, medium-term notes (MTNs) and asset-backed securities
6   includes US dollar-denominated bonds issued in Japan
n/a not available
The non-agency mortgage security series have been revised to reflect a change in source

Sources: Federal Reserve System Flow of Funds, US Treasury *Bulletin,* Euromoney *Inter-Bond Annual* of 1978, International Securities Market Association (ISMA), Moody's Investors Service, IDD Information Services, Orion Royal Bank Ltd., and Salomon Smith Barney Inc.

liability for public debt (see Article 104b). As the financing of homes is a matter of vital concern to electors, any formal pan-EU housing finance institution might be put under great pressure to equalize borrowing conditions to such an extent that it could become an engine of nation-building. That social and political role was apparent to the US Congress when it founded several agencies for this purpose (see Table 13.1).

The creation of quasi-government institutions that, in aggregate, could have obligations greater than those of the collective governments – as is now the case with the three relevant US agencies and the US Federal Government – could well be seen as a potential step in the *opposite* direction to 'subsidiarity', which is the EU doctrine of decentralization of political power. For perspective, the European Investment Bank (EIB) has outstanding obligations that are not even 5 per cent of those of the central governments of EU member states.

Another particular factor in the US experience is that the bulk of residential mortgages are at a fixed rate for the entire term of the loan – often thirty years – though they are subject to pre-payment possibilities. Few European markets combine that maturity with a fixed rate and a 'free' pre-payment option.

Given their potential scale – and the political implications which might flow from that – Europe's desire for closer union seems likely to stop well short of creating government-backed financial institutions designed to give similar access to funding for home ownership throughout the territory of the Union. Thus it seems most unlikely that public authorities will foster the development of a mortgage-backed security (MBS) market within the EU in the way that the agencies have in the US. Therefore, the European private sector will have to provide the credit support mechanisms, and analysis, to give investors the comfort necessary to invest in this type of market.

During the past century or more, the 'mortgage banks' in, for example, Germany, Austria, Denmark and Sweden have shown what can be achieved by a strict legal basis for lending and then collateralizing bond issues of the bank itself – the *Pfandbriefe* model – rather than a special-purpose vehicle. Typically, this type of bank bond issue has a greater volume outstanding than the central government of that country.

Can the 'mortgage banks' export this model throughout the EU? Those banks may find it difficult to ensure that there is a sufficiently similar legal basis in each state for taking a mortgage on a property and then putting it into a pan-European collateral pool. The alternative is to continue with a series of fragmented national markets which may not achieve wide enough distribution to ensure the liquidity that is necessary to minimize the yield spread versus government bonds of ECU 10–20 billion. Ten-year Jumbo *Pfandbriefe* continue to trade at more than 40 b.p. over corresponding Bunds, significantly above the spread that would be expected on the basis of their AAA credit rating.

That is the key challenge: if the 'special-purpose vehicle' model is seen by investors as giving sufficient security – perhaps via over-collateralization techniques – then mortgage originators may find that a more cost-effective form of funding. That opens the way to a more competitive offering to the citizen, which would be seen as a major benefit of EMU, given the significance of home-ownership costs to the average citizen.

In summary, the 'agency' element of the US experience of the move to securitize residential mortgage credit is unlikely to be a role model for the Eurozone, but the 'special-purpose vehicle' model may offer stiff competition to the *Pfandbrief* model.

Why does the euro make any difference?

On 1 January 1999 and at a stroke, the euro effectively abolishes the currency-matching rules which presently lock many countries' long-term savings institutions into domestic assets. For example, Europe's life insurance companies must match 80 per cent of their assets to the currency of their liabilities. Table 13.3 reproduces the table in the Bank of England's *Practical Issues Quarterly, no. 9* (Bank of England 1998) that illustrates these restrictions.

As the vast majority of those liabilities are denominated in national currency, so are most of the assets. Once those institutions can diversify their portfolios, they may look around the Eurozone for other investment opportunities that yield more than government bonds. Insurance companies are key, as their total assets match those of pension and mutual funds combined, yet insurance funds are most affected by the currency-matching rules. Some detailed implications of this are discussed later in this paper.

Asset-backed securities and corporate bonds should loom large on that menu of new opportunities, though it will take some years for that menu to build up. But there should be little doubt that it will happen eventually, as companies disintermediate the banking system, avoiding the costs and relative inflexibility of the 'covenant burdens' of bank loans, and go directly to the capital markets. So new investment opportunities for investors such as insurance companies should also be a new funding opportunity for corporations.

The key problem in launching a new sector is to reach the initial critical mass. Investors are reluctant to buy paper that is both unfamiliar in its credit nature and obviously destined to be illiquid. This is where EMU may have a crucial influence: Removing the importance of currency-matching rules should dramatically extend the range of institutions that can purchase new types of security. A modest initial step by many individual institutions then cumulates to a significant-sized market. Intermediating this process is the challenge that awaits the securities firms.

Table 13.3 Ivestment restrictions in the European Union

	Currency-based			Other (e.g. nationality, issuer etc.)		
	Pension funds	Insurance companies	Mutual funds	Pension funds	Insurance companies	Mutual funds
Austria	50% minimum in Austrian currency deposits or bonds	80% currency matching rule	None	35% ceiling on foreign financial assets	None	None
Belgium	None	80% currency matching rule	None	50% ceiling on foreign assets	None	None
Finland	80% currency matching rule	80% currency matching rule	None	None	None	None
France	None	80% currency matching rule	None	34% minimum of securities guaranteed by State; 5% ceiling on foreign assets	34% minimum of securities guaranteed by State; 5% ceiling on foreign assets	Tax-exempt share savings plans restricted to French shares
Germany	Penions Kassen: 80% currency matching rule	80% currency matching rule	None	Spezialfonds: foreign fund managers required to link with German unit trust fund manager	None	None
Italy	33.3% currency matching rule (but ECU assets can match any EU currency liability)	80% currency matching rule	None	None	None	None
Netherlands	None	80% currency matching rule	None	None	None	None

Table 13.3 continued

| | Currency-based | | | Other (e.g. nationality, issuer etc.) | | |
	Pension funds	Insurance companies	Mutual funds	Pension funds	Insurance companies	Mutual funds
Portugal	None	80% currency matching rule	None	20% ceiling on foreign securities	None	None
Spain	None	80% currency matching rule	None	None	None	None
UK	None	80% currency matching rule	None	None	None	None

Source: IMF 1997, Table 63 and p. 213

Future regulatory developments of the Eurozone financial markets

One of the under-reported events at the informal Finance Ministers meeting at York in March 1998 was a request to the European Commission to review the financial services legislation in order to make sure that the single market in finance is all that it should be. This was a call to modernize, because the package of measures that created the single market in financial services, including the Second Banking Directive and the Investment Services Directive, was designed ten years ago. Regrettably, the legislation is not yet in force in all countries because of delays in national implementation measures.

Commissioner Monti has been active in spelling out these issues. Further progress was made at the European Council Summit at Cardiff in June 1998. The Summit's conclusions invited the Commission to table a framework for action by the time the Vienna European Council met in December. To quote the Communiqué, these proposals should 'improve the single market in financial services, in particular examining the effectiveness of implementation of current legislation and identifying weaknesses which may require amending legislation'.

The European Commission published its Communication *Financial Services: Building a Framework for Action* on 29 October 1998, and it does indeed propose a collection of actions that should 'eliminate remaining capital market fragmentation to minimize the cost of capital raised on EU markets; [and] make the advantages of open markets available to both users and suppliers of financial services'.[1] Among the key proposals, the Commission has undertaken to: improve the cross-border acceptability of prospectuses; alleviate the burden of investment restrictions for institutional portfolios; clarify the definition of professional users of financial services to ease their access to cross-border services; and ensure that legal provisions on collateral are mutually compatible. Eventually some of these provisions should apply beyond the EU, but agreement with, say, the US authorities on recognition of prospectuses will have to await a corresponding recognition of accounting standards.

Realistically, these proposals may take up to two years to progress through the EU's legislative system, and then at least the same again before full implementation in all national law. However, an opportunity has opened to fix remaining glitches in the Single Financial Market, so the driving force of economic liberalization is likely to come back into play during the next few years.

Government bond markets: setting the example

The potential changes in the government bond markets are particularly important because they could set a crucial example to the private sector. A wider maturity range of government securities may acclimatize

Securitization in the Eurozone

Demographic effects

The population of Europe is ageing. The effects will begin to become quite pronounced within the next decade, in Europe as well as in the rest of the industrialized world. The process has several consequences for financial markets.

- *Ageing populations need funded pensions.* Public pay-as-you-go systems will not be able to cope, so a move to at least partial funding by individuals of their own retirement is generally accepted. That eventual imperative has been brought into sharp focus by governments' collective agreement to avoid 'excessive deficits' in the future, an immediate benefit of EMU. Though funded pensions do not solve all the problems that flow from an ageing population, an ultimate result of this trend was illustrated by the previous UK government's proposal for every citizen to build up a personal pension fund. For EMU, this has the practical result of enlarging the size – and therefore power – of the financial markets.
- *The majority of electors will fear for the safety of their pensions.* Picking an arbitrary age of forty-five for people to become concerned about retirement income creates a group comprising well over half the electorate: and they turn out to vote, unlike the younger age group. Once they have grasped that their self-interest lies in price stability and the safety of their capital, they are likely to vote for conservative financial policies.
- *Extra return will be sought.* The bulk of these retirement savings will be intermediated by financial institutions that sell their services on the basis of performance. For the fixed-income component of the savings portfolio, taking on the market risk of the underlying assets is an easy boost to performance versus the capital-certainty of a bank deposit. Is the public really prepared to 'rent' bank shareholders' capital to give a buffer of certainty against unexpected shocks in the markets? The answer is probably 'no', and that may build up a moral hazard problem for society if market risks do, in practice, crystallize in the future.
- *The preferred asset mix changes at the moment of retirement.* During the earning years, a saver may go for higher total returns in the equity market, but on retirement many people will buy a higher-yielding

annuity. Indeed, pension schemes often require that. At that moment, the insurance company that offers the highest annuity rate gets the business. What assets will they invest the money in? Bank deposits, government bonds and AAA corporates, or credit card receivables plus a leavening of really high yielders? Early retirement of the 'baby boomers' of 1946 onwards should have a rising impact after 2002. In effect, the rise in the number of retirements that will parallel the early years of EMU should prompt an institutional search in Europe for incremental yield.

If continuing price stability succeeds in keeping government bond yields at the lowest levels for a generation or two, demographics may trigger a scramble to obtain the highest yields possible. That scramble should provide the critical mass of investors to start up new security sectors denominated in euro.

investors to taking extra risk to earn incremental return. In today's climate that may well be just maturity risk, but credit risk may come along later. The key issue is whether the existing trend towards an increasing reliance on publicly-issued bond markets will continue. If so, how far could it go?

Liquidity is a key investor requirement

The recent peak spread of more than 40 b.p. between on and off-the-run US Treasury long bonds provided a vivid illustration. But is the US Treasury bond market still such an absolute benchmark for the global investment flows associated with the world's reserve currency?

Even in recent months, the Spanish government has built up its longer-dated bond issue to a size of about ECU/euro 17 billion equivalent. The current benchmark US Treasury ten-year is ECU 10 billion. As the US budget is in surplus, that will be the normal size, unless there is an unusual market opportunity to reopen an earlier issue. The French government has, as a matter of policy over many years, built up the size of its ten-year fungible bonds – OATs – to about ECU 16 billion. The largest German government bond in that maturity segment is about ECU 15 billion, as is the largest Italian bond, though the Italian Treasury plans to increase the issue size. A number of government debt managers are increasing the size of their bond issues with an implicit intention of making them as liquid (because they would be as large) as a US Treasury issue.

The trend to securitization of government debt is underway

Table 13.4 shows the current size of the individual bond markets and the percentage that they represent of gross government debt, as defined for the purposes of the Maastricht Treaty. The 44 per cent average conceals a wide variation between member states, from a high of more than 90 per cent in Denmark to a low of 26 per cent in Austria.

It seems unlikely that a government would go to 100 per cent 'bond' finance because there will always be some short-term debt and special instruments, such as inflation-linked securities. Also, governments are likely to provide retail savings vehicles with tax advantages or as a service to the 'un-banked' sectors of society. As an illustration, Table 13.4 shows the effect of a move to 75 per cent securitization, about the top end of the current range. That may seem a large change, but the average has already moved from about 30 per cent in the last five years, though it has declined from 47 per cent in 1998 as bonds outstanding (on this specific definition) declined in some states, most noticeably in Germany.

A securitization level of 75 per cent would have a startling impact. The total value of government bonds in the Eurozone would rise by two-thirds and become twice the size of the US market. Moreover, this rise would not be because of surging government deficits, but would be solely a re-arrangement of the existing debts of states without an 'excessive deficit': in other words, some of the world's best credits.

There are at least two powerful reasons why this trend to securitize government debt is likely to continue.

Table 13.4 Securitization of government debt

Country	Bonds as % of 'Maastricht' debt	Market value (ECU/euro billion)	
		current	75% of 'Maastricht'
Germany	35	415	864
France	57	422	545
Italy	31	390	943
UK	58	376	503
Netherlands	62	146	171
Belgium	50	130	195
Spain	50	169	249
Denmark	97	92	67
Sweden	52	81	121
Austria	27	34	98
Finland	66	40	46
Ireland	41	17	31
Portugal	36	20	43
Total	44	2,334	3,876
US	40	1,822	
Japan	28	1,007	

Sources: Eurostat, Salomon Smith Barney 1998a, 1998b

1   Debt managers will continue to be under relentless pressure to cut funding costs. One mechanism is to reduce intermediation costs such as those of the banking system. Another is to make their securities sufficiently liquid to avoid any illiquidity premium.
2   Many states are now looking at bond yields that are the lowest for decades. As many heavily-indebted states have an excessive exposure to short-term debts, this seems a golden opportunity to lock in, for as long as possible, the benefits of getting into EMU. These factors point to a surge in long-term bond issuance by governments, irrespective of their indebtedness. Already, this process seems to be getting under way, judged by the examples since 1997 of thirty-year bonds from Austria, Belgium, France, Germany, Italy, Netherlands and Spain.

This process should expand the maturity choices in the top credit category available to institutional investors. For insurance companies trying to match-fund annuities for an ever-ageing population, this trend should be highly welcome.

Non-government bonds in the Eurozone

Recent issuance patterns

Figure 13.4 shows that issue volumes in the euro's constituent currencies have already surpassed 1997's levels by a substantial margin, despite the recent global hiatus. A number of points emerge:

•   The Jumbo *Pfandbriefe* sector has grown dramatically and established itself as a major asset class.
•   The asset-backed market has shown spectacular growth, but this has been heavily influenced by a number of banks issuing collateralized loan obligations (CLOs) as a mechanism to shift low-yielding corporate loans off their balance sheet to economize on regulatory capital.
•   High-yield markets opened in 1997 but have suffered particularly badly from the rush to quality and liquidity.
•   The finance subsidiaries of some major companies, for example in the auto sector, continue to be major borrowers so that they can fund their parents' retail sales. This continues a process of disintermediating the banking system.
•   Governments and their agencies have been particularly active in the international market, quite apart from their domestic markets, as they have sought to initiate 'tributary' bonds that convert into euro and become fungible with their domestic issues once EMU begins.

ECU/euro billion

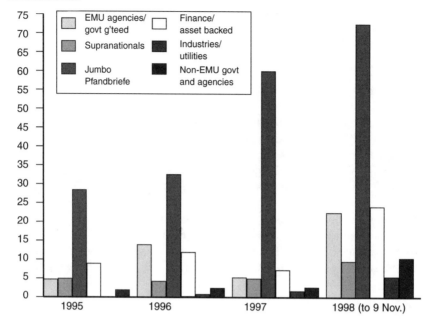

Figure 13.4 International issuance volume, EU-11 currencies, 1995 – 9 November 1998, ECU/euro billion
Source: Salomon Smith Barney 1998b

Catching up with the US?

Despite this upsurge in issuance, the US non-government bond markets continue to dwarf their EU counterparts. Salomon Smith Barney introduced the Euro Broad Investment Grade Bond Index (Euro BIG) in May 1998, as a counterpart to its long-established US Broad Investment Grade Index (BIG). These indices set out to provide performance yardsticks for institutional investors, and attempt to measure the performance of all bonds that are deemed sufficiently liquid to be traded by institutions. We believe that this criterion is met currently by the minimum size threshold of ECU 500 million outstanding, well above the US$ 100 million threshold in the US. Additionally, bonds must be fixed rate and have at least one year of life remaining.

Modern portfolio management techniques argue for active management, so liquidity is a major factor in the choice of investments. Indeed, this is a driving force in the development of government markets. But private-sector issuers cannot compete on sheer size, and so cannot match liquidity in the secondary market. There is a risk that investors may shun private-sector bonds for that reason alone. One of the major challenges flowing from EMU is to bring liquidity to smaller issues so that institutions will be prepared to invest in smaller-sized corporate issues. That would make the bond market an effective alternative source of capital for corporations.

Table 13.5 compares the characteristics of the Euro BIG and BIG indices, and Figure 13.5 sets out the comparative sizes, split into government and sub-sectors of the non-government component. Salient features include:

- the difference in size of the two central government sectors, now that all borrowings by European Governments in any euro-constituent currency are included
- the longer maturity of the US market, whether measured by duration, average life or maturity distribution
- the minimal size of the low-rated sectors in Europe, reflecting the much higher dependency of European corporations on bank finance and a tradition of less leveraged capital structures.

Whether European markets catch up with their US counterparts seems likely to depend on the non-government sectors. In the world of EMU, that development will be a balance between the access of new types of issuer to the market whose structure will be determined by the needs of investors.

Who can issue?

The simplistic, traditional concept of a market consisting largely of major companies issuing long-term bonds to a number of investors such as life insurance companies is already outdated, and indeed such issues will probably be only a fragment of the new market. There are likely to

Table 13.5 Characteristics of 'investible' bonds: EU versus US

	Euro BIG	US BIG
Number of issues	811	6,819
Market capitalization (ECU/euro, billion)	2,625	4,497
Average:		
modified duration, years	4.93	5.50
remaining life, years	6.75	8.05
yield, %	3.99	5.54
Sector breakdown (%):		
1–10 years	88.3	78.4
10+ years	11.7	21.6
AAA rated	60.0	79.7
AA rated	36.8	4.0
A/BBB rated	1.4	16.3

Note: criterion for inclusion in index: amount outstanding Euro BIG, ECU/euro 500 million; US BIG US$ 100

Source: Salomon Smith Barney 1998c

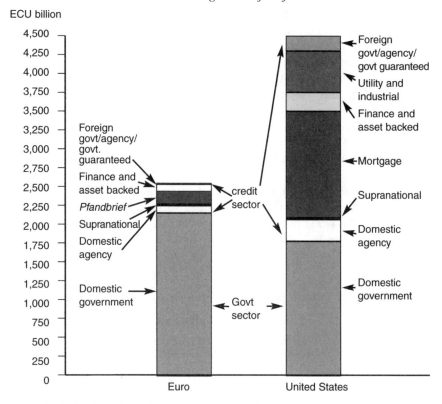

ECU billion

Figure 13.5 Bond markets: EU versus US

be two additional and key sources: pan-European banks and new types of issuer:

- Banks with technologically sophisticated administrative and sales systems may be able to offer their products throughout the Eurozone, giving them a major competitive edge. This may prompt even more restructuring of the European banking system.
- New types of issuer are already apparent from the US and UK models.
  - Companies that wish to sell their products on credit are well placed to economize on working capital by selling the right to the customer's payments, and the scale of issuance by financial corporations in recent years attests to the potential demand.
  - Regional governments are another sector of potential issuers, though the relationship with central government will be a key factor in determining the cost of funds. A straightforward guarantee is one approach. Or the region may have the power to raise taxes separately from the central authority. Market participants will examine very carefully those constitutional arrangements to ensure

that no adverse changes are likely during the life of any bond that may depend on those taxing powers for repayment. In the last year, a variety of European regions and cities have borrowed in the international markets, ranging from the cities of Stockholm and Vienna, to the regions of Andalucia, Azores, Ile de France, Lazio, Sachsen-Anhalt and Valencia. These issues are not large but show the willingness of regions to act on their own.

• Infrastructure projects that themselves generate cashflows, the classic example being a toll road or bridge. The regional government may wish to stimulate these.

Many different models have been tried in the global markets and there seems little reason why these techniques cannot be imported into the Eurozone. The key is more likely to be whether investors develop a sufficient appetite for securities other than those issued by their own central government.

Will some issuers be under pressure to re-open the market?

The loan exposure of European banks to the emerging markets is surprising: on BIS statistics, an amount equal to 75 per cent of their capital is so exposed. This has a historical resonance with the US where similar problems were a driving force in the mid-1980s. To the extent that European banks experience any corresponding problems stemming from the emerging markets, that would be a force which could stimulate the growth of asset-backed bond markets in the Eurozone. However, European banks collectively face sufficient pressures from low asset returns that such developments may be stimulated, even without extra problems from the emerging markets.

Investors also have a problem

Bond yields have fallen to remarkably low levels. For investors in formerly high-yielding bond markets, such as Italy, the problem is particularly acute: yields came down from 13 per cent in 1995 to just under 5 per cent in late 1998 (see Figure 13.6). For investors such as pension and life insurance funds, the problem of low interest rates is likely to be significant. Indeed, the greater the depth of any deflationary crisis that leads to a long period of low bond yields, the greater the difficulty in meeting the expectations of the underlying beneficiaries.

Many European insurance companies have to contend with the problem of guaranteed interest rates on their life insurance and annuity contracts (May, Pitt and Shea 1998). Moreover, some companies – especially in France – have to offer surrender values that are hardly penal. The current level of interest rates should mean that any new yield-enhancements should be attractive.

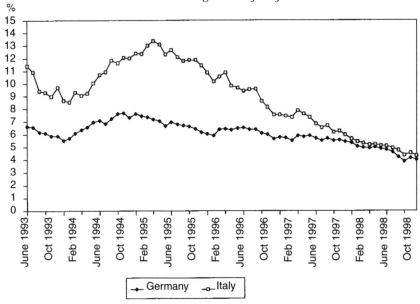

Figure 13.6 German and Italian government ten-year bond yields, June 1993 –
        November 1998

Source: Bloomberg

For life funds this could become acute if the company has promised a
minimum return to policyholders that is now difficult to achieve, especially
after allowing for administrative costs and taxes that may be up to 2 per
cent of income. Life insurers in Belgium are particularly affected, as they
have issued guarantees of a minimum return of 4.75 per cent, and ten-year
government bonds – a key asset – yield somewhat less than that. Perhaps
the next worst-affected EU life insurers are those in France, and many
companies have already had to take sizeable charges against profits to
strengthen their reserves.

With a net return that appears so unattractive, the investment managers
may have little option but to take greater risk. At this stage of low confidence, that may amount to nothing more than lengthening maturity in the
government market. In the Deutschmark market, lengthening from five to
ten years improves yield by 12 per cent, but going to thirty years gives a
36 per cent increase, from 3.6 per cent to 4.9 per cent. In the US dollar
markets, the five-to-thirty year pick-up is only 12 per cent.

The alternative strategy might be to take extra credit risk but – with
lingering concerns from the recent sell-off – that may have to await a
broader recovery in confidence. The incentive is clear. Figure 13.7 shows
the fitted yield curve of the German Government and also that of the
highest yielding EMU government, Italy. The increment in yield is relatively minor within the government sector, unless maturity is extended

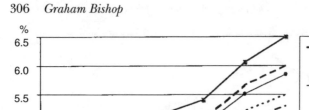

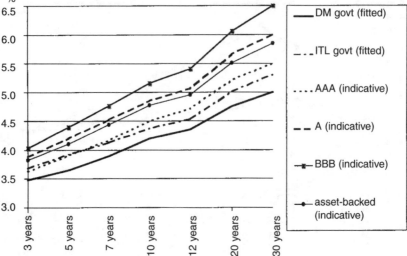

Figure 13.7 Yields: the risk/return trade-off

Source: Salomon Smith Barney estimates

substantially. However, taking credit risk can produce a 20 per cent gain in yield without increasing maturity, based on current indications of new-issue yields.

Additionally, investors (particularly insurers) seeking total return, rather than just yield, may reduce fixed income exposure altogether in favour of equities. This has already happened passively over the past few years as the value of equity investments has increased faster than that of bond holdings.

Institutional investors also face the problem of delivering superior investment performance when the availability of indices makes relative performance highly transparent. Equity investors are already grappling with the problem of re-balancing portfolios along pan-European sectoral lines, rather than the former national make-up. Bond investors may find that they are measured against pan-European indices – such as those of Salomon Smith Barney – where there are substantial differences from national benchmarks. Perhaps the most striking difference will occur when the UK joins EMU: the modified duration of the UK Government Bond Index is 6.83 years versus only 5.13 for the EMU Government Bond Index.

In summary, monetary union is likely to present investors with a new set of trade-offs between maturity and credit risk. Their response will determine whether EMU also opens up new funding opportunities for issuers – whether governments, corporations or consumers (using their credit cards) – as the low level of bond yields may prompt a reassessment of investment patterns in search of higher yields. That demand should eventually encourage the process of securitization.

Some implications of securitized credit in the Eurozone

Changing the structure of the financial system

Securitizing European credit may create a profound, and perhaps quite rapid, change in the financial structure. Two examples illustrate the possibilities:

1   Because of the differences between the short and long-term interest rate sensitivity of economies, the result could be a much more uniform financial structure right the way across the Eurozone. For example, judging by the speed with which UK citizens have shifted their mortgages to fixed rate – traditionally minimal but now 59 per cent of new mortgages – fears about a different financial structure in the UK could dissipate within a surprisingly short number of years after British entry into EMU. That has political implications beyond merely the structure of the banking system.
2   Those financial institutions that currently hold short-term government debt as an asset will find that they face an unexpected competitive threat as the governments reduce their short-term debt. Moreover, the technological revolution that is bringing Internet trading to many individual savers will open the way for them to participate in capital markets by holding directly longer-term, and thus normally higher-yielding, securities which can be easily and cheaply liquidated.

The political impact of 'market discipline'

Long-term investors seek a reward commensurate with the risks they bear. For investors, the political commitment to budget discipline has been a vital step towards EMU, because the bonds issued by these governments – newly disciplined by the pressure to accede to EMU – are the foundation of many investment portfolios. But there is a major political implication: fnancial markets of this scale are genuinely politically independent and cannot be controlled by an individual government, so they can act as a rolling referendum on the views of savers about the fiscal probity of a particular government. As the EU is founded on the principle of open and competitive markets, savers are free to move their funds to where they can get an adequate return for any risk perceived in answer to the simple question: will the state pay my interest and principal on time?

If there is any real doubt, a myriad of investment decisions taken by, or on behalf of, the ageing savers of Europe will shift those savings to safer havens. The European financial markets are no more than intermediaries for the retirement savings of ageing citizens, largely, of Europe. In a world of free movement of capital, any discipline over and above that of the electorate should come from the markets that finance any excess of spending, the national equivalent of the bank manager, rather than an external political power.

There can be no compulsion to lend to governments, because all EU members now have a liberal, market-based economic system. Moreover, the Treaty forbids compulsion: 'privileged access . . . to financial institutions shall be prohibited' unless based on prudential considerations (Article 104b of the Maastricht Treaty). These institutions may seem anonymous and remote to citizens, but they are merely convenient legal channels in which to pool the retirement savings of the electorate. Pension funds, life insurance companies, unit trusts, and so on hold a large slice of a government's accumulated debts. Banks take deposits from the electorate and invest some of it in government debt as well.

The existence of very large and liquid capital markets may well have profound political implications for the EU. Institutional investors – such as pension and life insurance funds – may neither be, nor feel themselves to be, restricted to securities offered by their own government. Instead, they will have several competing governments and a profusion of non-government issuers, whether regional governments, traditional corporate bonds or new securitized issues that underpin innovative credit opportunities for the Eurozone economy.

These two examples serve to illustrate the potential ramifications of EMU – in combination with the driving forces of liberalization, demography and technology – for the European Union.

Notes

This article is based on the ideas developed by the author in a number of speeches during 1996, 1997 and 1998, in particular at the Government Borrowers Forum, June 1996 in Luxembourg; the International Monetary Conference, June 1997 in Interlaken; the Second Euro Symposium at the Bank of England in January 1998 and the 21st Colloquium of Société Universitaire Européenne de Recherches Financières (SUERF) in Frankfurt, 14–17 October 1998.

The author is grateful to the many friends within, and outside, Salomon Smith Barney, who have participated in discussions on these issues. In particular, the following colleagues should be thanked: Jeremy Amias, Charles Berman, Phil Bennett, Philip Brown, Sean Byrne, Albert Desclee, Jim Forese, Ian Hall, Udo Herges, Christopher Hewitt, Paul Horne, Paul Jablanski, Costas Kaplanis, John Leonard, Paul Matthews, Sara McKerihan, Zoeb Sachee and Brian Shea. Finally, the author would like to thank Rachel Parry for her unstinting help in assembling the data and text into its finished state.

1 The author participated in DGXV's Strategy Review Group which provided background analysis in this process.

Bibliography

Bank of England (1998) *Practical Issues Quarterly, no. 9*.
IMF (1997) *International Capital Markets, Developments, Proseects and Key Policy Issues,*

International Monetary Fund, Washington, D.C. (November).

May, T., Pitt, A. and Shea, B. (1998) *Insurance Issues,* Salomon Smith Barney (22 October).

Salomon Smith Barney (1998a) *World Government Bond Index,* Salomon Smith Barney (November).

Salomon Smith Barney (1998b) *EMU Government Bond Index,* Salomon Smith Barney (November).

Salomon Smith Barney (1998c) *Fixed Income Indices,* Salomon Smith Barney (November).

14 The impact of EMU on portfolio management

Martin Brookes

Introduction

A considerable amount has been written about the impact of EMU on European financial markets. A broad consensus has emerged from this work about the impact. The main conclusions may be summarized as follows:

- Government bond markets will be more closely integrated and yields closely correlated.
- Non-government borrowers will increasingly borrow directly from investors by issuing debt securities rather than borrowing from banks, leading to a US-style corporate bond market.
- The national bias in equity and fixed income investments will diminish and funds will be increasingly managed against Euro-wide benchmarks, possibly involving some reallocation of existing investments.
- Equity markets will grow, as more companies go public and more investors seek to invest funds in equity markets.

There are a raft of additional conclusions which have emerged, and some writers make greater claims than others, but these are the core conclusions of research on EMU and financial markets.

This paper is not going to challenge this consensus. Instead it will highlight how EMU will change the behaviour of institutional investors, which is the key factor behind the expected changes to capital markets. It is useful to distinguish between factors influencing the supply of funds in different financial markets, and factors influencing the demand for funds. The aggregate approach usually taken often does not make this distinction clear. Most papers look at the size of the Eurozone financial markets and the barriers to their development caused by having distinct currencies. The aim here is to ask why EMU is expected to lead investors to change the way that funds are managed, prompting the changes outlined.

The plan of the paper is as follows. The following section considers the impact of EMU on a fixed-income fund manager: how does the introduction of the euro affect the behaviour of this fund manager, and how does this affect the demand for new financial markets? Subsequent sections discuss equity markets and EMU. There is evidence that EMU is already changing investor behaviour and will do so further. Evidence is presented from a survey of investors managing over US$ 2,500 billion of funds. After a discussion of investor behaviour, the paper describes transitional issues in fixed income and equity markets caused by potential flows of funds between national financial markets and interest rate convergence.

The penultimate section describes the current state of financial markets within the Eurozone, comparing them with the US and Japan. This serves to emphasize that an important feature of discussions about Eurozone financial markets is the size of the Eurozone economy. It is questioned whether financial markets within the Eurozone can realize their full potential and grow to match those in the US. Several barriers to integration remain, as do shortcomings in the regulatory environment. These are likely to remain for a considerable time, inhibiting the growth of Eurozone financial markets. None the less, as the conclusion remarks, the introduction of the euro paves the way for a substantial change in the way that investors in the Eurozone behave.

EMU and fixed-income markets

Government bond markets in EMU

The financial markets that have felt the impact of EMU most forcibly to date are the national government bond markets of countries joining the monetary union.[1] The key concerns of investors in these markets during the three years 1996 to 1998 have been the prospects for EMU going ahead, and the countries which would join any monetary union. Fluctuations in the prospects of EMU going ahead and of individual countries qualifying for entry have been a prime factor in influencing bond yields.

When EMU begins, all new government debt of the eleven countries in the Eurozone will be issued in euros. In addition, all governments are redenominating the vast majority of tradeable government debt.[2] Therefore, from the beginning of 1999 there will be no currency differences between (say) German and French government debt.

Denominating government debt in the same currency will remove an important distinction between bonds of different governments. Historically, an investor comparing a French government FFr bond with a German government DM bond needed to take into account foreign exchange risk, that is, the possibility of change in the DM/FFr exchange rate. This risk may have been low, but the different currency denominations of the two bonds made them more distinct assets. Consequently the correlations between yields on the two government bonds was lower.

Removing foreign exchange risk should increase the degree of substitutability and the correlations between bond markets of different governments. The prospect of EMU has already boosted correlations between returns in different markets.

An alternative way to make this same point is to use the expectations hypothesis of the term structure of interest rates. The current bond yield can be broken down into the current level of short-term interest rates and expectations of future interest rates. For example, today's two-year bond yield can be written as the average of the current one-year interest rate and the one-year rate expected in a year's time. (This is a linear approximation rather than an exact formula but it suffices for our purposes.) Additional factors such as the credit risk of the borrower and liquidity may also influence the current level of two-year bond yields, but this formula contains the dominant factor. Inside EMU, market interest rates and expectations about future interest rates will be determined by the monetary policies of the ECB. The dominant influence on government bond yields will therefore be common across all government bond markets, making the markets more closely correlated. It is the anticipation of this which has driven actual bond yields close to one another through the convergence of forward interest rates implicit in current yields (see Figures 14.1 and 14.2).

As well as removing the currency distinctions between government bond markets, governments are taking steps to harmonize the conventions on different bond markets, such as the way in which accrued interest is calculated and the settlement terms. This will remove another distinction between new issues of government debt, increasing the degree of substitutability yet further.

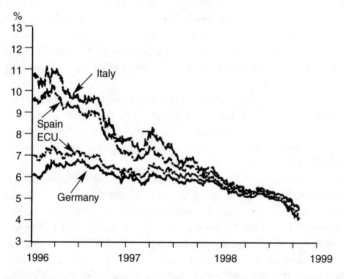

Figure 14.1 Benchmark government bond yields

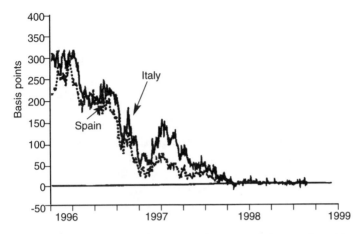

Figure 14.2 Five-year, five-year forward swap spreads over Germany

Some distinctions between different government bonds will remain. Two important distinctions will be issuance practice, which will remain the responsibility of national governments, and credit risk, with individual governments being responsible for the consequences of their own fiscal actions. These factors are likely to prevent the different government bond markets being perfectly correlated with another. Notwithstanding this, the impact of EMU on government bond markets can be summarized simply as higher correlations.

Increased correlations between the different national government bond markets should effectively result in one integrated euro government bond market at the beginning of 1999. This prospect changes the way in which investors will look at national government bond markets within the Eurozone. Increased correlations between national markets remove the differences between bond markets which were a key part of the process of investing in these markets until recently. This could markedly change the way in which fixed income funds are managed in the Eurozone.

Fixed-income fund management in EMU

Higher correlations between national government bond markets reduce the benefits of diversification. For example, a French investor holding a portfolio of French government bonds could alter the volatility of his portfolio by shifting some funds into foreign currency government bonds, such as DM bunds. So long as the correlations between the two markets was low this would reduce the volatility of the overall portfolio without reducing returns. Switching bond holdings into other government debt was also a means of seeking higher returns on a portfolio.

Table 14.1 illustrates the impact of higher correlations on bond port-folios. It shows the tracking error on a portfolio of either French or German government bonds relative to a benchmark of all Eurozone government bonds. These tracking errors are shown under different assumptions about the correlations between government bond markets in Europe. The correlations begin at zero and end at one, with perfect corre-lation between the national government bond markets. Intermediate values for the correlations are the actual correlations in January 1994, when EMU was an uncertain prospect, and January 1998, when the prospect of EMU had pushed correlations higher. The tracking error on a portfolio of purely French or German government bonds declines as the correlations increase from left to right. This is because the portfolio of French or German government bonds becomes a closer substitute for the aggregate Eurozone portfolio. When bond markets are perfectly corre-lated the tracking errors are very small.

This shifts the focus of fixed income fund management within Europe. A traditional method of managing a fixed income portfolio of government bonds within Europe was to decide whether to increase allocations to certain European markets to try to boost returns. The choice of country was the main decision variable for a fund manager.

EMU changes this. By increasing correlations between government bond markets, EMU makes the choice of country less important. An investor holding a portfolio of French government bonds who decides to try to boost returns by switching into Italian government bonds (say) changes the structure of his portfolio only slightly, as Italian government bonds are now closer substitutes for French government bonds.

Table 14.2 shows this change most starkly. Imagine an investor managing a portfolio of European government bonds who is not allowed to take duration risk, that is, has a 'market exposure' of one. This investor has a target tracking error for the portfolio relative to the benchmark aggregate Eurozone portfolio of 50bp. This represents the investor's appetite for risk. The investor takes the risk by switching funds between different government bond markets, for example moving out of France and into Italy. If correlations between the government bond markets are in line with those in January 1994, it is possible to construct a portfolio which has a tracking error of 50bp and achieves an expected out-performance relative to the benchmark of 30bp (30bp represents the pay-off for assuming additional risk in the portfolio). (All these

Table 14.1 Tracking errors decline as correlations increase

	Tracking Errors, bp			
	Corr = 0.0	*Corr: Jan 1994*	*Corr: Jan 1998*	*Corr = 1.0*
France	305	191	150	15
Germany	260	197	129	47

Table 14.2 Fewer opportunities to take risk

Portfolio	Market exposure	Tracking error	Projected performance
Corr: January 1994	1.00	50	30
Corr: January 1998	1.00	37	7

calculations are based on the Goldman Sachs Black–Litterman asset allocation model.)

If we use the higher correlations between the government bond markets of January 1998, the story changes. It is now not possible to construct a portfolio with 50bp of tracking error without taking duration risk. The different government bond markets are too close substitutes for one another to allow this. The maximum tracking error which is possible is 37bp. For this level of risk the expected out-performance relative to the benchmark portfolio is just 7bp.

Therefore, inside EMU it will not be possible to satisfy investors' typical appetites for risk by the normal process of switching between the different national government bond markets. The above scenario is a reasonably accurate presentation of investors' behaviour in the run-up to EMU, and highlights the need for a switch in behaviour as correlations increase. There are several possible responses. First, the investor actively managing a portfolio of European government bonds can manage the duration of the portfolio more aggressively than before. A second possibility is to change the parameters on the portfolio and manage the international exposure between the US, Europe and Japan more aggressively.

The third possibility is to look elsewhere within European fixed income markets to find opportunities to take risks and boost returns on portfolios. This is one key reason to expect the development of a corporate bond in euros in the future.

A Eurozone corporate bond market

Investors seeking new fixed-income opportunities to boost returns on bond portfolios will add to the demand for corporate credit inside EMU. This has already happened to some extent, but the process is likely to intensify. First, correlations of returns on government bonds should increase further between much of the EMU bloc. Second, unfunded pension liabilities and pension provision in the private sector will push fund managers into seeking higher returns on existing portfolios of pension assets. This will necessarily entail higher risk, partly in the form of greater credit risk. Third, the supply of government bonds may diminish as governments keep fiscal deficits low in line with the stability and growth pact, reducing further the available returns on portfolios of government bonds.

A final impact is through increased opportunities for diversification. By broadening the universe of domestic currency corporate bonds, EMU will increase the scope to diversify away any individual corporate credit risk. This increases the attractiveness of investing in a given corporate credit. The demand for a given corporate credit therefore increases at unchanged spreads, or in other words, the demand curve shifts rightwards.

An increased demand for credit risk will reduce the cost of raising debt in the corporate bond market; that is, it will reduce the corporate credit spread over government debt over time. This will boost the overall supply of corporate debt and will go some way to restoring the opportunities to take risk and increase returns on fixed income portfolios in Europe. However, the total size of the European corporate bond market depends on the supply of corporate credit as well as the demand. If a substantial corporate bond market is to develop in the Eurozone an increase in the supply of debt is desirable, independent of changes in demand. (See Figures 14.3 and 14.4.)

The corporate bond market in the Eurozone is currently woefully small. The corporate sector relies to a greater extent than its US counterpart on bank finance. Figures from the IMF show that two-thirds of every dollar raised by US companies comes directly from the capital markets, with the remainder coming from bank borrowing. The balance is exactly reversed in Europe: two-thirds of borrowing comes from banks and only one-third direct from capital markets. Moreover, most of the borrowing in capital markets is done by financial institutions. There is very little direct borrowing by non-financial institutions to finance their activities.

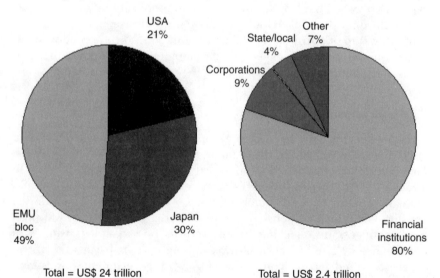

Total = US$ 24 trillion   Total = US$ 2.4 trillion

Figure 14.3 The market for bank loans   *Figure 14.4* The corporate bond
                                                market in EMU

One of the factors which has inhibited the development of a corporate bond market is exchange rate risk. Because of restrictions on investments in foreign currency assets, the possible range of investors for most companies has effectively been limited to domestic investors. This has raised the cost of issuing debt securities for most companies relative to the alternative of borrowing directly from the banking sector. EMU should broaden the investor base for European companies wishing to issue corporate debt. In addition, the foreign exchange cost of issuing debt in one main currency and then transferring the proceeds into various different local currencies to finance local operations will disappear (see Brookes and Winkelmann 1998 for more details). These factors should boost the supply of corporate credit independently of the increase in demand.

An increase in both the demand for, and the supply of, corporate credit will foster the development of a corporate bond market. Back-of-the-envelope calculations suggest that this market could grow fivefold or more from its current anaemic state.

The main consequence of EMU for fixed income investors is therefore a shift in focus from the national economic policies of individual governments towards corporate credit.

EMU and equity markets

Sector versus country

There is considerable evidence that investors in financial markets have a strong domestic bias and hold a very large share of their investment portfolio in domestic assets. Many studies show that the proportion of assets held domestically is suboptimal, and that a shift of some funds into overseas assets would reduce the volatility of portfolio returns without reducing the level of returns. These are unexploited benefits of portfolio diversification.

One of the barriers to such diversification of portfolios is exchange rate risk. Investors are either wary of shifting funds into overseas markets because of exchange rate risk, or are prevented from doing so by regulations which are themselves justified by exchange rate risk.

As has been noted, EMU will remove exchange rate risk between the national financial markets of countries joining the monetary union. The definition of the 'home' financial market should therefore shift from the national market to the Eurozone-wide market. For example, a DM-based investor with a portfolio of assets largely in the 'home' market of Germany should begin to consider assets in any Eurozone market as 'home'. Within equity markets this shift is likely to reinforce the move from managing portfolios of European equities along national lines towards sectoral lines.

Equity market strategists and academic researchers continue to debate the merits of distinguishing equity markets along national or sectoral lines for investment purposes. The issue here is whether (for example) an investor should compare the share prices of German banks with the share prices of other German companies, or with those of banks in other European countries. Although investment research has become increasingly organized along sectoral rather than national lines, this does not prove the case for sectors over countries.

The prospect of EMU has led to increased stability in exchange rates and convergence of bond yields and interest rates in the countries joining the monetary union. In principle this might have increased the correlations between national equity markets, as the determinants of corporate profits and risk premia move more closely. Simultaneously, one might expect correlations between equity prices within the same sector to increase as European economies become more integrated and trade flows between European countries increase.

Research by Goldman Sachs (Goldman Sachs 1998) suggests that sectors have indeed become relatively more important than countries in determining equity returns. This research looks at average historic correlations between equity returns within national equity markets and within equity sectors. Although there is no conclusive increase in correlations within sectors during recent years, there has been a decline in correlations within national markets. However, the evidence remains ambiguous as to whether sectors or countries have proved better asset classes. None the less, the research concludes:

> from a European perspective, and more specifically from the perspective of EMU, it seems likely that the ability of any analytical system to generate country rotation signals within Europe will fall as interest rate and exchange rate changes among countries included in EMU fade into history. Even if the sector signals do not improve, this suggests an increase in the relative ability of sectors to contribute to the investment decision process. . . . [W]e believe investors have a basis to assume that sectors will be better asset classes going forward.
>
> (Goldman Sachs 1998)

Ultimately the question of whether investors will look at sectors or countries when making investment decisions is empirical. Survey evidence strongly indicates that investors will base their decisions on sectors rather than countries. Together with the investment consultants Watson Wyatt, Goldman Sachs undertook a survey of our client base asking about the impact of EMU on behaviour (Rattray and Boomgaardt 1998; see Figures 14.5, 14.6 and 14.7). The aggregate value of funds under management covered by the survey was approximately US\$ 2,700 billion.

Out of the fund managers surveyed, a full 70 per cent said that EMU would lead them to reconsider their asset allocation. The fund managers

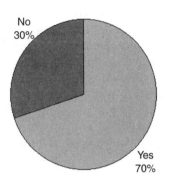

No
30%

Yes
70%

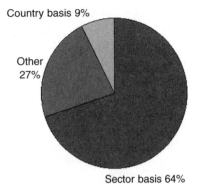

Country basis 9%

Other
27%

Sector basis 64%

Figure 14.5 The Goldman
Sachs/Watson Wyatt EMU
survey: will the estab-
lishment of the euro
prompt you to reconsider
your asset allocation?

Figure 14.6 The Goldman
Sachs/Watson Wyatt EMU
survey: post EMU will your
European equity portfolio
be organized on a country
or a sector basis?

3–5 years
10%

5+ years
2%

1–3 years
29%

0–6 months
30%

6–12 months
30%

Figure 14.7 The Goldman
Sachs/Watson
Wyatt EMU
survey: how long
do you expect
transition from
your current
portfolio to your
'EMU compatible'
portfolio to take?

were asked whether they would organize their European equity portfolio
on a country or a sector basis. Sixty-four per cent of managers said that
European equity portfolios would be organized on a sector basis. Only
9 per cent said that portfolios would be organized on a country basis, the
remaining 27 per cent saying 'other', probably indicating a mixture of
country and sector factors (Figures 14.5, 14.6, 14.7).

Linked to this finding there is strong evidence from the survey that fund
managers increasingly find the country of listing of a company within the
Eurozone to be irrelevant. This survey provides evidence that EMU will
lead to greater management of portfolios by sector rather than by country.

One factor which might stimulate change in the way funds are managed is changing regulations. EU based insurance companies are covered by the EU Third Life Insurance Directive which is reflected in national law in each country. This directive requires insurance companies to hold at least 80 per cent of their assets in the same currency as their liabilities. This forces insurance companies to hold the bulk of their equity portfolios in domestic equities. When EMU begins, the euro will become the legal currency of each country in the monetary union, and all equity markets will switch immediately to transacting only in euros. For any insurance company operating in a Eurozone country, this effectively removes the restriction on investing in equity markets in other countries within the monetary union.

There is no common framework of regulation for pension funds, and attempts by the European Commission to propose a framework continue to face opposition by individual countries. The impact of EMU on restrictions on pension fund investment is therefore less clear. However, it is expected that EMU will ease restrictions on pension fund overseas holdings by redefining the 'home' market, for example through changing the results of asset–liability studies.

One interesting feature of the survey was the speed with which changes are likely to be implemented. Almost 60 per cent of fund managers expected the transition period to take no more than one year, and almost 90 per cent expected it to be finished three years into EMU. This suggests a fairly rapid adjustment of equity portfolios. It is possible that this might cause some dislocation in some national equity markets as funds migrate from national portfolios into pan-Eurozone portfolios. This is one of the transitional issues for EMU discussed later in this paper.

Benchmark indices

Increased management of Eurozone equity portfolios along sector rather than country lines will bring into question the relevance of existing national equity market indices.[3] In the limit, if no investor holds a portfolio of only national shares what is the point of national equity indices? The corollary of this is a growing demand for pan-Eurozone equity indices. In anticipation of this demand there is already a burgeoning supply of such indices.

To date six different benchmark indices have been launched covering either the whole of Europe or just the EMU countries. It is possible that the number of benchmarks will decline as some prove more successful than others. It seems likely that many funds with existing designated benchmarks will not change to a new benchmark. This is largely because of the costs of changing benchmarks, in the form of the transaction costs of adjusting portfolios. Such funds are currently the dominant pools of equity money in Europe, which suggests that the adoption of new benchmarks will be more prevalent in new and smaller funds. What has been dubbed the 'battle of the benchmarks' is really about new money flows. One absolute winner is unlikely to emerge, as existing funds retain their existing benchmarks. Consequently, the range of benchmarks available to investors is likely to be permanently wider than ever before.

Transitional issues

Portfolio rebalancing

As was noted earlier, there is evidence that equity investors are planning to adjust their portfolios fairly rapidly within EMU. This prospect has led to some speculation about the extent of cross-border flows. In principle these flows might be substantial. If investors in each national equity market decide to adjust their portfolios into pan-Eurozone portfolios the majority of funds under management could change hands. Institutional holders of equities are more likely to adjust their portfolios than individual investors. (See Figure 14.8.) The concentration of institutional holdings of equities in particular countries, most notably in Dutch pension funds and German and French insurance companies, has raised the possibility of massive net flows between some markets.

Two distinct approaches can be taken to portfolio rebalancing.[4] First, one can consider rebalancing using a country approach. This would involve selling domestic equity holdings and investing the proceeds across

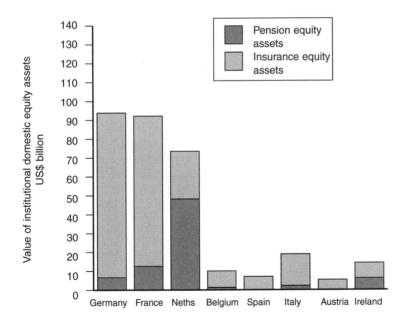

Figure 14.8 EMU zone domestic equity assets

the Eurozone on a country basis. If funds were to rebalance using such an approach, those markets with the highest level of institutional equity investment relative to their weight in the Eurozone would suffer most. There would be massive flows of funds out of the Dutch and French equity markets and into Spain and Italy. There would also be large selling of Irish equities. Figure 14.9 shows the net rebalancing flows and also the number of days trading volume assuming that 30 per cent of portfolios are adjusted. Flows from insurance companies and pension funds are shown separately, as pension funds may rebalance more slowly than insurance companies owing to the differences in regulation. The extent of flows of funds depends on the approach taken to rebalancing.

The alternative approach to portfolio rebalancing is to do it along sector lines. In this case institutional investors would rebalance away from their domestic country sector weights to Eurozone neutral sector weights. The country of portfolio holding is irrelevant here. The only interest is in whether sector holdings match the sector breakdown of the aggregate Eurozone equity index. Consequently, institutional investors remain biased on a country basis after rebalancing. Given the stated preference of equity fund managers for managing portfolios along sector lines inside EMU, this seems a more realistic approach to take. Figure 14.10 shows the net portfolio flows assuming 30 per cent of funds are reallocated on a sector basis across the Eurozone equity market. The flows are more muted than for a reallocation along country lines. This is because existing allocations of funds look less unbalanced when measured against a neutral sector benchmark. Moreover, on sector lines there are more flows which cancel out.

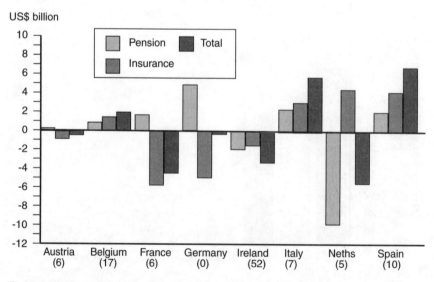

Figure 14.9 Net rebalancing flows using a country approach

The aggregate effect of portfolio rebalancing in equity markets may therefore be more limited than is widely thought. However, one feature of these potential flows is particularly worth noting. Typically, when investors rebalance portfolios they concentrate new purchases on large-cap names. This suggests that cross-border equity flows which result from rebalancing may be skewed towards large-cap stocks. One factor reinforcing this is that the most widely used benchmarks for pan-Eurozone equity investors are likely to be large-cap biased. Investors will therefore have an added incentive to concentrate purchases in large-cap stocks. The rebalancing effect within equity markets may have the most marked effect on stocks of different market capitalizations within the same sectors, rather than on different countries or sectors.

It is possible that there will also be substantial rebalancing flows within bond markets, but the arguments for this are less compelling. In particular, correlations between different government bond markets are very high, and the diversification benefits from switching between different markets will be very low. Perhaps the most compelling argument in favour of diversification is prudential considerations. Specifically, a French insurance company may reason that a portfolio of government debt heavily biased towards French government bonds represents an excessive exposure to the credit risk of the French government. None the less, the force of this argument is fairly limited and diversification of bond portfolios may be slow and protracted.[5]

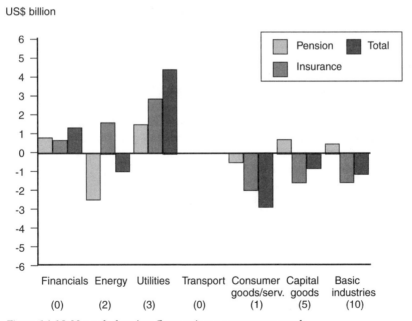

Figure 14.10 Net rebalancing flows using a sector approach

The shock of convergence

The creation of a monetary union necessarily requires the convergence of short-term interest rates.[6] At one point this looked likely to involve reductions in short-term interest rates in some countries and increases in other countries. Such changes in interest rates may be regarded as a 'convergence shock' to GDP growth. This convergence shock is an asymmetric shock impacting different economies differently.

Some commentators have argued that the convergence shock should lead equity investors to continue to concentrate on national economic performance rather than Eurozone economic performance when allocating funds. This is in effect an argument for maintaining the use of country rather than sector in asset allocation.

This argument is flawed. For interest rate convergence to provoke continued use of country models in equity allocation, the 'convergence shocks' to GDP growth must matter for equity market returns. If the convergence shocks have relatively little effect on equity markets then they can safely be ignored by equity investors. In fact, the contribution to equity returns from economic factors is frequently low. Other factors are often more important. Factors such as bond yields and the exchange rate usually dominate economic activity. These will be shared across equity markets, suggesting that equity markets will move closely together.

To illustrate this an analysis of variance was undertaken of the results of research explaining equity sector returns. This research used econometric equations to explain sector returns using several factors. These factors are growth in economic activity, bond yields, the exchange rate (against the US dollar), the oil price and a valuation term.

Analysis of variance involves calculating the amount of the variation in equity returns explained by the different factors in an equation. For each equation explaining the sector returns we calculated how much of the variation in returns is due to changes in each factor. Twenty-three distinct equity market sectors were considered. There were only three sectors in which changes in economic growth account for more than a quarter of explained changes in equity prices. These three are autos, beverages and tobacco, and health and personal care.

This confirms that economic growth is generally only a small contributor to the explanatory power of the equations for equity market returns. Note that this does not suggest that economic growth is unimportant. Rather it suggests that economic growth is primarily important in how it affects bond yields and exchange rates. Bond yields and exchange rates are strongly affected by interest rate sentiment which is affected by growth. Apart from this effect, however, there is little incremental information in changes in growth for equity markets within Europe.

One way to illustrate the relative insensitivity of equity markets to

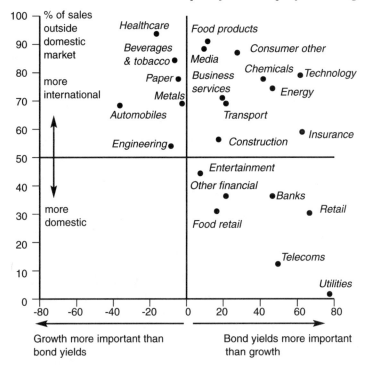

100 ┬ % of sales
      outside   Healthcare   Food products
90 ┤ domestic   ●
      market   Beverages   ● Consumer other
                      & tobacco ●   Media
80 ┤ more   Chemicals ● Technology
      international   Paper ● Business   ●
70 ┤   Metals   services   ● Energy
                        ●   ●
                    Automobiles   Transport
60 ┤   ● Insurance
                   Engineering ●   ● Construction
50 ┤
                              ● Entertainment
40 ┤   Other financial
                               ● Banks
30 ┤ more   ●   ●   ● Retail
      domestic   Food retail
20 ┤
                              ● Telecoms
10 ┤   Utilities
                                    ●
0 ┴────┬────┬────┬────┬────┬────┬────┬────┬
   -80 -60 -40 -20   0   20   40   60   80

Growth more important than   Bond yields more important
bond yields   than growth

Figure 14.11 Domestic cyclicals do not exist: relative importance of bond yields
          and growth in explaining returns

changes in economic growth is shown in Figure 14.11. Along the
horizontal axis is measured the difference between the proportion of
returns explained by bond yields and the proportion explained by growth
in the equations for sector returns. The vertical axis measures the
proportion of sales revenue in the sector which comes from the domestic
market. A truly domestic sector would be in the bottom left segment of the
graph, that is, with a low proportion of company sales overseas and
changes in economic growth dominating bond yields in explaining equity
market returns. None of the twenty-three sectors falls into this quadrant.
There are no equity sectors which can be regarded as cyclical, for whom
domestic sales account for the majority of company receipts. Given this, it
is difficult to make a compelling case for maintaining a strong focus on
national economic performance within EMU as opposed to the
performance of the whole of the Eurozone.

These results suggest that for equity investors, slight fluctuations in
economic growth are not particularly important for influencing equity
markets and so should not have a dominant effect on asset allocation.
The 'convergence shock' does not provide a reason for concentrating
on national equity market analysis as opposed to sector analysis.

A logical end-point?

Table 14.3 compares the Eurozone with the US and Japan. It is common to use the US economy as the benchmark for comparison for the Eurozone because the two are broadly comparable in terms of GDP; Eurozone GDP is roughly three-quarters of US GDP.

Some of the arguments about the future development of Eurozone financial markets stem from this fact alone. To illustrate this point, imagine that EMU did not involve eleven EU countries together forming a monetary union, but instead involved the sixteen German Länder with distinct currencies and financial markets coming together to form one country with a common currency, the Deutschmark. The key part of this process is exactly the same, that is, one of economic areas adopting a common currency. It is difficult, however, to imagine analysts making the same claims about the future development of DM-denominated financial markets as are made about euro-denominated financial markets. The qualitative claims which would be made may well be similar – greater liquidity and depth in financial markets leading to greater range of instruments and markets – but the range of instruments and markets expected to develop would be smaller than is the case for the Eurozone.

This reasoning highlights the fact that among the important factors behind some of the changes expected to take place are the economies of scale which arise from removing exchange rate differences and aggregating the eleven Eurozone economies into one. These exchange rate differences have fragmented pools of savings within Europe, and prevented borrowers from raising funds throughout Europe rather than within their local economies. As a consequence of this, financial markets have not fully developed and much financial intermediation has gone through the banking system. This has provided an important role to traditional commercial banks in Europe.

There are many barriers to the Eurozone developing financial markets and a fund management industry to match the US. The size of the economy is not everything. Many of these factors were highlighted in the recent report from the Centre for European Policy Studies (CEPS 1998). Two key factors are the lack of a common Eurozone regime for the tax

Table 14.3 The Eurozone comes close to matching the US

	Eurozone	US
GDP (US$ trillion)	6.8	7.6
Population (million)	288	261
Share of world trade (%)	18.6	16.1
Government bond market (US$ trillion)	2.3	2.2
Equity market (US$ trillion)	2.6	8.4

treatment of investors, and the lack of a common accounting standard. Although some governments have expressed an interest in making progress in harmonizing taxation policies in this area, any progress is likely to be slow. The role of accounting policies in inhibiting the growth of European financial markets was highlighted by the listing of Daimler Benz on the New York Stock Exchange (NYSE), pointed out in the CEPS report. In order to comply with NYSE listing rules Daimler Benz had to adopt US GAAP (Generally Accepted Accounting Principles). These led to markedly different results from those produced under German accounting rules. This raised the effective cost of capital for Daimler Benz. Progress is likely to be made in integrating accounting systems within the Eurozone, but again progress will probably be slow.

These factors will inhibit the growth of financial markets in EMU, and will likely detract from international investor involvement in these markets. Consequently, the size of financial markets within the US is probably an exaggerated end-point for the Eurozone. A further factor that could inhibit the growth of financial markets is the legal framework protecting shareholder rights in Europe. Recent research (Porta *et al.* 1997) highlights the role of investor protection in promoting or restricting the growth of capital markets. This research has highlighted differences in the degree of investor protection afforded by different legal systems. Porta *et al.* examine the links between four measures of the development of financial markets and a quantitative measure of the extent of investor protection. The measures of financial market are stock market capitalization, the number of listed companies per head of population, the number of initial public offerings of shares (IPOs) and a measure of debt finance. The hypothesis is that investors are more likely to provide funds if the legal system provides adequate protection for their investments.

The evidence suggests those countries with common-law legal systems, such as the US and the UK, provide greatest investor protection and also support the most developed equity markets. Countries governed by French civil law systems, such as France, Italy, Spain, the Netherlands and Belgium among the Eurozone countries, provide the weakest investor protection and support the smallest equity markets. Countries with legal systems of German and Scandinavian origin lie between these two extremes, and in turn support medium-sized financial markets.

This line of research is still relatively new, but the results to date highlight a further drawback for the potential growth of financial markets within the Eurozone. Eurozone countries are covered by legal systems which do not provide the same extent of legal protection as does the US. Therefore it is probably excessively optimistic to assume that the logical end-point for European financial markets is the size and breadth of the US financial system. The differences between the two are more than the exchange rate differences preventing the exploitation of economies of scale within Europe.

One area in which Eurozone financial markets are particularly restricted is equity markets. The number of publicly listed companies and the size of equity markets in the Eurozone is considerably smaller than in the US, even adjusting for the relative sizes of the two economies. As was noted in the introduction, one of the main conclusions of research into the prospects for Eurozone financial markets is that equity markets will grow and more companies will go public. A major reason for this expectation is the economies of scale argument mentioned earlier; this therefore has nothing to do with investor behaviour. Investor behaviour may help spur the growth of equity markets, as investors seek higher returns to plug gaps in pension provision, and to replace the high real returns previously available on government debt. These changes are however a subsidiary reason for the expected growth in equity markets.

It is received wisdom that the smaller equity markets in Europe are a reflection of the difficulties of small to medium-sized companies in Europe in gaining a listing. One way to test this is to see if the structure of the US equity market is markedly different to the aggregate of Eurozone equity markets. If it is true that small and medium-sized companies are restricted in their access to equity capital, one would find relatively fewer small and medium-sized companies listed on Eurozone stock exchanges than in the US. Figure 14.12 shows the number of companies listed on the NYSE and NASDAQ compared with the aggregate of the EU-11 countries. The figures for the EU-11 countries are scaled so that the aggregate number of listed companies is the same as the total for NYSE and NASDAQ. This is because our interest is in the distribution of companies, not the absolute number. There do not appear to be any marked differences between the two markets.

Figure 14.13 looks at the same issue from a different perspective. It takes the difference between the number of companies in each band of Figure 14.12 and weights this by the market capitalization of the band. Each bar represents the difference in market capitalization between the US and the Eurozone accounted for by that sector, again adjusting so that the aggregate capitalization is the same in each case. If small and medium-sized companies were under-represented in the Eurozone compared with the US, the bars on the left would be larger than those to the right. In fact there is no systematic pattern between the two.

This experiment suggests that the 'problem' of smaller equity markets in the Eurozone is not caused by small and medium-sized companies being deterred from listing. The distribution of listed companies in the Eurozone appears similar to that in the US. This research is preliminary but it reinforces the impression from other work that the constraints on the development of financial markets in the Eurozone are more than a question of scale and that there are fundamental factors which prevent or deter companies from seeking a listing in the Eurozone.

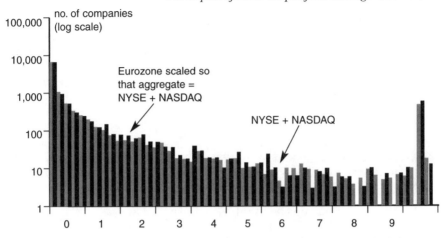

Figure 14.12 Number of companies: New York Stock Exchange and NASDAQ versus the Eurozone

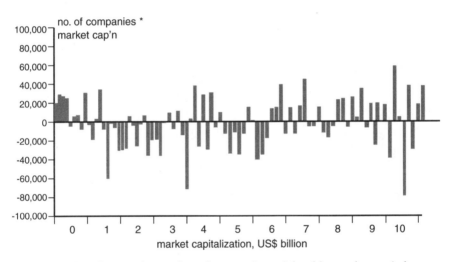

Figure 14.13 Difference in number of companies weighted by market capitalization: New York Stock Exchange and NASDAQ less the Eurozone (* scaled so market capitalizations are equal)

Conclusions

The advent of EMU undoubtedly promises great change for financial markets in Europe. For investors in all classes of assets, the key change is the removal of existing distinctions between national markets. Some of this change will be prompted by changes in regulations, such as the regulations covering insurance companies. Further changes will be prompted by the increased correlations between some national markets. In particular this will lead to growing credit markets.

Ultimately Eurozone financial markets may grow to match those in the US. However, this will take a very long time and there appear to be structural barriers to such growth. None the less, dramatic changes are likely to come. A key aspect to these changes is the way in which investors will change their behaviour when investing in European financial markets.

Notes

This paper draws upon much existing research of colleagues at Goldman Sachs. In particular, the work of Kurt Winkelmann, Sandy Rattray, Mike Young, Peter Sullivan and Francesca Massone is used. I am grateful to Joshua Rauh for research assistance in preparing the paper.

1 These sections draw on Brookes 1997 and 1998, and Brookes and Winkelmann 1998.
2 A report published in April by the EU monetary committee shows the share of tradable national currency government debt which is being re-denominated is over 80 per cent for all countries joining EMU except Finland (77 per cent) and Austria (34 per cent).
3 These comments draw on Rattray 1998a
4 The following draws on Rattray 1998b.
5 The effects of portfolio rebalancing within government bond markets are considered in Brookes 1998.
6 This section draws on Brookes and Massone 1998.

Bibliography

Brookes, M. (1997) 'Credit Risk and Bond Yield Spreads Within EMU', Goldman Sachs (March).
Brookes, M. (1998) 'Portfolio Flows Between Government Bond Markets in EMU', Goldman Sachs (February).
Brookes, M. and Massone, F. (1998) 'The Economics of Interest Rate Convergence in Euroland', Goldman Sachs (April).
Brookes, M. and Winkelmann, K. (1998) 'Government Bond Markets in EMU – The Supply and Demand for Corporate Credit', Goldman Sachs (March).
CEPS (1998) 'Capital Markets and EMU', Report of a CEPS Working Party, Centre for European Policy Studies.
Goldman Sachs (1998) 'Sector Versus Country – When is an Asset Class an Asset Class?', *Goldman Sachs Portfolio Strategy* (March).
Porta, R. La, Lopez-de-Silanes, F., Shleifer, A. and Vishny, R. (1997) 'Legal Determinants of External Finance', *Journal of Finance* (July).
Rattray, S. (1998a) 'Benchmarks for Europe: A New Age?', Goldman Sachs Equity Derivatives Research (April).
Rattray, S. (1998b) 'The Great European Rebalancing: Fact or Fiction?', Goldman Sachs Equity Derivatives Research (16 May).
Rattray, S. and Boomgaardt, R. (1998) 'The Goldman Sachs/Watson Wyatt EMU Survey – Summary of Results', *Goldman Sachs Equity Derivatives Research* (17 June).

15 Credit risk and ratings after the euro

Christopher Huhne

This paper aims to elucidate some of the likely changes in creditworthiness of different entities as a result of EMU. It is split into two parts. The first part deals with the immediate impact of the introduction of the euro on creditworthiness. The second looks at changes in the economic environment which are likely to impact rated entities.

The system becomes operational on Monday 4 January 1999. This is when the currencies are locked together at the fixed and invariable parities announced at the Brussels summit (the central rates of the existing exchange rate mechanism) and when each national currency becomes merely a 'legal expression' of the underlying (but at this stage not yet physical) euro. The second key date is the first six months of 2002, when the national notes and coin will be physically replaced by a euro note and coin issue.

The EMU area – or Eurozone – will become one area with one monetary authority, one currency and hence one set of foreign exchange earnings, which will be shared among the inhabitants purely on their ability to bid for foreign currency from those who have earned it. There will be no restriction on flows between member states and no entity within the area – whether sovereign, sub-national, corporate or bank – will have preferential access to that foreign exchange. Therefore there should be only one 'sovereign' ceiling rating (as the rating which measures the risk of transfer of money from local currency into the investors' currency). This transfer risk is small, given that the progress of fiscal consolidation has been sufficiently impressive to reduce the risks of a break-up of EMU, and given the Eurozone's net-creditor position, diversified foreign currency earnings, current account surpluses and the liquidity of its markets. (Indeed, the net weight of AAAs in the existing area – Germany, the Netherlands, Austria, France and Luxembourg – is two-thirds of the GDP of the eleven initial members).

However, there is an important caveat. The EMU area is not yet as credible a monetary union as, say, the existing German or American monetary unions. There remains a small risk that the EMU will break up. If part of the union breaks off, then it is likely to resume its previous sovereign ceiling, or even a lower one, given the potentially high costs of exit from the Eurozone and the lack of any procedures for doing so. This scenario is not too far-fetched: monetary unions have broken down in the past (for example, the Latin Monetary Union) although arguably they have not had the same support mechanisms and common institutions as are proposed for EMU.

During the transitional period between 1 January 1999 and the final replacement of national notes and coin, it will at least be practically possible for a member state to reintroduce monetary autonomy if it comes under a lot of political stress to do so. This might arise in a 'strong' member state like Germany, worried by the apparently inflationary tendencies of others, or in a weak member state which found that monetary policy was inappropriate for its needs.

Imagine, for example, that the Italian government was hit by a political crisis which in turn entailed a sharp loss of financial confidence that Italy would be able to sustain its membership in the currency union. In theory, speculation against the lire would be impossible. Within Europe, national currencies which participate will only be an expression of the euro after 1 January 1999, so that any other national currency or the euro itself can be used to repay debt. Speculators may however be able to use offshore centres to write futures contracts. Another means of speculative attack would be simply to move bank deposits to parts of the euro-area which are thought likely to continue with the euro, or which would appreciate in value if the euro area collapsed: probably Germany. For any big corporate, it might make sense to denominate liabilities in lire and assets in DM, just on the off-chance of a break-up.

This phenomenon is what broke the fixed exchange rate between the Czech and Slovak crowns (which was not a genuine monetary union, since they did not pool foreign exchange reserves). It is already apparent in Canada, where there is a lower ratio of bank deposits to GDP in Quebec than in the rest of Canada, in part perhaps because depositors prefer the assurance of being paid in Canadian dollars rather than a separate Quebec currency. It is very difficult for banks to assure their depositors on this score: legal tender regulations generally redenominate one currency into another during a monetary change or reform.[1] In principle, these potential shifts in bank deposits could lead to substantial shifts in profitability as banks in, say, Frankfurt become deposit-rich while others have to rely on the inter-bank market or, *in extremis*, on official provision of liquidity on less attractive terms.

None of this could be enough to break EMU apart on economic grounds: the system is bullet proof in the sense that the European Central Bank will be committed to providing liquidity anywhere within its jurisdiction to maintain the policy interest rates it wants. However, the political strains could become serious if some parts of the area are being drained of bank deposits, and there is also a potentially embarrassing demand for particular denominations of the euro, notably German marks. These risks are real but are probably, in the light of the European Union's commitment to the project and tradition of shoring up common policies, very small.

Within the Eurozone, sovereigns will no longer have preferential access to foreign exchange, but they will continue to have different credit characteristics, just as the US states have in the US capital markets. Sovereigns with low tax pressure, low spending, a track record of low deficits, and a low public debt are self-evidently better risks than those without such advantages, as are sovereigns with a relatively buoyant and well diversified tax base. So sovereign ratings will continue to differ, but the focus of analysis will be even more on their fiscal accounts and less on their external accounts. Indeed, the external accounts will gradually, as the monetary union strengthens, become irrelevant. (The external accounts will only be relevant in assessing the sovereign ceiling of the whole Eurozone).

What will those sovereign ratings look like? Much heat has been generated by the debate between Standard and Poor's and Fitch-IBCA on one side, arguing that they should be more like the foreign currency ratings today, and Moody's on the other side, arguing that they should be more like the local currency ratings. In reality, each country has to be assessed on a case by case basis, and the ratings which are resulting from that process in each agency are in fact not very different.

The case for awarding AAA to all participants is just that they will all have the power to tax in the new currency, unfettered by serious restrictions, at least on income tax, although there are some bands for VAT and excises thanks to EU concerns about trade distortion. However, there is an unwritten but important constraint on taxation, which is simply that economic actors – corporates even more than individuals – can get up and move if a particular national tax system gets too out of line. This is becoming more important in Europe as mobility increases. It is already noticeable at local authority level, where tax competition has become a fact of life. It is likely to be particularly important where large population centres can easily purchase goods across borders and where products can be supplied easily by mail order or purchased through the Internet. Corporates may also find it easy to reincorporate in lower-tax areas of the Eurozone, a factor that has recently benefitted Ireland.

Moreover, the existing local currency ratings are also generally higher than foreign currency ratings because of a second advantage: the ability to monetize debt. The right to print the money to assure debt service is a privilege not accorded to sovereigns which have to service foreign currency debt, and nor will it be accorded to post-EMU participants. True, the central banks of all member states that are likely to participate are now nominally independent and would not monetize debt today, so there should not be a dramatic change, but we have been skeptical about that argument in the past. (See Figure 15.1 for a summary of public debt ratios.)

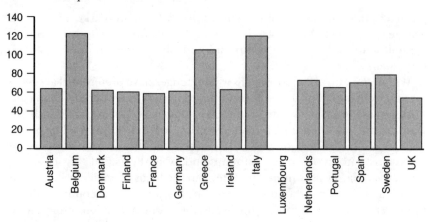

Figure 15.1 Public debt ratios as a percentage of GDP, end 1997

Source: OECD

What would the Banca d'Italia do if the Italian Treasury was faced with an investors' strike when it needed to roll over debt worth 4 per cent of GDP in one month, which is not so unusual? In theory, it would not lend the Treasury the money. In practice, it would probably indulge in open market operations to buy up the debt, and argue that it was merely smoothing disorderly markets and would be able to unwind the transaction soon afterwards. Nor need this type of liquidity support be inflationary, if it were subsequently possible for the Banca d'Italia to unwind its position by placing the bonds that it had bought. In any case, the option of substantial support in the market, ensuring timely debt service, has been one reason for rating Italy as AAA in local currency terms.

This liquidity support is particularly important for highly indebted sovereigns with high refinancing requirements: the extreme cases are Italy and Belgium. (See Figure 15.2.) Not only are their public debt to GDP ratios very high, but they also have a relatively high need to refinance short-term and medium-term debt coming due within one year. In the case of Italy, more than 29 per cent of the public debt is of such effective short maturities, representing a rollover requirement worth 35.6 per cent of GDP. (The monthly pattern of refinancing requirements over the year from May 1998 is shown in Figure 15.3, with a peak of 4 per cent of GDP requiring roll over in October 1998). In the case of Belgium, 26 per cent of the debt was coming due within the year, representing 32 per cent of GDP.

Until now, many of the holders of these countries' short term debt – insurers and banks – have effectively been locked into their national markets by virtue of their own need to match their liabilities and their assets in their own currency. After 1 January 1999, no such constraint will operate. The potential for a crisis of short-term funding will increase because investors will have a choice of competing sovereign issuers into

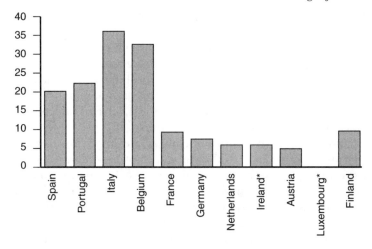

Figure 15.2 EMU members' short-term debt (general government debt maturing within the next 12 months) as a percentage of 1997 GDP

Source: national sources, or EMI*

whose paper they can now fly. Individual sovereigns can no longer rely on benefitting from a 'flight to quality' within their own currency. There will therefore be a substantial increase in the systemic risk posed by short-term debt within the new integrated European capital market.

The option of liquidity support – covert monetization, at least temporarily – may continue to be available to the European System of Central Banks: it is charged by the protocol setting out its objectives and functions with the promotion of 'the smooth operation of payments systems'. In addition, the Treaty itself says that 'The ESCB shall contribute to the smooth conduct of policies pursued by the competent authorities relating to the prudential supervision of credit institutions and the stability of the financial system' (Article 105(5)). These objectives might, with some legal legerdemain, be stretched to include the temporary support of

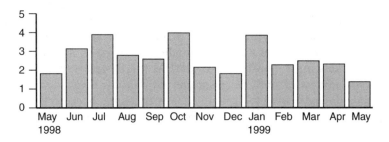

Figure 15.3 Italian short-term debt: amounts maturing in each month as a percentage of GDP

Source: Ministro del Tesoro

indigent member states via open market operations, since banks hold large amounts of government paper.

However, this is clearly not the intention, and monetization (or, more politely, liquidity support) would be substantially less easy in EMU. More direct forms of credit to the public sector are prohibited by Article 104, and each member state will only be able to count on one member on the council of the ECB. The independence of the ECB and the national central banks is explicitly guaranteed by Article 107 of the Treaty of European Union, and ECB council members are appointed for non-renewable terms of eight years, so that they are not beholden to anyone. Moreover, the ECB is likely to believe that any such support would be perceived as undermining its independence, its commitment to price stability, and hence its anti-inflationary credibility. Furthermore, there is an explicit no-bail-out clause which prohibits the Community from being liable for, or assuming the liabilities of, other public authorities, and also prohibits member states from doing the same.[2] In other words, the economic system definitely becomes less forgiving.

The high-debt countries – Belgium and Italy – argue that it will be easier to refinance their short-term debt because the market will be bigger and more liquid. Moreover, stress tests of substantial rises in short-term interest rates on their paper show that they could sustain a substantial financial price shock for a period. However there are times, even in big and liquid markets, when investors ration their purchases, and when rises in interest rates can send out signals which merely confirm market participants' desire to shun the paper rather than buy it. Markets like the short-term government paper market are particularly prone to this phenomenon, since they are markets in a close substitute for cash held in bank deposits. Investors want safety and liquidity above all else.

In these circumstances, markets may reach an equilibrium not by changing prices, but by becoming illiquid. A process of credit rationing can operate, particularly in the market for short-term paper. For this reason, it is common even for very well-rated borrowers in the United States markets to have back-up facilities for commercial paper programmes, without which a short-term rating will not be issued.[3] Yet neither Belgium nor Italy have yet stated that they intend to reduce their dependence on short-term financing, or that they have arranged any such back-up facility to deal with the eventuality of being shut out of the financial markets for a month or two. EMU is therefore likely to weaken the creditworthiness of both Belgium and Italy unless they undertake a programme of lengthening their maturities or arranging back-up facilities.

These liquidity concerns dominate the outlook for the high debt sovereigns, but if they are lifted the ratings of the high-debt countries could improve. There will undoubtedly be an improving solvency position for the high-debt countries, since the Maastricht Treaty (Article 104c) and the subsequent Stability and Growth Pact (Council Regulations nos 1466/97 and 1467/97 of 7 July 1997) commit member countries to a 'stability programme' which will normally entail a falling trend of public debt ratios. Notably, the member states will seek a 'medium term objective for the budgetary position of close to balance or in surplus' and will be subject to detailed Commission and Council of Ministers' surveillance about the prospects of doing so, including an examination of assumptions. The objective will be to ensure that they do not exceed the limit of 3 per cent public deficit to GDP even in recession years.

Partly because of these fiscal commitments and procedures, the nominal (and probably real) financing costs of even high-debt sovereigns are likely to fall even further. This in turn ensures that they will have some flexibility during the transition period, to ease discretionary public spending or taxation even while constraining their overall deficits. Alternatively, lower financing costs can be seen as a way of locking in the recent gains due to fiscal tightening to prepare for EMU. Figure 15.4 compares the interest savings for countries able to fund at the same rate as Germany – there will be some credit spreads added on here, of course, of maybe up to 100 bps for Italy – with the average rate over five years before the recent convergence of yields began in earnest. (The period taken is 1991 to 1995). In the case of Italy, for example, the anti-inflationary credibility of EMU is worth about 5 per cent of GDP in savings to its nominal interest costs.

There has been much commentary in the press about so-called 'fudges' to meet the convergence criteria, by member states anxious to participate, and there has indeed been a long list of special fiscal manoeuvres, almost all of which tend to reduce deficits and debt (the special France Telecom dividend, gold sales in Belgium, one-off taxes in Italy, changes in the basis of accounting from cash to accrual in Spain and so forth). However, these effects are in aggregate small, and are insignificant in assessing the sustainability of the fiscal positions of the member states. Indeed, the fiscal

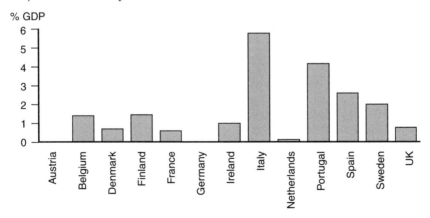

Figure 15.4 Reduced financing costs: estimated interest savings as a percentage of GDP

positions of Belgium and Ireland are already compatible with the provisions of the treaty on sustainability, while the progress made by other participants has been little short of dramatic.

The vast bulk of the fiscal consolidation necessary to meet the Treaty's objectives has been undertaken in all the southern European member states, as Table 15.1 shows. The first column calculates the fiscal balance required in each member state as a cyclical average, if that member state is to avoid breaching the 3 per cent deficit limit in a normal recession (defined as the average of the biggest gap between actual output and potential output recorded in that country between 1975 and 1997). This is the benchmark at which countries need to aim. The second column shows the OECD's estimate of the cyclically adjusted (or 'structural') budget balance in 1997: this is a measure of the deficit that would still exist if the economy were operating at full non-inflationary capacity. The third column shows the change in the structural balance required to attain the position in the first column. To put this further fiscal tightening into perspective, the fourth column shows the efforts that the country has already made to tighten its fiscal policy compared with its peak deficit. The year of the peak deficit is shown in the fifth column.

The overall message is that most of the fiscal consolidation in Europe has already been undertaken. In Italy, for example, a tightening worth a further 0.2 per cent of GDP is probably necessary, whereas the tightening so far since the Amato administration has been 9.5 per cent of GDP (admittedly including interest savings). This further tightening is insignificant: indeed, it is certainly within the margin of error of the calculation of

Table 15.1 Fiscal sustainability

	Fiscal balance req. to avoid 3% govt. deficit in recessions*	1997 structural general govt. balances (OECD)	Change in structural fiscal balance req. to attain 'stability pact-compatible' fiscal position	Change in structural fiscal balance recorded bet. 'peak' deficit and 1997	Year of 'peak' deficit
Germany	-1.6	-2.3	0.7	2.3	1991
France	-1.5	-1.8	0.3	2.5	1994
Italy	-2.1	-2.3	0.2	9.5	1990
Austria	-2.1	-2.3	0.2	2.3	1995
Belgium	-1.7	-1.4	-0.3	5.8	1991
Finland	-0.1	-1.2	1.1	2.2	1995
Greece	-2.1	-4.2	2.1	11.8	1990
Ireland	-1.1	-0.1	-1.0	9.5	1985
Netherlands	-1.9	-1.9	0.0	4.4	1990
Portugal	-1.1	-2.3	1.3	5.9	1991
Spain	-1.2	-1.6	0.4	5.4	1991

Note: * defined as average max. output gap recorded in recession 1975–97

the cyclically-adjusted deficit. Only three participating countries have significant fiscal tightening – of more than half a percent of GDP – still to come: Germany, Finland and Portugal. Even these are modest compared with what has already been done, in all cases save Finland.

However, these financial risks are not the only ones which must be considered in reassessing sovereign risks. Other risks of an economic rather than financial kind will be harder to tackle, and these affect countries such as Finland and Spain as well as Italy. The big question with EMU is whether a single monetary policy – a single exchange rate and interest rate – will be appropriate for all participants at least most of the time. This boils down to a question of whether these economies tend to move in tandem, or tend to have activity which is not correlated.

Much of the work in this area follows the results of an interesting study by Tamim Bayoumi and Barry Eichengreen (1992) on the extent to which demand or supply shocks over the period from 1962 to 1988 have affected different parts of the European economy in the same way. Their study was not comprehensive for all the likely member states. However, the International Monetary Fund (IMF 1997) recently undertook similar calculations, giving the correlation coefficients for each country's real GDP compared with the 'anchor' country, Germany. The data suggests that there is a reasonable degree of convergence between Germany, France and the Benelux but much less with Britain and southern Europe. (See Figure 15.5.)

It is important, though, to put this into context by looking at the degree of correlation in the demand or supply disturbances of regions in another big monetary union, the United States. (See Figure 15.6.) Here the anchor region is supposed to be the mid-east, and it can be seen that there is actually a greater degree of correlation between the anchor region and the most significant US regions than there is even in the core of the proposed

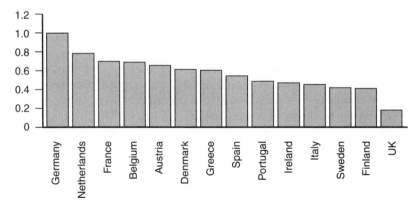

Figure 15.5 Does Europe share shocks?

Source: IMF 1997

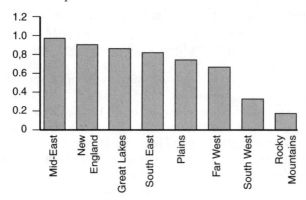

Figure 15.6 Do the United States share shocks?

Source: IMF 1997

EMU. However, it is also noticeable that three smaller US regions – the South East, South West and Rocky Mountain regions – have very little correlation with the supply shocks faced by the anchor core. Optimal currency area theory might suggest that they would benefit from a separate dollar and monetary policy if that were the only consideration.

Recent work by the OECD also suggests that fears about the inappropriateness of monetary policy in some participating countries – the critique that 'one size will have to fit all' – may be overplayed. The Bayoumi-Eichengreen and IMF works (Bayoumi and Eichengreen 1992, IMF 1997) look at correlations with a dominant 'anchor' area, which may be the appropriate basis for assessing the old European Monetary System. Correlations with the euro area as a whole have been closer, particularly during the period of German reunification.

There is another argument for a lack of concern about asymmetric shocks, which is that an independent monetary policy may not be a very useful or effective tool for dealing with them. Some proponents of monetary union have argued that most of Europe's experience is that devaluations of the exchange rate in nominal terms are very soon followed by rising domestic prices and wages, and hence the *real* exchange rate is rapidly left unchanged. That is particularly true for small open economies where much domestic expenditure goes on imports, and where devaluations therefore feed through very rapidly into prices. This is certainly the principal reason why European policy makers have historically tended to be in favour of fixed exchange rates: apart from the 1930s and the 1970s, modern European economic history is dominated by fixed systems of one sort or another. Once again, therefore, this argument may apply strongly to the smaller countries near to Germany.

However, it is surely hard to argue that nominal devaluations do not lead to real devaluations in the wake of the breakdown of the narrow bands of the exchange rate mechanism of the European Monetary System in 1992 and 1993. Britain, Italy and Spain all saw substantial falls in their real exchange rates. The inflationary impact of devaluations was much more muted than conventional econometric models had projected. (This in turn reflected the unusual degree of spare capacity which existed in those economies, and therefore the strong anti-inflationary competitive pressures.)

Therefore it can perhaps be tentatively concluded that the non-core countries – Ireland, Italy, Spain, Portugal, Finland – will be giving up a useful means of adjustment if they join EMU. Their response to shocks – either shifts in demand or supply – have to occur by means of price and wage changes, or labour and capital mobility, or fiscal transfers, rather than through a nominal exchange rate change which might speed up the real exchange rate change. In Canada, for example, the degree of real competitiveness (or real exchange rate) change between regions during the 1980s was as great as between countries in Europe, even though the Canadian regions shared a dollar (see Emerson and Huhne 1991).

Another key question is how effective are those other means of adjustment in Europe. The answer is mixed. There is limited room for fiscal manoeuvre at national level because of the commitment to the fiscal stability pact, and there is no mechanism for making transfers automatically to depressed regions through fiscal transfers. There is also surprisingly little labour mobility even within European countries, let alone between them.

The key factor is therefore wage flexibility, where the evidence is not encouraging. Judging a country's labour market institutions inevitably involves some subjectivity, but this is my judgement of how the peripheral members of the Eurozone fare. The small countries generally have flexible labour markets, not in the sense that it is necessarily easy to hire and fire, but in the sense that they react well and quickly to outside shocks, perhaps because they are small. Portugal, Finland and Ireland all have formal incomes policies which facilitate the setting of nominal wage increases in a non-inflationary and competitive manner. The problems are Italy and Spain, where labour market practices can be arcane, labour costs are relatively high, and unemployment has as a result been a serious problem, as Figure 15.7 shows.

The relative inflexibility of the labour market in Spain and Italy poses two types of risk post-EMU. The first is that unemployment may rise sharply in a recession, cutting tax revenues and boosting social security payments, thereby worsening the public finances. The second is that it may raise questionmarks about the sustainability of EMU membership itself. Until European labour markets have become more flexible, they will be an Achilles heel which could bring down the whole enterprise if they generate enough political tension.

In sum, therefore the post-EMU ratings from the participating sovereign states will draw some strengths from the existing local currency ratings.

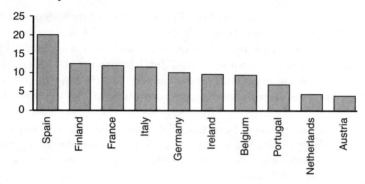

Figure 15.7 Unemployment rates as a percentage of the labour force, end-1997

Sovereigns will retain the power of taxation, if the tax burden is relatively low. Their finances may be reinforced because of the commitment to sound public finances, and the transparent and public surveillance procedures for ensuring them. Nevertheless, as we have seen, the post-EMU sovereign ratings also entail some of the weaknesses of the foreign currency rating, notably the lack of monetization and short-term liquidity support. Moreover, the changeover to an integrated Europe-wide capital market will increase the likelihood of liquidity problems for high-debt sovereigns. The removal of an adjustment mechanism which allows economies to respond to shocks will place the clear focus on labour market institutions and flexibility.

The environment for banks and corporates

In macroeconomic terms, the euro area is likely to be relatively stable. Simply because of aggregation, which means that one part of the economy can offset contrary effects in another, short-term interest rates are likely to be less volatile over long periods of time than they have been in individual member states. Given the exceptional independence of the European Central Bank – founded by international treaty rather than merely by national law – the goal of price stability is likely to be met in good faith. Indeed, the financial markets are already signalling their belief in the anti-inflationary credibility of the euro, since the ten-year bond yields of Germany and France are more than 60 basis points below those of the United States. Any short-term concerns about the weakness of the euro are therefore likely to be dispelled in time.

The early years of monetary union are likely to be favourable if the European economy can be insulated from Asian contagion. The upswing in the continental economies is already underway, and there is a margin of spare capacity to absorb before it hits constraints. In addition, the policy-makers at the European Central Bank are likely to set short-term interest rates nearer to the level appropriate for nurturing that recovery in

Germany and France than to an average of the short-term interest rates for the whole area. This means that there will be further falls in short-term interest rates still to come in the peripheral countries – at the time of writing in late 1998 for example, Italian three-month rates were still nearly 150 basis points higher than those in Germany – and that will in turn fuel growth in those countries. Further, as has been demonstrated, the bulk of the fiscal adjustment in the participating countries has now taken place. Therefore taxes no longer need to rise, and public spending can resume its growth in line with GDP, removing an important source of weak demand in the continental economies. In addition, there is the possibility that companies will anticipate the effects of monetary union by investing more, rather as they anticipated the effects of the single market at the end of the 1980s.

European domestic demand should therefore accelerate. However, there are some macroeconomic risks, notably for those companies reliant on trade outside the participating eleven member states. Europe begins to look very like the United States in all sorts of ways, including its relative immunity from shocks outside its borders. The European economy will increasingly resemble the US's continent-wide span. This has particular implications for the proportion of its GDP which is traded: Figure 15.8 shows that the share of external trade (exports plus imports halved) as a percentage of GDP in the Eurozone will fall from 23 per cent to 11.65 per cent, making its trade dependence look much more like that of the United States or Japan. This is going to be enough to make the members much less sensitive to changes in their nominal exchange rate, simply because it is likely to have much less significant effects on demand and supply than it does now. The European monetary authorities may begin to look on the yen–dollar–euro cross-rates rather as policy-makers in Washington and Tokyo do: with some insouciance. The implication is that the big cross-exchange rates between the major currencies may be more volatile. For European corporates with a heavy trade or investment dependence outside the Eurozone, this may mean a more volatile earnings stream and some increased credit risk.

Turning to the microeconomic impact of the introduction of the euro,

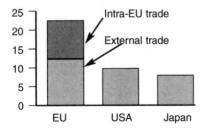

Figure 15.8 Trade as a percentage of GDP

it will clearly intensify sharply the competitive pressures at work in the European market. By making price comparisons much easier, consumers will be able to exert more market power and drive down the prices of manufacturers and service providers which have been able to shelter in niche national markets. The prices of significant consumer durables such as cars, washing machines and personal computers continue to diverge. The process of competition is also likely to put mounting pressure on the financial sector, where the Commission's evidence is that the divergence between the costs of standard banking operations has actually increased despite the single European market. Figure 15.9 shows the costs of a bank arrangement fee compared with the average of the European union, before and after the single market. One consequence will be a continuation of the strong trend towards the consolidation of European financial institutions as they attempt to reap scale economies.

Banks will come under pressure from the loss of their foreign exchange trading revenue from national currencies, and also from the likely loss of revenue from local debt trading. Local debt markets will no longer be segmented by the need of financial institutions to match national assets and liabilities in order to ensure that there is no open currency position. Instead, they will be able to diversify holdings throughout the Eurozone. This is likely to concentrate trading in a few important centres, to the disadvantage of small country banks with a strong local franchise at present.

The integration of the euro capital markets, however, will provide corporates with financial opportunities that have hitherto been denied them. Because investors will be able to diversify their portfolios over a much larger geographical area, they will also be able to put together

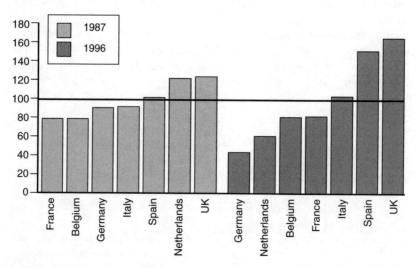

Figure 15.9 Costs of commercial loans in EU countries (as % of mean, 1987 and 1996)

substantial portfolios of higher-risk bonds while maintaining the same overall risk profile. This should increase the appetite for high-yield bonds. Indeed, the removal of higher yields on local currency instruments may also help to increase the appetite for higher-yielding instruments. Credit risk and liquidity risk become the only significant variables. These trends will in turn encourage further disintermediation from the banking sector, so that the European capital markets will increasingly come to resemble those in the United States (where mutual fund assets have just surpassed bank assets for the first time). As European governments also encourage private pension provision, the similarity is likely to become even greater.

The greater liquidity of the European capital markets may in turn become an attractive factor for official foreign currency reserve managers and others to increase their holdings of euro assets at the expense of the dollar. If this occurs, the rise in the euro real exchange rate may lead to greater competitive pressures on exporting companies.

It has been noted that short-term interest rates are likely to be less volatile because of the aggregation effect of EMU. A further consequence is that booms and busts in regions of EMU may the continue for prolonged periods until they work themselves out: there will be no separate interest rate or exchange rate to offset periods of irrational exuberance or despond. In this sense, the Eurozone will also resemble the United States, where the Massachusetts boom and bust and the Texas boom and bust are recent examples of more volatile regional activity than is usual in Europe. In theory, national regulatory authorities could use prudential regulation of their banking system (within the constraints of European law) to have similar effects to a local monetary policy. Capital requirements might, for example, be raised in countries undergoing a substantial and credit-driven property price explosion (as has been occurring recently in Dublin). However, regulators are very reluctant to develop in this direction, and any such variation would potentially put a country's credit institutions at a competitive disadvantage compared with others in the Eurozone which might move into the market.

In this context, it is therefore likely that banks' asset quality, particularly that of smaller institutions without regional diversification, may prove to be more vulnerable than at present. This longer-run trend is likely to be exacerbated during the early years of EMU by the intensification of structural change among companies, which will come about because of increased competition. It is often hard to predict how banks or companies will react to unexpected changes in their market environment, often after many years of relative stability. In this context, it would be surprising if there were not some high-profile and unexpected financial and corporate victims of the restructuring process.

This in turn puts a focus on the policy on bank rescues and support within the Eurozone. Hitherto this has been the responsibility of the separate member countries' central banks, regulatory authorities and finance ministries. In recent years, however, an increasing influence has been exerted by the EU competition authorities in the shape of the European Commission's DG IV, as has been particularly exemplified in the Crédit Lyonnais case. There is also a growing consensus among the authorities in all the G-10 countries that support of banks should be prompted by the necessity to preserve the smooth operation of national payment systems, and not by economic or political expediency. The most recent and most telling example of this was the unwillingness of the UK authorities to rush to the rescue of Barings plc in 1995. It has also become noticeable that central banks in these countries have not recently acted as 'lender of last resort' in cases of bank support; they have left attempts at this function to the state and have provided only liquidity support. There has been no regulatory forbearance of the sort conducted after the 1982 debt crisis.

The requirement of Article 3.1 of the European System of Central Banks (ESCB)/European Central Bank (ECB) Statute that the ESCB should, *inter alia*, 'promote the smooth operation of payment systems', and the requirement of Article 3.3 that it should 'contribute to the smooth conduct of policies pursued by the competent authorities relating to the prudential supervision of credit institutions and the stability of the financial system', have already been mentioned. This probably means that the ESCB will not countenance the failure of a bank, the sudden disappearance of which could endanger the 'smooth operation of payment systems' within the Eurozone. However, the ECB may also leave the actual support to the national financial authorities concerned, and confine itself to providing liquidity support against the required collateral. (The national central bank in question will no longer be able to provide such assistance independently.)

Although Article 104a of the Maastricht Treaty prohibits 'privileged access', or state financing which distorts markets, Article 2 of EU Council Regulation EC no. 3604/93 exempts such financing prompted by 'prudential considerations', or in other words, promotion of 'the soundness of financial institutions so as to strengthen the stability of the financial system as a whole and the protection of the customers of those institutions'. Thus, national governments will, in the circumstances supposed, be permitted to support banks, but such support may be less readily available than it has been in the past in some of the EMU member countries. There has been a considerable number of mergers in the Eurozone's banking sector in the run up to EMU. This process has been particularly remarkable in Italy, France and, for their size, in Belgium and the Netherlands. Such moves will strengthen the banks involved and make them better able to face the sorts of challenges arising from EMU that have been already touched on. However, they will not eliminate the possibility of bank collapses.

National considerations will not be as significant as they were, but national politics will, nevertheless, still have a considerable part to play. It is difficult to believe that even the smaller members of EMU will be prepared to countenance the elimination of their most important banks: they will no doubt use all the somewhat limited powers available to them and all their political wiles to prevent it. But, in certain imaginable circumstances, they might have to accept the demise of banks that are not attractive as merger or acquisition candidates; in some cases this could result in politically uncomfortable losses by depositors who are not fully covered by the national insurance schemes obligatory in the EU.

Summary of key points

- Until now, each country's rating for foreign currency debt has also been a ceiling for the ratings of entities based in that country, because sovereigns have had potentially preferential access to foreign currency. From 1 January 1999, sovereigns will no longer have preferential access to foreign exchange. It is therefore important to draw a distinction between the rating of the sovereign issuer – its default risk – and the risk that any entity will be unable to transfer funds to an international investor because of a lack of foreign exchange available to the economy. All the major credit rating agencies will therefore assess the ceiling rating for the whole area – representing transfer risk – separately from the rating of government bond issues.
- The ceiling rating for the whole area will be AAA for all three major agencies (Standard and Poor's, Moody's and Fitch-IBCA) reflecting the Eurozone's net creditor status, diversified foreign exchange earnings, deep markets and strong liquidity position. The risks of a break-up of EMU, with some weaker member states leaving the system, are so small as to be encapsulated within the AAA rating category. However, an increase in social and political strains within the system could lead to the reintroduction of a sovereign ceiling rating below AAA for member states whose participation appears to be at risk.
- Because entities in the Eurozone will suffer negligible transfer risk in paying debt service to international investors, and will therefore be subject to a AAA transfer risk ceiling, there will be no distinction between local and foreign currency ratings. (Local currency ratings rate debt issued in local currency and payable within the jurisdiction of the sovereign; foreign currency ratings apply to foreign-currency-denominated debt payable outisde the sovereign's jurisdiction in, say, London or New York.) Only one set of ratings will be published from 1 January 1999 within the Eurozone.
- The focus of sovereign analysis will increasingly be fiscal (budget deficits, financing requirements, public debt levels and public debt service relative to revenue and GDP) rather than the balance of payments (total public and private external debt service to exports, export growth, reserves and current account balance). Other

important criteria will be the ability to withstand shocks that would single that country out from the rest of the euro area, and the vulnerability of the structure of government debt to refinancing risk.

- The solvency position of European sovereign states is underpinned by the Maastricht Treaty and by the Growth and Stability Pact targets for low deficits and falling debt ratios. In the medium term, therefore, sovereign ratings should improve towards AAA.

- However, the short-term risks of a sovereign liquidity crisis increase for two reasons. First, investors no longer have an incentive to hold their own government's paper in a crisis: a flight to quality may result in a flight out of one government's paper and into another's, because investors will for the first time have a choice of competing sovereigns in their own currency. Second, each government will no longer be in a position to encourage its central bank to support its paper in the market. As a result, an important liquidity support for sovereigns is removed just as the liquidity risks increase. The practical consequences of these changes are that the most highly indebted sovereigns – Italy and Belgium – will become more vulnerable. They should lengthen maturities, reducing short-term debt, or arrange back-up facilities.

- Policy on bank rescues – the lender of last resort function – is opaque and is likely to remain so. However, it is clear that ultimate liability will devolve on national fiscal authorities, and that this may make bank rescues less likely for second-rank banks. There will be a perceptible change, indicating lower support probabilities, because support will have to be fiscalized immediately. Regulatory forbearance – the response to the banking crisis of 1992 following Mexico's default – will be less of an option.

EMU's effects on the economic environment for corporates and banks

- EMU will gradually increase the competitive pressure on European banks and corporates by making prices easy to compare. Margins will suffer, and consolidation to take advantage of economies of scale will be essential. Entities which are slow to react to this new environment will see ratings downgrades.

- Banks will be particularly affected by EMU because of the substantial difference in their prices for simple financial products, their loss of foreign exchange revenue, and in many cases their loss of revenue from local debt market trading.

- Because of the lack of separate interest and exchange rates for different parts of the union, countries are likely to undergo booms and busts (like the Massachusetts and Texas booms and busts in the US over the last twenty years). The first such asset price boom is under way in Ireland.

- Companies which earn a lot of revenue from outside the euro area will need to hedge fully if they are not to suffer greater earnings volatility. The euro–dollar–yen cross rates are likely to be more volatile, because policy makers will care less about the exchange rate: the tradeable sector will be smaller and imports will be a less significant source of inflationary pressure.

Notes

1 Although a bank could specify to its depositors that it intended to continue to pay euro on a particular account, it would presumably also have to find borrowers prepared to make a similar commitment if it was not to have the potential for a mismatched balance sheet.
2 Article 104b states:

> The community shall not be liable for or assume the commitments of central governments, regional, local or other public authorities, other bodies goverend by public law, or public undertakings of any member state, without prejudice to mutual financial guarantees for the joint execution of a specific project.

3 See for example Fitch-IBCA 1998.

Bibliography

Fitch-IBCA (1998) 'Rating Corporate Commercial Paper', Fitch-IBCA (April).

Bayoumi, T. and Eichengreen, B. (1992) 'Shocking Aspects of European Monetary Unification', *Discussion Paper no. 643*, Centre for Economic Policy Research, London.

IMF (1997) *World Economic Outlook*, International Monetary Fund, Washington, D.C. (October).

Emerson, M. and Huhne, C. (1991) *The Ecu Report*, London.

16 Prospects for the exchange rate of the euro

Robert N. McCauley

With the imminent introduction of the euro, much discussion has focussed on the prospects for the exchange rate of the euro. In particular, how will the euro trade against the dollar? In the foreign exchange market, the dollar/euro rate will surely represent the busiest pair of currencies in the world (Table 16.1). At almost two-fifths of all trading, it looks set to claim a share twice as large as the US dollar/Deutschmark pair *had*, and twice as large as the US dollar/yen *has*. Consistent with its importance in terms of transactions, this exchange rate will prove an important determinant of the performance of investments denominated in the euro and euro-based currencies relative to those denominated in the dollar and dollar-based currencies. Like all exchange rates, however, changes in the dollar/euro rate will affect not only the performance of investments, but also the relative prices of exports sourced in Europe on the one hand, and the Western hemisphere on the other hand. Thus, changes in the dollar/euro rate can be expected to shift global demand from one continent to another with unparalleled force.

Any prospective analysis of a currency which was still at the time of writing in the planning stages, whether by academic economists, those in

Table 16.1 Foreign exchange turnover by currency pair and the euro in April 1998 on the hypothesis of the euro's existence

Currency pair	Turnover (US$ billions/day)	Percentage
US dollar/euro	540.8	38.8
US dollar/yen	266.6	19.1
US dollar/sterling	117.7	8.4
US dollar/Swiss franc	78.6	5.6
US dollar/Canadian dollar	50.0	3.6
US dollar/Australian dollar	42.2	3.0
All other pairs	297.6	21.4
Total	1,393.5	100

Source: BIS

policy jobs or in the private sector, runs obvious risks. This paper surveys the questions that have been posed, provides an account of the argumentation, and in some cases offers tentative answers.

It considers the response of three classes of portfolio managers, official reserve asset managers, private asset managers and public and private liability managers, during (at least) three phases of monetary union: the period which covered the irrevocable fixing of conversion rates between existing European currencies and the euro, the period before the European Central Bank has consolidated its credibility, and the steady state beyond that. Monetary union itself carries three important changes: it eliminates exchange risk, creates much broader financial markets and introduces a new central bank with credible antecedents but no independent reputation. Such a mixture, with three actors, three stages and three transformations, leaves plenty of room for reasonable disagreement.

To help assess what the euro might mean for the dollar, a two-drawer toolkit is employed. First, the determination of the exchange rate is approached as a price that balances the demand for and supply of financial assets denominated in different currencies (Branson and Henderson 1985). These assets are taken to be imperfect substitutes, so that their supplies and demands affect the exchange rate. Still, the quantitative impact of substantial portfolio shifts can be fairly subtle.

Another drawer in the toolkit is an empirical regularity, rather than theory. The observation, first made in the late 1970s (Brown 1979), is that when the Deutschmark weakens against the dollar, most other European currencies also fall against the dollar, but strengthen a little against the Deutschmark. Conversely, when the dollar falls against the Deutschmark, it also falls against most other European currencies, but in lesser measure, so that they fall somewhat against the Deutschmark.[1] Figure 16.1 shows the estimated coefficients from a regression of the percentage change in the dollar exchange rates of eleven currencies on the percentage changes in the dollar/DM exchange rate, estimated in a sliding window of 125 working days. An observation near one means that a currency moves with the DM, while an observation near zero means that it moves with the dollar. Typically, the currencies of Germany's neighbours – and more recently the escudo and the peseta – track the DM quite closely, while sterling, the Italian lira and the Swedish krona share half or more of the DM's movements.

In the discussion that follows, the first organizing principle is time. A separate section for each of the three periods assesses the effect of the behaviour of private investors and central banks (and global liability managers in the steady state) on the level of the dollar's exchange rate.

The transition period

By the summer of 1998, European policymakers had answered many of the questions whose resolution, only months before, had seemed to have great

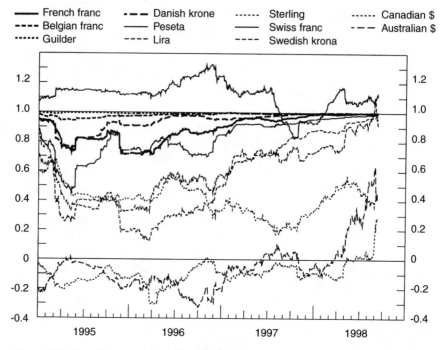

—— French franc	‑ ‑ ‑ Danish krone	······ Sterling	······ Canadian $
‑‑‑‑ Belgian franc	—— Peseta	—— Swiss franc	‑ ‑ Australian $
······ Guilder	‑‑‑‑ Lira	‑‑‑‑ Swedish krona	

Figure 16.1 Sensitivity to movements in the mark against the dollar

Note: Each point represents an estimated elasticity derived as the parameter β in the regression $\log X/\$_t - \log X/\$_{t-1} = \alpha + \beta(\log DM/\$_t - \log DM/\$_{t-1})$ over the current and previous 125 working days. By definition, the DM/$ sensitivity to itself is unity, and that of the dollar is zero.

Source: Datastream

potential to roil markets. The choice of the eleven initial participant countries in monetary union and of the six initial members of the ECB's board did not move market prices. The choice of members confirmed expectations which had firmed up as long ago as the early summer of 1997. The broad membership reduced the importance of the question of the nature of the exchange rate mechanism linking the euro and other currencies, in that only Greece wanted to be part of such an arrangement. The muted reaction to the less anticipated '50 per cent solution' to the Franco-Dutch difference over who should head the ECB suggested that market participants were not shocked at the sight of politicians weighing in.

Thus by mid-1998 monetary union had the look of a done deal. Nevertheless, important portfolio and policy questions remained. International holders of DM bank deposits were about to experience the disappearance of the DM, and those holding French and Belgian francs, lire, guilder, and pesetas would no longer need separate balances to make payments in these currencies. Moreover, the attitude of the European authorities toward the foreign exchange value of the euro was still an unknown.

Private asset managers

Private deposits might be shifted toward the dollar in this transition period. This possibility gains plausibility from one reading of the distribution of bank deposits across the currencies to be melded into the euro (Table 16.2). While Germany accounts for about a third of the GDP of the Eurozone, DM deposits represent almost half of international deposits held in the euro's predecessor currencies. It should be recalled that returns on a number of the participating currencies have in recent years exceeded those on DM deposits. If these balances are interpreted as investments, then they would seem to have a defensive character, seeking stability of principal rather than income. The portfolio bias toward the DM

Table 16.2 International holdings of bank deposits at end-1997

Currency	Residence of holder							
	European Union countries				Rest of the world		Total	
	Euro area		Other					
	US$ billion	%	US$ billion	%	US$ billion	%	US$ billion	%
Euro area currencies	200.9	100.0	93.1	100.0	165.5	100.0	459.5	100.0
Deutschmark	109.4	54.5	37.3	40.1	72.4	43.7	219.1	47.7
French franc	21.7	10.8	9.8	10.5	28.4	17.2	59.9	13.0
Italian lira	20.1	10.0	19.6	21.1	14.3	8.6	54.0	11.7
Dutch guilder	18.2	9.1	5.6	6.0	15.6	9.4	39.4	8.6
Belgian/ Luxembourg franc	11.3	5.6	9.9	10.6	17.3	10.5	38.5	8.4
Spanish peseta	6.9	3.4	5.2	5.6	5.7	3.4	17.8	3.9
ECU	11.4	5.7	3.1	3.3	9.9	6.0	24.4	5.3
Other[1]	1.9	0.9	2.6	2.8	1.9	1.2	6.4	1.4
Other EU currencies	30.0	14.9	8.1	8.7	88.4	53.4	126.5	27.5
Pound sterling	28.7	14.3	2.7	2.9	87.3	52.7	118.7	25.8
Other[2]	1.3	0.6	5.4	5.8	1.1	0.7	7.8	1.7
Total EU currencies	230.9	114.9	101.2	108.7	253.9	153.4	586.0	127.5
US dollar	158.1	78.7	122.3	131.4	470.9	284.5	751.3	163.5
Japanese yen	20.3	10.1	31.6	33.9	28.9	17.5	80.8	17.6
Swiss franc	23.1	11.5	5.5	5.9	32.7	19.8	61.3	13.3
Grand total	432.4	215.2	260.6	279.9	786.4	475.2	1,479.4	321.9

Note: Non-banks' holdings only; holdings abroad of a given currency by residents of the country of issue (for example, German residents' DM holdings in Luxembourg) are excluded. Only the cross-border position in domestic currency is available for Austria, Denmark, Finland, Ireland, Spain and Sweden. Portugal and Greece do not report banking data to the BIS, but cross-border liabilities to non-banks resident in Portugal are included in euro area holdings, and those to non-banks resident in Greece are included in other EU holdings.

1   Austrian schilling, Irish pound and Finnish markka.
2   Danish krone and Swedish krona.

Source: BIS

could evidence a risk aversion that might lead to shifts from DMs to dollars in the transition.

An alternative reason for the bias toward the DM, however, suggests less of a portfolio shift than a reduction of holdings. The DM has played the role of a key currency in Europe, and the bias toward holding of DM deposits could reflect this role. The 1995 survey of foreign exchange turnover showed that the DM was on one side in almost every exchange of one European currency for another (US$ 140 billion per day out of US$ 150 billion per day). Thus a corporate treasury with payments to make in francs, guilder and pesetas might well hold DMs which could cheaply be exchanged for any one of these. Instead of evidence of a bias in investment demand, disproportionate holdings of DMs represent on this interpretation the ease with which DMs can be transformed into transactions balances in other European currencies.

If deposits in the euro's predecessor currencies are transaction balances, one can estimate the reduction in their holdings that will result from the euro. The basic result here is that of Baumol (1952): the transaction demand for money rises with the square root of spending. Thus when a variety of currencies merge into one currency, transaction balances at banks will decline.[2] Honohan (1984) analyses the opposite case, the increase in money demand that followed the split of the Irish pound from pound sterling. For instance, spending of US$ 16 million in one currency and US$ 9 million in another would lead to money balances proportion to the sum of their square roots, US$ 7 million. In a single currency, however, the transaction demand would be proportional to the square root of the sum of spending, or US$ 5 million, a reduction of two-sevenths. Applying this logic to the aggregate holdings on Table 16.2, one might see transactions demand fall from US$ 460 billion to US$ 240 billion. The logic does not strictly apply to an aggregate, however, so that this almost halving of demand can be taken to be an upper bound on the reduction. (Note that the bias toward the DM tends to limit the shrinkage of money balances with the euro.) If this transaction perspective is correct, the funds released by smaller holdings of euro would be more likely to be distributed over the whole of the portfolio than shifted into dollars.

Central banks

Official reserve holdings of non-industrial countries show the same bias as private portfolios toward the DM, and similar behaviour might be anticipated (Table 16.3). Note that a transaction motive would not seem to account for the concentration of DM holdings in non-industrial country official reserves, in so far as these currencies trade predominantly against the dollar (Galati 1998: 35).

Central banks in the euro area face particular incentives to shift into dollars (or sterling or yen) in the transition period. Their holdings of DMs (and French francs and ECUs), amounting to about US$ 100 billion, will

Table 16.3 Composition of non-industrial country reserves, in billions of US
dollars and percentages, at end-1996

Currency	Developing countries	of which: Taiwan	Eastern Europe	Total	Memo item: global total
US dollar	531.9	50.6	34.1	566.0	1,041.5
	71.5%	57.5%	51.0%	69.8%	68.6%
Japanese yen	60.8	13.0	0.0	60.8	105.3
	8.2%	14.8%	0.0%	7.5%	6.9%
Core EU currencies	101.0	20.3	31.2	132.2	303.6
	13.6%	23.1%	46.7%	16.3%	20.0%
Of which:					
Deutschmark	87.1	20.3	30.5	117.6	246.1
	11.7%	23.1%	45.6%	14.5%	16.2%
French franc	10.1	0.0	0.7	10.8	23.2
	1.4%	0.0%	1.1%	1.3%	1.5%
Dutch guilder	3.8	0.0	0.0	3.8	5.1
	0.5%	0.0%	0.0%	0.5%	0.3%
Pound sterling	36.4	0.0	0.9	37.3	52.1
	4.9%	0.0%	1.3%	4.6%	3.4%
Swiss franc	13.9	4.0	0.7	14.6	15.4
	1.9%	4.6%	1.1%	1.8%	1.0%
Total	744.0	88.0	67.0	810.9	1,517.8
	100.0%	100.0%	100.0%	100.0%	100.0%

Note: Developing countries include Hong Kong and Taiwan. Taiwan's disclosed dollar
share as of April 1996 is applied to end-1996 holdings; disclosed shares of yen,
marks and Swiss francs as of August 1995 are reduced proportionately to accommodate the (higher)US$ share of April 1996. Core EU currencies include holdings
of private ECUs. Dollar reserves of developing countries are reduced by the
current value of the Brady bond collateral held at the Federal Reserve Bank of New
York and by advance payments for US military exports as reported in the *Treasury
Bulletin.* The reserve composition of Eastern European countries is estimated. The
global total includes industrial countries.

Sources: Hong Kong Monetary Authority, BIS *Annual Report* 1996, Central Bank of China as
reported in *Reuters*, 6 June 1996, US Treasury *Bulletin*, March 1997, Table IFS-2, IMF,
and BIS estimates.

become domestic euro assets with the arrival of the euro, and some may
wish to sustain their international reserve holdings by converting DMs into
dollars. Several considerations will however work to limit these shifts. Only
dollars (or yen) can be used in the initial reserve pooling, which will be for
39.5 billion euros equivalent, split into 85 per cent foreign exchange and
15 per cent gold. At the same time, no European central bank needs to buy
dollars to have enough to earmark for the ECB. Some European central
banks may foresee excess foreign exchange reserves in the long run (an
issue discussed later in this paper) and permit the conversion of reserves
into domestic assets with equanimity.

Early years of the ECB

In this second phase, extending from the inception of the euro at least until the disappearance of the former national banknotes and coins (scheduled for 2002), the ECB will refine its operating procedures, build an independent record with regard to the maintenance of stable prices, and give evidence of its exchange rate policy. Much of the discussion of this period centres on whether the ECB will pursue a tough interest rate policy, or will react with unusual vigour to a weakening of the euro against the dollar. At the same time, other uncertainties could arise: interest and exchange rates could show volatility, as the ECB and market participants grope for a common understanding of policy targets and instruments and their nuances.

Private asset managers

Private asset managers could shift funds into the euro upon demonstration of, or indeed in anticipation of, a firm interest rate and strong currency policy on the part of the ECB. The European Commission (1997b: 9) casts doubt on 'an often heard argument . . . that the ECB would attempt to establish early counter inflation credibility by adopting a tight monetary policy stance' on the grounds that 'there is . . . no reason to assume that the Bank will not enjoy counter inflation credibility from the outset'. The former Bundesbank chief economist, now chief economist for the ECB, dismissed as a 'nice idea' the notion that the new ECB would pursue a particularly restrictive policy despite high unemployment in Europe.[3] It will probably be very difficult even after the fact to know whether the ECB has shown a bias towards firm rates.[4]

With respect to exchange rate policy, one can debate how much European monetary policy will respond to exchange rate movements in the steady state, but several considerations suggest that the ECB might put considerable weight on the exchange rate in its early years. Were the euro to weaken in this period, not only financial market participants but also domestic wage and price setters would look to the ECB's reaction for evidence bearing on its credibility. Put another way, the first 'referendum' on the ECB could be conducted in the foreign exchange market and the authorities might respond vigorously, whatever the cyclical circumstances.[5]

At the time of this writing, the danger of such an acute dilemma for European policy makers seems less than it once did. With the European economies accelerating, and the US economy possibly decelerating, many market participants anticipate that business cycle developments will lend support to the DM/euro against the dollar. The uncertainties surrounding the ramifications of the strains in Asia, however, mean that some such dilemma cannot be ruled out.

Central banks

The introduction of the euro will make it easier for central banks to invest in the world's second-largest reserve currency. Until recently, the Bundesbank's opposition to short-term finance has kept the German finance ministry from floating part of its debt as treasury bills. As a result, many risk-averse central banks were denied their natural investing habitat of short-term government bills, and with some discomfort had to deposit their DM reserves with banks. Some central banks used bond futures to shorten the duration on holdings of German government bonds or currency forwards to convert US Treasury bills into synthetic DM bills. However, by no means all central banks are able and willing to employ such strategies.

Whatever the debt management policy of the German government, the other triple-A governments in the Eurozone will ensure a supply of euro-denominated treasury bills that is ample enough to satisfy all central bank demands. Central banks should probably not be expected to reallocate their portfolios abruptly in January 1999, in response to this new menu item in the world's second-largest reserve currency, but this could make it easier for central banks, particularly in emerging markets, to diversify into the euro thereafter.

Summary

The early years of the ECB may see portfolio reflows towards the euro. Private market participants may anticipate a tilt towards a firmer interest rate policy and a bias against euro depreciation in a period in which the ECB is consolidating its credibility. Central banks will enjoy in short order the opportunity to invest in a liquid market for high-quality treasury bills denominated in the euro. Monetary policy operations conducted in a variety of markets may of necessity adopt a rate-setting procedure that avoids leaving private market participants guessing at the ECB's intentions, with implications for money market volatility and knock-on effects in the bond market and foreign exchange market. Still, the inevitable process of defining in practice the new central bank's foreign exchange policy could prove a source of market volatility.

Toward the steady state

The steady state role of the euro in relation to the dollar and yen is a subject that attracts more attention than it produces consensus. In the early 1970s, at the beginning of the period of general floating, Triffin (1973: 78) foresaw that the 'Community's unit of account would also be likely to be used more and more, in lieu of the Eurodollar, in private lending and borrowing operations'. But a generation later, 'The surprise in this history is that . . . there was no general revulsion against lending in depreciating dollars . . . The world stayed with the dollar as a limping standard *faute de mieux*' (Kindleberger 1996: 187–8).[6] The '640-billion-euro' question is whether the euro, offering a more heavyweight alternative to the 'limping standard', will attract a large net portfolio shift from the dollar.

In the steady state, four slowly evolving developments could bear on the level and volatility of the dollar. First, the increase in the liquidity of the financial markets denominated in euros could lead private portfolio managers to shift assets from the dollar and into the euro. Second, the same structural change in European financial markets could lead central banks to reduce their heavy weight of the dollar in their foreign exchange reserves in favour of the euro. Indeed, the large size of the euro area could lead to a wider use of the euro as an anchor for the exchange rates of smaller countries, the third development discussed in this paper. Many analysts stop here and conclude that the euro will attract large net portfolio shifts from the dollar. However, more liquid euro financial markets and more anchoring to the euro can change the choice of currency denomination by debt managers, the fourth development discussed here.

Private asset managers

There is little disagreement that the introduction of the euro will create broader, deeper and more liquid financial markets in Europe. Observers differ, however, on the prospects for an integrated government bond market in the euro area. A full discussion of these prospects can be found in McCauley and White (1997). The briefer review given here first highlights the size of the euro money market and swap market, demonstrating that these markets in euros will bulk large in comparison with their counterparts in dollars and yen. It then summarizes the evidence bearing on the prospects for an integrated government bond market in Europe.

Ranging from an overnight rate, which will be strongly affected by the monetary policy operations of the ECB, to interbank rates for placements lasting from one week to one or two years, a single reference money market yield curve for euros can be expected. Its liquidity, as measured by derivatives transactions, will surpass that of the yen money market. A considerable gap will remain between the US$ 40 trillion per year turnover (in 1996) in euro futures and forwards, and the corresponding volume of dollar transactions, which exceed US$ 100 trillion.

At longer maturities, the most frequently used private interest rates will be the yields on the fixed rate side of interest rate swaps. These standard and liquid prime-name rates extend from two years out to ten years in maturity, and already serve as the most important private reference rates in today's bond markets. Swap yields for contracts in Belgian francs, Deutschmarks, Dutch guilders, French francs, Spanish pesetas and Italian lire have converged over the past two years (See Figure 16.2). At the introduction of the euro, the now nearly identical swap curves will collapse into one single swap curve. This private capital market in euros is also likely to be a very liquid market from its inception. On current evidence, even a narrow monetary union would offer a swap market about as active as those in the dollar and yen, with something like US$ 5 trillion per year in transactions. Even if it is recognized again that convergence trades are providing a temporary boost to European transactions, the euro looks set to offer a private yield curve with world-class depth, breadth and liquidity.

Those who argue that the government bond market in euros will be fractured, point to the municipal bond market in the United States, where different states' bonds offer different yields as a result of widely differing credit standings and tax rates.[7] European bond market pricing and ratings, however, seem consistent with the development of nearly uniform valuations for certain European governments' bonds, which could then be interchangeably delivered into a futures contract (McCauley 1996). Until quite recently, the gap between the nearly identical swap rates and the Dutch, French and German government bond yields was nearly the same in the three markets. Never in the history of the swap market had this spread been so similar, for so long, across so many markets.[8] This observation suggests that the euro-denominated debt of these governments could trade with nearly identical yields. Furthermore, major rating agencies assign the same top rating to the debts of Austria, France, Germany and the Netherlands (See Cantor and Packer 1996). Market participants want, and thoroughgoing integration would require, European treasuries to cooperate in establishing common market practices and conventions (European Commission 1997a, Dammers 1997). Joint auctions would not be necessary to build large benchmark issues; instead European treasuries could simply match each other's terms, in effect 'reopening' each other's issues. The potential benefit of integrated trading is evident when one considers that transactions in exchange-traded futures and options on German, French and Italian bonds amounted to a face value of over US$ 20 trillion in 1996, well above the US $16 trillion of such transactions based on US Treasury securities or the US$ 14 trillion based on Japanese government bonds. At the time of this writing, it appears most likely that the German government bond and its associated futures contract will emerge as the benchmarks for the European bond market, but a more inclusive futures contract might yet do more for the liquidity of the market.

The more integrated the government bond market in euros is, the more liquidity and depth should improve. Both European residents and foreign investors could enjoy narrower bid–offer spreads, an ability to buy or sell larger amounts with no price effect, a richer array of instruments and deeper repurchase markets. The euro bond market might be served by two active futures contracts, one at the medium term and the other at the long

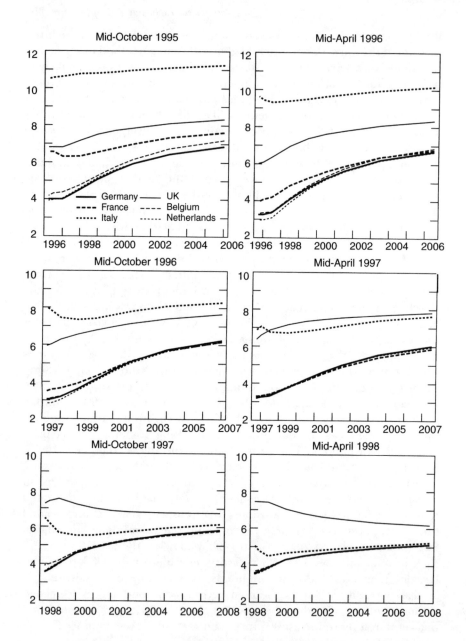

Figure 16.2 Private interest rates in Europe in per cent per annum

Note: The yield curves are based on eurodeposit rates and, for longer horizons, on swap (midpoint) yields

Sources: Datastream, Reuters and BIS

term, as the US bond market now uniquely features (Jeanneau 1996). Foreign investors might come to enjoy trading opportunities in all major time zones, similar to those now available to holders of US Treasuries.

Portes and Rey (1998) have put forward an ingenious argument linking structural change in European financial markets to the international roles of the euro, dollar and yen. Essentially, they claim that if the European government bond market becomes as cheap to use as the US Treasury market, then the former could attract funds looking for a temporary resting place in the course of effecting international trade and portfolio transactions, and the euro could displace the dollar to some extent as the vehicle currency in the foreign exchange market. The respective roles of the euro and the dollar simultaneously reflect and determine the costs of using markets. Even if the argument does not convince, it can change the way one thinks about the problem.

The first response to this argument must be that the premise that the European government bond market will become as cheap to use as the US market is, as the authors acknowledge, unlikely. The preceding argument has sketched an optimistic view of the effect of structural change in European financial markets resulting from the arrival of the euro, but at best the costs of using the European government bond market can be expected to approach from above the costs of using the US Treasury market. Without a federal borrower that refinances all the national governments' debts (or joint and several liability of the national governments), it is unlikely that the European government bond market can match the low costs of using the US Treasury market. The authors dangle the benefits of this unlikely scenario in order to argue for a Bank-of-England-style promotion of the euro market, instead of the more distant Continental approach to financial market development.

While the conception of the argument is a wow, the execution is often an ouch. The benefits to Europe of the unlikely outcome seem overstated. The promised flow benefit of 0.2 per cent of the Eurozone's GDP is much larger than the gain in seigniorage to Europe if global cash holdings were to shift from dollars to euros. It is hard to see how this amount could largely represent savings on the real costs of transacting in the European government bond market. The authors cite turnover of US$46 trillion in European government bonds, and a bid–ask spread of four basis points. If the dealer shows a bid–ask spread of four basis points, then the resource cost of each transaction can be taken to be two basis points: it takes two transactions for the dealer to get the bid–ask spread. If the bid–ask spread were squeezed to zero, then US$ 9 billion of savings would result from the US$ 46 trillion (.0002 x US$ 46 trillion). If the Eurozone's output is worth about US$ 10 trillion, a tenth of a per cent is over US$ 10 billion. Of course, under the authors' hypothesis, there would be more transactions (many by non-Europeans), but the welfare gain on transactions induced by a narrower bid–ask spread would not be the entire reduction of the spread.

It is hard to see how the benefits add up to the amounts proposed.[9] That said, the authors' basic message is correct: the role of the euro will depend on the extent of the financial market changes to which it gives rise.

In considering the consequences of such changes for possible shifts by private portfolio managers into the euro, a difficult question arises as to whether interest rates in a large euro bond market might show a smaller correlation with US bond yields than is displayed by current European government bond rates.[10] This is an interesting question because private portfolio managers would find the euro bond market particularly attractive if it were to offer diversification benefits superior to anything available in the constituent bond markets. Large size and investor diversity could provide ballast to a European bond market now exposed to spillovers from New York (Borio and McCauley 1996a, 1996b; Domanski and Neuhaus 1996).[11] However, the trend towards higher correlations across European bond markets in recent years has not to date brought any diminution of the correlation between the German and US markets.

Greater liquidity and depth could increase demand for bonds denominated in euros relative to the total demand for bonds in the constituent currencies, but the scope for a potential reallocation of private portfolios from the dollar to the euro is necessarily extremely conjectural. One starting-point is provided by the shares across G-10 currencies of GDP, trade, foreign exchange reserves and international assets, including both international bank deposits and international bonds (See Figure 16.3). The G-10 members of the European Union produce about one-third of G-10 output and would show a slightly smaller share of international trade net of their EU trade. After a similar consolidation, however, the share of international assets denominated in euros would be only about one-eighth of the G-10 total. For the euro share to match the output and trade shares of the G-10 members of the European Union would require a shift of some US$ 0.7 trillion. This figure should not be taken too seriously; the calculation ignores the non-resident holdings of one-quarter of US Treasury securities and also the non-resident holdings of about a third of German public bonds. The figure serves to make the important point that shifts in private portfolios could prove to be much larger than any possible shifts in official reserves. Similar figures are produced on the back of different envelopes by Bergsten (1997a) and Thygesen *et al.* (1995: 135).

Central banks

Two hypotheses about the diversification of official reserves away from the dollar by non-industrial countries may provide an indicative range. If non-oil developing countries – admittedly a heterogeneous group, but the lack of available data constrains the discussion here – were to follow Taiwan's example in its diversification of the last ten years by increasing their portfolio weight on core Europe to 25 per cent, about US$ 50 billion could be

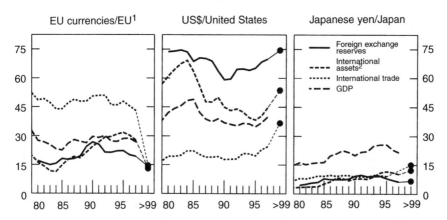

Figure 16.3 The international role of the euro, dollar and yen: currency and
country shares, in percentages

Notes: EU = the European Union. Hypothetical shares beyond 1999 are computed by
netting out from most recent observations, respectively EU holdings of EU currency
reserves, EU holdings of EU currency bank assets and EU issuers' bonds/notes in
G-10 EU currencies; and G-10 EU trade with EU countries. Total reserves, assets
and G-10 GDP were US$ 1.58 (1.48), 5.5 (4.5) and 19.7 trillion respectively in 1997;
G-10 trade (vis-à-vis the G-10) was US$ 3.2 (2.1) trillion in 1997 (consolidated totals
in brackets).

1   G-10 EU countries only
2   Includes international bonds, cross-bonrder bank liabilities to non-banks, foreign
     currency liabilities to domestic non-banks (from 1984) and euronotes (from 1989)

Sources: IMF, OECD, BIS and national data

shifted out of the dollar and into the euro.[12] Were all non-industrial countries to put equal weight on the euro and the dollar, some US$ 200 billion
could be shifted. This latter scenario ignores the potential for reserve
diversification by Asian central banks into the yen, however.

After monetary union, European central banks may find that they have
more dollars than they need. All that has been agreed is that up to
50 billion euro in reserves – consisting of dollars and other non-EU
currencies – will be put at the disposal of the ECB in the first instance by
the participating central banks. Various authors have tried to estimate
some concept of reserve excess. Emerson *et al.* (1992) put the excess of
reserves at between US$ 200 and 230 billion, but Kenen (1995: 115), shows
that such figures imply excess *dollar* holdings of something like US$ 40–70
billion. Gros and Thygesen (1992) use US reserves as a benchmark to
suggest excess reserves of about ECU 50 billion at one point in their
discussion (ibid.: 254) but revisit the question (*ibid.*: 403) and use reserves
not pooled to suggest excess reserves of ECU 80 billion.[13] The excess of
reserves over each country's share of the 50 billion euros to be pooled
initially cannot be taken as the measure of this surplus, however, because
calls beyond the ECU 50 billion can be made in the future. Unpooled

reserves left at the national central banks, moreover, are not necessarily useless. Some countries, including Austria, Belgium and Italy, have dollar debt outstanding. Furthermore, national central banks could conceivably carry out foreign exchange intervention as long as they act 'under instructions from the ECB'.[14]

One crude but very popular benchmark against which to measure the potential excess is the shrinkage of EU members' international trade by about 60 per cent when intra-EU trade ceases to be international. The fraction of EU members' trade with each other, however, is shrinking because their trade with fast-growing countries whose currencies are anchored to the dollar is expanding most rapidly, albeit from a low base. One can imagine that EU countries would desire to reduce their international reserve holdings by something like one-half. However, it should be recalled that EU reserve holdings denominated in core EU currencies amount to one-third of total holdings. If this fraction of international reserves is allowed to become euro-denominated assets, then EU countries would already have lost one-third of their reserves. Given this potential for passive reserve reduction, active reserve management in Europe might yield a reduction of one-sixth in current reserves, about US$ 55 billion.[15] Most analyses of this question by economists at banks and securities firms have taken something like this approach (Table 16.4).

The trade benchmark is an anachronism, however: a vestige of thinking from the Bretton Woods era, when capital controls made imports the first and often the last claim on reserves. Usha Thorat, the head of reserve management at the Reserve Bank of India, takes another view, which might not be irrelevant for industrial countries:

> The precautionary motive which stems from the desire to have a cushion against unforeseen reversal of capital flows would depend on . . . the share of volatile capital flows to total; portfolio investment, short-term debt, including short-term non-resident deposits, are usually considered volatile elements . . . With the opening up of economies and increasing integration of word money and capital markets, the traditional measure of adequacy of reserves in terms of import cover, with three months cover as a rule of thumb is clearly not satisfactory. One alternative is to look at the ratio of short-term debt to reserves.[16]
>
> (Thorat 1997: 28)

In practice, many central banks accumulate and hold reserves as much as a by-product of other policies as owing to a reserve policy *per se*. Machlup's likening of reserve size and composition to the contents of his wife's closet – a collection of by-products of decisions rather than the object of an independent optimization – suffers more from changing social norms for acceptable images among economists than from any loss

Table 16.4 Surplus foreign exchange reserves of euro area: various recent
estimates (in US$ billion)

Source	Surplus			Benchmark
	Core EU	Other EU	Total EU	
CS First Boston *Keating (1996)*			none	US reserves as a ratio of trade with non-dollar area
JP Morgan *Persaud and Dambassinas (1996)*			30–70	average ratio of reserves to imports for 23 industrial countries
Goldman Sachs *Brookes (1996)*	30	93	123	1994 reserve/import ratios for individual EU countries
Paribas *Parsons (1996)*			none	current aggregate reserves/ import ratio for the EU
Nomura *Golden (1996)*			100	current aggregate reserves/ import ratio for the EU
Union Bank of Switzerland *Adler and Chang (1996)*			some reduction plausible	'reserves are a residual that results from central banks leaning against the wind of dollar depreciation' (p. 22)
Salomon Brothers *Lipsky* et al. *(1996)*			none	'in a world of free capital movements, trade flows are not a good guide to the desired scale of reserves' (p. 39)
Morgan Stanley *Bulchandani (1997)*			possibly a deficit	larger portfolio shifts with larger, more liquid euro financial markets
Deutsche Bank *Deutsch (1997)*	50–90	150–110	>200	US reserves of 1–1½ months' imports
Deutsche Bank *Hoffman and Schröder (1997)*			130	US reserves of 1–1½ months' imports

Note: Estimates presented in chronological order of publication

in truth value. A recent attempt to model European reserve holdings, done
under genteel duress, produced little in the way of robust results (Leahy
1997). Contrary to the assertions of some market analyses, reserves are not
expensive to hold for countries with good credit ratings.[17] Even if surplus
reserves can in some sense be identified, is it safe to presume that they will
be sold?[18] Moreover, caution would suggest deferring any paring of
reserves until the process of union is very far advanced and the credibility
of the ECB well secured. These considerations, in combination with the
amounts involved and the time horizon, suggest that any reserve liquidation will prove to be modest in scale and limited in effect.

Even as figures on possible reserve shifts are contemplated, it should be
recalled that official reserve status and currency strength are far from

necessary companions. The Swiss franc has tended to appreciate in real terms in recent years, with the result that the Swiss franc's internal purchasing power tends to be well below its external purchasing power. Yet the fraction of official reserves accounted for by the Swiss franc has fallen from a peak near 3 per cent in 1980 to 1 per cent in 1996.

The euro as an anchor currency

Some observers imagine that, backed eventually by the world's largest single economy, the euro could provide an anchor for a broad range of countries outside the Eurozone proper. With currencies linked to the euro, private traders might increasingly denominate their transactions in the euro, a practice that would lead them to hold working balances in euros, and would ultimately reinforce any tendency for private and official portfolios to shift into the euro. Eichengreen (1997) approaches this prospect historically and argues that inertia is easy to underestimate. This prospect can be approached in terms of currency geography, by considering the respective roles of the dollar and Eurozone currencies as anchors, recognizing the current flux in East Asia.

A currency anchor is the major currency whose movements against other major currencies are largely shared by another (the anchored) currency. Going beyond a quick look at the IMF's *Exchange Arrangements and Exchange Restrictions* (1997) compilation to conclude that 'only a limited number of smaller countries' peg to the dollar (Krugman 1984), several recent studies have investigated the behaviour rather than the officially announced linkage of exchange rates. Following, apparently often unknowingly, on the seminal work of Brown (1979), analysts have adopted a number of approaches to this question including multiple regression (Frankel and Wei 1993, 1994; Kawai and Akiyama 1997, Bénassy-Quéré 1996a, 1996b, and Galati 1998), variance ratios (Bénassy-Quéré 1996a, 1996b), and bilateral elasticities (BIS 1997b, McCauley 1997).

These studies show broadly defined currency zones as pictured in Figure 16.4. The proto-Eurozone includes the Eurozone proper, most of the rest of Western Europe, most of Eastern Europe, some of the countries bordering the Mediterranean and Francophone Africa. Sterling varies in its proximity to the DM on the one side and the dollar on the other, but it is shown as part of the Eurozone. Most of the rest of the world, with the exception of Japan, lies in the broadly defined dollar zone. Thus, the euro will not arrive amidst the chaos suggested by formal exchange rate arrangements, which make floating exchange rates the overwhelming norm. Rather, well into 1997 it appeared that the euro would come into existence surrounded by a 'dollar zone, [which] far from breaking up since the collapse of the Bretton Woods system, . . . encompasses the American continent[s], Asia, the Persian Gulf, Australia and New Zealand' (Ilzkovitz 1995: 93). In an exhaustive analysis, Kawai and Akiyama (1997, Table 5a)

Figure 16.4 Currency geography
Source: author's calculations

estimate that 47 per cent of world GDP in 1990–6 was produced in the dollar area (less than half of that in the United States), 33 per cent in the proto-euro area (including the UK) and 18 per cent in the yen area (essentially Japan).

The crisis in Asia has dated this observation by unhinging currencies from the dollar. At stake is the output in the heretofore dollar area in Asia, amounting to 7 per cent of world GDP, according to the study mentioned earlier. As a result of the crisis, the debate regarding the appropriate anchoring of Asian currencies has intensified. Many observers take the view that the dollar peg of Asian countries was part of the problem (Ito, Ogawa and Sasaki 1997). A somewhat different view is that the reversal of the dollar's long-term decline against the yen carried East Asian currencies upward, and thereby undermined their competitiveness and set them up for currency attacks.[19]

Even before the crisis in East Asia, many economists recommended against the linkage of Asian currencies to the dollar and looked forward to these currencies weaning themselves from it. Kwan (1994) concluded that patterns of international trade argue that the currencies of Hong Kong, Korea, Singapore and Taiwan should be pegged to the yen. Eichengreen and Bayoumi (1996) suggested that the yen is a marginally better peg than the dollar for the currencies of Indonesia, Korea and Thailand, and a not much worse peg for the currencies of several other currencies. They suggest that 'Even Hong Kong, which has resisted greater flexibility to date, may have to contemplate it after the resumption of Chinese control in 1997', a notion that the Hong Kong authorities vigorously disputed.[20] This analysis, however, does not take into account the fact that other currencies, outside as well as inside Asia, are anchored to the dollar. Most

Asian currencies are almost completely surrounded by currencies anchored to the dollar. This circumstance is recognized by Williamson's (1996) proposal that Asian countries adapt a *common* currency basket for pegging, consisting of something like 40 per cent dollar, 30 per cent yen and 30 per cent DM (then euro).[21] The analogy that Eichengreen and Bayoumi (1996) draw between Europe's movement away from the dollar in the 1970s and East Asia's situation today does not respect an important difference. From the outset of floating, a number of currencies in Europe aligned themselves with the DM right away, so a currency that later moved into the DMs orbit was joining an effective DM zone larger than Germany. In Asia, by contrast, the yen bloc has had just one member.

Hamada asked whether each Asian 'country was driven by a purely economic rationale in its exchange-rate policy. In practice . . . political considerations may have motivated the pegging policy' (Hamada 1994: 330). This interpretation might suggest an increased willingness to anchor to the yen with the passage of time, much as Taiwan switched some of its dollar reserves into yen (Table 16.3). Taguchi of the Bank of Japan elaborates on the non-economic considerations:

> To what extent, and at what pace the Japanese yen will become an anchor currency in Asia hinges on many economic and noneconomic factors: e.g., how intraregional trade and investment will develop, the future military presence of the United States in this region, whether political ties among Asian countries become close and the development of the U.S. economy . . . [and, in particular, whether] the U.S. economy remains sound and its inflation rate low.
>
> (Taguchi 1994: 354)

In summary, the euro arrives in a world still half-anchored to the dollar. Looking forward, Asia is a question mark. Russia's trade with the Eurozone and an increasingly DM/euro anchored Eastern Europe raise the question of whether, after its recent unpegging from the dollar, Asia will renew its dollar orientation.

Global liability managers

Many analysts foresee that portfolio shifts by private investors and official reserve managers from the dollar into the euro will drive up the euro against the dollar and push the euro area from a current account surplus into a current account deficit (Bergsten 1997b, and Alogoskoufis and Portes 1997). This argument resembles that of Triffin (1960), who observed that the growth of world trade meant a growing demand for dollar-denominated bank accounts with which to settle the transactions.[22] If the only way for these dollars to reach the hands of traders outside the United States were for the latter to run deficits, Triffin argued, then the necessary succession of deficits would undermine the credibility of the link between the dollar and gold. Take away the problem of the gold link, and the line of reasoning put forward by Bergsten and Alogoskoufis and Portes is very Triffinesque: a portfolio shift into the euro entails deficits for the euro area.

Kindleberger (1965) and Despres, Kindleberger and Salant (1966) denied Triffin's claim that the United States had to run deficits in any reasonable sense of the word in order to provide the world with dollar balances. If the US banking system were to extend long-term credits to foreign companies and governments, and the funds were to accumulate as short-term bank deposits, then the needs of trade could be met.[23] In application to the present case, the shift of private asset managers and official reserve managers into the euro need not pressure the euro upwards in the exchange market or push the euro area into current account deficit if willing borrowers of euros come forward.

This is likely because, in addition to having strong attractions for asset managers, a more integrated bond market in Europe would also attract debt managers in the steady state. (Debt management does not fit into the sections discussed because the arguments apply to both official and private debt managers.) The development of a broad and deep euro bond market could potentially affect debt management more strongly than asset management, and the greater supply of euro-denominated assets could place downward pressure on the euro.

It may seem strange that something as welcome as the development of broad, deep and liquid markets could adversely affect the currency concerned, but portfolio theory holds that the shift of funding from one currency to another will result in some combination of a higher interest rate and a lower exchange rate in the currency experiencing the increase in asset supply. For instance, were Korea to issue new DM securities and to use the proceeds to buy in all its dollar debt, private investors would need to be induced to hold more DM and fewer dollar assets. Depending on the size of the operation, some combination of higher DM interest rates and a lower DM exchange rate might be required to make the investors willing to hold newly supplied DM securities. A flow model of exchange rate determination agrees with the result: as the Koreans exchanged the newly borrowed DMs for the dollars required to pay off their outstanding dollar debts, the demand for dollars would rise. A parallel analysis would apply to a Carter bond issue by the US Treasury, in which bonds were sold in DMs (or euros) instead of dollars (see the discussion later in this paper). The current choice of currency for large issues by global debt managers, and the current financing habitat of emerging economies, make the prospect of heavier use of the euro by debt managers plausible.

The relation of the size of international bond issues to the choice of currency denomination suggests that more liquid European bond markets might attract more borrowing. As things stand, international bond issuers favour the dollar for large deals (Table 16.5). If an underwriter of a large

Table 16.5 International security issues by size and currency, in billions of US$, 1990–5

Currency of denomination, by region	Size of issue		Total
	< $1.0 billion	>$1.0 billion	
Developing countries	141.7	10.5	152.2
US dollar	96.8	7.4	104.2
EU currencies	17.6	0.0	17.6
Japanese yen	27.3	3.2	30.5
Developed countries	1,555.7	209.1	1,764.8
US dollar	554.9	119.5	674.4
EU currencies	660.1	58.9	719.0
Japanese yen	340.8	30.6	371.4
International institutions	117.1	39.9	216.9
US dollar	34.1	15.0	49.1
EU currencies	113.9	15.3	129.3
Japanese yen	29.1	9.5	38.6
Total	1,874.5	259.5	2,134.0
US dollar	685.8	141.9	827.7
EU currencies	791.6	74.3	865.9
Japanese yen	397.1	43.3	440.4
Grand total, including offshore centres	2,078.6	276.9	2,355.5

Note: including bonds and medium-term notes

Sources: Euromoney Bondware and BIS

bond in euros could more easily hedge against movements in the underlying euro yields by shorting large blocks of European government bonds, issuing costs might fall, eliminating this bias, and inducing more issuance in euros. While there is no guarantee that borrowers do not offset any constraint on their choice of currency for large debt issues by appropriately managing their other liabilities and assets, including those off balance sheet, the evidence suggests that market fragmentation in Europe might be diverting debt from the euro's predecessor currencies.

With a broader, deeper and more liquid bond market in Europe, moreover, debt managers outside Europe could be interested in increasing the proportion of their debt that is denominated in euros. The estimated currency composition of international debt (Table 16.6) owed by countries in Asia and Latin America shows a very low share of European currencies.[24] Even if the euro does not displace the dollar – or in Asia, the yen – as a reserve currency, there is great scope for additional borrowing in euros.[25] Currently, the weight of the European currencies in the reserves of non-industrial countries (Table 16.3) is noticeably heavier than in the debt of those countries.

It is thus possible that a larger supply of euro-denominated assets, which on portfolio balance reasoning would push down the value of the euro,

Table 16.6 Currency composition of developing country debt, in US$ billion and %, at end-1996

Obligor	Currency				Total
	US $	Yen	EU	Other[1]	
Latin America	421.1	66.0	72.0	65.2	624.3
	67.4%	10.6%	11.5%	10.4%	100.0%
Banks[2]	100.3	2.2	7.1	4.2	113.7
World Bank[3]	320.8	63.8	65.0	61.0	510.7
Asia	344.7	243.4	71.7	85.4	745.1
	46.3%	32.7%	9.6%	11.5%	100.0%
Banks[2]	135.7	80.1	10.6	16.9	243.3
World Bank[4]	209.0	163.3	61.1	68.5	501.9
Eastern Europe	138.0	42.6	101.9	90.9	373.4
	37.0%	11.4%	27.3%	24.3%	100.0%
Banks[2,5]	7.3	0.5	14.3	5.3	27.4
World Bank[6]	130.8	42.2	87.5	85.6	346.1
Total[7]	1,044.5	377.1	329.4	331.4	2,082.5
	50.2%	18.1%	15.8%	15.9%	100.0%
Banks[2]	245.0	73.9	32.9	22.3	374.1
World Bank	799.5	303.2	296.6	309.1	1,708.4

Note: Obligor total includes other developing countries. World Bank figures for 1996 are preliminary and refer to debt maturity greater than one year. Multiple-currency debt reported by the World Bank is distributed among underlying currencies according to the composition of the World Bank currency pool. Figures may not add due to rounding.

1   Including unidentified
2   Excludes bank claims of more than one-year maturity, including medium-term debt with remaining maturity of less than one year. Semi-annual maturity distribution applied to quarterly currency distribution. Includes author's estimates of currency breakdown of debt to banks in offshore centres and other debt to banks for which no official currency breakdown is available.
3   World Bank subtotal for Latin America and the Caribbean
4   Comprises World Bank subtotals for East Asia and Pacific and South Asia
5   Includes former Yugoslavia
6   Comprises World Bank subtotals for Europe and Central Asia
7   Includes Africa.

Sources: World Bank and BIS

could outweigh a larger demand, which would push it up.[26] At any rate, one should not attempt to calculate the effects of the greater attraction of the euro for official and private asset managers without considering that it might exert a similar attraction for debt managers.[27] If one takes seriously the possibility that there will be a large net portfolio shift away from the dollar toward the euro, what would be the appropriate policy response? Such concerns are articulated against the background of the tension between Brussels and Frankfurt regarding exchange rate policy in the Maastricht treaty. A full exegesis can be found in Kenen (1995), but suffice it to say that finance ministers have the right to enter formal exchange-rate arrangements and to set general orientations for exchange-rate policy, subject in the latter case to the primacy of the ECB's responsibility to deliver price stability. The prospect of large portfolio shifts into the euro causing unwanted euro strength points to a larger role for finance ministers. For some of those who foresee such shifts the conclusion is that the ECB must be flexible, or that international co-ordination arising out of meetings at Bercy or the Plaza Hotel (if no longer the Louvre) must be contemplated.

Rudi Dornbusch reminded those attending the Economic Policy panel on the euro in 1997 that the US Treasury could sell something like Carter bonds, in this case, euro-denominated bonds, to accommodate any port-folio shift without letting the euro rise sharply. Given that the euro's exchange rate may for some time be more important to the European macroeconomy than to its US counterpart (as discussed later), European finance ministers might consider shifting their debt management by 'over-funding' their deficits with euro-denominated bonds and investing the proceeds in dollar bonds. This would be equivalent in many respects to sterilized intervention by the ECB. One might argue that the accommo-dation of the portfolio shift by finance ministers would have the advantage of greater transparency and political accountability.

Summary

There is no immediate prospect for the euro's use as an anchor currency outside Central Europe and the Mediterranean. Still, a successful euro could deepen Europe's financial markets and conceivably make the evolution of European bond prices more independent of developments in New York. Both greater depth and better diversification possibilities could attract more international investment to the euro. The prospect of substantial portfolio shifts into the euro, however, does not by itself justify forecasts that the new currency will appreciate against the dollar over an extended period. Liability managers outside the euro area should also find the enhanced liquidity and improved diversification possibilities of euro-denominated debt attractive. Thus, in response to a shift in demand, global financial markets are capable of producing euro-denominated assets by changes in the currency habitats of international borrowers.

Conclusions

Broad monetary union in Europe will introduce a euro that will generally carry more weight as an international money than the Deutschmark carries, but less weight than currently adheres to the sum of the euro's constituent currencies. In the foreign exchange market, the euro is likely to be on one side of 50 to 60 per cent of all transactions, more than the DMs 37 per cent share but less than the 70 per cent share of all EU currencies at present. In the invoicing of international trade, the euro is likely to denom-inate something like one-quarter of world trade, more than the DM's sixth, but less than the combined EU currencies' third. As a reserve currency, the euro is likely to claim a share of about one-sixth, much the same as the DM, and lower than the one-fifth claimed by all EU currencies (including sterling). In terms of international private assets, the euro's likely share of one-seventh would be no higher than the DM's current share and would be half of the EU currencies' joint share. When one compares the euro's prospective role to the one-third share of EU G-10 countries in G-10 GDP or international trade, one can readily conclude that the new currency's economic base would support a larger role of the euro as an international money. Add to these comparisons an increase in the breadth, depth and liquidity of the European financial markets, with the possible implication of greater independence of returns in European fixed income markets from those in New York, and the potential for the euro as an international money comes into view.

However the very act of union will tend to push up the dollar's share on all these measures (Table 16.7). In the foreign exchange market, 92 per cent of transactions would have the dollar on one side. In trade invoicing, the dollar would serve as the currency of contract for 59 per cent of all transactions. As a reserve currency, the dollar would represent three-quarters of all holdings, and among international private assets, the dollar's share would rise to 50 per cent. From one perspective, the prospective rise of the dollar on these measures is uninteresting, reflecting as it does the merely arithmetic effect of treating the EU as a single monetary area. After all, although intra-European foreign exchange transactions will indeed disappear – to the considerable benefit of Europeans (Emerson *et al.* 1992) – a Martian would discern no visible change in economic activity. European trade would continue, and might grow faster; European central banks would have domestic assets instead of foreign assets; and European borrowers would continue to sell their bonds to Europeans in other countries, even if they were no longer denominated in a foreign currency. But from another perspective, the rise of the dollar's share on these measures points to the limited, regional success of the DM as a vehicle currency in transactions and trade denomination, as an official reserve currency, and as a standard of deferred payment. In a world of unbalanced growth, this regional focus of the DM as an international money has consequences for the prospective role of the euro.

Going into 1997, the rapid growth of output and international trade in Asia and the general dollar orientation of Asian exchange rate policies implied that the dollar area had been growing faster that the world economy as a whole. To be sure, the introduction of the euro will effec-tively enlarge the European currency zone by eliminating the gravitational effects of the dollar on the economies at the edges of Europe (Figure

Table 16.7 International uses of major currencies before and after the introduction of the euro (%)

Use	Currency	Before	After
Official reserves[1]	EU currencies/euro	24	16
	US dollar	69	76
	Japanese yen	7	8
International assets	EU currencies/euro	34	13
	US dollar	40	53
	Japanese yen	12	15
Foreign exchange	EU currencies/euro	70	56
market transactions[2]	US dollar	84	92
	Japanese yen	24	26
Denomination of trade	EU currencies/euro	34	22
	US dollar	48	59
	Japanese yen	5	6
Memorandum items:			
GDP as a percentage	Euro area G-10	36	36
of total G-10 GDP	United States	37	37
	Japan	23	23
International trade	Euro area G-10	55	32
as a percentage of	United States	23	34
G-10 trade	Japan	13	20

Notes:
1   Components sum to 100% despite the Swiss franc's 1% share owing to rounding
2   These figures represent the turnover in which a given currency appears on one side of a transaction; consequently the percentages sum to 200% (including currencies not shown)

Sources: Central Bank Survey of Foreign Exchange and Derivatives Market Activity 1995, Hartmann 1996: 7 (citing Ilzkovitz 1995), United Nations, IMF, BIS and author's estimates

16.1). But this enlargement, which may occur in several stages and eventually include the countries of central Europe, is contrary to the general movement in the opposite direction produced by faster growth in economies more oriented toward the dollar. Dollar Telephone and Telegraph is installing many new lines in young countries, while Euro Telephone and Telegraph will not on current trends enjoy such customer growth after it has finished rewiring Central Europe.

Some analysts have therefore discerned signs of a levelling-off or even reversal in the 1990s of the long decline in the dollar's role (Oppers 1995, Frankel 1995, Eichengreen and Frankel 1996), which in any case was subject to overstatement (Kenen 1983). Changing the metaphor, the plate tectonics of the global economy, adding to the economic mass of parts of the world where wealth is still measured in dollars, may serve to sustain and even to increase the dollar's role.

Looking further ahead, there is no guarantee that the dollar area will continue to grow more rapidly than the world as a whole. Both the dollar anchoring of East Asia and the more rapid growth there are in question. Many observers see a larger role for the yen and the euro.

What needs to be borne in mind, though, is the ambiguity of the relationship between the respective international roles of the euro and the dollar, on the one hand, and the exchange rate between them, on the other. Were the euro to figure more importantly in the management of industrializing economies currently anchored to the dollar, asset managers *and* liability managers there would be more likely to shift their portfolios towards the euro. Since these countries are generally running current account deficits and thereby accumulating international debt, however, such a portfolio shift from the dollar to the euro would tend to produce a lower exchange rate of the euro against the dollar.

In sum, one should be skeptical of claims that the euro will be a strong currency by virtue of large, unidirectional portfolio shifts. Still, looking across the business cycle, there is a reason to expect the euro to be a strong currency. Travel is narrowing, wrote Chesterton, and those who tour the world sampling McDonald's Big Macs would seem to confirm his anti-adage. But those who have done so find a systematic relationship between the international wealth (the net foreign asset position, technically) of the country and the cost there of the archetypal burger. If you go around the world, the product tastes much the same but varies in price, measured in a common currency. Countries running current account surpluses and building up net claims on the rest of the world feature relatively expensive Big Macs. Those countries running current account deficits and building up net liabilities to the rest of the world, by contrast, feature cheap Big Macs. For example, Switzerland, running a current account surplus of US$ 2,400 per year per man, woman and child, has the distinction of serving some of the most expensive McDonald's hamburgers in the world (Figure 16.5).

Qualitatively, the euro area will look more like Switzerland than the United States in this regard. In December 1997, the OECD (OECD 1997) looked at the economic area consisting of those countries actually chosen to form the Eurozone in May 1998. The OECD projected that the Eurozone would run a current account surplus of 2.7 per cent of domestic product and experience inflation of no more than 2 per cent in 1999. In effect, Europeans will be saving more than they invest. The United States, by contrast, is expected to be running a current account deficit about as large in relation to its output, investing more than it saves, with inflation no lower than in Europe. In terms of Figure 16.5, the Eurozone will tend to drift upwards along the regression line, while the US drifts downwards. The pace is glacial, a few cents every five years, but still one can expect the euro over time to behave more like the Swiss franc than the dollar. Europeans will tend to find vacationing abroad cheaper than vacations at home, while Americans will have to pick their destinations carefully not to find the reverse.

Thus, however the euro, dollar and yen stand in relation to each other as international moneys a generation from now, the best prediction is that

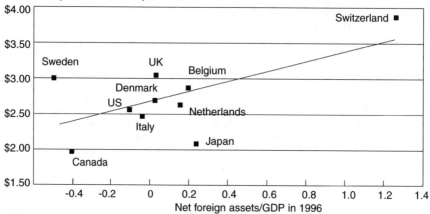

Figure 16.5 Net foreign assets and Big Mac price in US$

Source: IMF, International Financial Statistics; *Economist*

the exchange rate between the dollar and euro will reflect inflation outcomes, growth performance and long-term developments in net foreign asset positions on either side of the Atlantic. A sustained advantage in growth performance for the US economy would tend to support the dollar with higher interest rates, but undermine it with a more rapid build-up in external liabilities. Over shorter horizons, the relation between business cycles and associated cycles in monetary policy will figure importantly in variations in the dollar/euro rate. Portfolio flows between the euro and the dollar might at times exert a powerful force, but they are unlikely to run long enough and strong enough in a single direction to predominate in setting the dollar/euro rate.

Notes

This work has benefited from discussion at the BIS but should be viewed as the work of the author. He would like to thank Svein Andresen, Steve Arthur, Florence Béranger, Henri Bernard, Joseph Bisignano, Claudio Borio, Andrew Crockett, Paul De Grauwe, Gabriele Galati, Giorgio Glinni, Serge Jeanneau, Peter Kenen, Jean-Marie Kertudo, Charles Kindleberger, Frederick Marki, Denis Petre, Georges Pineau, Fabrizio Saccomanni, Jeffrey Shafer, Frank Smets, Kostas Tsatsaronis, Jürgen von Hagen, Axel Weber and William White.

1 Subsequent observations and accounts include Frankel 1986, Giavazzi and Giovannini 1989, Group of Ten Deputies 1993, and Galati 1999. The Swiss franc, by contrast, tends to amplify the DM's movements against the dollar, falling against the DM as the DM weakens against the dollar, and, conversely, appreciating against the DM as the DM rises against the dollar, as in 1995. See Ettlin 1996.
2 Rother (forthcoming) argues that the decline in transaction balances will be

larger (smaller) if prices and output are negatively (positively) correlated across countries in the Eurozone.

3 Otmar Issing, speaking before the European Summer Institute, quoted in Stüdemann (1997: 2).

4 One approach would be to look for deviations from a Taylor rule for ECB policy. See Clarida, Gali and Gertler 1997.

5 Masson and Turtelboom 1997, and Funke and Kennedy 1997 speak of the privileged policy position that the exchange rate might occupy in the euro's early days.

6 Or, as de Boissieu (1996: 130) puts it: 'Since the end of the 1960s . . . the dollar has been challenged without being replaced.'

7 The appropriateness of this analogy may be questioned in view of the strong clientele effects created by state tax codes' exclusive tax exemption for interest on home-state municipal bonds.

8 The spread reflects not just the relative creditworthiness of the respective government, but also cyclical factors, such as the strength of construction spending. In 1998, the yield on the German government ten-year bond has fallen below that of the Dutch and French government bonds, but this development is ascribed to the increasing concentration of futures and other hedging activity in the German government bond, rather than to credit developments.

9 Their quantification encounters other objections. Thus, one of the biggest flows in the world bond market, that between New York and London, is taken by the authors to involve two different currencies when in fact to a very substantial extent it involves trans-Atlantic trading in dollar bonds. The authors view foreign exchange transactions as reflecting no more than fundamental demand arising from international trade in goods and assets, which are multiplied as dealers play 'hot potato' with the exposures imposed on them by such customer transactions. In the real world, however, major banks use the foreign exchange market to take positions on their own account, and indeed they often find the consequent exchange of one currency for another a nuisance. As a result, they are considering limiting their settlement exposures by entering into so-called contracts for difference: instead of exchanging marks for dollars to settle a forward transaction, the losing party would transfer the losses to the gaining party.

10 See also European Commission 1997b. Masson and Turtelboom 1997 simulate the change in the correlation of returns on short-term instruments only, deriving ambiguous results depending on the ECB's intermediate target. However it is well known that returns on short-term instruments are much less correlated than returns on bonds, so the interesting question remains wide open.

11 A contrary view is expressed by Thygesen *et al.*:

> Confidence in the insulating properties of flexible exchange rates was shattered from the first half of 1994 by the transmission of higher US interest rates to Europe at a time when such a linkage seemed inappropriate because of different positions in the business cycle on the two sides of the Atlantic. At a time of high uncertainty in the foreign exchange markets investors appear to compare national interest rates more directly, discounting anticipated, but very uncertain exchange rate changes strongly in comparing the yield on assets denominated in different currencies . . . A larger market share of the ECU [euro] in international financial portfolios and hence more symmetry between the dollar and the ECU [euro] would not really mitigate the problem.
>
> (Thygesen *et al.* 1995: 126)

12 Taiwan's reserves were 95 per cent US dollars as recently as end-1986. See Seth

and McCauley 1987: 37. Tavlas and Ozeki (1992: 40) report that even as Taiwan was diversifying away from the dollar 'selected [unnamed, unnumbered] Asian countries,' presumably not including Taiwan, were raising their holdings of dollars from 48 per cent in 1986 to 63 per cent in 1990, at the expense of the yen and European currencies.

13   Could the inconsistency have arisen from different treatments of the dollars 'swapped' for official ECUs, more a nominal than a substantial transaction?

14   EMI (1996: 56), based on Article 31 of the ESCB/ECB Statute requiring ECB authorisation for national central banks' foreign exchange operations.

15   Golden (1996) and Parsons (1996) obtain different numbers using this same trade benchmark, while Brookes (1996) uses current ratios of reserves to imports of individual EU countries in recognition of the wide range of observed ratios: from 0.8 months' imports for France; through 3.4 for the EU on average; and as high as 7.0 for Greece. Keating's (1996) approach has much to recommend it. He uses the United States as a benchmark but measures US reserves against US trade with the non-dollar area.

16   This alternative differs from the ratio of M2 to reserves, which is based on a notion of a domestic run on reserves rather than a foreign run. See Sachs, Tornell and Velasco 1996.

17   'Excess reserves represent an economic loss,' according to Persaud and Dambassinas (1996: 2).

18   Kenen (1995: 114): 'The EC countries may be stuck with redundant dollars, just as they were stuck with gold after it was demonetized officially by the Second Amendment to the Articles of Agreement of the IMF'. (European central banks could easily take a different view of gold acquired at US$ 35 an ounce, although total returns on dollars and gold measured from a late-1960s base have been converging for some time.)

19   The Thais devalued the baht in 1984 (after a period of dollar appreciation) and adopted a basket peg thereafter, only sharply to reduce the weight of the yen in their basket in 1985 when the dollar started to fall against the yen. Another consideration, pointed out by Ueda (1994: 356) is that a stable CPI in Japan implies a negative inflation rate for Japanese export prices, 'creating strong deflationary pressure on other countries' linked to the yen. This argumentation is similar to that of Mundell (1993), p. 24, who argued that 'the deflationary stance of the [European] Community . . . will impose too tough a monetary standard for the countries of Eastern Europe to match. They are far more likely to adopt the easier standard that would be set by modest US rates of inflation.'

20   Yam (1996) termed the notion that Hong Kong will have to abandon its dollar peg 'Myth Number Four.'

21   This sounds like the son of the Special Drawing Right (SDR): the IMF's hybrid basket currency. The introduction of the euro may provide the opportunity or excuse for a recasting of the SDR. At the 1997 IMF conference, Philippe Maystadt of Belgium (1997) raised the question whether the SDR should be based only on the dollar, euro and the yen. Governments propose but markets dispose, and markets have not embraced the SDR (Eichengreen and Frankel 1996).

22   I am indebted for this parallel to Paul De Grauwe, commenting at a CEPR seminar on exchange rate policy for the euro.

23   While it is tempting to say that 'Triffin had the better of the argument', (Garber 1996: 2), it is fairer to say that 'the cogency of that position [of Despres–Kindleberger–Salant] has been thoroughly undermined by the fact that the United States has now developed a real [that is, a current account] deficit' (Kindleberger 1985: 295).

24   Compare Bénassy-Quéré (1996a, 1996b), who relies on World Bank data alone.

25 Small EU countries such as Ireland and Portugal may be tempted to borrow exclusively in the broad and deep euro market, instead of using local currencies, DM, dollars and other currencies. (For some EU countries, such a policy might miss an opportunity to use debt management as a substitute for exchange rate flexibility. If a country has larger than EU-average trade shares with the dollar area, it is more exposed to a loss of exports resulting from a dollar depreciation. Whereas, before, the tendency of the currency to fall against the DM served to buffer the economy against dollar depreciation, going forward, the economy could benefit from the interest savings on dollar-denominated debt in the event of dollar depreciation.) Working in the opposite direction, it must be admitted, is the new World Bank policy of offering its borrowers a choice in the denomination of credits. Previously, the World Bank mixed a currency cocktail, heavily weighted towards low-interest-rate currencies in Europe and the yen, and gave its borrowers no choice but to accept the cocktail. Evidently, the World Bank will be lending a higher share of dollars under the new policy. I am indebted to Jeffrey Shafer for pointing out this 'dollar-negative' factor to me.

26 See Alogoskoufis and Portes (1997) for the argument that the shift of assets into the euro should be expected to occur faster than the offsetting shift of liabilities. Their argument, however, ignores the importance of short-term international debt (as Thailand's difficulties remind us), the capacity of currency swaps to transform extant exposures, and the euro's stimulus to short-term securities markets in Europe.

27 Portes and Rey (1998) suggest that the demand shift by asset managers toward the euro can be expected to be faster than the supply shift by borrowers. Their argument is based on the notion that international debts have long maturities and can only be redenominated at maturity. However, many international debts have short maturities and currency swaps can transform outstanding debts before maturity.

Bibliography

Adler, O. and Chang, K. (1996) 'The Myth of an EMU-Related Reserve Sell-Off', Union Bank of Switzerland *Currency Briefing*, 26 November, 1–23.

Alogoskoufis, G. and Portes, R. (1997) 'The Euro, the Dollar and the International Monetary System', in P. R. Masson, T. H. Krueger and B. G. Turtelboom (eds), *EMU and the International Monetary System*, International Monetary Fund, Washington: 58–89.

Baumol, W. J. (1952) 'The Transactions Demand for Cash: An Inventory Theoretic Approach', *Quarterly Journal of Economics* 66: 545–56.

Bénassy-Quéré, A. (1996a) 'Exchange Rate Regimes and Policies in Asia', Centre d'études prospectives et d'informations internationales, *Document de Travail*, no. 96–07 (July).

Bénassy-Quéré, A. (1996b) 'Potentialities and Opportunities of the Euro as an International Currency', *Economic Papers*, European Commission, no. 115 (July).

Bergsten, C. F. (1997a) 'The Impact of the Euro on Exchange Rates and International Policy Cooperation', in P. R. Masson, T. H. Krueger and B. G. Turtelboom (eds), *EMU and the International Monetary System*, International Monetary Fund, Washington: 17–48.

Bergsten, C. F. (1997b) 'The Dollar and the Euro', *Foreign Affairs* (July/August): 83–95.

BIS (1993) *Central Bank Survey of Foreign Exchange in April 1992*, Bank for

International Settlements, Basle, March.

BIS (1996a) *66th Annual Report*, Bank for International Settlements, June.

BIS (1996b) *Central Bank Survey of Foreign Exchange and Derivatives Market Activity, 1995*, Bank for International Settlements, Basle, May.

BIS (1997a) *International Banking and Financial Market Developments*, Bank for International Settlements, Basle, May.

BIS (1997b),*67th Annual Report*, Bank for International Settlements, Basle, June.

BIS (1998) *68th Annual Report*, Bank for International Settlements, Basle, June.

Borio, C. E. V. and McCauley, R. N. (1996a) 'The Anatomy of the Bond Market Turbulence of 1994', in F. Bruni, D. E. Fair and R. O'Brien (eds), *Risk Management in Volatile Financial Markets*, Kluwer Academic on behalf of the Société Universitaire Européenne de Recherches Financières, Dordrecht: 61–84.

Borio, C. E. V. and McCauley, R. N. (1996b) 'The Economics of Recent Bond Yield Volatility', *Bank for International Settlements Economic Papers no. 45* (July).

Branson, W. and Henderson, D. (1985) 'The Specification and Influence of Asset Markets', in R. W. Jones and P. B. Kennet (eds), *The Handbook of International Economics*, vol. 2, North Holland, New York.

Brookes, M. (1996) 'EMU's Excess Foreign Reserves', Goldman Sachs *EMU Briefing*, Issue 6, London (4 September).

Brown, B. (1979) *The Dollar/Mark Axis*, Macmillan, London.

Bulchandani, R. (1997) 'More on the Euro as a Reserve Currency', Morgan Stanley Investment Research – U.K. and Europe, Economics *EMU Insights* 7 (March): 10–12.

Cantor, R. and Packer, F. (1996) 'Determinants and Impact of Sovereign Credit Ratings', *Economic Policy Review*, Federal Reserve Bank of New York, 2(2) (October): 37–53.

Clarida, R., Gali, J. and Gertler, M. (1997) 'Monetary Policy Rules in Practice: Some International Evidence', paper presented to the European Summer Institute, Berlin, 10–13 September.

Dammers, C. R. (1997) 'Should a Single Currency Mean Harmonisation of Market Conventions?' Presentation to the Government Borrowers' Forum, Dublin, 12 May.

De Boissieu, C. (1996) 'Stability in a Multiple Reserve Asset System', in M. Mussa, J. M. Boughton and P. Isard (eds), *The Future of the SDR: In Light of Changes in the International Financial System*, International Monetary Fund, Washington, D.C.: 122–44.

Despres, E., Kindleberger, C. P. and Salant, W. (1966) 'The Dollar and World Liquidity: A Minority View', *Economist* 218 (6389) (5 February), reprinted in C. P. Kindleberger (ed.), *International Money*, Allen and Unwin, London (1981): 42–52.

Deutsch, K. G. (1997) 'EMU and Reserve Management at European Central Banks — Consequences and Unanswered Questions'. Deutsche Bank Research, *EMU Watch* no. 29 (12 March).

Domanski, D. and Neuhaus, H. (1996) 'Bond Market Volatility in Germany', in *Financial Market Volatility*, BIS Conference Papers, vol. 1 (March): 113–28.

Dornbusch, R., Favero, C. A. and Giavazzi, F. (1998) 'Immediate Challenges for the European Central Bank', *Economic Policy* (April) 15–64.

Eichengreen, B. (1997) 'The Euro as a Reserve Currency', paper presented to the

NBER–TCER–CEPR Conference on The Future of the International Monetary System, Tokyo, 19–20 December.

Eichengreen, B. and Bayoumi, T. (1996) 'Is Asia an Optimum Currency Area? Can It Become One? Regional, Global and Historical Perspectives on Asian Monetary Relations', University of California, Berkeley, Department of Economics, *Center for International and Development Economics Research Working Paper no. C96–081* (December).

Eichengreen, B. and Frankel, J. A. (1996) 'Implications of the Future Evolution of the International Monetary System', in M. Mussa, J. M. Boughton and P. Isard (eds), *The Future of the SDR: In Light of Changes in the International Financial System*, International Monetary Fund, Washington, D.C.: 337–78.

Emerson, M., Gros, D., Italianer, A., Pisani-Ferry, J. and Reichenbach, H. (1992) *One Market, One Money*, Oxford University Press, London.

EMI (1996) *Annual Report* 1995. European Monetary Institute (April).

EMI (1997) *Annual Report 1996*, European Monetary Institute (April).

Ettlin, F. (1996) 'On the Fundamental Determinants of the Swiss Franc Exchange Rate for the D-Mark', in *The Determination of Long-Term Interest Rates and Exchange Rates and the Role of Expectations*, Bank for International Settlements, Conference Papers, vol. 2 (August): 18–27.

European Commission (1997a) 'Report of the Consultative Group on the The Impact of the Introduction of the Euro on Capital markets' (Giovannini Report), *Euro Paper no. 3* (July).

European Commission (1997b) 'External Aspects of Economic and Monetary Union'. Commission Staff Working Paper, SEC(97) 803 (23 April).

Frankel, J. A. (1986) 'The Implications of Mean–Variance Optimization for Four Questions in International Macroeconomics', *Journal of International Money and Finance* 5 (March): 553–75.

Frankel, J. A. (1995) 'Still the Lingua Franca: The Exaggerated Death of the Dollar', *Foreign Affairs* 74(4) (July–August): 9–16.

Frankel, J. A. and Shang-Jin Wei (1993) 'Trade Blocs and Currency Blocs'. *NBER Working Paper no. 4335* (April).

Frankel, J. A. and Shang-Jin Wei (1994) 'Yen Bloc or Dollar Bloc? Exchange Rate Policies of the East Asian Economies', in T. Ito and A. Krueger (eds), *Macroeconomic Linkage: Savings, Exchange Rates, and Capital Flows*, University of Chicago Press, Chicago: 295–329.

Funke, N. and Kennedy, M. (1997) 'International Economic Implications of the Euro', *OECD Economic Outlook* vol. 61 (June): 24–30.

Galati, G. (1998) 'The Role of Major Currencies in Emerging Foreign Exchange Markets', in *Bank for International Settlements, International Banking and Financial Market Developments*, (February): 34–7.

Galati, G. (1999) 'The Dollar–Mark Axis', *Bank for International Settlements Working Papers no. 74* (August).

Garber, P. M. (1996) 'The Use of the Yen as a Reserve Currency', Institute for Monetary and Economic Studies, Bank of Japan, *Monetary and Economic Studies*, 14(2) (December): 1–21.

Giavazzi, F. and Giovannini, A. (1989) *Limiting Exchange Rate Flexibility*, MIT Press, Cambridge, Mass.

Golden, C. (1996) 'The Effects of EMU on the Major Trade Currencies'. Nomura *Fixed Income Research, September*.

382 *Robert N. McCauley*

Group of Ten Deputies (1993) *International Capital Movements and Foreign Exchange Markets* (April): 25.

Gros, D. and Thygesen, N. (1992) *European Monetary Integration*, Longman, London.

Hamada, K. (1994) 'Comment on Yen Bloc or Dollar Bloc?', in T. Ito and A. O. Krueger (eds), *Macroeconomic Linkage: Savings, Exchange Rates, and Capital Flows*, University of Chicago Press, Chicago: 329–33.

Hartmann, P. (1996) 'The Future of the Euro as an International Currency: A Transactions Perspective', *Centre for European Policy Studies Research Report no. 20.*

Hoffman, R. and Schöder, U. (1997) 'The Euro – A Challenge to the Dollar?' Deutsche Bank Research *EMU Watch no. 33* (25 June).

Honohan, P. (1984) 'The Break-Up of a Currency Union Increases the Demand for Money', *European Economic Review* 25(2) (July): 235–8.

Ilzkovitz, F. (1995) 'Recent Developments in the International Use of Currencies: Towards a Tripolar Regime?', in ECU Institute (ed.), *International Currency Competition and the Future Role of the Single European Currency*, Kluwer Law, London: 67–95.

IMF (1997) *Exchange Arrangements and Exchange Restrictions: Annual Report*, International Monetary Fund, Washington.

Ito, T., Ogawa, E. and Nagataki Sasaki, Y. (1997) 'How did the Dollar Peg Fail in Asia?' paper presented at the NBER–TCER–CEPR–TRIO Trilateral Conference on International Monetary Regime in the 21st Century, Tokyo, November.

Jeanneau, S. (1995/1996) 'Interest Rate Futures: Characteristics and Market Development', in Bank for International Settlements, *International Banking and Financial Market Developments* (November 1995, February 1996).

Kawai, M. and Akiyama, S. (1997) 'Empirical Analyses of Exchange Rate Arrangements: Changing Influences of the World's Major Currencies', paper presented to the NBER–TCER–CEPR Trilateral Conference on International Monetary Regime in the 21st Century, Tokyo, 19–20 December.

Keating, G. (1996) 'Forex Reserves After EMU: Ample Dollars', *Economic Research – Europe*, Credit Suisse First Boston, London (4 June).

Kenen, Peter B. (1983) The Role of the Dollar as an International Currency, *Group of Thirty Occasional Paper, no. 13*, Group of Thirty, New York.

Kenen, Peter B. (1995) *Economic and Monetary Union in Europe*, Cambridge University Press, Cambridge.

Kindleberger, C. P. (1965) 'Balance-of-Payments Deficits and the International Market for Liquidity', *Princeton University Essays in International Finance no. 46*, Princeton University, Princeton, N.J. (May).

Kindleberger, C. P. (1981) *International Money*, Allen and Unwin, London.

Kindleberger, C. P. (1985) 'The Dollar Yesterday, Today and Tomorrow', *Banca Nationale del Lavoro Review* 155 (December): 295–308.

Kindleberger, C. P. (1996) *World Economic Primacy, 1500–1990*, Oxford University Press, New York.

Krugman, P. (1984) 'The International Role of the Dollar: Theory and Prospect', in J. Bilson and R. Marston (eds), *Exchange Rate Theory and Practice*, University of Chicago Press, Chicago.

Kwan, C. H. (1994) *Economic Interdependence in the Asia–Pacific Region: Towards a Yen Bloc*, Routledge, London.

Leahy, M. P. (1997) 'The Dollar as an Official Reserve Currency under EMU', *Open Economies Review* 7 (January): 371–90.

Lipsky, J. *et al.* (1996) 'Managing Convergence: Market Implications for 1997 and Beyond', *Economic and Market Analysis*, Salomon Brothers (December).

Masson, P. R. and Turtelboom, B. G. (1997) 'Characteristics of the Euro, the Demand for Reserves, and Policy Coordination Under EMU', in P. R. Masson, T. H. Krueger and B. G. Turtelboom (eds), *EMU and the International Monetary System*, International Monetary Fund, Washington, D.C.: 194–224.

Maystadt, P. (1997) 'Implications of EMU for the IMF', in P. R. Masson, T. H. Krueger and B. G. Turtelboom (eds), *EMU and the International Monetary System*, International Monetary Fund, Washington, D.C.: 146–53.

McCauley, R. N. (1996) 'Prospects for an Integrated European Government Bond Market', Bank for International Settlements, *International Banking and Financial Market Developments* (August): 28–31.

McCauley, R. N. (1997) 'The Euro and the Dollar', *Bank for International Settlements Working Paper no. 50* (November). Also in International Finance Section, Department of Economics, Princeton University, *Essays in International Finance no. 205* (November).

McCauley, R. N. and White, W. R. (1997) 'The Euro and European Financial Markets', *Bank for International Settlements Working Paper no. 41* (May); also in P. R. Masson, T. H. Krueger and B. G. Turtelboom (eds), *EMU and the International Monetary System*, International Monetary Fund, Washington, D.C.: 324–88.

Mundell, R. (1993) 'EMU and the International Monetary System', in G. de la Dehesa, A. Giovannini, M. Guitián and R. Portes (eds), *The Monetary Future of Europe*, Centre for Economic Policy Research, London.

OECD (1997) *Economic Outlook no. 62*, Organisation for Economic Cooperation and Development (December).

Oppers, S. E. (1995) 'Trends in the International Use of the US Dollar', International Monetary Fund, Washington, unpublished.

Parsons, N. (1996) 'The "Euro" and Central Bank Reserves', in *EMU Countdown*, Paribas Capital Markets International Research (9 September): 14–18.

Persaud, A. D. and Dambassinas, D. (1996) 'Euro, FX Reserve and Vehicle Currencies: Some Unusual Findings', *J. P. Morgan Foreign Exchange Research*, London (29 August, revised 13 September).

Portes, R. and Rey, H. (1998) 'The Emergence of the Euro as an International Currency', *Economic Policy* 26 (April): 305–43.

Rother, P. (forthcoming) 'European Monetary Integration and the Demand for Money', *Journal of International Money and Finance*.

Sachs, J. D., Tornell, A. and Velasco, A. (1996) 'Financial Crises in Emerging Markets: The Lessons from 1995', *Brookings Papers on Economic Activity* 1: 147–215.

Seth, R. and McCauley, R. N. (1987) 'Financial Consequences of New Asian Surpluses', *Federal Reserve Bank of New York Quarterly Review* 12 (Summer): 32–44.

Stüdemann, F. (1997) 'Political Pressure "Likely to Hit ECB"', *Financial Times* 12 September.

Taguchi, H. (1994) 'On the Internationalization of the Yen', in T. Ito and A. O. Krueger (eds), *Macroeconomic Linkage: Savings, Exchange Rates, and Capital Flows*, University of Chicago Press, Chicago: 335–55.

Tavlas, G. and Ozeki, Y. (1992) 'The Internationalization of Currencies: An Appraisal of the Japanese Yen', *International Monetary Fund Occasional Paper no. 90*, International Monetary Fund, Washington (January).

Thorat, U. (1997) 'Purposes of Reserve Management', Appendix A to *Reserve Management and the Euro*, Central Banking Publications, London: 27–31.

Thygesen, N. *et al.* (1995) 'The Implications for the International Monetary System of EMU with the ECU as its Single Currency', in ECU Institute (ed.), *International Currency Competition and the Future Role of the Single European Currency*, Kluwer Law, London: 117–36.

Triffin, R. (1960) *Gold and the Dollar Crisis*, Yale University Press, New Haven.

Triffin, R. (1973) 'The Role of a Developing European Monetary Union in a Reformed World Monetary System', in A. K. Swoboda (ed.), *Europe and the Evolution of the International Monetary System*, A. W. Sijthoff for Institut Universitaire de Hautes Études Internationales, Geneva: 69–80.

Ueda, K. (1994) 'Comment on "On the Internationalisation of the Japanese Yen"', in T. Ito and A. O. Krueger (eds), *Macroeconomic Linkage: Savings, Exchange Rates, and Capital Flows*, University of Chicago Press, Chicago: 355–6.

US Treasury (1997) *Treasury Bulletin* (March).

Williamson, J. (1996) 'The Case for a Common Basket Peg for East Asian Countries', paper presented to Centre d'Études Prospectives et d'Informations Internationales (CEPII)/Association for the Monetary Union of Europe (AMUE)/Korean Institute of Finance(KIF) conference on 'Exchange Rate Policies in Emerging Asian Countries', Seoul, Korea, 14–16 November.

Yam, J. (1996) 'Hong Kong's Monetary Scene: Myths and Realities', speech before Bank of England Seminar, 10 September, London, in *Hong Kong's Monetary Arrangements Through 1997*, Hong Kong Monetary Authority, Hong Kong: 11–20.

Index